The New York Times

SUNDAY CROSSWORD OMNIBUS VOLUME

1

Edited by WILL WENG

Random House
Puzzles & Games

Basically, a good crossword puzzle is timeless. That is why it can provide so much pure enjoyment and escape from the cares of the day.

But that doesn't mean that it ignores the outside world. It simply makes the best of what's there. Current names in politics, literature and sports are bound to crop up. Some of these are timeless, like Babe Ruth, and others aren't, like Roman Hruska, who used to be a senator from Nebraska, or Hildegard Knef, who wrote a best seller in 1971.

Names do go out of style, and that is one of the minor woes of reprinting old puzzles. Newsom and Newsome (both baseball pitchers) and the like crop up every so often and nothing can be done about it.

These instances are rare, though, and it is doubtful that the puzzles in this book—all reprints from the Sunday New York Times—will show their age.

This is the first omnibus collection of Times Sunday puzzles and, unless you are gifted with contest-caliber speed, it should take care of the leisure-time problem for a couple of eons, to use a puzzle word. And enough pleasure for a good part of a lifetime, it is hoped.

Will Weng

SOLUTIONS TO THE PUZZLES ARE FOUND AT THE BACK OF THE BOOK.

Copyright © 1984 by The New York Times Company

The puzzles in this book first appeared in **Will Weng's Special Crossword Puzzle Book,** © 1979 by Will Weng, and in **The New York Times Sunday Crossword Puzzles,** Vols. 1-3, ©1969-1972 by The New York Times Company. Reprinted by permission.

All rights reserved under International and Pan-American Copyright Conventions. Published in the United States by Random House, Inc., New York, and simultaneously in Canada by Random House of Canada Limited, Toronto.

ISBN 0-8129-1139-3

Manufactured in the United States of America

23rd Printing

1 ID Cards by Eugene T. Maleska

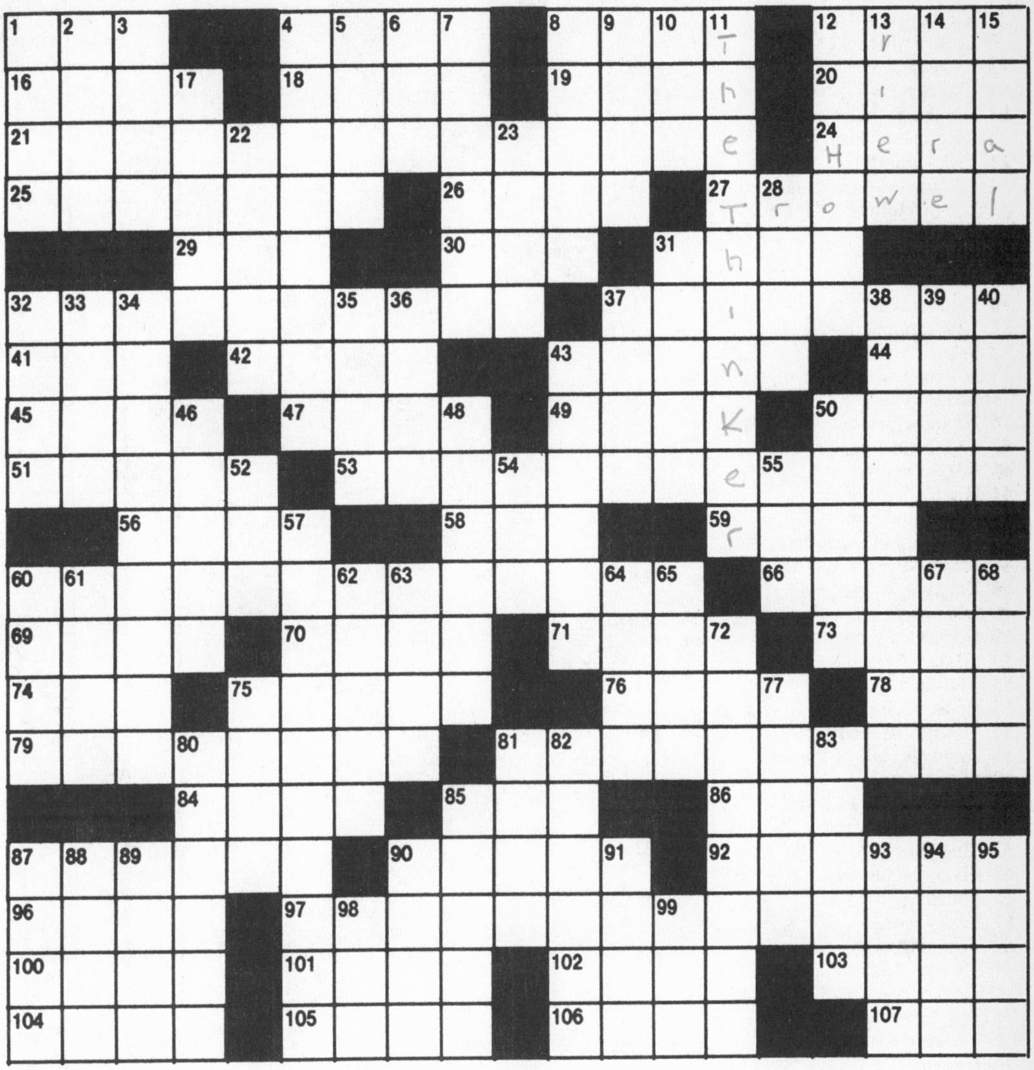

(Crossword grid with handwritten entries: 11 Across area reads "The Thinker", and 27 Across reads "Trowel")

ACROSS

1 Faulty
4 Balustrade
8 Light thud
12 Pulpy fruits
16 Guinness
18 Wagnerian earth goddess
19 Madcap
20 Like Nelly
21 Laurence Harvey
24 Greek counterpart to Juno
25 Bowlers
26 Geometer's term
27 Tool for plastering
29 Japanese outcast
30 Superlative ending
31 Scatter the chickens
32 Aaron Chwatt
37 Long-legged insect
41 Didn't go hungry
42 Do a K.P. job
43 Hollows
44 Fury
45 Puff
47 Square heraldic bearing
49 Stench
50 Water plant
51 English county
53 Leila Koerber
56 Birdbrain
58 Rhyme for bleak or seek
59 Viscous
60 Sidney Leibowitz
66 Gumption
69 Lucius Domitius Ahenobarbus
70 Suffer, in Scotland
71 Barring
73 Fiber for yarn
74 Onassis
75 Dunderheads
76 San __, Italian resort
78 Trifle
79 Manufactured
81 Charlotte Brontë
84 Linen marking
85 Part of R.P.M.
86 Box-score initials
87 Source of mohair
90 Ricky in a TV series
92 Hotel Bible name
96 Topsoil or gossip
97 Titian
100 Jai __
101 Lead
102 __ Bator
103 Fleece
104 Botch
105 Drover's concern
106 Pungent humor
107 Ronsard creation

DOWN

1 Ready for a hairpiece
2 Wings
3 Earl __ Biggers
4 Prepared leftovers
5 Clumsy boats
6 Gilbertian princess
7 __ Peak, Calif. volcano
8 Figured dress
9 Northern whiting
10 Seagoing initials
11 "Le Penseur"
12 Detach
13 Panorama
14 Ptolemais of the New Testament
15 Signet or cachet
17 Pepper cigarette
22 Keep late hours
23 "__ and make up"
28 Missiles having television apparatus
31 Dexter or bullock
32 Shipment to a paper mill
33 Peary's winter headquarters
34 First name of 90 Across
35 Abound
36 Stewpot
37 Yukon vehicle
38 William S. Rosenberg
39 Yen
40 Equipment
43 Ben-Gurion, originally, and Verdi
46 City in Utah
48 Brothers, in Bordeaux
50 Soft wood
52 Town in Nigeria
54 Iconoscope, for short
55 Scion
57 The Devil
60 Breeze of a kind
61 Alaska's former status: Abbr.
62 Upbeats, in poetry
63 Spurry or yarrow
64 Real name of writer Carter Dickson
65 Invariably
67 Stringed instrument
68 Jewish month
72 Suddenly appearing
75 Jascha Heifetz's teacher
77 Spherical
80 Hindu loincloths
81 Last Supper portrayal
82 Herschel's discovery
83 Sojourns
85 Snooped
87 Eden name
88 El Bahr
89 Mardi __
90 Sky-blue: Fr.
91 Parisian novelist: 1840-1902
93 Nevada city
94 Odiferous
95 Lowest pinochle card
98 O'Neill play
99 Kind of lace

ACROSS

1 Kind of room
6 Little earthquake
12 __ fideles
18 Contract
19 Fill the potholes
20 Certain trackmen
21 Talks bluntly
24 St. John's — (midsummer)
25 "__ of Hoffmann"
26 Ohio city
27 W.W. II agency
28 Rhode Island fowl
30 Kind of wind
31 Law's companion
32 Sect
33 Is wrong with
35 Woodwinds
36 Hindu widow sacrifice: Var.
37 Coxswains' boats
40 Silkworms
41 Hood's weapon
42 Color qualities
43 Granny and sheepshank
44 Wayside Inn and others
48 Relative of "Ah, me"
49 Old school __
50 Noncom's sleeve wear
52 "Bali __"
53 Certain cage
54 Rock: Prefix
56 __ with (backed)
57 Baseball Hall-of-Famer
58 Slippery one
59 Traveling, as an actor
61 Husing or Knight
62 Blue-pencil
63 Fixes the turkey
65 Pulled
67 Leaky vessel
68 Tennis hiatus
69 Musical finales
70 Finicky one
71 Serious crime
74 Eateries
75 Amerind
76 Drink made from holly
77 "Playin' on the old __"
78 Good Feeling, for one
79 Calif. wine valley
83 French article
84 Garden spot
85 British guns
87 Air-defense initials
88 Cache of a sort
92 Certain son
93 Group of nine
94 Goodnight girl
95 Fixes the clock
96 Bows' opposites
97 Passé

DOWN

1 Gantry or Rice
2 French or two-weeks'
3 Kind of Alaska or potato
4 Chemical suffix
5 "How the __ Was Won"
6 Fishes from a moving boat
7 Recalcitrant one
8 Group of poems
9 Isle of __
10 Certain cooked meats
11 Dwells
12 "Forever __"
13 Vaya con __
14 Elected, in St. Lo
15 Proceed
16 Extra-base hit
17 Country place
22 Fastens securely
23 October drinks
29 Store offerings

31 Newspaper items
32 Shrewd
34 French pronoun
35 Spanish gold
36 Practiced prudence
37 Gazed
38 __ than thou
39 Make possible
40 Before febrero
41 Yawned
43 Saint __-Nevis
44 __ over (endured)
45 Home for a colossus
46 "My __ land"
47 Parents' aide
49 Belief
51 Ceremonies
54 Polish city, to Germans
55 What Hamlet called the time
60 Agnes De Mille opus
62 Iron, in the Saar
64 Gin or plum

66 "Able __ I . . ."
67 Sweet girl
69 Certain teeth
70 Parisian money
71 Entertaining one
72 Irritate
73 Mounts
74 Roman orator
75 Nicene and Apostles'
77 Mattress fillings
78 One of the Allens
80 Black-ink item
81 Almost, to Cicero
82 Performed
84 Hanger-on
85 Ending, with gang and spin
86 Moved precariously
89 Kind of way
90 Direction: Abbr.
91 __ pro nobis

3 Lateral Passes by Evelyn Benshoof

ACROSS

1 __ luego
6 Bedouin
10 "Take it easy!"
16 Friends, in Brittany
17 Vogue
18 Mysterious
19 Pool-ball destination
21 Energetic one
22 Like some wine
23 Spotted African cat
25 Doctrine
26 Pester
27 Word with wood or water
28 Pa. lake port
30 Compass point
31 Easy-gaited horse
33 Moored
35 Pipe gadget
37 Self-reproach
40 Golf's Palmer
41 Purport
42 Orient
45 Treaty
46 Inspire
47 "__ yellow ribbon . . ."
49 Mal de __
51 Apportioned
52 Codicil
53 Broke forth
55 Rouse
56 Dangling ornament
59 Lessens
60 __ mode
61 Coaster
63 Old S.A. empire
64 Place for three men
67 Kind of service
68 Plan
70 English composer
71 Glamorous
74 Home-grown crimes
76 Fodder
77 Actress Barbara
78 Taiwan port
79 Photography gear
80 Palm fruit
81 Wield

DOWN

1 Son of Fatima
2 Spanish girlfriend
3 Furtive look
4 Got the golf ball ready
5 Cobra
6 Cupid, for one
7 Did lawn work
8 Askew
9 Midler
10 Racetrack-window worker
11 Food scrap
12 Wood sorrel
13 Open-handed
14 Existing
15 Phrased
20 Reddish yellow
24 Tree-lined
27 Graf __
29 Gaelic
32 Left out
34 4 P.M. or so, to some
35 Light blow
36 Latin-class word
37 Renew a lease
38 Growing out
39 Full of specks
41 Devil, for one
43 Relative of the crawl
44 Minor age
48 Dexterity
50 Periods
52 Sub __
54 Loosened
55 Confronted
56 Most feeble
57 Panacea
58 City of Italia
59 Auto driver
62 Partner of cut
63 Secondary map
65 Open
66 Make intoxicated
69 Brazilian tree
70 Trojan War hero
72 Start a beer keg
73 "But __ on forever"
75 French season

4 Finishing Touches
by Elaine D. Schorr

ACROSS

1 Corny leftovers
5 Seaweed
9 Narrow valley
13 "It's a __!"
17 Word with sesame
18 Kind of bag
19 Indian prince
20 __ breve
21 "I __ man with . . ."
22 Yegg's target
23 Stravinsky
24 Legislative togetherness
25 Pinocchio was __
29 Sea god
30 Buts' companions
31 Take heed
32 First U.S. Chief Justice
35 Irritate
39 Alternates
42 Won a court point
44 __ king
45 Famine's counterpart
47 Rail holder
48 Peter Pan __
52 "__ la vie!"
53 Sometimes they're fishy
54 Type of test
55 Gets the short straw
56 Part of I.T.T.: Abbr.
57 Woody or Ethan
59 Tanning agent
60 Group of three
63 Bit of land
64 Seat of the Duke of Normandy
68 Pressed the doorbell
69 Humpty Dumpty __
72 Cold item in Coblenz
73 Son of Zeus and Europa
74 Direction: Abbr.
75 Fork-tailed flier
76 Intelligent
78 See 49 Down
81 __ culpa
82 Rigged out
83 Gal of song
85 Cake or meal
87 Cinderella put __
96 Split
97 Elihu or cube
98 Exhaust
99 "__ what I eat"
100 __ homo
101 __ Royale
102 Went like the wind
103 Mets' home
104 Barely managed
105 Miserly
106 Nanook's transport
107 William or do

DOWN

1 Torpor
2 Fuel cartel
3 One of the Marches
4 Slow goer
5 Imbibe
6 Autumn fall
7 Fisherman's spear
8 Dill herb
9 Distress
10 Port of Nigeria
11 Organic compound
12 Ointment
13 Vehicles for talking animals
14 Consigns
15 Father Time is __
16 Sail a zigzag course
26 Chick or cow
27 Go apace
28 Harte
32 Lone-shark film
33 One-__
34 Gypsum: Var.
36 Deep-sea stingers
37 Priestly wear
38 D or Doris
39 Monologist Mort
40 Superlative ending
41 Achieves a bridge reverse
43 Like the trapeze man
45 Suggestion to Gridley
46 Actor Richard
49 With 78 Across, mint condition
50 ". . . __ no dog bark!"
51 Nick of "Rich Man, Poor Man"
52 A Harvard president
55 Oner
57 __-ran
58 Stock-price listings
59 __ Paulo
60 Pioneer's migration
61 Sadie Thompson needed a __
62 Cheek
63 Torment
64 Worry
65 The same: Lat.
66 Dried out
67 Miss Best
69 Get an Oscar
70 Light-Horse Harry
71 Attack vessel: Abbr.
73 Lunch time in Toulon
77 __ off (evaded)
78 Ziegfeld
79 Performed an air-show stunt
80 Corny unit
83 Garment for Agrippina
84 Kind of glow
86 Story slant
87 Nutmeg or family
88 What to do when you bear it
89 Fireplug tie-in
90 Takes one's pick
91 Implement
92 To the __ (headmost)
93 Wimbledon winner in 1975
94 Roll with the punch
95 Pass the cards

5 Focal Point by Threba Johnson

ACROSS

1 Mountain passes in India
6 Recess for a statue
11 Chair part
16 Proportion
17 Stupid one
19 Japanese verse
20 Last work of 59 Across
22 Potter's clay
23 Radar location: Abbr.
24 "__ kingdom come"
25 Boundary: Prefix
26 Concerns of 59 Across
28 Prefix for copter
30 French direction
32 __ de menthe
34 "__ shame!"
35 Christmas __ of 59 Across
37 Fodder
38 No longer active: Abbr.
40 Drink
41 Zodiac sign
43 Part of a warm cap
46 Early English tax
48 Not noticed
50 Frost flower
53 Kind of history
56 Resources
58 Island off Sumatra
59 Well-known name
62 __-Ra
63 Man's nickname
64 Santa's entry
65 German empire
67 Chaperon
69 Fruit stones
70 Pent up
72 Thrice: Prefix
73 __ Yat-sen
74 Opposite of taboo
75 Erode
77 59 Across, for one
82 Woman soldier of W.W. II
85 Beam, in ship measuring
87 "__ my brother's . . .?"
88 New Zealand owl
89 Hell
91 Little one
93 Yale
95 Err
96 Metric measure in Britain
97 Home of 59 Across from 1708 to 1723
101 Pillages
102 Sayings of Jesus
103 Fruit from the tropics
104 Explanatory note: Abbr.
105 Gypsum used for painting
106 Malicious burning

DOWN

1 Writing: Prefix
2 John Brown visited his ferry
3 King of the Huns
4 Uncle, in Spain
5 Kind of ware or soap
6 Never, in Berlin
7 Inside dope
8 Where 59 Across worked
9 Flight from Mecca
10 __ de Cologne
11 One-hoss vehicle
12 1735 work of 59 Across
13 Lehar's kind of opera
14 Tamiroff and others
15 Oklahoma city
17 Nature: Prefix
18 Suffix for pachy
21 "Over __"
27 Mister, in Germany
29 1735 work of 59 Across

31 Tropical balsam
33 Embroidery hole
36 Ancient
39 Park tree
42 Make possible
44 House part
45 Yielding
46 Dwarf of folklore
47 Onomatopoeic
49 Early ascetic
51 Output of people who tat
52 Pale
53 Partly open
54 Compass point
55 Hebrew letter
57 Czech measure
60 Dodged
61 Caper
66 Word after boo

68 Alms box
71 Kind of broker
73 Pleasant look
76 Clothing
78 Greek letter
79 Miss Anthony and Miss Glaspell
80 "__ bragh"
81 Writer Damon
82 Miss Cather
83 Negative atom
84 Burns's river
86 Big Ten team
90 Ease
92 Lights-out signal
94 __ la Douce
98 Kind of head or plant
99 Greek letter
100 Deface

6 Pads by Ruth W. Smith

ACROSS

1 El __, Texas
5 Anger
8 Trick takers
12 Dance step
16 Brim or dragon
17 Turner and Pendleton
19 Byron poem
20 __ au lait
21 Frying pan's habitat
24 Nimbus
25 Fighter Muhammad
26 Monkey
27 Well ventilated
28 Yokum heir
29 "Hiawatha" abode
34 Classified documents: Abbr.
35 Peaceful
36 ". . . is one with __ and Tyre"
38 "Bus Stop" author
41 Shipbuilding wood
44 Proper
45 Kind of store or cupboard
48 Skimps
50 Church part
53 Compass direction
54 Except
57 Termite: Var.
58 Blind parts
59 Consumed
60 Ring Lardner locale
63 Landed
64 Kelly and Rayburn
66 Fame
67 Melody
68 Partner of Maugham's cakes
69 Writer Bombeck
70 Caruso and others
72 Kind of bullet
74 Useful quality
76 Chemical endings
78 D'Urbervilles girl
79 "Tempest" character
81 What dieters do
85 "__ longa . . ."
86 Shaw's abode
92 City in Illinois
94 Verdi opera
95 French month
96 Soak
97 Woodwind
98 Famous relative's abode
102 Japanese coins
103 __ from the blue
104 Sword
105 "Two Years Before the Mast" author
106 U.S. cartoonist
107 Roman date
108 Public notices
109 Singles

DOWN

1 Expression of irritation
2 Lizard
3 Creamy: Ger.
4 Begin, to poets
5 __ only
6 Apportion
7 Numerical suffix
8 Happy as __
9 Grand or Diablo
10 Work unit
11 So, in Scotland
12 Strike figure
13 Poe's eerie dwelling
14 Again
15 First and reverse
18 Certain meetings
22 Glacial ridges
23 Grande or de Oro
28 Cruising
30 Osterreich capital
31 __ to be tied
32 More vague
33 Insides of buildings: Abbr.
37 Container for perfume
38 Glacial epoch
39 Pater __
40 W.H. Hudson's tropical dwelling
42 What the Forty-niner dwelt in
43 Citizen's name
46 Properties: Abbr.
47 Cheer
49 Zola novel
51 Country crossings
52 Chemical compounds
55 Roman province
56 Biblical town
58 Dust or fish
61 Sioux
62 Meet
65 __ Lynne
70 Ribbon: Suffix
71 Notched
73 Polynesian god
75 London district
77 __ eye to eye
79 Lawrence's place
80 Delphi feature
82 Blocked up
83 Czars' edicts
84 Stylish
85 Kind of squash
87 Inclines
88 Military unit: Abbr.
89 Citified
90 River of France
91 Heating devices
93 ". . . I will give you __"
98 Where: Lat.
99 Partner of Wynken and Blynken
100 F.D.R. agency
101 Confusion

7 Sequels by Mel Taub

ACROSS

1 Club sport
5 Hodyssey hauthor
9 Did a takeoff on
13 Take it easy
17 Don Juan's preoccupation
18 Madre's little girl
19 Big name in pineapples
20 E.A. Robinson's Mr. Flood
21 Novel about a beggar who struck it rich
24 Take notice of
25 Right out of the oven
26 Thick and sweet: Var.
27 Earth
29 Us, in Spain
31 Enormous
32 Droopy-eared dogs
35 Scandinavian capital
38 Giveable share of one's mind
40 Of the Blue
41 General of the Gray
42 Scott's novel on the value of raising dogs
44 Ill-wisher
45 Volubility
47 Carbohydrate suffixes
48 Took a taxi
49 Cause suffering to
50 Van man
52 Applesauce maker's instrument
53 Perform an ablution
54 "Lady's Book" publisher
55 Capital of ancient Elam
56 Strict Mennonites
58 Anglo-American poet W. H.
59 Got a furnace going
62 Primary action
63 Baseless
64 Derived from Cicero's tongue
65 Ordinal suffix
66 Play about a woman married to a drunkard
69 Miss Fabray, familiarly
70 Oil or sugar plant
72 Former Turkish president
73 King at Runnymede signing
74 Lincoln's Secretary of War
75 Tighten with ropes
76 Royal mattress irritant
78 Small shoot
79 Hebrew letters
81 Fly catcher
85 Gay sound
87 Novel about a marooned singer
90 Breslau's river
91 Port of Yemen
92 "I cannot tell __"
93 Edomite's forebear
94 Tidings
95 Porter ingredient
96 Head of France
97 Dexterous

DOWN

1 Sharp metal spur
2 Sharif
3 Traditional knowledge
4 San Joaquin Valley city
5 Undivided
6 Wire measures
7 Brightens
8 Mad scramble for success
9 Make suitable
10 Kind of glot or gamy
11 Shade tree
12 Bombe, parfait et al.
13 Bethlehem, Pa., campus
14 Novel of a town's search for a beauty queen
15 Last of 26
16 Tackle's neighbor
22 Song hit from "Sunny"
23 Thrush's relative
28 Egad, e.g.
30 Banquet-goer's travail
32 Intrusive insect
33 Deteriorate
34 View with a curled lip
35 Muscovite girl
36 Personal interest
37 Chronicle of the Ericson family
39 Briefly, part of M.I.T.
40 Prying
42 Pielike Jewish delicacy
43 Made on a loom
46 Satiated
48 Two-time A.L. home-run champ
50 Archetype
51 Keats opus
52 Radium pioneer
54 Ravine
55 Becomes attentive
56 Insists it's so
57 Sacred choral composition
58 Bedeck
59 Goatish deity
60 Young state
61 Founder of Philadelphia
63 Relative of a hieroglyph
64 Name for Groucho's lawyer
66 Con
67 Prowl-car equipment
68 Speaks sharply to
71 Spiritual
73 Shook up
75 City of Michigan
77 Platonic letter
79 Original victim
80 Fit of pique
82 Yorkshire river
83 Airman's initials
84 Belmont "adviser"
85 Greeting to Crazy Horse
86 Brouhaha
88 Harem room
89 Bee follower

8 Self-Starters by Paul R. Barnes

ACROSS

1 Atomic reactor inventor
6 Get around
11 Sleeping-car inventor
18 Eskimo boat
19 Place for a boutonniere
20 Mediterranean playground
21 Slow, in music
22 Old-womanish
23 Late news-story additions
24 Harbor craft
25 Memos
27 Refined guy
29 Obtain
30 Sioux
32 Bandleader Brown
33 Seagoing ray
34 Swordsmen's dummies
35 Cuddled up
37 Type assortments
38 Pale
39 "__ the season to be merry"
40 Kind of pie or meat
41 Separating membranes
43 Intimidated
46 "A votre __!"
47 Turkish cavalryman: Var.
49 French soul
50 Neighbor of Wash.
51 Direction to the Orient
53 Footlike part
54 Early computer inventor
56 Jet __
57 Fully
60 League, in Spain
61 Summer on the Left Bank
62 Restraints
63 Modern hairdos
64 Belgian W.W. I battleground
66 "Christ of the __"
67 Of bees
68 Little: Fr.
69 Astronaut Grissom
70 Studied
71 Hopeless situation
75 Contemptuous cries
77 More reasonable
78 State or fountain
79 Mexican tribe
80 Make __ of it
81 __ bien
82 Roams
84 Sizes below large: Abbr.
85 Feelings of extreme disgust
88 French river
90 Brave, in Soho
92 In succession
93 Thing given to a waiter
94 Main artery
95 Stethoscope inventor
96 Like some gases
97 Dynamite inventor

DOWN

1 Steamboat pioneer
2 Uprising, in France
3 Beatles' Starr and others
4 Wrestler's milieu
5 Sacred image: Var.
6 Overjoyed
7 Windmill arms
8 Sacred bull
9 Actress Dolores __ Rio
10 Tasteful opulence
11 Lithographs
12 Utah range
13 Departs: Abbr.
14 Trygve __
15 Linotype inventor
16 Soviet co-op
17 Political cartoonist and family
26 Corrida cheers
28 Grafted, in heraldry
31 Feminine suffix
33 Balloon inventor
34 Custard apple
36 Teapot part
37 Of better quality
38 Cried
40 Go to the altar
41 Flat-tire noise
42 Charge with gas
43 Matadors' decoys
44 Cattle viscera
45 Air-brake inventor
46 Kind of food or music
48 Rims
51 Urge
52 Cries of triumph
54 Mrs. Truman
55 Mongol tribe
58 River of Asia
59 Travel ways: Abbr.
63 "__, le déluge!"
64 In addition
65 Holing-out stroke
67 First-rate
68 Window piece
70 Interstellar space measure
71 Go back
72 Swallow again
73 Silicate mineral
74 Adding-machine inventor
75 Switchboard unit
76 Guam's capital
77 Declare
78 Tough question
82 Makeshift
83 O'Casey
86 Lure for mad dogs and Englishmen
87 German article
89 Sea bird
91 Down Under animal

ACROSS

1 Over: Ger.
5 Fundamental
10 Specified task
13 Actress Louise
17 Frenchman's income payment
18 Kind of diet or program
19 The Eternal City
20 Legree
21 Well-known campaign song
25 White poplar
26 "Grave Alice, and __"
27 Nostrils
28 Colleen's land
29 Vase handle
30 Slippery one
31 Make lace: Var.
32 Enters
35 Wander about
36 Brilliance
38 "__ for Sergeants"
42 Atlantic or Indian
47 Japanese apricot
50 Israeli dances
52 Divest of weapons
54 Norway's capital
55 Ancient: Prefix
57 Partner of order
59 Fabulous bird
60 Baghdad natives
62 Italian Riviera resort
64 American banker
66 He's Li'l
68 Shakespearean people
73 Dinner time in a play
74 Jot or whit
75 West African republic
77 French province
80 Onager
82 Knight's title
84 Like the girl with the curl, at times
85 Concerning
86 Witchy town
88 Golden king
90 Urban lines
91 "Like Niobe, all __"
93 "And don't __ the water"
96 Titter
98 Newborn lamb
100 "He that __ rosy cheek. . ."
102 Neighbor of Va.
106 Religious day: Abbr.
109 Babylonian goddess
111 Chance: It.
112 Stupid one
113 Weep bitterly
118 Foreign
119 Popular movie of 1963
121 Like treacherous shallows
122 Weird
123 Aristocratic
124 Peau de __
125 High notes
126 Psyche parts
127 Indian litter
128 Spanish queen and namesakes

DOWN

1 Former U.N. Secretary
2 "__ black sheep . . ."
3 Connoisseur
4 Sated
5 Between a and e
6 Russian sea
7 "__ prayer for me"
8 Editions
9 Mortification
10 One of the apostles
11 The end
12 French poet
13 Buster Brown's dog
14 Likeness
15 Bête __
16 Record, old style
19 Bridle part
20 Argentine river
22 Affirmative
23 Big beast
24 Miss Maxwell
32 Pessimistic one
33 Rower's need
34 Common abbr.
37 "Ta-ta!"
39 European flatfishes
40 Cadmus's daughter
41 Large parrot
43 More rough
44 Title for H.M. Pulham
45 Muhammad
46 Some votes
47 Partner of downs
48 Thank-you __ (road bump)
49 French city
51 Bahia's capital: Abbr.
53 Hiawatha's beloved
56 Impede, in Paris
58 "Alas and alack!"
61 Rudolph's feature
63 Famous jurist's initials
65 Inner: Prefix
67 Twice, in music
69 Balbo
70 Pierre's hunger
71 Legendary monster
72 Complain
76 British V.I.P.'s
77 Cherry feature
78 United
79 Gershwin
81 Japanese coin
83 Ceremony
87 Symbol of Christ
89 __ Moines
92 "Has Anybody __ Gal?"
94 Frighten
95 French dramatist
97 Fence in
99 Kind of code
101 Hex
103 Achilles' teacher
104 Miss Earhart
105 Types of script
106 __ facias (legal writ)
107 Russian cooperative
108 ". . . and two if __"
110 "Arabian Nights" character
111 Peter Rabbit's creator
112 Cutting tool
114 Blockheads
115 "I'm all __!"
116 Shield boss
117 Sort of tale
120 Early Algerian governor

ACROSS

1 Discoverer of Labrador
6 Wampum
11 Razor leather
16 Sight that isn't there
17 Heartened
19 Resembling the real thing
20 Follows Sir Francis Drake's route
22 Wild sheep of Asia
23 Job or trade: Abbr.
24 Deadly
25 Precarious situation
27 As __ (customarily)
29 Seed coats
31 Deck a boxer
32 Coterie
33 Apartment sign
34 Native of Baghdad
36 Small paid notice
38 Aide: Abbr.
40 Productive
42 Swirled
45 French shout
46 On a pension: Abbr.
48 The birds
50 Monkeyshine
52 Makes over
54 Old woman
55 Georgia __ Clark, ex-Treasurer
56 What Liberace or Charo goes by
57 Caffeine
58 Panic starters
59 Actress Hagen
60 Repetitive rat race
63 Greek letters
64 Loch monster
66 Neck or wrist ruffles
67 Plane's home port
69 Part of the rhythm section
70 City and county in Nevada
71 Adorned, as a Christmas tree
72 Silken
73 Fly alone
74 Sharp taste
75 Sanctified ones: Abbr.
76 Books awarded to top students
79 Fisherman, at times
81 Agitate
83 Historic age
85 Get rid of rodents
86 Peculiarity of speech
89 Impresario Hurok
92 Undesirable element
94 Ceremonies
96 Permission
97 Ways of doing things
100 Buy __ (Wall St. choice)
102 Singer Cole
103 Sinus cavities
104 Mysterious area of sea disasters
107 Carved pole
108 Cuban town of a hit song
109 Karl Marx collaborator
110 Packs cargo
111 Sad sign at a service station
112 McQueen or Lawrence

DOWN

1 Total of radians in an angle
2 Curved line
3 "Swan Lake" and "Giselle"
4 Curved molding
5 Seed covering
6 Cream the opposition
7 Brain-wave reading, for short
8 Lash mark
9 Have __ over one's head
10 Galaxy
11 The do-si-do folks
12 Sudden fright
13 Police calls, usually sudden
14 River to the Missouri
15 Sky captain
16 Prefix for an oven wave
17 Bossed the meeting
18 Do a black-chamber job
20 Layer of paint
21 Saving graces
26 "__ that tiger!"
28 Injury
30 One whose aim is honesty
35 Bills
37 Ringworm
39 Underwater concrete machine
41 Menace of the comics
43 Classic love tangle
44 Recitative artistes
45 Exactly in the middle
47 Energy source: Abbr.
49 Prophet
51 Levied a tax, in England
52 Boxing units
53 International tennis competitors
54 Laughed quietly
57 Port near Marseilles
58 Partners of Hamlet's arrows
61 Vexes
62 Biblical brother
65 Hit hard
68 Parallel to
71 Most biting
74 Holder for a snack
77 Highway
78 Cleans vigorously
80 Electron tubes
82 Cultivation of the soil
84 In this
87 Elliptical shapes
88 Measure out
89 Gaiters
90 "Here I come, ready __!"
91 Board game
93 __-Croatian, Yugoslav language
95 Ecological periods
98 Ship's company
99 Air pollution
101 Coat-pocket accumulation
105 Miss Merkel
106 Desert state: Abbr.

11 Before the Thaw
by Hugh McElroy

ACROSS

1 Little scamp
4 Heating unit: Abbr.
7 "The Forsyte __"
11 Kind of roofing
16 Land mass
17 Make headway
18 Kind of heating
19 Black or Valentine
20 Garment for Stevenson's Silver
22 Games to get a party going
24 Charm
25 __ de Leon
27 Kind of heat
28 Work of poetry
29 Line of pickets
30 Doer: Suffix
31 Hepburn movie, with "The"
35 Relative of "Eureka!"
36 "__ 'nuff!"
39 Author Hammond
40 Carney
41 Fireplace crackler
42 Organic compound
43 Insect
44 Hair's counterpart
46 Son of Isaac
48 Seat for Elizabeth
50 Stadium shout
51 Brown or Paul of music
52 Prayer endings
53 Tiny centipede
54 Anne and Bernadette: Abbr.
56 Joseph C. Lincoln's Cap'n
57 Rancor
58 Kind of gin
59 Villa d'__
61 Advice to a procrastinator
63 "Das Rheingold" role
65 Wagons-__ (French sleepers)
67 Newsman Pyle
68 Hearthside residue
71 Uses a solarium
73 Lacking a behavior code
75 Quoted
76 Vintage auto
77 A __ in the air
78 Per __
79 Parka feature
80 Some say "Welcome"
82 British medal
83 Manner
84 Marshall, for one
86 Neighbor of Md.
87 Comfort
89 McMahon et al.
90 On the __ (punctual)
91 Trail at Vail
95 Ankle warmer of yore
97 Entices
98 Sea bird
99 Goes by plane
101 Eastern womens' quarters
102 Misbehaves
106 In, like the spy
109 Money for overshoes?
112 Asian capital
113 Matadors' targets
114 Like chilblains
115 Early auto maker
116 Relating to
117 __ up (be secretive)
118 Have
119 Be regretful

DOWN

1 "This one __ me"
2 This is often over matter
3 Place for a weather ear
4 Scrooge's cry
5 Kind of ear or horn
6 Like money in the bank
7 World Cup game
8 Mariner's word
9 Gift of __
10 Train schedule abbr.
11 Do a figure eight
12 L.A. basketeer
13 Kind of code
14 Student's time span
15 Half ems
16 Hearty brew
17 Bridge expert
18 From the time of
21 Somewhat green in color
23 Lovers of finer things
26 Neighbor of Que.
29 F.D.R. broadcast
30 Mateo or Sebastian
31 Some fishermen
32 Hereditary
33 Ready to go, as skiers
34 Hip boot
35 Moving-in parties
36 Knee-deep in work
37 "__ soit. . ."
38 A Cassini
41 Poem part
42 Editors' concerns
45 __ de France
46 Removed the contents
47 Fished with a net
49 American patriot
52 "It's __ Tell a Lie"
55 Recipe words
60 Coup d'__
62 Constellation
64 Cordial flavorings
66 Like haphazard work
69 Closes securely
70 Like a toddy
72 Seed cell
73 Highest point
74 Robin Hood's Marian
81 Ironing mishap
85 Land purchase
86 Allows as correct
88 Seek out
91 Zigzag downhill thrill
92 Mideast-area people
93 Pique
94 Stop
95 Neil or Paul
96 Kind of larceny
99 Friend of Kukla and Ollie
100 Kind of wolf
101 Now, to a Spaniard
103 Sea off Borneo
104 Wavy, in heraldry
105 City depts.
106 U.S. home agency
107 Catchall abbr.
108 Mountain pass
110 Kind of bridge or blow
111 Vessel for Keats

ACROSS

1 Small drink
5 Louder, in music: Abbr.
10 Humorist Nash
15 Sixth-sense feelings
19 Jot
20 Soak out
21 Gloat
22 Harbor boat
23 This is heard in November
26 American Indian
27 Intensive inflections
28 Artist Max
29 Subject
30 Invariably
31 Peevish
32 Kipling locale
34 Kitchen utensil
37 Call up
38 Deep bow
39 Things to know
40 Made one aware of
42 Indian tent: Var.
45 "__ Town"
46 Scorch
48 Headland
49 Connective
50 Grows up
52 Make abundantly clear
56 Hole in three, on a par five
58 Ones who deny
60 Garish lights
61 Took it on the run
62 Finnish Olympic star
63 Kind of raving mad
64 __ diem
65 Trounce
67 April 1 people
68 Hair-raising stories
71 Hindu princess
72 Expelled ignominiously
74 Ostrich's cousin
75 Doer: Suffix
76 Roman bronze
77 Nervous
78 Small fish
79 Bungle
81 Took pot shots
85 Welcome
87 Dictate
89 Arabian chiefs
90 Stylish
91 Playwright Shelagh
93 Family members, for short
94 Appear to be
95 Between Tinker and Chance
96 Corn chip
97 Pursued a court case
101 Gave credit
102 Wound up badly
105 Sole time
106 __ aves (unusual things)
107 Siren call
108 Splotch
109 Brit. money
110 Pauses
111 Freshet
112 Stew

DOWN

1 Make a splash
2 Leeway
3 Eagerly awaiting
4 Sugarcane knife
5 More handy
6 Direct attention to
7 Dines
8 Learning place: Abbr.
9 Root for the team
10 Sailing room
11 Vulgar
12 Kind of store: Abbr.
13 Slippery one
14 Compass point
15 Reversion of property
16 Fit of nerves
17 Verses
18 Like Sue
24 Roof parts
25 Tine
29 __-la
31 Fascinate
32 Specious
33 Wholly
34 Show despair
35 Item of cosmetics
36 A meaningful lull
37 Baby buggies
38 Does sewing
41 Critter for a buster
43 Tent need
44 Provoked
46 Noisy bite
47 Mata __
51 Fry lightly
53 Insect study: Abbr.
54 Domain
55 Race or dark
56 British peer
57 Capacious
59 Accurate
61 Common folk
63 Drunkard
64 Engine sound
65 Hat part
66 Lessen
67 Jacques, for one
68 Buffalo Bill et al.
69 Advises, old style
70 Full of fat
72 Vassar-chain material
73 Loved ones
80 More knowledgeable
81 Opponent
82 Ridicules
83 Singer Pasquale
84 Towns in Minn. and Miss.
85 Miss Garson
86 Orders back
88 Stances: Abbr.
90 Delegate
91 Apollo's isle
92 Occurrence
93 Kind of Dane
94 Show off
96 Belonging to a W.W. II President
97 Confused
98 Usurer's offering
99 Small case
100 Obligation
102 Stray
103 Scottish denial
104 High peak

13 Running a Temperature by David A. Scully

ACROSS

1 Michigan county
7 Drinks
11 Buck's partner
14 Las Vegas machine
18 Concluding part
19 Hindu garment
21 Kind of laundry
23 Fire: Prefix
24 Guardian of the tree of life in Eden
26 Site of Sam McGee's cremation, with 38 Down
28 Evergreen
29 Green Mountain boy et al.
30 Capri and Elba, e.g.
32 Bodies of knowledge
33 Will __, first Hollywood czar
34 "Sabrina __"
35 Dismounted
36 __ and con
39 Decays
40 Oast
41 Hams it up
45 Flavoring oils
47 Hot time in the Midwest
50 Direction for a left turn
51 Stevenson and father
52 Without help
53 Neighbor of Vietnam
54 Have concern
55 Untruthful ones
56 Cut of meat
57 __ terrier
59 He wrote about Poker Flat
60 Donkey, in England
61 Insect eggs
62 Go __ (deteriorate)
63 Lasso
64 Compass point
65 Smokey's concern
68 Component
69 Tower of Pisa, for one
71 Parts of a dilemma
72 Agenda
73 Booth Tarkington boy
74 What troubleshooters do
76 Explorer Johnson
79 Heavy swords
80 Columbus's port
81 Odds and __
82 Newts
83 Burns midnight oil
84 Math ratios
85 Dwellings
87 Bistros
88 Gay and sprightly
89 "The __ Love"
90 Head cavity
91 "__ Under the Elms"
92 Henpeck
93 Explosive device
96 Cuban V.I.P. and family
97 Contrivances
99 Century plant
100 Trucks
101 City lines
102 Indonesian islands
103 Scent
104 French dances
105 Jack or his wife
107 Fiddle from Cremona
108 Disavowed
110 Drinking place
113 ". . . falsely shouting fire __"
115 What three Biblical Babylonians fell into
118 Top-drawer
119 Pollutions
120 Crimean meeting place
121 Was befitting
122 Debtor
123 "__ Little Teapot"
124 Loch __
125 Remains

DOWN

1 Uncertain
2 White or Blue river
3 Bite persistently
4 Radioman
5 "I cannot tell __"
6 Cough-drop flavors
7 Metal analyses
8 Grassy places
9 Love god
10 Preachment: Abbr.
11 Roadside cafe
12 Table scraps
13 Anglo-Saxon letter
14 Capital of Laconia
15 Early harp
16 Assns.
17 __ the line
20 Impressive structure
21 Dealing out in dabs
22 Shouters
25 Sights on the Ganges
27 Rippled fabric
31 Sitting room, in Spain
35 Plane over the Seine
36 Biblical songs
37 CB's and transistors
38 See 26 Across
39 Louis XIV and others
40 Tight curl
41 Work __
42 Elijah's vehicle to heaven
43 Steak or sauce
44 Kind of potato
46 Like a day in June
47 Teacher's charge
48 Short term of endearment
49 Miscellanies
52 Change
54 A la __
56 Inspired, with "up"
57 Animal horn
58 "Don't make __ of yourself!"
59 Worn-out horses
61 Forbidden things
62 Beginners: Var.
63 Fortifies the punch
65 Ex-boxer Tommy and family
66 Ultima __
67 Relatives of pix
68 Ernie and Gerald
70 One's own worst __
72 Has a meal
73 Outcast
74 Black Friday occurrence
75 Leg bone
77 Solid alcohol
78 Evaluate
79 Looks over
80 Lonesome trees
82 Bridge seat
84 Puppeteer and family
85 Take to the trail
86 __ in a million
87 Kind of pool
89 Record of a meeting
90 Purify, as gold
91 Tallchief, for one
93 Iranian empress
94 Electronic finders
95 "Thanks __"
96 Western state: Abbr.
98 Trade
100 Chekhov's Uncle and others
103 The end
104 Lahr and Wheeler
105 Kind of job
106 Window part
107 Minute quantity
108 Take out
109 Ear part
110 Restrain
111 Maple genus
112 Cerises, etc.
113 Honey-eating bird
114 Friend, in France
116 Writer Fleming
117 Point of a pen

14 Tricky Treatment

by Tap Osborn

ACROSS

1 Word with whip or back
5 Foundation
10 Gushes
15 Close ones
19 Siouan
20 Turn away
21 Tuck
22 Crazed
23 First line of a verse
27 Pear-shaped instrument
28 Fastidiously neat
29 At one's elbow
30 Stress factor
31 Delhi money
32 Antagonize
33 Supply's partner
36 Cockeyed
37 Arpeggio
38 Neck, in Nice
41 Khachaturian
42 Fry, as onions
43 Lumberjack's contest
44 Attila follower
45 Second line of verse
50 Home: Prefix
51 Kind of footed
52 Zenith
53 Uncommon
54 Cakewalk dancer
56 Cold victim's need
58 Amtrak worker
60 Walter or Jean
61 Ribald
62 Corona
63 Beach-club adjunct
66 Roadshow worker
67 Order to a little dogie
71 Singing brothers
72 Emden or Memel
73 NOW members
74 Nash or Reo
75 Third line of verse
81 Lummox
82 Banish
83 Financial windfall
84 Tide
85 Nazi leader
86 Bare
87 Roof or screen, e.g.
88 Throw into a tizzy
90 Partner of forget
91 Hugh of N.Y. politics
92 Fleshy fruit
93 Appearance
96 Ordinary
97 Its child has to work
101 Last line of verse
104 Defeat soundly
105 Food chemical
106 Escape
107 Wild plum
108 Times past
109 Lachrymose
110 Man-made fabric
111 Layer

DOWN

1 Rich soil
2 "__ boy!"
3 Male child, in Coburg
4 Unit on an auto front
5 Serenader's piece
6 Miss
7 In stitches
8 Pique
9 Approach boldly
10 Like a cactus: Var.
11 Level
12 Slithery
13 Hebrew letter
14 Abstract sculptures
15 Outdated
16 Both: Prefix
17 Stentorian
18 Terrier
24 Bird on a fish diet
25 Small child
26 Word with jack or jacket
31 Awaken rudely
32 Pocahontas's John
33 Entries on a calendar
34 Straight up
35 Estate sight
36 Cargo shipper
37 Spacious
38 Mulct
39 Exaggerated
40 Racing's Al or Bobby
42 Derisive look
43 Oscar-winning film
46 With frequency
47 Extreme
48 "Annie" role
49 Leon of films
55 Kiev edict
56 "Poker Flat" author
57 Cereal bristle
58 Church plate
59 Warner of Chan films
61 Unit of pressure
62 Encircle
63 Plot group
64 Divert
65 Ross or Palmer
66 "The Friends of Eddie __"
67 Like in a big way
68 Singing group
69 Like some voices
70 Complaint
72 Egotistical feeling
73 Aviator Post
76 "Death in __"
77 Joyous
78 Beyond ethics
79 Nightlong celebrant
80 Passbook item
87 Songbird
88 Putrescent
89 Asian boundary river
90 "Twelfth Night" clown
91 Chair worker
92 Child: Prefix
93 Cockeyed
94 "Vamoose!"
95 Serve, in a way
96 Code word
97 Deacon's carriage
98 Modern artist
99 Stub __
100 River to the North Sea
102 ". . . __ that tiger!"
103 Power authority

15 Wall Writings by Raymond F. Eisner

ACROSS

1 Charley or Crazy
6 Gather in
10 Counterweight
14 Kind of head or point
17 Critical
18 Preposition
19 Cupid
20 River of the Left Bank
22 Range animal
23 Graffiti question
26 Chicago suburb
28 Records
29 A __ color (profusion)
30 White vestments
33 Cheer in Granada
34 Where countries get together
35 Graffiti statement
42 Like Pisa's tower
43 Gypsy's horse
44 Dilapidated
45 Portable seat
48 Spanish uncles
49 Lasso
52 Airboard initials
53 "There __ tavern in . . ."
54 Salamander
55 Graffiti statement
61 __ Carlo
62 Dull
63 Golfer with an army
64 Cuts short
66 Beetle
67 Ulysses S. and family
68 Ex-Mayor Abe of N.Y.
69 Western plateau
70 Honkers
71 Graffiti reply to 55 Across
75 Dry, as wine
78 N.Y. time
79 Languid
80 Moving about
81 Flying prefix
82 Football holder
83 Crackerjack-box offering
85 Campus in Troy, N.Y.
86 __ nous
87 Graffiti retort to 35 Across
92 Entices
94 Cartoonist Irvin
95 Sings softly
96 Is unable
97 Blaze or Ringo
99 Wish upon __
101 Graffiti question
104 Respiratory ailment
108 Cafe lights
109 Hercules's captive
110 Dies __
111 Writer Bret
112 Elected, in France
113 Overwhelms
114 Predatory fish
115 Matriculate

DOWN

1 Kind of been
2 One of twelve: Abbr.
3 Street, in Paris
4 Patterns for printing letters
5 Most uncanny
6 Take a taxi
7 Space monkey
8 Had a bite
9 Actor Tom
10 Home of a brave
11 "Rule Britannia" composer
12 Nessen and Ziegler
13 Vane direction
14 Michelangelo masterpiece
15 Cases for geishas
16 Hildegarde __
20 Anvil
21 French school
24 Island east of Java
25 "Common Sense" was one
27 Trip-inducing initials
30 Small type
31 Underlying theme
32 Stupid one
36 Beautiful birds
37 Sharp ridge
38 Mexican President Porfirio
39 Stymied
40 Bonnet monkey
41 Subway stops: Abbr.
45 Permitted
46 Tray contents
47 "__ as you go"
50 Hebrew letters
51 Come __ friend (run into)
55 Opera by Bellini
56 Prefix for continental
57 King of Tyre and others
58 Kitchen gadget
59 Remove
60 Actress Bancroft
61 Extinct birds
64 Maltreat
65 Miss Davis
67 __ of (discard)
69 Founder of Egypt's first dynasty
70 Suitcases
71 Use the parimutuels
72 Chide
73 Bronx cheer
74 Italian bell town
75 "Ready, __" (race-starting words)
76 Mistaken: Abbr.
77 Campus girls
81 Native of a Pyrenees land
83 Mountain climbers' pegs
84 Remainder, in Seville
86 Result of hearing a rock combo
87 Curtain material
88 Ichabod and Stephen
89 Possessive
90 Small centipede
91 Outer: Prefix
92 Swiss city
93 Variety of pear
96 Movies, for short
97 Win, place or __
98 Tattler's offering
99 Remote
100 Sanctified women: Abbr.
102 Spanish aunt
103 Writer Wolfert
105 Scrap
106 Western Indian
107 __ diem

16 In Residence by Alfio Micci

ACROSS

1 Spanish ladies: Abbr.
5 Neither fem. nor neut.
9 Declare
14 Queenly term of address
18 Marco et al.
20 Within: Prefix
21 English isle
22 Skink
23 Organic compound
24 Glacial trough
25 Author Joyce Carol
26 Frees of
27 __ the future (tell fortunes)
29 Second
31 Up the __
32 Italian Miss
34 Velvetlike fabrics
36 Hockey star Bobby
37 Solar disks
38 Unworthy of
39 Something often raised
42 Hebrew month
43 Haitian voodoo deities
44 Testing quarters
47 Heightens
50 American Miss
54 Early historical period
55 Caravansary
56 Medit. port
57 Tender
58 Prodded
61 Nabokov Miss
62 Words of understanding
65 Swiss Miss
68 Single
69 Easter __
71 Overrun
72 Spanish river
74 Walking __ (elated)
75 Deserter
76 Cold symptom
80 Mexican Miss
85 Minnesota Fats's milieu
86 ". . . __ I saw Elba"
87 In __ (in place)
88 Downs or salts
90 Just
91 Boned item
92 Zoo beast, for short
93 Naval monogram
95 Camper's gear
98 Pennsylvania Miss
103 Presented a movie twice
104 Town crier's light
106 Of less importance
107 Fairway club
108 Do a grammarian's job
109 Handle manuscripts
111 Common homemade candy
112 Join
113 Harden
114 Famed fiddler
115 S.O.S. item
116 Peggy and Gypsy Rose
117 Experiments
118 Rive
119 Secondhand

DOWN

1 Tic
2 Paris's rival
3 Foreign
4 Connecticut Miss
5 French wine
6 Upward: Prefix
7 Main and Wall
8 Pone source
9 Faints
10 Opera headwear
11 Go-betweens: Abbr.
12 Keats' "__ St. Agnes"
13 French connectives
14 Bone content
15 Ta-ta, in Toulouse
16 Viper
17 Disguises
19 Man of Mexico
28 Bus-rider's scrip: Abbr.
30 He wrote "Divine Poems"
31 Near
33 Poker move
35 Biblical ruler

38 Golden-haired one
39 Thing, in law
40 Canadian prov.
41 Exclamation of surprise
42 Mideast desert
44 Vladimir Ilyich Ulyanov
45 Loos
46 Kind of metabolism
48 Prefix meaning modern
49 Insert mark
51 Turns thumbs down
52 Concerning
53 Island Miss
58 Between Arthur and Doyle
59 "We're __ see the
   wizard . . ."
60 Ripen
61 Of the lips: Prefix
62 ". . .to fetch her poor dog__"
63 Ace or king
64 Trap
66 Rid of mustiness
67 Asp's weapon
70 Geologist's concern
73 Fill the gas tank: Abbr.

76 Parody
77 Swedish county
78 Building addition
79 Foxy
81 "__ 'er up!"
82 Resembling a star
83 Roi's spouse
84 Evident
89 Metrical foot
91 Certain bun occupants
92 Grand and others
93 City on the Danube
94 Body of officers
95 Flatfish
96 Unworldly
97 Male bee
98 Beginning
99 Celebrated Lady
100 As __ the hills
101 Red grouper
102 As slim as __
105 War god
108 Western time zone: Abbr.
110 Author Levin

17 Quiz Time by Maura B. Jacobson

ACROSS

1 Dexterous
6 Jellied side dish
11 "The mouse __ the clock"
16 Junta
21 Dickens's Heep
22 After-bath item, at Caracalla
23 Operational
24 Kukla's buddy
25 What did the villainous flagman say?
27 Where do Eskimo horsemen play?
29 One of the Starrs
30 Word on a proof
31 Under the weather
32 Does originals
33 Teasdale
35 Fool's __ (futile enterprise)
37 O'Casey and namesakes
38 Fort __, Calif.
41 Bernstein-Sondheim song
43 Picnic pest
44 Squirm
45 N.Y.C. skyline letters
48 What did the basketball coach say?
52 Floe
53 City on Norton Sound
54 Costello
55 Call __ day
56 Marquis de __
57 Flutter above
58 Detroit name
60 Myths
62 Await judgment
63 Dahl or Francis
64 Wives of rois
66 Zilch
67 Spongy mushroom
68 Stowe villain
69 Concorde
70 What is a party-pooping sailor?
73 Xmas paste-on
75 Sniggles
76 Cheer up
78 Part of the head
80 Long for
82 Cartoonist Goldberg
84 Umps' compeers
87 What do showy dancers wear on their feet?
90 Guevara
93 Items on the slate
95 Auto grease jobs
97 "Arabian Nights" bird
98 High regard
100 What was said when Kitty awakened?
101 Chemical endings
102 Senate aides
104 Restaurant request
105 __ alia
106 What Hester Prynne wore
107 __ Lanka
108 Forenoons: Abbr.
110 Cut of beef
111 Humorist George and family
112 Why is it wrong to whisper?
116 Cato's hearth god
117 Giggle
118 Ballpoint
119 Glyceride, for one
120 Metric units: Abbr.
121 Wading birds
122 Montmartre attraction
124 Saragossa's river
126 Masthead listings
129 Asphalt's kin
130 "__ deal!"
132 Bridge positions
135 Who host gangland shindigs?
137 What is paid for chickens?
140 Anoint, old style
141 Acclimate
142 Alpaca's cousin
143 Lady love, in Lyon
144 Nuzzled
145 Discourage
146 Miss Glasgow
147 Father Damien's parishioner

DOWN

1 __ wiedersehen
2 Beat soundly
3 De Valera's land
4 Becomes uninteresting
5 "Did he who made __ make thee?"
6 One __ time
7 Is droopy
8 Mesa
9 Less cordial
10 Striking differences
11 Attack verbally
12 "You can't teach __ dog . . ."
13 Partner of void
14 Canteen initials
15 Discern
16 Forcible
17 Pseudonym
18 Rorschach image
19 Senior: Fr.
20 Minus
26 Push off the track
28 Do a blackboard chore
34 Jargon
36 Novelist Seton
37 Wrap the baby
38 Proprietors
39 Home of the Colossus
40 What did the Aswan surveyor report?
42 Tennessee Williams's lizard
44 Scottish titles
45 Where do you look up Biblical data?
46 Opening in a parapet
47 Is of the same mind
49 High-school age
50 Gives way
51 Addict
52 "Where's Charley?" star
57 Charlemagne's legacy: Abbr.
59 Siberian river
61 Adjective for Abner
62 Hit a shallow fly
63 Assert without proof
65 Petty tyrant
67 Certain skirts
71 Letter
72 Takes the car
74 Author Rand
77 Opticians' items
79 Narrow waterway
81 Aide: Abbr.
82 Ethnological
83 Answer to "Me goose?"
85 Swindles
86 Fountain order
88 Gluttonous one
89 Surfers' sites
91 Balloonist's need
92 Makes corrections
94 Hard, in Nice
96 Geste or Brummell
99 Kind of tale or order
102 Precept
103 Struck hard
106 Worked up again
107 Viewed
109 Soprano Eleanor
112 Holly feature
113 Not as dense
114 Fleshly
115 Lineup
117 Decorated a book binding
121 Stone marker
122 Pivotal troop unit
123 Lagoon locale
125 Actor Davis
126 Zest
127 __ De Laurentiis
128 Currier's partner
129 Race-track figure
131 Egyptian dancing girl
133 Small mound, in England
134 River duck
136 "__ if by land. . ."
138 Relative of ecru
139 Delhi weight

18 Digital Computing by Sidney L. Robbins

ACROSS

1 Look daggers at
6 Art school
10 Refer to
14 Like an SST
18 Unsocial one
19 Spanish fingers
20 Change for a five
21 Nastase of tennis
22 Joined the cast
23 Era
24 Neighbor of Mont.
25 Hawaiian goose
26 New Korean method of counting by hand
29 Taj Mahal city
30 Actual being
31 Bridge seat
32 I.R.S. collection
33 Certain kind of penny
35 Oklahoma or Ohio
37 Box
39 Fine Italian marble
40 Welcome __
43 Lyon seasons
44 Opposite of a rave
45 Sally Rand's cover
46 Baby carriage
47 Run off
49 Sinister movie role
52 High-__ (easily unnerved)
54 Annamese measure
55 Picnic pest
56 Pinball woe
59 Camping item
60 Cuban ballerina Alicia
63 __ Grande
64 Unique figure
65 Smell __
66 Piano feature
69 Type of chest
71 Old English letters
73 "__ lamps for old"
74 Choosy words
75 Preposition
76 Active one
77 Hindu title
78 Fool
79 Highly decorated
81 Beauty salon item
85 Monsters
86 Russian range
89 Ref. book
90 Mineral rock
91 Icelandic writing
94 Medics: Abbr.
95 Wind instruments
97 In any way
98 Requirements
100 Bargain
101 Before: Prefix
102 Anna's destination
103 Ancient chest
107 Coal, for one
108 Basic operation in 26 Across
112 Pretzels' partner
113 Casino currency
114 Gooey mess
115 Miss Moorehead
116 Irish exclamation
117 Breathe heavily
118 Lena tributary
119 Lateen boat: Var.
120 Org.
121 Painting, sculpture, etc.
122 Bread and whisky
123 Skilled

DOWN

1 Candied
2 Lomond and Ness
3 Opposers
4 Pee Wee and family
5 Wagnerian goddess
6 Ousts
7 Take on
8 Severinsen et al.
9 Pale
10 Get joint billing
11 Back part of a textbook
12 Mets or Dodgers
13 Igloo dweller: Abbr.
14 Step in booking a prisoner
15 Put on guard, in Spain
16 Frank or Nancy
17 Golfer's place
19 Exchange pros and cons
27 Clean
28 Position
29 Opposite of dep.
33 Sudden pain
34 Dixie edible
36 Pimple time
37 Wife, for one
38 Pard
39 Eddie and Ida
40 Mostest hostess
41 Changed
42 Link between Kansas and Oz
45 Spire ornaments
48 Do a Mafia job
49 "West Side Story" event
50 Atlantic island people
51 W.W. II zone
53 Arabic letter
54 In the chips
57 Bernstein
58 Roosevelt Raceway entry
61 Classified-ad totals
62 Gold, in Spain
67 More heroic
68 __ volente
70 Wind-deposited soil
72 __ Lanka
80 Type of hog
82 Type of book
83 Type of rug
84 Exist
86 Alas, in Bonn
87 Certain shoes
88 Ones who wrangle
91 Mysteries
92 Saturate with noise
93 Type of tasse
96 Building wing
97 Explodes
99 Drooped
101 West or pin
102 Sarcastic
104 French income
105 Crawl
106 Thing of value
108 Scorch
109 Russian ex-V.I.P.
110 Poorly
111 Space initials
112 Bleat
113 Bookkeeper, first class

19 Nonsked Flights   by Arnold Moss

ACROSS

1 Fellow, in England
4 One of the Mohicans
8 Vex
12 Layer of paint
16 Shrill instrument
17 Performers' union
19 Resin
21 Heavenly one, in Anjou
22 Campus military org.
23 Debussy birdsong
25 Require
26 Awestruck
28 Mr. Rathbone
29 Fees for keeping goods
31 Insect science: Abbr.
33 Golfer's depredation
35 Before febrero
36 Frank Lloyd Wright center
39 Leaf part
41 Without aches
44 Caesar's wrath
45 "__ work" (road sign)
47 Archeologist's find
49 Pranks
50 Evergreens
52 "__ and a bone. . ."
54 Drink mixes
56 Suffix for Henri
57 Like some bargain antiques
59 Harness parts
61 Spanish direction
63 Drink in Paris
64 Deteriorate
66 De France and du Diable
68 Goes over the hill
70 Dark-complexioned, to a poet
72 Whitman's flower
74 Chant
75 Nonanalytic
76 Dissertation material
77 Christmas song
78 Number of coins for Trevi
79 Handbills: Abbr.
82 Old Greek pillar
84 Begets
88 Cans, in Canterbury
90 To the subject
92 Raw or New
93 Yield
94 Agreed
96 Seven, in Milan
98 Hair tufts
101 One of the Khans
102 Uprising
104 U.S. flag parts
106 Events at Lourdes
108 Michigan's Ann
110 Give a lecture
112 Nine, to Cicero
113 Stormy cape
116 Coral island
118 Hoist with one's own __
121 Mitch Miller's instrument
122 What an avian brother might do
125 Etcher's need
126 N.Y. commuter line
127 Zoological classes: Suffix
128 Of an ecological cycle
129 Political cartoonist
130 Hodgepodge
131 National burden
132 R. I. birds
133 Farm animal

DOWN

1 Life history: Abbr.
2 "Rape __" (Pope's avian offering)
3 Of the dean's side of the choir
4 Milk sugar
5 Labor initials
6 Make a __ at (try)
7 Group of three
8 Heads for Gretna Green again
9 Neighbor of Mo.
10 Durocher and others
11 Ham it up
12 Section of Brooklyn
13 Deserving water bird
14 Awry
15 Kennedy and Williams
16 Filippo Lippi
18 Upbeat, in music
20 Turkish statesman
24 One doing a gainer
27 Stern's counterpart
30 Split
32 Talkative musical trios
34 Eagle's weapon
36 Quarrel
37 Sills specialty
38 Honshu city
40 Neighbor of Venice
42 Take turns
43 Of a birthright seller
46 Language in Sri Lanka
48 Grosbeak's wrongdoing
51 Inn for caravans
53 Frosty
55 Pitman expert
58 Hog
60 Psalm word
62 Kefauver
65 Narrow groove
67 Glutted
69 Of an old Greek race
70 Ariel, for one
71 Winged remodelers
73 Cavalier poet
75 Rose perfume
80 Louder, in music: Abbr.
81 Argument
83 Mangle
85 Genuine parrot
86 TV's "__ of Night"
87 Red and Black
89 Contemptuous laughers
91 Famous docking spot
95 River to the North Sea
97 Muse
99 Drives forward
100 Use a piggy bank
103 Sculptor's piece
105 Puts away
107 Colorless oil
109 __ City, S.D.
111 Kind of statesman
113 Eleanor or Celeste
114 Rose's love
115 Radio's Vic and __
117 Money in Venice
119 Singer Stevens
120 Insecticide
123 Johnny __
124 Kind of dog or hatter

20 Like the Driven Snow by Frances Hansen

ACROSS

1 Madrid gallery
6 Something to strain at
10 Door part
14 Agreement
18 Making all stops
19 Columnist Barrett
20 The Tentmaker
21 Gosh!
22 Cave, to poets
23 Heated discussions: Abbr.
24 Miss Turner
25 Remove a wrapping
26 Start of a verse
30 Convex moldings
31 October stone
32 Garish gas
33 Mulligans
34 Kind of dance or room
36 Fuss
38 Having wings
39 Inlet
42 __-me-up (short snort)
45 Served with ice cream
49 Greek peak
53 More of verse
57 Pointed arch
58 Fairy-tale start
59 Part of K.K.K.
60 Eddie Albert's wife
61 Classiness
62 Cigarette stub
63 Ardor
64 Sprayed the house plants
65 Attic salt
66 Young 'un
67 Approximately: Abbr.
68 Gardening tool
72 Peak point
74 Karl or Chico
76 Bourbon, rye et al.: Abbr.
80 "The Broken Nose" sculptor
81 Off balance
82 Farm building
83 Port Moresby's territory
84 More of verse
88 European blackbird
89 Mosaic piece
90 Companion of Ares
91 Unfold, poetically
92 Dayak tribe
94 Tree feller
96 "The Second __ Tanqueray"
98 Belle or Ringo
100 Deer track
103 Speak gratingly
106 Word with tattle or tell
110 End of verse
114 Tilting, at sea
115 Campaigner's objective
116 Bare
117 "Age of Reason" author
118 Mythical king of Crete
119 State firmly
120 Italian wine center
121 Fuel ship
122 "East of __"
123 Barber's call
124 Musial
125 Girl in a pool

DOWN

1 Braid
2 Sonata movement
3 Man in a cast
4 "Oh, shucks!"
5 Kitchen staple
6 Comprehension
7 __ Jean Baker (Marilyn Monroe)
8 Luanda is its capital
9 Chore
10 Zsa Zsa's mother
11 "Gabriela, Clove and Cinnamon" author
12 Massenet opera
13 Breakfast cereal
14 Western pines to think about
15 Permit
16 Thunder crashes
17 Do a hunt-and-peck job
21 __-percha
27 Theme
28 __ Gay of W.W. II
29 Medicine's Sir William
35 Church area
37 Dinesen or Borge, e.g.
38 __ Olam, Hebrew hymn
39 Melee
40 Classic villain
41 Idi of Uganda
43 Political muscle
44 Rockwell __
46 Invited
47 "__ 18," Uris book
48 Stadium shape
50 Ilk
51 Purple or scarlet
52 Footless
54 Greeting to Caesar
55 Take steps
56 Norse giant
62 Puppeteer Baird
63 Slate-cutting tool
64 Cooking direction
65 Go one's way
66 You need a reservation to sleep here
67 Bop on the head
68 Shipshape
69 A Kennedy
70 River to the Baltic
71 "Tarka the Otter" author
72 "__ well that ends well"
73 Luau dishes
74 Russian village
75 Lily plant
76 Swedish county
77 __ facto
78 Bon mot
79 In one's right mind
81 Choir response
82 Tunisian port
83 Impoverished
85 Eared seal
86 In a snit
87 Sylvan maiden
93 Neighbor's children
95 Hemingway or Pyle
97 Gide's "__ Is the Gate"
98 Kind of geometry
99 Stout cord
100 Rude push
101 Synthetic rubber
102 Open
104 Artery
105 Poet Gertrude
107 Spry
108 Napery
109 Spanish month
110 Moniker
111 Terrible one
112 "Amo, __, I love a lass"
113 Body of poetry

21 Flying Lesson by Herb Risteen

ACROSS

1 Educated cook
5 Gossip
9 Show pleasure
13 Rose-to-be
16 Of hearing
18 Helper
19 Little or Sid
21 One: Prefix
22 Henry James novel
25 Dixie initials
26 Roman time period
27 Dutch painter
28 Captured
30 What Ulysses's men wound up as
32 __ on it (hurries)
34 Mouthlike openings
36 Motor trips
37 Tropical birds
39 Manchurian port
40 Marine fish
41 African outing for T.R.
42 Main force
43 Kind of store: Abbr.
46 Work unit
47 English tree
48 Before stock and barrel
49 Bird call
50 Spider work
51 Sharpens
52 Sour and seedless
54 Clue
55 Legal plea
57 Monarchs
58 Use an epee
59 Master a mountain
60 Old woman
61 Versatile Victor
62 Joint
63 Fissure
64 Anchored
66 Eating place
67 Disturb
69 Actress Debra
70 Ginger or Adam's
73 Greek god
74 Admit
75 Scornful ones
77 Negative
78 Weight of India
79 Vehicles
80 Overdoes a role
81 I know: Lat.
82 Teeth
84 Low places
85 Violinist Isaac
86 Over-the-hill race horses
88 Leg parts
89 __ Haute
90 Singer Lehmann
91 Kind of companion
92 Famous frontiersman
94 Black bird
95 Afford protection
103 Recent: Prefix
104 Scanty
105 Bank of type
106 Strange
107 Sea eagle
108 English river
109 Fuss
110 Valley

DOWN

1 Popular pet
2 Exclamation
3 Sooner than
4 Being servile
5 Hockey puck's destination
6 Radiator sound
7 Wedding words
8 Ship-shaped clock
9 Highlanders
10 Ohio athletes
11 Prefix for bar or pod
12 Nautical abbr.
13 Vaudeville performer
14 Like loose gems
15 Moon goddess
17 Kind of share
19 Cowboy garb
20 Sharp reply
23 Compass point
24 On __ (at top speed)
29 French soul
30 Village high point
31 Football lineup
32 Hurries away
33 Weight allowance
34 Gander's due
35 Clinking sounds
36 Large number
37 One of fifty
38 Following
39 Eye and gum
41 Young hog: Var.
42 Trumpet sound
44 Coventry coins
45 Mal de __
47 Thrash
49 "Over __"
53 Blow one's top
56 Hay units
57 Very: Fr.
58 Wayne and Donelson
59 Entangle
60 Balls of yarn
61 Mafeking fighters
62 Fearless fliers
63 Bumpkins
64 Dull finish
65 Curved moldings
67 Of the cheek
68 Extras
69 Milieus for strokes
71 French river
72 Harrow's rival
76 Arab country
79 Is wintry
81 Scattered
83 Baseball's Mel
84 Was prominent
85 Be aware of
86 Kind of geometry
87 Howard Hughes, for one
88 Toper
89 Southern part of Italy
91 Swiss city
92 James or savings
93 Get __ (go aboard)
96 Skillful
97 Miss Francis of films
98 Salamander
99 Aussie animal
100 Gershwin
101 Nothing
102 __ whiz

22 Two on the Aisle by Louis Baron

ACROSS

1 Hitching post
6 School shindig
10 Northern highway
15 Of the peak
21 Bulls, to a Roman
22 Miss Ponselle
23 Old Italian coins
24 Wedlock, overdone
25 Writer Asimov
26 River by the U.N. complex
27 Utah city
28 Cajun locale
29 Marital-column question
33 Orig. writings
34 Line judge's call
35 Famed alarmist
36 Large gong
40 Gentle and Big
42 Fool
44 Pizarro's loot
45 Warplane crewman: Abbr.
48 "__ economy is always
beauty" (James)
49 Abner
50 Domineer
53 Poison
54 Ham __ (deli order)
55 Of yesterday
56 Millay
57 With it
59 "__ tale's best for winter"
60 U.S. Pacific base
61 Old bard
62 Tryout for a car buyer
64 Italian resort
65 Neighbor of Sask.
66 A Mongolia
68 Tup's mate
69 Parisian
71 Gull's cousin
73 Lowed
77 U.S.A.F. dept.
79 Mutilates
80 Bargain for two
85 Roman priests of Mars
86 Long time
87 Shinto gateway
88 Deliver
89 Miss Nightingale's milieu
91 Gamblers' place in N.Y.
93 Work on greasy pans
95 Farm moocher
99 Bullets, briefly
100 Lassie biography
105 Sailors
106 Author Victor
107 Simba
108 Spanish bear
109 Algerian port
110 Resident: Suffix
111 Israeli native
112 Children's zoo ride
113 Wise polygamist
115 Robe size: Abbr.
116 Did a lube job
117 Plank curve
118 Shoe width
120 Concubine's room
121 U.N. initials
123 American landscapist
124 Displayed
126 Objective
127 Windy City's nickname
128 Society-column phrase
138 "Messiah" composer
139 Curved
140 Four-star review
141 All-stops train
142 Bony
143 __ honors (officiate)
144 Deodar or baobab
145 ". . .with __ bodkin?"
(Hamlet)
146 Rowboat
147 Pledged
148 Bark
149 Well-known epigrammatist

DOWN

1 Ending for problem or morgan
2 Town in Italy
3 Sir, in Malaysia
4 Smell __ (suspect)
5 Gold digger's target
6 One of the media
7 Meander
8 Peak in Greece
9 Married lady
10 Use __ (do barbecuing)
11 Bee proboscis parts
12 Obstruct
13 Unfavorable
14 Weeper of myth
15 One who degrades
16 Roguish hero
17 "__ at the office"
18 Juniper
19 Surrounded by
20 __ de Putti, of silents
30 Doctrine
31 Backfield man, at times
32 Elicits
36 N.Y. county
37 Undo a marriage
38 Corday's "hit"
39 Matchmaker's advice
40 Intolerant one
41 Furtive marriages
42 Christie or Held
43 Garden tool
45 Of an arm vein
46 Stop __ (brake quickly)
47 Red wines
49 Hiatuses
51 Tokyo's old name
52 Sexy cake
53 The wife, to some
58 Press run of a book: Abbr.
61 Spore clusters
63 Newlyweds, to misogamists
67 Aussie animal
70 Prayer word
72 Great Lake
74 Frequently, to poets
75 Habitat: Prefix
76 June bug
78 Covered, in a way
80 Walter Scott hero
81 Divorce item
82 Baby words
83 City in Yugoslavia
84 Comparative suffixes
85 Tepee trophies
90 Fuss
92 Hematologist's concern
94 Horse opera
96 Kiev cash
97 Story heavies
98 Blue-dye herbs
101 Demineralized bone
102 Miss La Douce
103 U.S. farm agency
104 Yawn-inducing states
111 Relative by marriage
114 Uncultivated one
118 Ingratiate
119 With maleficence
122 Kind of pants
123 N.Z. fish
124 Less normal
125 Relatives of ods bodkins
126 Priscilla's John
127 Party pooper
128 Monday burden
129 Heraldry word
130 Prefix with morph or plasm
131 Glass oven
132 Steak order
133 Knievel
134 Shamo's alias
135 Suffix with dialect or myth
136 Ointment
137 Kind of club
138 "__ now, brown cow?"

23 Weather Ears by Virginia Wilson

ACROSS

1 Heart-test initials
4 Alleviated
9 Footless
13 Fall guys
18 Indian of the Dakotas
19 Ring, in Rheims
21 Nevada city
22 Heavenly path
23 Aged: Lat.
24 Advocate of the status quo
26 Town of Saudi Arabia
27 Playful, in Paris
29 Ole of vaudeville days
30 Burned
32 Early slave
33 __ down (squelch)
35 Moslems, collectively
37 Aver
38 Beginner
40 N.Z. bird
42 Leatherneck
44 Indian salt deposit
46 Tall garden flowers
48 Cold month in Madrid
49 Tax expert
52 Warned
54 Follower of err and fan
56 Flush
57 Emoter
58 Derisive cry
59 Neck of land: Abbr.
61 Song
63 Hindu cult adherent
65 Extinct bird
66 Arafat's org.
67 Elusive saucers
69 Curly dogs
71 Acts like a startled deer
75 Dumps
76 Historic period: Sp.
77 Scottish river
78 U.S. humorist
79 Malodor
80 Before
81 Less-holy one, in saying
83 Empty
85 Kind of bark
86 Work units
89 Calm, in Cologne
91 Cactuses of the Southwest
94 Cheer
95 Mixes eggs
97 Burke's subject
99 Dog noise
100 Indirect hit
101 Current
102 Chevalier movie
104 Relaxed
107 Jump-off for Columbus
109 P.I. cordage tree
111 Household pests
114 Silly talk
116 Town in northern Michigan
118 Rush of water
120 Maltese weight
121 "Baby, it's __!"
124 Highest note
125 Quart's relative
126 African lily
127 Accustomed
128 Part of a journey
129 Huge, once
130 Dusk's counterpart
131 Mimes
132 Actress Myrna

DOWN

1 Clean the slate
2 Strongholds
3 Call Moscow from the White House
4 Orient
5 Opposite extreme
6 Military muddle
7 Poetic contraction
8 Pedestal part
9 U.S.S.R. co-op
10 Fido or Tray, e.g.
11 United
12 Beetles
13 Was handed a line
14 Ultimatum words
15 Remain
16 Stove mechanism
17 Town, in Germany
20 How Kipling's dawn comes
25 Famed Italian birthplace
28 Ferdinand I, for one
31 Sadat's seat
34 Ring victory
36 Squalid
39 Purchase ack.
41 Familiar Latin verb
43 Electrical unit
44 Yell
45 Basic
47 Roman officials
49 Improbable situation
50 Slender cigar
51 Pile up
53 "The Age of __"
55 Confuse matters
60 Sprinkle
62 Horned viper
64 Handsome
66 Graduate degree
68 Govt. agency
69 Soul
70 Grecian urn's offering
71 Keen enjoyment
72 Capture violently
73 Comparative ending
74 Fuss
80 Prevent, in court
82 Take warning
84 Intuitive initials
87 Resist
88 Sal, for example
90 __ good
92 Sunny side up, for one
93 Six, in Naples
96 Accept naively
98 Shade of anger
100 Pancake base
103 Balloon hoister
104 Teacher's reward
105 Prepare for the Olympics
106 Keep an __ the ground
108 Burdened
110 Ardent
112 Whole: Prefix
113 Theatrical
115 Modified organism
117 Heating lamp
119 Moslem Easters
122 Wave, in Spain
123 Eat late

24 Convention Sites
by Bert Kruse

ACROSS

1 To the nautical left
6 Golden calf
10 Currency
14 Indian of Colombia
18 Orator's first word
20 Perceives
22 __ spumante
23 Drive
24 Site for a U.S. Cheerleaders' Congress
26 Dental Society site in Conn.
28 Timetable abbr.
29 Hot Mexican dish
30 More under the weather
32 Hosts
33 Mère's mate
34 Kind of boat
35 Circus attraction
36 Railway part: Abbr.
39 Place, in the past
40 Brazilian trees
41 Wane
42 Take a dip
46 Capitol Hill figure
48 Cousins of regulations
50 S.R.O., for one
51 Kind of way
52 Congo headstream
53 Bartenders Unlimited site in Ohio
57 Place for a whisper
58 Neighbors of Sooners
60 Marie Saint and Braun
61 Political columnist
62 Dutch commune
63 Keep
64 Tears down: Var.
66 River of France
67 Column supports
69 Silkworm
70 Diamond Merchants Assn. site
75 Francis I and Louis XVI
76 Stays motionless, as a ship
78 Cereal unit
79 Lafayette College site
81 M*A*S*H star
82 Site of Yachtsmen's Jamboree
87 Juliette Low org.
90 Tidies up
92 Certain guns, for short
93 Desert havens
94 Deserter
95 Like an iron to be struck
96 Miss Stritch
99 "__ take arms against. . ."
100 Kind of film
102 Time of life
103 Traffic Safety Engineers' site
107 Intervening, in law
108 Ear addition
110 Inferior
111 Broad, in Bonn
112 More pure

114 Writer Thomas
115 Be off
116 Poker openers
117 Injure
118 TV parts: Abbr.
119 African fox
121 Fastens with a belt
122 Whisky source
123 Quick impression
126 Intelligence
127 Turn
129 Card game
132 Jockeys of America site
134 Calisthenics Teachers' site
137 Lubricated
138 Actress Virna
139 Discernment
140 Shed poundage
141 Tickled
142 Editor's term
143 Dread
144 Loved ones

DOWN

1 Medieval poem
2 Henry's sixth
3 Repute
4 Japanese coin
5 Education tool
6 Toward the center
7 He made a study in scarlet
8 Western Indian
9 Celtic Neptune
10 Sea-bottom lines
11 __ as a beet
12 Ado
13 Secreted

14 Sailing-ship spar
15 Thine, in Paris
16 Additional
17 Certain fine items
19 Get with it
21 Captain
23 Simple
25 Arabian commanders
27 Heavyweight Tony and family
31 Dog-walker's need
34 Soupy of comedy
35 Take on city hall
36 African fly
37 Take up a burden again
38 American Critics Society's site
39 Laurel
41 Archeologists' concerns
43 National Cyclists' site
44 Moslem decrees
45 Rumanian river
47 Wings
48 Composer Maurice
49 Official proclamation
50 City near Florence
54 "Ben-Hur" portrayer
55 Danish king
56 Brief quaffs
59 Indian titles
65 "__ boy!"
66 Recorded deeds
68 Bill's partner
70 Tilted
71 Australian jumpers, for short
72 Row
73 Cause
74 Long green
77 Cantor name

80 Disrespectfulness
81 Speech defect
83 Furniture worker
84 Hic, __, hoc
85 Russian author
86 __ home (dine in)
88 Shakespearean work
89 Changes
90 Captivate
91 Rises
94 Tavern orders
97 Worship
98 Stravinsky
99 Court hearings
101 Mosque priest
104 Construction pieces
105 Most hackneyed
106 Beetle
109 Like old oaks
113 Suggested
116 Word with an artist's signature
117 Lode or Goose
120 Run before the wind
121 Canadas, e.g.
122 Terra __
123 Excited
124 Container for Jill
125 Raines
126 Struck
127 Deception
128 Patient spouse
129 __ Grey, Chaplin's wife
130 Unusual person
131 Bookmaker's study
133 Map lines: Abbr.
135 Bumpkin
136 Actress Ruby

25 Frustration · by Anthony B. Canning

ACROSS

1 "__ which will live in infamy"
6 "Coffee __?"
11 Poet royal of Charles IX, Jean __
16 Very, in France
20 Sacred anthem
21 Requires
22 Senseless
23 Melee
24 Nonanswer to "Who was the 'Forever' gal?"
28 N.C. college
29 Take out
30 Please, in Bonn
31 Owner of the Chicago-fire cow
32 Thing, in law
33 Suffix for hippo or velo
34 Weight of Guinea
35 Like a clear night
36 Nonanswer to "Who created Sherlock?"
40 Kitchen cupboard units
44 Heavy blow
45 Curbs
46 Foot: Suffix
49 Smarter
50 Packaged, as cotton
52 Novelist Charles
53 Make a mulish sound
54 Abalone
55 Held sway
56 Inferno expert
57 Writer's output
58 French articles
59 Kind of series or war
60 Carrie Chapman and family
61 Censures
62 Thy, in France
63 Appeared
64 Miffed
65 Roman 552
66 Nonanswer to "Who was a musketeer?"
73 Reminder
74 Fictional king
75 Wadkins of golf
76 Quencher
78 Prop for Will Rogers
81 __ City, town on the Ohio
83 Deposed a king, at chess
84 Do last-minute studying
85 Believer: Suffix
86 Got along
87 Mnemosyne's offspring
88 Hispaniola unit
89 Wrench
90 English writer of 1800's
91 Physician of old
92 One doing mending
93 Family member
94 What matadors sometimes get
95 Injure
96 Fence fixers
97 Nonanswer to "Who created Nero?"
101 Carolina river
104 British anthem composer
105 Mosquito genus
106 Ways: Abbr.
109 Woodrow or Flip
110 Allay
112 __ sanctum
113 Siouan
114 Where to find the answers
118 Cow's stomach
119 Coal deposits
120 "He's __ loser"
121 Fished
122 Roof pieces
123 Cairo leader
124 French fathers
125 Sandarac trees

DOWN

1 Cape __, Malagasy point
2 "Sir Nigel" author
3 Holy Greek mountain
4 Youthful suffix
5 Greek letter
6 Heavy
7 Give a new title
8 Hardy girl et al.
9 Ernie's widow
10 One of the Wednesdays
11 Goes-into word
12 Kind of truck
13 Be bombastic
14 Get in the poker game
15 Kind of house or pot
16 City on the Mosel
17 Speeder's nemesis
18 Palace storage room
19 Finish off a dragon
23 Organizations' rules
25 Church order-keeper
26 Tolerated
27 ". . . __ cent for tribute"
33 Jacques Cousteau, for one
34 Languished
35 Base
37 Did a cobbling job
38 He had a last case
39 "Endymion" author
40 Pub drink
41 Pugnacious insect
42 Tangle up
43 Munchausen's accounts
46 School event
47 Slow up
48 Anil et al.
50 Saclike cavity
51 Gracie or Ethan
52 One making assessments
53 Hair adornment
55 Barnyard lodging
56 Brave one
57 Roman author
59 Kind of watch
60 Yankee Doodle Boy
61 Fair
63 Tatar or Mongolian
64 Bayard or Traveller
65 Units of force
67 Epic poem
68 Of yore
69 Sated
70 Used up
71 Guadalcanal invader
72 Beetle
77 Mideast nobles
78 Frying aid
79 One multiplication result
80 Bartender's item
81 Gay city
82 Plowed land
83 Much: Prefix
84 Boxing lineup
86 Military group
87 River near Paris
88 Behaves ghostily: Var.
90 "I have __ wickedness"
91 African coastal region
92 Abandon
94 Take a certain elevator
95 Fall moon
96 Up-to-date ones
98 Principal ore of lead
99 "A __ All Seasons"
100 Poe girl
101 Photo for a locker
102 Fragrant resin
103 __ Park, Colo.
106 Roman woman's gown
107 Leaning or ivory
108 Elates
109 Had on
110 New York ball park
111 Like the Negev
112 "__ lost without my glasses"
113 European river
115 Video sets: Abbr.
116 Siesta
117 Vote

26 Lake Tour by Adelyn Lewis

ACROSS

1 Grass units
7 Steer clear of
12 Give
18 Emerald-green mineral
19 Chili con __
20 Little girls
22 Louisiana lake
24 Easily molded
25 Alamogordo's county
26 Thugs
27 Asian weights
29 Of copper or bronze: Abbr.
30 New York lake
32 Fleecy clouds
33 "Or __!"
34 Tiller
35 Slattern
36 Water buffalo
37 Scandinavian
39 Congressional bill letters
40 Small evergreen tree
41 Bay window
42 Black Sea port
43 Seine sights
44 __ out (sends to the minors)
45 Aftermath of a scrape
46 Deepest lake in the U.S.
49 California-Nevada lake
50 Large number, in India
51 Follower of Mar.
54 Tanker
55 Strength
56 Counterweight
57 Seed wings
58 New Jersey lake
60 Minnesota lake
62 Sweetsop
63 Metals' sources
64 South Africans
66 Renée's shopping reference
67 Coin collectors' orgs.
68 Professional charges
69 Washington lake
70 Connecticut lake
71 Aspersion
72 Kind of chair
73 Surfeit
74 Make ragged
77 Diaphanous
78 Radial or flat
79 Opposite of vert.
82 Suppressed
83 Works on edging
84 African title
85 Final Indian count
86 Carved Indian poles
87 Sour substances
89 Florida lake
91 __ slow boat to China
92 Mild cigar
93 __-de-lis
94 Suffixes for toothed animals
95 Mosque tower
97 New Hampshire lake
100 Kind of dye
101 German port
102 Still and humid
103 South Pacific island
104 Calhoun et al.
105 Imposes a burden on

DOWN

1 Fellow member
2 Direct descendants
3 Sinus
4 Plant with two seed leaves
5 Ordinal suffix
6 Jonathan Livingston et al.
7 Put in performance
8 Bulgarian port
9 Old English moneys
10 Classification suffix for animals
11 Tooth tissues
12 Verb mood: Abbr.
13 Maine lake
14 Before omegas
15 __ rule (generally)
16 Lewd persons
17 Planned progress
18 Historic periods
21 New York lake
23 Form of croquet
28 Russian sea
31 Late-blooming flower
32 Urban problem
33 Jewish holiday eve
36 Directional sign
38 Harem room
40 Warn
41 Missouri River dam
43 Willows
44 Rattlers' weapons
45 Hindu garments
46 George M.
47 Vivid color displays
48 Basses ou Hautes
49 Fork parts
50 Bert and family
51 Like a storm-tossed ship
52 Trattoria specialty
53 Lengthen a dress
55 More painful
56 Relative of 'twixt
57 "This is __ romance. . ."
59 Idaho lake
61 Make proud
64 Presages
65 Glacial ridges
68 Run away
69 Encounters
70 Of atmospheric weight
71 Norms: Abbr.
72 Detective, at times
73 Kind of time or year
74 Lake named for two states
75 Amino acid in muscle
76 Oberon's wife
77 Commotion
78 Traffic stoppage
79 Neighbor of Jersey City
80 Unity
81 Baseball's Pee Wee and family
84 Bundles of yarn
85 Lump
88 Provide food
89 Secretary of State under Cleveland
90 Miser's delight
92 Theater review: Abbr.
93 One who establishes: Abbr.
96 Rep. Ullman and others
98 Ship in 1917 disaster
99 Pueblo people of N.M.

27 Ouch by Ruth W. Smith

ACROSS

1 Disconcert
6 Egyptian gold alloys
11 Lugosi and others
16 Light craft
17 Wife of the 34th President
18 Anoint
19 Tongue-twister sifter
22 N.Y. time
23 Roman meal
24 Wilder
25 Fragrance
27 Spanish queen
28 Old World roses
34 Young ladies in Granada: Abbr.
38 Stupid person
39 Vex
41 Leprechaun land
42 List
45 Relative of pekoe
47 Kind of proceeds
48 Yucca
51 Tennis term
54 Cry of amazement
55 Alone
59 Other: Lat.
61 Palm starch: Var.
62 Greek letter
63 Pronouncements
65 Table utensil
70 ". . . to the __ of the party"
72 More infrequent
73 Flatter
78 Church part
79 Prefix with amble or historic
82 Items in Ophelia's garlands
85 "For want of __ the horse. . ."
86 Year: Fr.
87 Aix partner in good news
88 Spanish coins
89 Prophets
90 Uncanny

DOWN

1 Part of a Molière play
2 Scrooge exclamations
3 Dill herb
4 __ Canals
5 Jazz performer
6 Musical key
7 Sandwich meat
8 Flightless bird
9 Drizzle
10 __ Thomas
11 Children, in Aberdeen
12 Capture
13 Baltic resident
14 Other: Prefix
15 "Has anybody here __ Kelly?"
20 Sage, for one
21 Tool for Edwin Markham's man
26 Famous duelist
28 Transmitter: Abbr.
29 Court
30 Urban lines
31 Girl's name
32 Hoosier poet
33 Kind of eyes or gin
35 Kind of hat or god
36 Common verb
37 Bridge tragedy
40 At loose __
43 Old name of Tokyo
44 Cheers
45 American Indian
46 The, in Italy
49 College degrees
50 Star in Pegasus
51 "When I was a __"
52 Wallach
53 Twitching
56 Sticky substance
57 Communication: Abbr.
58 Tibetan beast
60 Beat __ against (pelt repeatedly)
64 Passages
66 Painter Jan __ Meer
67 Moslem decrees
68 Leningrad river
69 Gray goods
71 Female deer
73 __ out of it (recover)
74 Bacteriologist's wire
75 Sea-depth measures: Abbr.
76 King of Judah and others
77 Window part
79 Wharf
80 Italian painter
81 This, in Madrid
83 Direction: Abbr.
84 Pronoun

ACROSS

1 Give short __ (brush off)
7 Eight: Prefix
11 Sound of laughter
15 Wiles
19 Spinets or grands
20 Kublai __
21 __ even keel
22 Fellow
23 Sagging
24 Shine's predecessor
25 Early Briton
26 Miss Louise
27 Small anvil
28 Enriched drink in Valletta
30 Berlin productions
31 Bridge declarer's rival: Abbr.
33 Miss Horne
34 Napoleon's space
36 Abode in Agaña
40 Pair
42 Shade maker
43 Former draft org.
44 On fire
45 Norma or Moira
49 Mauna __
51 Sadat's capital
52 One with speech troubles
54 Of hearing
58 Bean or Welles
59 Make effervescent
60 Organ covering
62 Electrical unit
64 Having no page nos.
66 Jack of movies
67 A Caribbean bouncer
71 Runabout for a colossus
73 Land known for cedars
74 Reciprocal of WNW
77 Caravan stops
78 Winter wear
80 Exact satisfaction
82 Strikebreakers
87 Lake Erie victor
88 Fought
90 Kovacs
91 Continent near Eur.
93 ". . .to set the __ a roar?"
94 Blue-penciler
95 Honshu city
98 Seoul soldier
100 Scottish explorer
101 Obesity on an exotic isle
102 Philippine beetle of sorts
105 Malayan sir
108 Upward: Prefix
109 Metric measure
110 Fibs in Cowes
113 Saucerlike bells
118 Mah-jongg piece
119 Rani's mate
120 Fleming and Hunter
121 Etna's milieu
122 Singer Adams
123 Big to-do

124 Closing word
125 Arthur's paradise
126 Grange and Barber
127 Jeanne and Marie: Abbr.
128 Sniffer
129 Bastes again

DOWN

1 Quarrel
2 Start a child's game
3 Infrequent
4 Cadmus's daughter and others
5 Ready for action in Manila
6 Recipe amt.
7 Gumbo material
8 Ague symptom
9 Discernment
10 Lawrence Welk's Alaskan intro.
11 Arizona Indian
12 Old womanish
13 Fishing fly
14 Picnic invader
15 Emoter
16 Zoo beasts, for short
17 Cugat offerings

18 Tics
28 Apple-pie maker
29 Miss O'Hara
30 Philanthropist's motto in Pago Pago
32 Possess, in Scotland
35 Legal degree
36 Texas city
37 Construction beam
38 Dormouse genus
39 Yepremian of football note
41 "__ the deep blue sea"
45 Take second, à la Lou Brock
46 Obstacle
47 Flight-plan initials
48 Radiation unit
50 Mystical halos
52 N.Y. resort lakes
53 Relaxed
55 Declaim
56 Action: Suffix
57 Ogle
61 Have it __ (succeed)
63 Irish battle cry
65 Right away
67 Askew
68 Dream, in France
69 Above, in Berlin
70 Sandbar, in Spain

72 Golfer Walter
75 Day of rest
76 Alaskan islands' unfolding
79 Tiny one
81 French summer
83 Cheat
84 Stage org.
85 Sci. course
86 Sonora Indian
89 Spoil
92 Pilfer
94 Billion years
95 Belfast's region
96 Happen
97 Contact-lens contact
99 OPEC member
101 Dance step
103 Corners
104 W.W. II guy
106 Cottonwood
107 Mets and Giants
111 Gang rods
112 Old slave
114 Wood sorrels
115 Blue or White
116 Radiate
117 Opp. of antonyms
119 Carriers: Abbr.
121 Men's org.

ACROSS

1 Old Norse poems
6 Cap or bear
11 Colorado's __ Park
16 Religious house
17 Demean
18 Cascade peak
20 Prisoner's final trial pleas
22 Hat measurement
24 Inhabitant: Suffix
25 Western oak
26 Wet-cellar problem
28 Maritime: Abbr.
29 Quantity of fish
31 First duke of Normandy
33 Gleans benefits
34 Act the coquette
35 Fed the kitty
37 Dangles
39 Original mold
40 Groom
41 Hail and Rolling
43 Stigmatized
45 Light cotton fabric
46 Numerical prefix
48 __ antique (green marble)
49 Unshared
50 Complete meal
55 Phony stone
59 Ethiopian city
60 Recent: Prefix
61 Withdraws
63 __ polloi
64 U.S. reformer
65 Glance off
67 Detachable trailers
68 Kind of swallow or storm
69 "Close Encounters" subject
70 British sailor
72 Case of a subject: Abbr.
73 Bogged down
74 Social events girls prefer
76 Stentor and others
79 Snake eyes
80 Act servilely
81 Ahmadabad attire
82 Hyde or Roberts
85 Rutabagas' cousins
88 Haphazard
92 Chose
93 Bell or fly
94 Reproductions, for short
96 Animals, in Germany
97 Starting places
98 Mountain lakes
100 Gazelle's larger cousin
102 Use a radar beam
103 Wood sorrel
104 Type of lens
106 Greek assembly
108 Itinerary: Abbr.
109 Sheep's horn, in a way
111 Effect of department-store sales
114 Shade of red
115 Pyle
116 More diminutive
117 Blood __
118 Takes a picture
119 Pro golf veteran

DOWN

1 Composer Lecuona
2 Underworld god
3 Glum
4 Round Table wear
5 Dove, as related to peace
6 Kneecap
7 Sash
8 Vientiane is its capital
9 TV's Lou Grant
10 Started a new lawn
11 Word with artist or mechanism
12 Certain rugs
13 Masking or video
14 Sibilant consonant
15 Brandy drink
16 Vigorous
19 Colorful bush flower
20 Deep sleeps
21 Set apart
23 Counterparts of odds
27 Follower of pre or post
30 Madames, in Madrid
32 Former Twin slugger Tony
34 Waiter's notation
36 Theatrical scenery
38 Puppet Mortimer
40 Picks up sneakily
42 Erwin or Symington
44 Candleberry and catalpa
45 Protective channels
47 Male kinsmen
49 Undersized people
50 Play monotonously
51 Mideast port
52 Pleiades' sky neighbor
53 "__ how!"
54 Deceive
55 Greek island
56 Busiest U.S. airport
57 Kitchen utensil
58 Types
62 Remain unsettled
65 Purvey
66 Tooth
68 Cynosures on bathing beaches
70 Like a lion or a horse
71 Communities
73 French revolutionary leader
75 Lavishes love
77 Couple
78 Word with phone or drum
80 Kilns
82 Kind of cade
83 Purgative root
84 Like some clams
85 Acrimonious
86 Taste centers
87 Duse's medium
89 Belittled
90 Demosthenes or Bryan
91 "Prevalence of Witches" author
93 Raillery
95 Quick drinks
98 Trunk
99 Disdain
101 Exhaust
104 What boisterous ones raise
105 Sandwich filler
107 Facial affliction
110 Con's counterpart
112 Short drink
113 Mexican aunt

30 Relatives by Raymond F. Eisner

ACROSS

1 Melodic passage
7 Cite
13 Rotary engines, for short
19 Delay again
20 Jacob's eldest son
21 Wraparound, in bookbinding
22 English poet
24 Street or carpet
25 Ocean: Abbr.
26 Couturier's creation: Abbr.
27 Opening dice throws of 7 or 11
29 Self
30 Accomplishes, in Aberdeen
32 Charm
34 Exasperate
35 Between Mont. and Minn.
36 State of India
38 Show a weak bridge hand
39 Name for Hemingway
40 Bellwether state, once
41 Wiconsin city
43 Pine or ice cream
44 Mr. Polo et al.
45 Vane direction
48 Black: Prefix
49 Autumn pear
50 __ out (waited)
51 Garden bloom
53 Inane
55 Tropical tree
58 "La Vie __"
59 __ far niente (sweet idleness)
60 Brought upon oneself
62 Spirit lamp
63 Proposed
65 Single
66 Cue card, e.g.
69 Iron, in Essen
70 Freedom, with strings attached
72 Word part: Abbr.
73 __ Winkelried, Swiss hero
75 Well liked
76 Helps with the dishes
78 German river
79 Riding __
80 Med. men
81 Insurgents
83 Miss West et al.
84 "Ay, __ the rub"
86 Daredevil Knievel et al.
87 Bounders
88 Creeks
89 White: Prefix
93 Gives a bad review
94 Word with ahoy
95 Gave a sly look
97 Uppity one
98 G.I. dog-tag initials
99 Explain in detail
101 Lively, in music: Abbr.
103 Onager
104 Afternoon pauses
106 English historian
109 Walks unsteadily
110 Antoinette, for short
111 Works on a cavity
112 Joins
113 Mixes a salad
114 Atelier accouterments

DOWN

1 Fleet
2 Lariats
3 Plant fibers
4 Mel
5 Gotham's new Bohemia
6 Hat or glasses
7 River in Central Brazil
8 German article
9 Actress Irene and family
10 Sea raider
11 Primitive chisel
12 Stamina
13 Tutu material
14 Western Indians
15 British historical org.
16 Revolutionary general
17 Cookery seasoning
18 Golfers' countings
21 Florida city
23 The Barretts' street
28 Suitable
31 Sat. or Sun.
33 W.W. II landing craft
35 Delhi dress
37 Notes
39 Owner
40 Island in Taiwan Strait
42 __-majesté
43 Dreams up
44 One of a grammar trio: Abbr.
45 Brews tea
46 One on guard duty
47 "Five Towns" author
49 Norman or Barbara
50 Dispatch
52 Prowl
53 Soak
54 Legal right
56 Lasso, in Spain
57 Larry and Stella
59 Spanish silver dollar
61 N.Z. bird
63 Congress V.I.P.'s
64 Big casino
67 Buckets
68 Three, in Toledo
70 Like a church mouse
71 Fencing move
74 Western shrub
75 Admission fee to a wedding
77 Electric units
79 Parlor game
81 Glue again
82 Act of dodging
83 Kind of order
84 Fasten
85 His, in Le Havre
87 Mover's game
88 Double-checks one's addition
90 Helpless
91 TV's Howard
92 Preoccupy
94 Bickers
95 Alfred and Lynn
96 Electron tube
99 Suffix for spin or young
100 Mountain: Prefix
102 Gore Vidal character
105 Sault __ Marie
107 No-no for George
108 Constantine's birthplace

31 Wising Up   by William Lutwiniak

ACROSS

1 Low I.Q. scorer
6 Castle buffers
11 Induced yawns
16 Cadets' alma mater
20 Man without a country
21 TV's Dickinson
22 Accrue
23 Northern highway
24 Daily airwave words
28 Potato buds
29 Plug-uglies
30 Reviles
31 Reduces, as ore
32 Flushed
33 Easter visitor
34 Disparaging
35 Skyline features
36 High quality
37 Too familiar
38 Revue bits
39 F.D.R.'s trust
41 Martin or Acheson
42 Vibratory sound
43 Tennis unit
46 Long-distance words
53 Stands well
54 Nomadic group
55 Solos
56 City of Florida
57 Tennysonian lady
58 __ up (titivates)
59 Fish in an active way
60 Percussion cap
61 Portray
62 Part of a full house
63 Make over
64 Opposite of ant.
65 Weekly words
75 Neighbor of La.
76 Smell __
77 Festive affair
78 Cleo's quietus
79 Cracks a crime case
82 Uses an auger
83 Massachusetts port
85 Cassava
86 Serve
87 Eau __ (brandy)
88 "Fiddler" star on stage
89 Kepi feature
90 Printed words
94 Yore, of yore
95 Insect eggs
96 Fee-takers
97 __ a time
98 White poplar
100 Josh
102 Paderewski and Kosciuszko
104 Art of coloring: Suffix
106 Fargo's partner
107 Kind of green
108 Understand
111 Small space
112 Flower feature
113 Israeli port
114 Detonator

115 Source for words from space
119 Virgilian hero: Var.
120 Feed greedily
121 Quickly
122 Wystan Hugh of poetry
123 Retreats
124 Arrests
125 Female insects
126 Wallace or Noah

DOWN

1 Counting device
2 Daisy
3 Vexed
4 Endings with peti and aure
5 Neighbor of Ariz.
6 James and Pamela
7 Bermudas
8 Travail
9 Lizzie and Woodman
10 Proxmire or Javits: Abbr.
11 Lament
12 __ kick, in football
13 Moscow money
14 Goofs
15 __ volente
16 Gastric woes
17 Conquer Mt. Everest
18 Marina sights
19 Noun endings
23 Receive
25 Large lizard

26 Verdi opera
27 Have ambitions
33 Ecstasy
34 Condition
35 Pelts
36 Worked with rattan
37 Posts
38 Sandbank
39 Neighborhood library
40 Like the rhea and emu
41 Like Bette Davis's victory
42 Erst
43 Grand word in bridge
44 La femme
45 Peter or Nicholas
46 Pick up the tab
47 Possessive
48 Peter of films
49 He wrote of Celia
50 Goads
51 Common cold
52 Berry parts
58 Miss America pageant V.I.P.
59 Weight allowances
60 Sacred song
62 100%
66 Nit-pick
67 Birthmark
68 Entourage
69 Appointed
70 Lit
71 Hibernians
72 Feeling of revulsion
73 Beau

74 Servicewomen
79 Notorous marquis
80 Facial shape
81 Put
82 Remainder: Fr.
83 What "ibn" means
84 Chimpanzees
85 Kennel sounds
87 With irony
88 Learners
89 Copter features
91 Kind of show
92 NASA program
93 Civil
98 Bouquets
99 Horse pill
100 Seven, to Cato
101 Famous Georgia town
102 Home, to Elizabeth
103 Indulges in grandiloquence
104 Beldam
105 Muscle flexers
106 Shuttle around in traffic
107 Pound's "__ Cantos"
108 Tour-bus host
109 Chemical compound
110 Very small
111 Made a hole in one
112 "Aroint thee!"
113 Make out
114 Chimney feature
116 April 15 heavy
117 Xanthippe, for one
118 R. & D. area

32 In Tune by Alice H. Kaufman

ACROSS

1 Carried
6 Ethereal fluid
11 One who enjoys nightclubs
18 Make amends
19 Immerse
20 Temporary prison grad
21 Well-known clarinetist
23 Click beetles
24 Dramatist O'Casey
25 Conflicts
27 Insect egg
28 Extent of surface
32 Command for an admiral
35 Tennis serve
36 Singles
37 Thing cast in the fall
39 Cheer
40 __ Boys of Crosby days
42 Biblical exclamation
43 To be: Lat.
44 Stoat
47 Tailless cat
49 Kind of steak
53 Mr. Marner
54 Philippine native
56 False gods
58 Kind of board or joint
59 Australian bird
60 Musical adaptation
64 English cathedral locale
65 Remunerates
67 Man of great wealth
68 Shrinks from
70 House for Nanook
72 Small fragment
74 A.L. player
75 Lost one's enthusiasm
77 Seines
79 Animal of tropical America
83 Glum
86 Buzzing insect
87 Aide
88 Curved supports
90 Combo instrument
91 Aim snide attacks at
93 Strive for
94 Old English money
95 U.S. Vice President
97 Hatfield or Twain
99 Football statistic
101 Musical brother
108 New England community
109 Foreign
110 Audience at a theater
111 Female animal
112 British author
113 Fluffy bits

DOWN

1 Marble
2 Indian of Nebraska
3 Before many cooks
4 Finish
5 North African rulers
6 Standard of excellence
7 Places for stop signs
8 Murmur
9 Explorer Johnson
10 Tear
11 Banquet accompaniment
12 Freshwater game fish
13 Gershwin and others
14 Negative
15 Bandleader lost in
   W.W. II crash
16 Weird
17 Relaxes
22 Weight
26 Old Mideast initials
28 Not present: Abbr.
29 Scottish explorer
30 Building wing
31 Aspen of Southwest
33 Bridge position

34 Phenomena of the '30's
   and '40's
36 Of an electrical unit
38 John or Maureen
41 Corporate officers: Abbr.
43 Actors in crowd scenes
45 Fastens firmly
46 Catch sight of
48 Teutonic goddess
50 Type of poem
51 __ de guerre
52 Puts into office
54 Insect stage
55 Late Mr. New Year's Eve
57 Kind of shoe or goose
59 Heroic
61 Rudiments
62 Conjunction
63 Doubly
66 Achieves a flying
   milestone
69 Organic compounds
71 Finished, to poets

73 Serf
76 Medicine-bottle listings
78 Decorated
80 Darwin subject
81 Golf area
82 Annoy
84 Lumbermen
85 English river
87 Large number
88 __ Canadians
89 Native of Teheran
92 Actor John __
95 Mr. Brubeck
96 Headliner
98 Eye makeup
100 Juan or Rickles
102 Arena cheer
103 Miss Farrow
104 Louis XVI, e.g.
105 Baltimore newspaper
106 Superlative ending
107 Indeed

33 Pipsqueaks by Stephanie Spadaccini

ACROSS

1 Moving aimlessly
7 Detecting device
12 Relatives of sultans
17 Caama
21 Skier's disappointment
22 "__ Mio"
23 City for April
24 Of an acid: Prefix
25 Rigorous
26 Weeps noisily
27 Get going
29 Snake
30 Quantity of laughter
32 Prefix for phyte
33 Sass
34 Dull finish
35 Green
40 Eur. country
41 Crumpet time
44 "Come up __ my etchings"
45 Sink, old style
46 Walls, in Lille
47 Related
48 Penny __
49 Concealed
51 Belgian town
53 Icy-walk mishaps
54 Use a fountain coin
55 __ for size (gets a fitting)
57 Rope fiber
58 L.A. player
59 Wildcat
61 What bikini wearers show lots of
64 Nigerian people
66 Performing
68 Ocean liner: Abbr.
69 Process: Suffix
71 Draw, as a crowd
74 Drags
75 Yale name
77 Pointed instrument
79 Pinnacle
80 Swelling ailment
82 Expiate
84 Taken __ (surprised)
85 Siesta
87 Kind of session
88 "__ old cowhand"
89 Reads
91 Hog plum
92 Munched
94 Actress Thorndike
96 Corrida sounds
97 New Year party wear
100 Wine: Prefix
101 Do sums
102 German girl's name
106 Fizzles
108 160 square rods
110 Kind of thief
111 Underneath
112 __ for the course
113 Garden evictee
114 Put wheat in bundles
115 Tusked animal
117 Ship-shaped clock
119 Dostoevski
121 Plods through wet snow
122 Swedish name for Turku
123 Sob stuff
126 Misrepresent
128 Author Josephine
129 Treasure-trove king
130 Be in cahoots with
131 Org. in Patty Hearst case
134 Raspberry
137 Gingko trees
139 Conference in a tepee
141 Garish
142 Stone: Prefix
143 Intended
144 Complete
145 Inner: Prefix
146 Came up
147 These, in Mexico
148 Leaned

DOWN

1 Celestial handle
2 "Handsome is that handsome __"
3 Invitation initials
4 Feminine suffix
5 "__ sake!"
6 Made a bird sound
7 California oak
8 __ rule (usually)
9 Blue
10 Former Chilean leader
11 Does lawn work
12 Globular body: Abbr.
13 Selassie
14 Bandman Shaw et al.
15 Click
16 Library sound
17 Harbor of Guam
18 Kind of wedding
19 Usher, at times
20 Bitter-__ (diehards)
28 Print measures
31 Arab garment
35 Impudent twerp
36 Holbein
37 Iran's capital
38 Hawaiian fern
39 Early German cavalrymen
41 Leftover item
42 That, in old Rome
43 Faint light
46 Fishy goings-on
48 Sharpshooter's forte
50 Society girl
52 Distress call
54 Basket or paper
55 Baseball's Speaker
56 Black buck
58 Riviera's Eden __
60 Hindu teaching
62 Mallorca, etc.
63 Relative
65 Kind of processing
67 "Look!"
70 Wall St. purchases: Abbr.
71 Old gold brocade
72 Kind of steamer
73 Four: Prefix
74 Grassland
76 Eur. capital
78 Weight deduction
81 Dismal, to poets
82 Uganda's Idi
83 Lyric poem
86 First segment
88 "__ you a million!"
90 Days of yore
93 What Twain said people do nothing about
95 "__ Grand Old Flag"
98 Lamprey
99 Cooking meas.
101 Chair or band
103 Wife of Jacob
104 Stash away
105 Makes do, with "out"
107 Blockheads
109 Jung or Reiner
110 Quick drink
111 Hit the silk
113 Offers as proof
114 Unexpected success
115 Prate
116 Actress Merle
118 "__ be you and me"
120 Prompt
121 Compact-car abbr.
123 Put the whammy on
124 Ones fixing shoelaces: Var.
125 Kilns
127 Word form for an Asian land
131 Actress Loretta
132 History
133 Amazed
135 Accountant: Abbr.
136 Caviar
138 Three __ match
140 Lb. and oz.

34 Sea of Troubles by Mel Rosen

ACROSS

1 Palmer House or Ritz
6 Trail through mud
12 Mid-American Indians
18 Charge with oxygen
19 Blast-furnace product
20 Like Moby Dick
21 Source of annoyance while dressing
23 Snooze
24 Carpenter's tool
25 Munich's river
26 Mil. award
27 Austrian psychiatrist
28 Short time, for short
29 Annoyances in the park
34 Common verb
35 Old verb form
37 Partial: Prefix
38 Comparative word
39 Agreeable
40 Lifters' burdens: Abbr.
42 Summer drinks
45 Maroon
47 Characteristic
49 Tennis's Arthur
51 Annoyance for Goren
53 Annoyance on the court
58 Home of the Cotton Bowl
60 Container
61 She's as good as a mile
62 Verve
64 Lake, in Italy
65 Type of Dr.
66 Filled up
68 One who takes a chance
70 Like Reynard
71 Paid performers
73 Lugs
75 Well-known Mohican
77 Kind of sickness
78 Wailed
81 Annoyances on the street
84 Catches
86 Holiday
87 Worthless matter
88 Wave
90 Tamarisk tree
92 Religious day: Abbr.
93 Natural fiber
95 Stumble
97 Prince of opera
100 Fuel
103 Act the stoolie
104 Annoyance on July 4
108 Zodiac sign
110 Lead-in
112 Like some verbs: Abbr.
113 Spanish rope
114 Raucous sound
115 Traditional
117 Annoyance for a party-giver
120 What sedatives soothe
121 Marked with stripes
122 River of many ghats
123 Having the least vermouth
124 Isolate
125 Advantages

DOWN

1 Did a sheepdog's job
2 Mexican painter
3 Income at the gate
4 Summer, in Nice
5 Longtime Red Square resident
6 Lifelike scenic exhibit
7 Ripen
8 Miss Gray of silents
9 Catch on
10 Footnote notation
11 Compass point
12 More, to Pedro
13 Of the pelvis
14 Retired
15 Annoyance for the shortsighted
16 Medical trainee
17 Flew high
18 "Down with!": Fr.
19 Periodic state
22 J.F.K. visitors
29 V.I.P. among Huns
30 Kind of wave
31 Leaders: Abbr.
32 Abyssinian weight
33 "The Lady __"
36 Deck mop
39 Toll
41 Holds back
43 This, in Spain
44 Ultimate gambling loss
46 Collection
47 Corrida figures
48 Annoyance in the garage
50 Football sweep
52 Young baldies
53 Overweight
54 Arbitrary ruling
55 Put __ to (halt)
56 Levy on an interstate purchase
57 On the way out
59 Sauce beans
63 Square, for one: Abbr.
67 Skin layer
69 Incursions
72 Done away with, as a dragon
74 Card game for three
76 Tough spot
79 Der __könig
80 Greek letter
82 Long Island city
83 Port of Honshu
85 Fern spore cases
89 Pick the right horse
91 Uniformity, in France
93 Kellogg-__ Pact
94 Forest monitor
96 __ the neck
98 Use a soapbox
99 Tear down
101 Assert
102 Pesters
104 Parts
105 Singer Lopez
106 English composer and family
107 City to avoid in Kansas?
109 Baseball great and family
111 Wander
114 Wine-cask stopper
116 N.Y.C. clock setting
117 Rubber tree
118 Worth: Abbr.
119 Kind of fly

35 Take Your Pick by Anthony B. Canning

ACROSS

1 Big Board listing
7 Ottoman subject
11 Treaty
15 Not up yet
19 "__ aside is human" (Burns)
20 Thames district
21 Kind of thing
22 African republic
23 Great hobby of one: Schiller, Schliemann, Schubert
25 It's often round, on Amtrak
26 Son of Zeus
27 Recap or spare
28 Of the skull
30 Sugar: Suffix
31 Bar-bucket contents
32 Organic compound
33 Dues for Uncle Sam's club
34 Cliff home
36 Aleutian island
37 Forthwith
38 Ready for shipment
39 Two of these: Shirley T. Black, Bob Hope, Benjamin Franklin
41 Predetermined
42 Kind of balloon or lawyer
43 Hiawatha's carrier
44 Role for an angry Zola
47 Large goose
48 Desertlike areas
50 Chicago team
51 Pivots
52 Limper's aid
53 Two of these: Copernicus, Ptolemy, Fuad I
56 Shows presumption
61 Ladder, in England
62 Pilewort fibers
63 Burr
64 Vicinity
65 Stamina
67 Two of these: T.E. Lawrence, Cosimo de' Medici, Casanova
69 Old Irish stronghold
70 Pigtail
71 Rain-forest growth
72 Feeble
76 Home-run star
77 Smear
79 Prepare for a bout
80 Exclude
81 Units of loudness
82 Two of these: Hurok, O'Neill, Todd
85 Hammer parts
86 Four qts.
89 Eternal-hope poet
90 Kind of acid
91 Metric measure
92 Bleak
93 For
94 Penpoint
95 Carpenters, at times
97 Partner of ready
98 Fifth-century pope
100 Anatomical tissue
102 One of these: Schnabel, Scheherazade, Schlegel
104 Gaelic
105 Chemical endings
106 Boyer's head
107 Leblanc's Lupin
108 Compass points
109 This, in Toledo
110 Toward the mouth
111 Schoolbook

DOWN

1 New York island
2 City near Milano
3 Bond held by a third party
4 A Kennedy
5 Pasture
6 Observe a sports event
7 At ease
8 Made up for
9 Hindu ascetics
10 Writer Seton
11 Western time: Abbr.
12 Radiant
13 Touch-and-go situation
14 Early Plains sights
15 Doctors' org.
16 One of these: Andy Williams, Mel Torme, Jim Nabors
17 Atom constituent
18 French reciters of songs
24 Bet-taker by word of mouth
29 Vampires
35 Abba
36 Hebrew month
38 One of these: Chagall, Chaliapin, Chaplin
39 Rhone city
40 Land units
41 Like many animals
42 Travel packages
44 Disconcert
45 Jai-alai basket
46 Supply what is wanted
47 Point Barrow sights
48 Munchausen, e.g.
49 Concerning
51 Success on Broadway
52 Provided for
54 Nursemaids
55 "Golden Boy" author
56 Cup of a sport
57 Sharp-billed finches
58 Hill nymph
59 European capital
60 Loom-bar worker
63 Robin __ of song
66 Vernon's partner
67 Tapestry
68 German lancers: Var.
70 Large ape
72 Paints with dots
73 Weapon makers
74 Squaw's burden: Var.
75 Loren's cash
76 Chow __
77 Cocktail wine
78 State nickname
80 Trifling sum
81 __ out (ended slowly)
83 South Carolina river
84 Textile city on the Somme
85 Jai alai
86 Like a Hawthorne house
87 Miss Francis
88 Facemaking one
91 Bishop's headdress
92 Light wood
96 Regarding
99 Plural endings
101 Red __ beet
103 Before

36   K Ration   by Herb Risteen

ACROSS

1 Money in Minsk
6 Emigré to Miami
11 Snakecharmer's favorite
16 Gridiron exchanges
21 City in Japan
22 Decree
23 Tire capital
24 Inactive
25 Brewery product
26 Zachary Taylor and Col. Sanders
28 Track-meet event
29 Period
30 Soissons summers
32 Heraldic bearing
33 Office piece
35 Diamond girl
36 Takes up an abode
38 Himalayan goat
39 Supermarket worker
41 Set system
42 BB-gun propellant
43 Lime tree
44 Game for Minnesota Fats
45 Corsica, e.g.
47 Two-state city
50 Napkin fabric
52 Shin's terminus
56 Unless, to Cicero
57 "Othello" ensign
58 Sacred book
59 City in Kansas
61 Game animal
62 Florida region
63 Large pieces
64 Speaker of Hall of Fame
65 Work unit
66 Journalists
68 Jockeys' wear
69 Where Mt. Ida is
70 __ de mer
71 Evil spirits
72 Wall piers
73 Motive
74 Otherwise
75 Part of O.A.S.: Abbr.
76 Places for garbage cans
78 Roman 102
79 Kind of flint
81 Advice to a clown
83 Frosty coatings
84 Nile temple site
87 Container
88 Places of trade
89 Pimlico entry
90 Atelier equipment
91 Unlucky
92 Bird calls
93 Bides one's time
94 Kind of eye or lady
95 Salty relish
96 Transfers, in law
98 Plains Indian
99 Dollar
100 Blockhead
101 French river
102 Join up
104 Large parrots
106 __ Gardens
108 Lighten
109 Oddball
110 New Zealand bird
111 Shetland export
114 En __ (Ahead, in France)
116 Old weapon
117 Escape, as a bit of news
121 French soul
122 Common Latin word
123 Martin
124 Legal writ
125 Mailing address
126 Barnyard fowl
128 Like a close horse-race finish
132 Glacial ridge
134 Military cloth
135 German city
136 Reception
137 Catkin
138 Caesar's dish
139 Kind of naked
140 Everlasting, to poets
141 Money

DOWN

1 Tropical trees
2 Western Indian
3 Actress Debra
4 Supplement
5 Soviet republic
6 Vegetables, for short
7 Music makers
8 Prohibit
9 City in Oregon
10 Of a sense system
11 Sponge or layer
12 Iroquois spirit
13 Apparel item
14 Short poems
15 Goose genus
16 Scottish church
17 Chemical suffix
18 Orchestra instrument
19 Snake of Asia
20 Manner
27 Metric measures: Abbr.
31 Cairn and fox
34 Join the Aspen crowd
37 Vehicle
38 Gambling game
39 Stupors
40 Bank business
41 Western city
43 Labels
44 Estes and Menlo
46 Slip
47 Diacritical mark
48 Arctic abode
49 Medford and Francis
50 Lifting device
51 New Mexico people
53 Khrushchev, Lenin and Stalin
54 Turkish pounds
55 Old U.S. coin
56 Exigency
58 Old Russian farmer
60 Tiny bit
62 Fay Wray's King
63 Obstacle
64 Bind
67 Anguished
68 Hindrances
69 Skeleton group
72 Touches on
73 Stupid
74 Where Sligo is
77 Body passage
78 Make watertight
79 "Blue __"
80 Arabian weight
81 French city
82 Had origin
84 City in Illinois
85 Energy sources
86 Castle section
88 Fibber of radio days
89 Medieval guild
90 Shovel's partner
93 Wasp __
94 Hockey disk
97 Very black
98 Part of K.K.K.
99 Between bell and candle
100 "__ the rich"
103 Most tidy
104 Small crown
105 Seer's reading matter
107 Part of a Tolstoy duo
109 Light
111 Hikers' burdens
112 Western city
113 India's neighbor
115 Copter parts
116 Clamor
117 Compare
118 Old bucket of song
119 Defeat
120 Civil wrongs
122 Miss Bagnold
123 Cold and damp
124 Maple genus
127 Turkish weight
129 Jeff Davis's domain
130 Prefix for plop
131 Time of day
133 Dallas school: Abbr.

37 Relaxation Time by Staneley A. Kurzban

ACROSS

1 Aries
4 Channel
7 Puts on
13 Shade
17 Writer Kingsley
19 Take one's winners, at bridge
20 Benedict or Matthew
21 Holly
22 Composition for nine
24 Seasoning herb
25 Core groups
26 Detective's quest
27 Cakes
30 German's refusal
31 Sports-page listings
32 Genus of auks
33 Wavering, in music: Abbr.
34 Spanish basket
36 Ian Fleming work
40 Eur. country
41 Prepared to travel
45 Prefix for puncture
46 Wireless: Abbr.
47 Legal degree
49 Playful
51 Lunar crater
54 "__ been had!"
57 Heavy vehicles: Abbr.
60 Small openings
61 Pres. Arthur, as a gamesman
63 "__ and yet so far"
65 Lair
66 Theater district
67 Legal thing
69 Subtle distinction
71 Prefix for meter or grade
72 Miss Ullmann
74 Diplomacy
76 Cry of triumph
77 Command to a horse
80 Very old: Abbr.
81 Auditors in Peking
86 Fled
87 Clever one
88 Adherent: Suffix
89 Jacques of films
90 Part of Congress: Abbr.
91 Mimics
93 Monopoly group
95 Swiss river
97 Primate
99 British title: Abbr.
102 Type style
104 Units in a chain-reaction effect
106 Burn sluggishly
109 German city
110 Doctors' org.
111 Being concerned
114 Merchandise held for a customer
116 Govt. department
118 Troy, N.Y., campus
120 Recent: Prefix
121 Latin fish
122 Miss Hogg
125 Fill in
130 Worked on dough
132 Japanese aborigine
133 Back
134 Type of board
137 Network
138 Barren land
143 Composer Bartók
144 Do a Detoit auto job
146 Flimsy mat
147 Vexed
148 Guinness
149 Napoli's land
150 Name for Ovid
151 Iron or black
152 Office piece
153 More brief
154 Old English letter
155 French season

DOWN

1 Resounded
2 Mine, in Paris
3 Neighbor of Wis.
4 Mirth: Var.
5 Eritrean capital
6 "The farmer in __"
7 American Indian
8 Dazed state
9 Of a mountain chain
10 Comeuppances for matadors
11 Form of Helen
12 Puget and others: Abbr.
13 X and O game
14 Jar
15 Gender: Abbr.
16 Former spouses
18 Town in Argentina
19 Certain religionist: Abbr.
23 Sea eagle
24 Ski-slope sights
28 One espousing violence
29 Refines metal
31 Gazed
35 Seed: Prefix
36 Instance, in France
37 Top banana in sports
38 Brief
39 The long and short __
42 Oven
43 Le Gallienne
44 Scottish river
48 Lung-feeder connector
50 Perennial board game
52 Talk
53 Spiral: Prefix
55 Spirit
56 Prior to
58 Football's Rockne
59 Weddell, for one
62 Gamy kind of confinement
64 Biblical giants
66 Italian painter
68 Geting a base, in a way
70 Front-page box
71 Cornfield sound
73 Motionless
75 Perform
77 __ the skids (facilitating)
78 Merit
79 Letters
82 Latin-exercise word
83 Stone slab
84 Pigment: Prefix
85 Pacific island group
92 Docking place
94 __ Mahal
96 City in Oklahoma
98 One who arouses
99 Behaves shyly, old style
100 Weapon
101 Girl's name
103 "Come with me to the __"
105 Border: Abbr.
106 U.S. political group: Abbr.
107 French month
108 Relaxation
112 Org. for teachers
113 Elephant group
115 Cocktail
117 Daughter of King Minos
119 Composer Grainger
123 Iron, aluminum, etc.
124 Species of penguin
126 Encroachment
127 Like a fop
128 German hair
129 Town in Iraq
131 Mountain ridge
134 Bible book: Abbr.
135 African river
136 De France and de la Cité
139 Road sign
140 Disconsolate
141 Afforded
142 Rim
144 Slower, in music: Abbr.
145 Roman spirit

38 Berlin Diary by Eugene T. Maleska

ACROSS

1 Roundup stick
5 Malayan masters
10 Carved symbol
15 Food fish
19 Actor's reward
20 L.I. resort town
21 Bangor neighbor
22 Fitzgerald
23 "A Fella with __": 1948
25 "Somebody's __ House": 1913
27 Winged maple fruits
28 Wagnerian goddess
30 "God Bless __": 1939
31 Breeding place
33 Merit
35 Cisterns
36 Hit song of 1932
42 Part of H.O.M.E.S.
43 Slangy refusals
44 "Sticks __ Hick Pix" (Variety headline)
45 It lurks sub rosa
50 Dancer with only a few fans
51 Lariat
53 Flocks of mallards
55 Supermarket offering
56 Bankbook abbr.
57 Famed Wagnerian conductor of 1800's
58 Song from "Top Hat": 1935
61 Dignitary protected by the Swiss Guard
63 Asian evergreen
64 Steering blade
65 "I Left My __ Door Canteen": 1944
70 "__ Hate to Get Up in the Morning": 1918
73 Name on a green stamp
74 Town near Lancaster, Pa.
78 Classic since 1933
81 Do not delete
82 Capek play
83 "Faust" finale
84 Family branches
85 Subsequently
87 Muttonfish
88 "Give __ horse he can ride"
90 "Le Coq __"
91 "__ Rag Picker": 1914
92 Star in Draco
93 Hit song of 1914
99 Trumpet's sound
102 Attitudinize
103 Aggrandize
104 Corrects
107 "Say It __ So"
109 Nationality of Berlin's Marie
113 "At the __": 1912
115 "The Girl __": 1946
117 Level
118 Ford or Pyle
119 Harold __, Berlin contemporary
120 Sharp
121 As it __ (so to speak)
122 Word with pug and snub
123 Oodles
124 Singer Nelson

DOWN

1 Mardi __
2 Chaplin's widow
3 Astringent
4 Necessitated
5 Screed
6 Spends
7 "__ Alone": 1924
8 Egypt's lifeline
9 "Woodman, Woodman, __ Tree!": 1911
10 "Nobody Knows and Nobody Seems __": 1919
11 Coronado's quest
12 Liberian group
13 Truly, to Tacitus
14 Co-winner of Nobel Peace Prize in 1907
15 Became prevalent
16 Ticker
17 Gluck et al.
18 "It's a Lovely __ Today": 1950
24 Canapé spread
26 Artist Wood
29 Morse code signals
32 Moses's Mount
34 Ninefold
36 Fine Afghan carpet
37 Relative of spinach
38 Recoil
39 Held a session
40 Nancy and Sofia, for example
41 Corporate V.I.P.
46 Word with pot or cigarette
47 Reeking
48 Film-director Clair
49 Top money-winning horse in 1950
51 Sign on a garage
52 Perpetually
53 Brother of Cain and Abel
54 Pan cleaner
57 Contemporary of Berlin
59 Very unpopular
60 __ to (should)
62 Unit of intensity of light
66 Table for a P.M. collation
67 Sewer device
68 Refrain syllables
69 Mal de __
70 Where Hercules died
71 Injure
72 First Chinese dynasty
75 Tilled land, in Texas
76 Swollen
77 Hit song of 1915
79 Pastoral staffs
80 Primitive
81 Not newsworthy
86 Viper
87 The Dead Sea is one
89 T.S. Eliot's "cruelest month"
91 Show disapproval
94 Abate
95 No longer immaculate
96 Left
97 Morning prayer
98 Ancient Asian land
99 Longest modern note
100 Crowbar
101 Of the birds
105 Saragossa's river
106 Word with culotte or souci
108 By way of, for short
110 Angered
111 Cézanne's "Boy in __ Vest"
112 Gotham initials
113 Morning moisture
114 Twisted tale
116 Neighbor of Miss.

39 From Mr. Malaprop
by Bert Kruse

ACROSS

1 Old German-African coin
5 Morocco's capital
10 Costly stones
14 Struck
18 Part of Q.E.D.
19 Aviator-statesman Balbo
20 Verboten
21 Head
22 Lomond, e.g.
23 Mr. Malaprop's inflamed throat
25 Rds.
26 Kind of conclusion
28 Isle of Wight channel
29 Comedian Bert and family
30 Growing out
31 Group of witches
32 "Not with __ but a whimper"
34 First born
36 Finishes the dishes
37 When Mr. M. is angry, he's this
40 Medieval lyric
41 A loner, to Mr. M.
44 Connective
45 "Gang aft __"
47 What Hemingway bade farewell to
48 Writes
49 Old Persian capital
50 No, in Nuremburg
51 Explosive
52 Gumshoes
53 Questionable
54 Make tediously long
56 Lady of Spain
59 Weep
60 Mr. M.'s broken bones
64 Rat race, in a way
65 French laces
66 Take back
69 Wine settlings
72 Early auto maker
73 Incipient rose
74 Thither: Lat.
75 Lasso
76 Before, in old Rome
77 Spoken
79 Okra
80 "__ my brother's keeper?"
81 Heinous felony, to Mr. M.
85 Universal: Prefix
86 Small rich cake
88 Cruel one
89 Satan
91 Giving the once-over
92 Wild buffalo
93 Dieter's no-no
94 Court decree
96 More simple
98 Provide explanatory remarks
101 Parts of glasses
102 Mr. M.'s words for New York subways

104 College subj.
105 Personal: Prefix
106 French notions
107 Fumble around
108 Use a library
109 Org.
110 Incline
111 Like some jugs
112 Fast planes

DOWN

1 Money
2 Ending for stink or switch
3 Back, to Mr. M.
4 Olympian deity
5 Rice dish
6 Make up for
7 Expose
8 Brew
9 Targets of farmers' plows
10 Greek physician
11 Israeli name
12 Westerners
13 Boston's are Red
14 Leaped
15 Einstein, to Mr. M.
16 Roman highway
17 Hardy woman
20 Writer Gay
24 Humble dwelling
27 Like long-winded orators
29 Put down
31 Stuff
33 Kinds of generals: Abbr.
34 African antelope
35 Beer
36 Gossip
37 Emetic plant
38 Snack
39 Breakfast support, for some
42 Poem division
43 "Manon" and "Louise," e.g.
46 Devour
49 Place of exile
51 Cluster
52 Zipped
53 Worth or Oglethorpe
55 Obligation
56 More nasty
57 Morocco-covered books: Abbr.
58 Grid org.
59 Took to court
61 Shortage of a tank's contents
62 Gertrude Ederle, to friends
63 Mr. M.'s words for skiing events

67 Region
68 __ fro
69 Small drink
70 Capital of Italia
71 Famed Greek theater's site, to Mr. M.
72 Fruit quaff
73 Sparrow, for one
76 School V.I.P.
77 Immigrants' ship quarters
78 Teen problem
79 Word form for a Benelux nation
81 Move like a butterfly
82 Arabian demons
83 Forty-__
84 Like some police
87 Keep one's __ (watch)
90 Librarians' tools
92 Pale
93 Marsh wader
94 Solo
95 Dispenses with
97 Sailing
98 Hebrew instrument
99 Suit __ (serve nicely)
100 Windups
102 Wire measure
103 F.D.R. agency

40 Dye Job by Alfio Micci

ACROSS

1 Benches
5 Barracuda
9 African antelope
14 Believe, old style
18 Unbleached
19 Hebrew spy
21 Papal cape
22 Angelic headwear
23 Channel sight, almost
27 Long period
28 Sheltered
29 Vinegar: Prefix
30 Wind-borne
31 Mimicked
32 Ugandan name
33 Certain metal, in olden days
34 Expensive wrap
37 Bakers' needs
38 Mrs. Leonowens
39 Brooks or Torme
42 Crane title, almost
47 Miss Horne
48 Pin down
49 French wine growths
50 Work units
51 Cockney's pad
52 Fine or liberal
53 Etonian's parent
55 Inter __
56 Family __
57 City on the Rhone
58 Credit extension
60 Irish ditty, almost
66 Prepare to fire again
67 __ solemnis
68 Pastures
69 Midianite defeated by Gideon
70 Social class
71 Pause
72 Test site
75 Places
76 Uncovered
77 Prefix for john
78 Student pilot's milestone
79 Fairy-tale figure, almost
85 Physics and biology: Abbr.
86 Landed
87 Old ceremonial apron
88 Sudden leap
89 Cheshire cat's remnant
90 Certain votes
91 Pair of horses
93 "All the world's __ . . ."
96 Disgorge
98 Small case
99 Tap word
102 Prokofiev title, almost
106 Wine: Prefix
107 Town near Salerno
108 French battle site
109 Facts
110 Grate
111 Architectural style
112 Derisive cry
113 Essence

DOWN

1 Seeger
2 Repeat
3 English architect
4 Standby, for short
5 Climb
6 Emulated an expectant father
7 Miss Sommer
8 Gumshoe
9 Displeasure
10 Huck Finn's transit
11 __ many words
12 Halloween sound
13 Hells
14 Oar fulcrum
15 Shankar
16 Olive genus
17 Threadbare
20 Reproached
24 Coat part
25 Cake topping
26 Wien's river
31 Duchess of __
32 Grandparental
33 Bring on
34 French town
35 Attention-getter
36 Nota __
37 Geisha items
38 With renewed vigor
39 Game fish
40 __ on (urging)
41 "Gil Blas" author
43 Ignorant
44 Trencherman
45 Double quartet
46 Cowboys' gear
52 Length times width
53 Ordinariness
54 Code word for "a"
56 Small-time
57 Opposed: Abbr.
58 Slays
59 Smell __
60 Folklore dwarfs
61 Brave
62 Makes a choice
63 Turkish inn
64 Japanese-American
65 Gum resin
70 Summer retreat
71 Foxx
72 Diving bird
73 Sleep like __
74 Augur
76 Had faith in
77 God: Sp.
78 Avoid
80 Handel favorite
81 Word for non-brand-name drugs
82 Solar-lunar differential
83 Meter
84 Egg-white coating
89 Lively dance
91 Office worker
92 Western Sound
93 Doer: Suffix
94 N.Y. stadium
95 Wallet items
96 Get an __ excellence
97 Pretty, in Marseilles
98 Saarinen
99 Chief
100 Hep
101 Peter or Paul
103 Nigerian
104 Cheer
105 Tokyo, formerly

ACROSS

1 Myrt's radio partner
6 Guru's relative
11 Marches
17 Ascent
21 Along a center line
22 Prussian lancer
23 Tolkien character
24 Scarlett's home
25 Japanese movie, 1966
29 The Gloomy Dean
30 Arm bones
31 Secondhand
32 Chemical suffix
33 Football gadget
34 Baseball's "Penguin"
35 Covering plate: Prefix
36 "Be that __ may"
37 Use up
39 1964 match-up
45 Beached
48 Unfolded
49 Neighbor of Calif.
50 Drenched
53 "Star Trek" weapon
54 Dim with tears
55 __ facias (judicial writ)
56 Lennon's mate
57 Plaster supports
58 Lists
59 Laminar rock
60 Tout le __
62 North Pole aide
63 East African lake
64 Tropical fish
65 Town near Hattiesburg, Miss.
66 Et __
68 Generation gap
70 Abe's characteristic
71 Allen and Frome
73 Smith of Rhodesia
74 Quarterback toss
75 Nahuatlan people
77 Rivalry leading to Appomattox
81 Phono record
84 Set sail
85 __ Mrs.
86 "__ you so!"
87 Legal girl
88 Stupefy
89 Rumpelstiltskin's growth
90 Great and Terrible Ivans
91 Carried
93 Ltr. container
94 Singer-actor Mario
95 Gratuities
96 Vacuum tube
97 Dentists' degrees
99 Helper
100 Actress Anouk
101 Track contestant
102 Clash of 1862
107 Pupa's surrounding
109 Type of type: Abbr.
110 Furor
111 Math abbr.

114 Kin of N.Y.S.E. and Amex
115 "Vive le __!"
117 "No man __ island"
118 Precious violin
120 Fiji's capital
121 Historic Supreme Court case
126 Comedienne Martha
127 Kite
128 Hall-of-__ (enshrined one)
129 German poet
130 Kind of dist. atty.
131 Like "Cleopatra" on film
132 Woke
133 City of France

DOWN

1 Kind of wand or lantern
2 Nerve-cell process: Var.
3 Like a washboard
4 Watch stars
5 Cantab's rival
6 Downcast
7 Tennis-shot sounds
8 Part of T.A.E.
9 Part of Einstein's equation
10 Bank-account addn.
11 "__ of the Cross" (De Mille film)
12 __ the occasion (coped)
13 Sleeping
14 Graduate degree
15 Strong cotton
16 From eolithic to neolithic
17 Low notes

18 Title bout of 1962
19 Inexperienced
20 Vied in a regatta
26 Reformation name
27 European soldier
28 Succeeding
35 Tender spots
36 Jet fuel
38 Legume
39 Kid around
40 Soviet division
41 City on Lake Winnebago
42 Pinpoint
43 Without humor
44 "__ off to see. . ."
45 Cop __ (beg off)
46 "We __ Overcome"
47 Feud of note
51 Bit of gossip
52 Art of verse
54 Suitors
55 Chase flies
58 French city
59 Bias
60 He played Pasteur
61 Mountain nymph
63 Village on the Hudson
64 Mind one's __ q's
65 Studied intently
67 ". . . cake and eat __"
69 Piece of food
70 Contemptible ones
72 Hundred: Prefix
74 Then: Fr.
75 Equipped with pipes

76 Upright
77 Cow, at times
78 __ avis
79 Moslem dignitary
80 Less original
82 Leather
83 One who gives in
85 "The evil that __ . ."
89 Taunt
90 Dromedary
91 Cease-fire
92 Sty sound
94 Awaiting resolution
95 __ vigor
96 Like "Othello"
98 __ Locks
100 Phoenician goddess of love
103 Norse goddess of fate
104 Having a travel permit
105 Decrees
106 Grown up
107 Snake in a basket
108 Others: Sp.
111 Tail feather
112 Summon
113 Great dogs
116 Polynesian unit
117 New Rochelle college
118 At a distance
119 Office note
120 Hoosegow
122 Bedew
123 Dull noise
124 Birds __ feather
125 Parseghian

ACROSS

1 Garden tool
4 Afr. or Eur.
8 Bridge-use charge
12 Color
15 British anthem composer
19 Ambassador's armful
21 Hebrew bushel
22 "Alpha, omega; it's __ to me"
24 How some footnotes are printed
25 Ah Sin
27 Riddle
28 Evening prayers
30 City in Nebraska
31 Eccentric
32 Treas. division
33 Elevator name
35 Mountain nymphs
37 Catchall abbr.
39 River duck
41 Drum sound
43 Evergreens
46 Bank vaults
50 "Made in the __"
52 African tribesmen
54 __ de Janeiro
56 Juárez miss: Abbr.
57 Of a TV network
59 Muffin for Henry VIII, maybe
62 Work the bar
63 Dispose of quietly
64 Fencing sword
65 Sugar source
66 Writer Ferenc
68 Ending for buck or flop
69 Recipe instruction
70 Factory, in Paris
72 Gumshoes
73 From a certain time
74 Charged particle
75 On the mother's side
76 Plain people
78 Relatives of planktons
80 Out of favor
81 Literature pupil, at times
84 Tibetan tongue
85 Film shots
86 Thickness measure
87 __ contendere
88 Court cry
89 Navigational aid
90 Expense
91 Backtalk
92 Tugboat and Orphan
94 R.N.'s concern
95 Sharpen
96 Orbital point
97 Bock or root
98 What Aleksandr Pushkin was called
102 Behind time
103 Although, to Ovid
104 Apple-cider girl
105 Toad or frog

106 Actor Wallach
107 Rich loam
109 Historical times
111 Nests
114 Unfeeling
118 Coal scuttle
120 Incense spice of the Bible
122 Sheltered
124 Hilo food
125 Traffic tie-up
128 Questionable
131 Furnishes
133 Actress Leslie
135 1, 2 or 3
138 Nae-saying?
140 Amscray or ixnay, e.g.
141 Animal shelter
142 Ernie or Williams
143 Revise
144 Likely
145 Employs
146 Whilom
147 Poetic word

DOWN

1 Balzac
2 State of India
3 Ending for kitchen
4 Neighbor of N. Mex.
5 Miss Newton-John
6 Most genteel
7 Sleep fitfully
8 High-grade Persian rugs
9 Musical works, in Rome
10 Himalayan city
11 Map abbr.

12 Blood: Prefix
13 Arm bone
14 Spanish city
15 Onassis
16 Western city
17 Require
18 Squeezed out
19 Singing bird
20 Gambling game
23 Mountain ranges of India
26 Panty or fire
29 Thick soup
34 Word before la
36 Study of racial decline
38 Alhambra and Alcázar
40 Celtic "cess"
42 Doubleday
44 Court order
45 Dad's girl
47 "A votre santé!"
48 Lab burners
49 Star in Cygnus
51 Opp. of NNW
53 Not chewed into
55 Electrical unit
57 Kind of maid or shark
58 "Toity-Toid Street," e.g.
59 Simple sugar
60 City in China
61 Bloodsucker
63 Orson or lima
67 Of the ear
69 Invest, as money
70 Antirust shield on cars
71 Finnish bath
75 Eulogist
76 On high

77 Soften
79 Exude
80 Emerald and Capri
82 Famous cow
83 Diana or Betsy
86 Infection, for short
88 __ a customer
90 Horn-shaped bone
92 Cain's victim
93 __ Lanka
94 Russian ruler
95 Star cluster in Taurus
96 __ one (together)
99 Ulan __ (U.S.S.R. city)
100 Old-style messenger
101 Hard nutty candies
106 Compass point
108 Capital of Bulgaria
110 Lopsided: Prefix
112 Cup and __
113 Mr. John and others
115 Ascent
116 Infatuated one
117 Drinking spree
119 Authoritative statements
121 Certain hairdos
123 __ homo
125 Make sport of
126 Jejune
127 Manger figures
129 Cut
130 Pursue game
132 Bone: Prefix
134 Charlie Chan words
136 Sandwich initials
137 Old French coin
139 Explosive

43 Possessions by Dorothea E. Shipp

ACROSS

1 Variety of myrtle
6 Sauce ingredient
11 Fast transports
15 Fly's nemesis
18 On the level
19 Florida city
20 Twenty: Prefix
22 Give the __ (fire)
23 First shouts over a phone
26 Hawkshaw
27 Kidney: Prefix
28 Feel one's __
29 Cove
30 Spot
32 Authenticate
34 Roman bronze
36 Bruit
37 Litigant
38 Ex-child star's witchcraft
44 Word with hop or port
47 R.A.F. hero
48 __-poly
49 __-toe
50 Got even with
52 Agree with
53 One with a lot of past
54 Hemingway character
55 Harper Valley org.
56 Cambridge campus
57 Sullivan et al.
58 Beethoven's "Für __"
59 Lobster source
61 Aspect
63 Writer's steak
70 Table sets
71 Hdkf. additions
72 Mrs. Berlin
73 Marriage: Ger.
76 Writers' output: Abbr.
77 Bishopric
78 Having pointed arches
79 Philippine palm
82 Cole and Turner
84 Like O'Neill's interlude
86 Trap again
87 Scottish island
88 Hebrew letter
89 Spread hay
90 Columnist's mailing necessity
95 Have a __ for news
96 Unit of hope
97 Alfonso's queen
98 Sleeping-sickness carrier
102 Honshu metropolis
104 Wasting disease
106 Gardner and namesakes
108 Spirit noises
109 Gibbon
110 TV star's spades
114 Scottish uncle
115 Clothing decoration
116 The end
117 French maid
118 Perfume: Abbr.
119 French donkeys
120 Farm machine
121 Bury

DOWN

1 Bow or Barton
2 Sublease
3 Go-between
4 Wee folk
5 Airport-board initials
6 Musical conclusion
7 Chemical compound
8 Zoroastrian
9 Letters
10 1944 Nobel physicist
11 In a stupid way
12 Part of the eyeball
13 Spree
14 Vane letters
15 Well-known D.C. address
16 High official, for short
17 Call's counterpart
21 Took for granted
24 Bulletin-board item
25 Make possible
31 Steeple sounds
33 Kind of leather
35 Neighbors of Israelis
37 Helter-__

39 Sea or Cross
40 Turf
41 Preferences
42 Unpublished: Abbr.
43 U.S.N. officers
44 Playwright Karel
45 Spanish province
46 Started the fire again
51 Poet Ogden
52 Eye afflictions
55 What Sam made too long
56 Dull finish
59 Blunder
60 Roof embellishment
61 French __
62 Products of Pythagoras
64 Feeling of guilt
65 Ready to emote
66 Gymnast Korbut
67 Abounding in: Suffix
68 Beleaguerment
69 Closed out
73 Common French verb
74 Blood: Prefix

75 City and lake southeast of L.A.
80 City land not on a corner
81 Has good results
82 Later
83 Group of anecdotes
84 Harbor city: Abbr.
85 "Is __?" ("Really?")
87 Portuguese saint and others
91 Resident in Delphi
92 Hard finish
93 Feral
94 In __ (in the flesh)
99 Ridicule
100 Porcupine's defense
101 Chemical compound
102 Swiss artist
103 Sweet potatoes
104 Kind of bed
105 Post
107 Open
111 Sky Altar
112 Wee: Scot.
113 Baseball stat

Getting Over

by H. Hastings Reddall

ACROSS

1 Loose robe for women
6 Horse quarters
12 Secular
16 "Open ___"
17 More vivacious
18 Chef's need
20 Auction follower
22 Overseers of manors
24 Asian sea
25 Enticed
26 Mohammedan noble
28 Before
29 Network
30 Like a football grid
31 Stimulates
32 High or eye
33 Military award
34 Trig ratios
35 Greek letter
36 Reacts emotionally
37 More exacting
39 Green quartz
40 Small Italian coins
41 Japanese dramas: Var.
42 Run-down area
43 West Indies native
44 Return payment
47 "Some of ___ days. . ."
48 Casbah country
51 Acquires the hard way
52 Tracts
53 Carousal
55 Wind that blows no good
56 Soft cheese
57 European roses
59 Roman 402
60 Antiquity
61 Beauty's friend
62 Unkempt
63 Palm starches
64 Young swans
66 Heaps
67 Mother or father
68 Pearl Buck's was good
69 Lemon, orange et al.
70 Proof of payment: Abbr.
71 Numbered-card game
72 Serpents' weapons
74 Levantine area
78 Drums' partners
79 Backyard privacy provider
80 Four: Prefix
81 French wheat
82 Girl
83 Musical closings
84 Turkish porter
85 Musical piece
86 Prefix for form or verse
87 Bounce off
88 Card catalogue worker
89 ___ souci
90 Tidal floods
92 Specialized crossing
96 Participate
97 Of a mountain chain
98 Wears away
99 Wearing boots
100 Gets hot under the collar
101 Scandinavians

DOWN

1 Capitol Hill figure
2 Basket fiber
3 Disfigure
4 "I ___ Camera"
5 Enjoys an easy chair
6 Fencing swords
7 Partner of sick
8 Dry
9 One club, e.g.
10 Envoys
11 Hermit of old
12 Household gods
13 Mime
14 Anger
15 Colorful New England crossing
16 Most peeved
19 Perfume oil
20 ___ and spades
21 TV dial
23 Mends tears
27 Period of time
30 Supple
31 "What a crying ___!"
32 Disguise
34 Skye people
35 Crossing with special supports
36 Do a bit of check cheating
38 Pointless
39 Fold in a skirt
40 Auction and white
42 Component of a quire
43 Cash and ___
44 Stringed instrument
45 "___ to bed. . ."
46 Venice crossing
47 Very, to a Parisian
49 Ancient Troy
50 Tilting
52 Under water
53 Locations
54 Family additions
57 All ___ go (ready)
58 Chest sounds
59 ___ blanche
61 Lance, Lahr et al.
63 Pelvic bones
65 Cager Archibald and others
66 Throes
67 Miss Bailey
70 Held back
71 Tropical vines
72 Hats for detectives
73 Unswerving
74 Valley near Corinth
75 Irritates
76 Holders for some skiers' arms
77 Comb hair in a way
78 Chimney part
79 Sunset point: Abbr.
80 Claws
83 Appraised, as a joint
84 Man's name
85 Actors' device
87 Mackerellike fish
88 Kind of market
91 Cheer
93 Chemical suffix
94 Part of a two-piece suit
95 Nessen

Relatively Speaking

by Betty Leary

ACROSS

1 Kind of waist
5 Depot: Abbr.
8 Rickety plane
13 Warbucks or Longlegs
18 Mirages
21 Harp on the unpleasant
22 __ as a beet
23 Unflappable
25 Rolled teas
26 Hillock
27 Puppets
28 Lively
30 Calendar abbr.
31 Mantelpiece fillers
34 School subj.
35 Literary initials
37 Fictional pirate
38 Pinch
40 Tackled a problem
43 Secures, in a way
45 Rorem and Sparks
47 Prepared potatoes
48 Here and there
49 Performing lions and others
53 Approach
54 __ Dame
55 Writer Bombeck and others
56 Virginia river
58 Carryall
59 Colonizes in a small way
60 French menu word
61 Pitcher Maglie
64 Like a poor speaker
66 Comme ci, comme ça
69 Russian political unit: Abbr.
70 Small container
71 Orchard yields
72 Egyptian season
73 Scene of Hessian defeat in 1776
76 Abounding in streams
77 __ garde
78 Kind of coal
79 Mundane
81 Short items, often
82 Desired
84 Nigerian tribe
85 Pentateuch readings
86 Arranged
88 "Beat it!"
91 U.S. military women
92 Anglo-Saxon letter
93 Squeal
95 Repeal
97 State of the Keys: Abbr.
100 Embroidery hoops
104 Unicorn fish
105 "Not __!" (Once is enough)
107 Kind of closet
108 Rather racy
111 Miss Castle
112 Leave out
113 Art masterpieces, e.g.
114 Krupp location
115 Lecher
116 Fast plane
117 Defeat

DOWN

1 Oil-lamp parts
2 Like Robinson Crusoe
3 Sailboat
4 Influence
5 Family member
6 Sycophants
7 Canal Zone town
8 Quality of bread or curmudgeons
9 Grog
10 French cleric
11 Indeed, in Paris
12 Make bread more healthful
13 Kind of bank
14 Staff person: Abbr.
15 Like the Prohibition era
16 Like female compared to male
17 Gridiron units: Abbr.
19 Siberian landmark
20 Shows ill humor
24 Ball of yarn
29 Australian hut
32 Split
33 Chance-taking, for short
36 Approved model: Abbr.
37 Horse mackerel
39 Biblical tower
41 __ Dinmont terrier
42 On the ocean
43 Sings lullabies
44 Like the dog days
46 Western flower
48 Ones opposed
49 Wedding-song offering
50 To __ (everybody)
51 Book of the N.T.
52 Lacking uniformity
55 Represent as the same
57 Legendary Celt and namesakes
59 Very small area: Abbr.
62 Catkins
63 Baltic people
65 Came out ahead
66 Parched
67 Form of Louise
68 Relishes
71 Butcher's customer
74 Carry on
75 Beaks
77 "The hopes __ of all the years. . ."
78 Ornery animals
80 Cape near Lisbon
81 Kind of belt
82 Diminutive suffix
83 Spanish peso
85 Splashes
87 Takes five
89 Wild buffalo of India
90 Damp
94 Singing sounds
96 Things often shifted
97 Make, in Montmartre
98 Verse units
99 Feeling of dread
101 Flowing hair
102 Gun
103 Aperture
106 Chow
107 French co.
109 Nonpermanent assignment: Abbr.
110 Wear away

46 Togetherness

by Sidney L. Robbins

ACROSS

1 Lizard
6 Mr. Rather and others
10 Type of heat
15 Type of devil
19 Hack poet: Var.
20 John, in Wales
21 Prepares dinner, at times
22 Did a hatchet job
23 Unlike: Prefix
24 Lima's land
25 Basis for assessment
26 Hollywood and __
27 Circus pair
30 Plains animal
31 Frenzy, in zoology
32 Copier
33 Type of pole
34 Youth org.
37 This, in Spain
38 War god
39 Confinement, usually vile
43 Rivulets
45 Self
46 In a calm manner
47 "Othello" villain
48 Comic pair
53 Defy, in Scotland
54 Altitude: Abbr.
55 Escort
56 "That __ hay!"
57 Concede
58 Type of conclusion
60 Night bird
61 Type of negligence
62 Alder tree
63 Concurs
67 Be sickly
68 Ferber and Millay
70 Golf-card listing
71 Attacked
76 Geraint's wife and others
77 Smeltery leaving
79 Efts
81 __-de-camp
82 Standard
83 Radio pair
85 Not kosher
86 Evacuate
88 Southern tuber
89 Ridicule
90 Lobe pendant
91 __ stockings
93 Poker stake
96 Corsica's neighbor: Abbr.
97 Fish eggs
98 Sleuth Wolfe
99 Traps
101 Bookkeeping word
104 Legendary friends
109 Region
110 Interrupt
111 Istanbul region
112 Type of laugh
113 Type of worm or leader
114 Declaim
115 Cylinder
116 Maternal kin
117 Head, in France
118 Propelled a gondola
119 Ancient kingdom
120 Material for jeans

DOWN

1 One of Lawrence's friends
2 Lollobrigida
3 Turkish V.I.P.
4 Intermediate
5 Awakens
6 What Kipling's captains and kings do
7 Fifth or Park
8 Aromatic plants
9 Treat with disdain
10 Skunk decoration
11 Greek philosopher
12 Consumer
13 Far off
14 Linguistic degree
15 Biblical twosome
16 Earth line
17 Divorce city
18 Paradise
28 Andes or Rockies: Abbr.
29 Brother of Moses
30 Type of back or bones
33 Sod
34 Lawyer's submission
35 Saliva: Prefix
36 "Sink or Swim" author
38 Culture medium
39 Apt
40 Approaches
41 Hints
42 Medieval court
44 Song couple
45 French season
46 Japanese money
48 Cosmic particles
49 Defense arm: Abbr.
50 Tea genus
51 It came, in the silents
52 Leave at the altar
57 Solo
59 Mardi __
60 Poetic word
61 Like many orators
64 Health places
65 Classic tale
66 Cut
68 __ Gay
69 More drastic
72 Criterion: Abbr.
73 Syrian moneys
74 Swelling disease
75 Postpone
76 Word ending
77 Self-satisfied
78 Fortune
79 Neighbor of Minn.
80 Greek org.
83 Top-notch
84 Stocking material
87 Disturbance
89 Boiled
91 Mideasterner
92 Did a laundry job
93 Del Sarto
94 Type of bomb
95 Attempt
98 Of birth
99 Show contempt
100 Was outstanding
101 Type of board
102 Niagara River feeder
103 Crooked
104 Spanish money
105 Harbor of Guam
106 Tabriz's land
107 Italian wine city
108 Appear
110 Whistle blower

47 Nostalgia by Tap Osborn

ACROSS

1 Spellbound
5 Sound of sorrow
9 Necessity
13 Do some sewing
17 Inter __
18 Contrived excuse
19 Opposed
20 Wheel holder
21 Jolson hit revived in '29 by Helen Morgan
25 Enrolled
26 Gourmet's concern
27 Attach
28 Sloth, for one
29 Artillery man
30 Like some winter days
31 W.W. I hit revived in '28
36 Profound
37 Before
38 Regret
39 Marble
42 Miscalculate
43 Implore
45 Hemingway, to friends
48 F.D.R.'s sidekick·
49 Moved slowly
51 1909 hit revived in '39
54 Dvorak
55 Formal departure
56 Valley for a LEM to explore
57 Hit of 1929 revived in '43
59 Remark
61 Donkey, in Düsseldorf
62 Cloud on the horizon
63 Unique
64 Nizer's forte
65 Rollaway or trundle
66 Paver's need
68 Intention
69 Musician Fountain
70 1919 hit revived in '45 and '52
76 Underwrite
79 Ending for mort or polit
80 Old Mideast initials
81 ". . . __ reason why"
82 Proclivity
83 Trade sanction
87 1914 hit revived in '30 and '50
91 Ali's milieu
92 Mother of F.D.R.
93 Winged
94 Groupie hero
95 Western Indian
96 Weather bad news
97 Road hauler, for short
98 Refuse

DOWN

1 Comedienne Martha
2 Bates or King
3 Early Britisher
4 Adopts as a hobby
5 Goddess of wisdom
6 Bestow kudos
7 Kind of star game
8 Nautical measure
9 Orono campus
10 Straighten, as hair
11 Part of N.Y.S.E.: Abbr.
12 __-dye
13 More unhappy
14 Emanate
15 Apportion
16 U.S. labor patriarch
22 Seed case
23 Anise or rue
24 Temporary New Havenite
29 Spiteful woman
30 Dallas campus
31 Iced drinks
32 Steak __

33 Mad
34 Droplet
35 Mecca native
39 Furniture support
40 Estrange
41 Peaked
43 Find it heavy going
44 Italian painter Guido
45 Fasten, as a medal
46 Constellation
47 Shepherd's __
48 Shoot
50 Type style: Abbr.
51 Morse had one
52 5, 6 or 7, to a golfer
53 Frost
55 Machine part
57 Cotillion star
58 Bloodcurdling
59 Perry
60 Shrill note

63 Elsa or Leo
66 Pulsate
67 Beame or Lincoln
68 Christie and namesakes
69 Build paper profits
70 Power loss
71 Small farmer in Puerto Rico
72 Headpiece used for hangovers
73 Miss Foch
74 Upper arm bones
75 Indulge
76 Word with spect
77 __, no-run ball game
78 Office worker
83 Hindu land grant
84 Made fun of
85 Hired thug
86 Just
88 Nincompoop
89 Water-control device
90 Cheer

48 Word Juggling

by Louis Baron

ACROSS

1 Conforming
7 North Dakota city
12 Chinese objet d'art material
16 "__ victor. . ."
21 Disavowal
22 "It's __!"
23 Arabian port
24 Garden pest
25 Stale comic
27 Anti-divorce lawyer
29 Poe's Annabel
30 Damascene
31 Hashish plants
33 Regional bird life
34 Clarinet socket
35 Sign on a house
36 Cleaving tool
37 Machine piece
40 Old Dutch measure
41 Iota
42 Changing scene
46 Easygoing
48 Burst of activity
49 Synonym man
50 Kind of artist
51 Cue
52 What dieters are shown
54 Macbeth, for one
55 __ water (on the spot)
56 Between 12 and 20
57 Drams
58 Citizen Tom
59 __ bene
60 Red wine
61 Arkin and Paton
63 Like some bills
64 Relating to: Suffix
65 Winner's stable
67 Entangled
68 With trills
70 Common street name
71 City near Cologne
72 "__ where the heart is"
73 Cloud-nine tie-up
77 Cap
80 A strait is named for him
81 Some stars
82 Implement
83 Kind of bat
84 Works for
85 Sound's cohort
86 Abbot's aide
87 Beat
88 Monkshood
89 Guitar rock
92 "__ her wrong"
93 Driving place
94 Czech town
95 Metric measure
96 Odalisks' digs
97 Accuses
99 Quail group
100 Auction word
101 N.Y. time
102 Barracuda

103 Las Vegas bandit's arm
104 Domineer
105 Occupy
107 Mr. __ of minstrel shows
108 Spanish explorer
110 Cote sound
113 Apache cemeteries
115 Jail-diary title
118 Overhangs
119 Some dancers
120 Blackbird
121 Scottish cap tassel
122 Color changers
123 Jug
124 Sad
125 Plains Indian

DOWN

1 Object of adulation
2 River in England
3 Snick and __
4 Twitching
5 Up to one's __
6 Cooperate
7 Asian ascetics
8 Madison Ave. type
9 Hold in
10 Started, à la Chaucer
11 Rosinante, for one
12 Stuck
13 Take on
14 __ ex machina
15 Noun suffix
16 Foundation for growth

17 First move
18 Siamese
19 Lush sounds
20 Dutch town
26 Arson or rustling, e.g.
28 Stinger
32 Resin
35 Relents
36 Beech-tree genus
37 Gambling place
38 Musical key
39 Indian chief with angst
40 As blind as __
41 Cupboard, in England
42 Exhausts
43 Like a witch with cauldron burns
44 Was listless
45 Staked
47 Celebes ox
48 Hebrew Hades
49 Lorelei milieu
52 A Roosevelt
53 Strain at a __
54 Hebrew letter
56 Lindens
58 Kashmir wool
60 Words for a top exec
61 Halls
62 Deflated
63 Hickory's kin
65 English guns
66 Buona __
67 Barbara or surgery
69 Idi and family
71 Role taker

72 Mobster's gat
73 Balkan capital
74 Balanced
75 Stage rabbit
76 More aloof
78 Battle sites
79 Not pushy
80 __ retreat
81 Ointments
83 Verdi girl
85 Be miserly
86 Diner on pumpkins
87 Incline
89 In a learned way
90 Gauntlet
91 Half a sawbuck
92 Grasped
94 Like flapper figures
96 "__ the Greek"
98 Letter-closing words
99 Suppress
100 Exclusively
103 Local chapter
104 Kind of beam
105 Cart
106 Quick greeting
107 Low or high
108 Egyptian drink
109 Works like __
110 Mistral's cousin
111 Dye shrub
112 Bewildered
113 Flowers' home
114 Middle or jazz
116 __ Morgue
117 Lt. __

ACROSS

1 Vanzetti's co-defendant
6 Auction sign-off
10 __ facto
14 Repress
19 Normandy beach
20 Foil's kin
21 Matrix
22 Like a lion's coat
23 Easy gaits
24 Test tube
25 Before: Prefix
26 Stay __ spot (be stationary)
27 Landfall figure
31 Not in, in Scotland
32 Con
33 Single: Prefix
34 Televise
35 Filched
37 Certain Renaissance oils
40 Iter's relative
42 Illustrious
45 Overture figure
50 Track habitué
51 Prefix for pod or color
52 Scrape by, with "out"
53 Kings' payments, traditionally
55 Looked after
56 Angel's prop
58 Canal Zone town
60 State bird of Hawaii
62 Cargo
63 Red Sea port
65 Chosen: Fr.
67 Tired routines
69 Total of the figures listed
78 Mountain lake
79 Forwarded
80 Top sheiks
81 Newts
85 Himalayan Bigfoot
87 Dostoevski subject
90 Et __
91 Champion of the dance
93 Calif. city
96 Greek letter
98 "C'__ Si Bon"
99 Gladiators' milieus
101 Slogan figure
104 Signified
106 "Tale __ Tub"
107 Most efficient
108 Nylon fabric
110 After zeta
112 Pastoral place
113 Prefix for sphere
117 Tunisian ruler
119 Address figure
123 Soviet range
125 Umiak, e.g.
126 "Miss Lulu __"
127 Crème de la crème
128 Knife inventor
129 Transistor's predecessor
130 City on the Oka
131 Do a tailoring chore

132 "There's __ spinning wheel. . ."
133 Nailhead
134 Ablush
135 Banquet ritual

DOWN

1 Syllabic system, in music
2 "__ for the Misbegotten"
3 Head, to Caesar
4 Treasure
5 Kiln
6 Booth Tarkington figure
7 Word from the bench
8 Sprat's fare
9 Artemis
10 Endangers
11 Ship's objective
12 Does a hit job
13 "Swan Lake" role
14 Squealers
15 Singer Janis
16 N.Y.C. dialing figure
17 __ account (never)
18 Russian veto
28 Archimedes's version of "Success!"

29 "Moon's a Balloon" author
30 "Blessed is the fruit of thy __"
36 Inner, in anatomy
38 Snacked
39 Honers' needs
41 Anthony Eden's earldom
43 __ care in the world
44 Trampled
45 Wharton hero
46 Basra native
47 Region of India
48 "I __ girl just like. . ."
49 Honorably retired ones
54 Cozy
57 English honor: Abbr.
59 "The __ Monte Cristo"
61 Ordinal ending
64 Thai coin
66 U.S.N.A. grad
68 Between Sault and Marie
70 Fodder
71 Neighbor of Provo
72 Olympian
73 ". . .to the __ perfect day"
74 Miss Sumac
75 Bath-floor repairman
76 Place for a watch

77 Suffix for pomp or verb
81 Mild oath
82 Not aft
83 Catch figure
84 Málaga mister
86 Personal: Prefix
88 In a lavish way
89 Bobbin holding
92 Approved
94 Brought about
95 Condition, in Capri
97 Conditions
100 Dry in Jerez
102 Monastery people
103 Iago's boss
105 Misgivings
109 Stream denizen
111 Shady place
114 Mrs. Perón
115 Apportions
116 Like some gases
117 __ au rhum
118 N.C. campus
120 Elephant-boy portrayer
121 Saarinen
122 Do an usher's job
124 Be under the weather

50 Gone With the Wind by Frances Hansen

ACROSS

1 Reindeer herders
6 Mulligatawny
10 Kind of ribs or parts
15 Where cheese comes from
20 Soprano Lucine
21 Of an arm bone
23 Less well
24 Of birds
25 Stand off
26 Prefix for phone or scope
27 Mrs. Meir
28 Knight's gear
29 Start of a limerick
33 "__ with flagons. . ."
34 Traveler or Rosinante
35 Gloss
36 Author Anita
37 High note
39 Room guarded by eunuchs
41 A code we live by
43 Take __ (acknowledge applause)
47 Where curry comes from
51 Knievel
54 Adorn with spangles: Var.
59 More of limerick
64 Sun: Prefix
65 Comes closer
66 Harsh
67 Mischievous ones
68 "__, one land, one heart. . ."
70 D-sharp on the keyboard
72 Dockworkers' org.
73 Casey's position
74 Angkor __
75 Bit of sediment
77 Bagels' partner
78 Cleo's way out
79 Lady Nancy and John Jacob
80 More of limerick
84 Where bassos meet sopranos
87 Crow's craw
88 His wife turned to salt
89 Pedestal part
90 __ Vegas
93 "Tell me where it __"
94 Invitation
95 Trembly tree
97 Eden resident
99 Greenland base
100 "It is __ wind. . ."
102 Trojan hero: Var.
104 Ancient Greek region
105 More of limerick
110 Mt. Everest guide
111 Late grandpa of "The Waltons"
112 Declare
113 Namesakes of Alfonso's wife
114 Where oil comes from
117 Zag's opposite number
119 Heat: Abbr.
121 Miss Pitts
125 Juan's waters
128 Woman raised to blessedness
132 Jai-alai ball
137 End of limerick
141 Indian of a low caste
142 Trap
143 Painter Andrea del __
144 Town for a coven's reunion?
145 Dress up
146 Metrical stress
147 Cook's tear-jerker
148 January, in Madrid
149 Matchmaker of "Fiddler"
150 Galleys and galleons
151 Boleyn or Bancroft
152 Lets up

DOWN

1 "__ Song," from "Zhivago"
2 Flower cluster
3 Port Moresby is its capital
4 College biggie
5 She danced for Herod
6 Oriental painting substance
7 Potpourris
8 Like some diamonds
9 Do a grammar job
10 Omen
11 Tills the soil
12 Mohammed's god
13 Moses parted its waters
14 Solver's aid
15 Cloy
16 Profit
17 Beatles' Starr
18 He-man type
19 Dill herbs
22 Man's slipper
30 Museum exhibit
31 Totted up
32 Cyclops's feature
38 "I Married __"
40 Belay's relative
42 Collection
43 "__ my heart beats. . ."
44 "You Must Have __ Beautiful Baby"
45 Small hooter
46 Orphan of the storm
48 Religious degree
49 Dies __
50 Wind current caused by motion
52 "I love __," said the ram, sheepishly
53 Generous
55 __ cock (rail)
56 Tree of Argentina
57 Wall St. phrase
58 Musical pauses
60 Welds
61 City near Malmo
62 Barked sharply
63 Bikini part
69 Sandy's barks
71 Dorothy Hamill's leaps
73 Waldorf-__
76 Zodiac sign
78 Comes to the ball
79 Nurse's assistant
80 Come-__ look (flirt's glance)
81 Kind of pool or bird
82 Steve or Elmo
83 U.S. painter Mary
84 Fischer's forte
85 Rabbit's residence
86 "__ Ben Jonson!"
90 Red Square figure
91 Santa __
92 Corset bones
94 Scrooge's word
95 "__-vous-en!" ("Get lost!")
96 Salamander
98 Wicked Wasp of Twickenham
101 Size after med.
103 "So!"
106 Finial part
107 Early Indians of Ecuador
108 African antelope
109 Musical beat
115 ". . . cycle of the __ renewed"
116 Slake
118 Plaster of Paris
120 French reflection
121 Full of ginger
122 Cognizant
123 Razor clam
124 Not rented
126 Valuable violin
127 Pancake topping
129 Yoga position
130 City on the Po
131 Chemistry Nobelist, 1922
133 Tarzan's viny swing
134 Makes eyes at
135 "Over __"
136 Kind of self-winding clock
138 Prong
139 Army meal
140 Elegance

51 Choice Words
by William A. Lewis Jr.

ACROSS

1. Winds
6. Somber shades
11. Embarrass
16. Outing
17. Pointless
18. Lost sight of
20. Most happy place
22. Griddle cake
24. Cover-up name
25. Revealed
26. London area
28. Shelter
29. Drying place
30. What company does
32. Melt off
33. Mention
34. Dawn goddess
35. Hails
37. Many times
38. Made with sections
39. Furtive ones
41. Cease
43. Kind of grove
44. Poker move
46. Three-abreast area in plane
47. Arias
48. Kiev comrade
51. Theory of behavior
56. Camel fabric
57. Deceptions
59. Glossed word
60. Pace
61. Good: Lat.
63. Pile
65. Useful things
67. Practice boxing
68. Too-too
70. Throng
72. Held
74. State: Abbr.
75. N.C. and S.C., for two
78. Congress in-betweens
80. Actress Fay
81. Farms
83. Writing Pere
84. Qualified
87. Atlantic republic
89. Sask. city
92. Be generous
93. —— Wednesday
94. Isn't alert
96. Cake
97. Skein
98. Holders
100. Bulls: Sp.
101. Number
102. Id ——
103. Show life
105. More: Mus.
106. Tuckered out
107. Send another way
109. Rural feature
112. Swift's home
113. Word of welcome
114. Fazes
115. Distance
116. Peace offering
117. Unreliable

DOWN

1. Police, postmen etc.
2. Map area
3. Places to stay
4. Not dark
5. Group
6. Weight-watcher's word
7. Items of interest
8. Take on
9. Massage
10. Helpful quality
11. Cause changes
12. Carried
13. Jejune
14. York's rank
15. Emergency wire
16. Centaur's home
19. Partner of totter
20. —— alive
21. Rich soil
23. Tall and thin
27. Spat
30. Caesar's enemy
31. Utah lilies
33. Pooches
35. Go rapidly
36. Slow one
38. Fly
40. Good rating
42. Group
43. Island dish
45. Pure pleasure
47. Not moving
48. Bans
49. Greek coins
50. Enthusiasm
52. Lover
53. What cannot be
54. Extra
55. Habits
58. Jotter's material
62. Illustrations
64. Hepburn sobriquet
66. Fastens
69. High abode
71. Is noisy
73. Greek communes
76. Squeal
77. View
79. Give
82. Annoying people
84. Attendant
85. Introduced gradually
86. Child's outburst
87. Mother of Horus
88. Andrea ——
90. Forces
91. Shortened verb
93. Steve, Woody, etc.
95. Old oath
98. Pin-up girl
99. Office worker
101. Fail
103. Attraction
104. Uses up
106. Color
108. Japanese item
110. Letter
111. Companion of dit.

52 Stepquote
by Eugene T. Maleska

ACROSS

1. Start of an eight-word quote descending in stairstep fashion to 150 Across
7. Small-time operator
13. Parnassians
18. Road job
19. Crisp cracker
20. Soirees
22. Gets one's bearings
23. Franken heroine
24. Chilean desert
25. Money player
26. Bach opus
28. Exceeded the resources of
30. Needlefish
31. Standstill
33. —— Gay, historic plane
34. Trifling
35. Together
37. Took pleasure in
39. Part of Stepquote
42. B'way group
43. Sweeten the pot
44. Proven
46. Put in relief
48. Utter
49. Author of Stepquote
50. Bills
52. Roundabout way
54. Construct
56. D-Day vessel
57. Certain rummy cards
60. Moved swiftly
62. Mind over platter
64. Science fiction site
65. Social asset
67. Hits hard
69. Raid
73. Eastern title
74. Very funny!
76. Actress Massey
77. Turkish city
78. Zero
80. Stubborn
83. Southern France
84. Prayer
86. Part of an antler
87. Tupelo or wicopy
88. Family member
89. Rich repasts
90. Knitted cape
92. Whoop
94. Mailed
95. Sweetsop
97. Printers' double daggers
99. Geological period
101. Cold cubes
104. Sheep
106. Hags
108. Sullen
109. David's daughter
111. A.M.A. members
113. Gide's "—— Is the Gate"
115. Figures of speech
119. Turkish standard
120. Man-made lake
122. Part of Stepquote
124. —— umber
125. Opp. of fortis
127. Fervent
129. Partner of fish
131. Utah flower
132. Neither Dem. nor Rep.
133. Do-it-yourself man
136. Shouts
138. D.C. group
139. Unyielding
141. End of a K.O. count
143. Krypton, for one
145. Indigenous group
146. Dodgers
147. Rank symbols
148. Ballerina Jeanmaire
149. Perceives
150. End of Stepquote

DOWN

1. Tell
2. Memorial Stadium team
3. Three in Roma
4. Hence: Latin
5. —— dark
6. Part of Stepquote
7. Stabilized
8. Gums
9. Very short pencil
10. Trapper's cache
11. Mystery
12. Ronald and family
13. Moderate
14. Tilled land
15. Army group: Abbr.
16. Twill weave
17. Of word meanings
18. Items for heads with tails
19. Cooked, in a way
20. Reinvested stakes
21. U.S. painter
27. Some Richards
29. Place for a frontal
32. Coaches
36. Principle
38. Ivy League team
40. Rosters
41. Part of Stepquote
45. Part of O.T.
47. Vain
49. Tire mark
51. Famous southpaw
53. Wry reply
55. Intended
57. Sir Rabindranath
58. Sister of Clio
59. Steep slopes
61. Tenfold
63. Shipshape
64. —— few words
66. Symbol of discipline
68. Glossy fabric
70. Gone up
71. Water nymph
72. Follower of a belief
75. Not forming an angle
79. Artificial satellite
80. Take out stitches
81. Makes a debut
82. Sniggled
85. Coat fur
91. Category
93. Boodle
94. Like an antitoxin
96. Parts
98. Customs officers
100. Check
101. Romance language
102. "Pudd'nhead Wilson's ——," source of Stepquote
103. Correct mss.
105. Hold forth
107. Draws off
110. "What —— bid?"
112. Russian length units
114. European linden
116. Maxim
117. Airport roarers
118. Ermines in brown
121. Infer
123. Part of Stepquote
126. Rung
128. French writer: 1823-92
130. Adriatic island
134. Arrow poison
135. Colors
137. Belgradian
140. Sixty secs
142. Kickoff gadget
144. Twice DI

53 Changing World
by William Lutwiniak

ACROSS

1. Quagmires
5. Tincture
10. Outer wear
14. Right-hand man: Abbr.
18. Quiz
19. Originate
20. Angel gear
21. Tete-——
22. Annual phenomenon
25. Bucephalus
26. Application
27. Exclusively
28. Disentangle
29. Perplexes
30. Denials
31. Garagemen: Abbr.
32. French city
33. Bantu-speaking Africans
36. Swiss city
37. Open-air
41. Peak in the Cascades
42. Checker-berry
44. City on the Danube
45. Lamp item
46. Como or Garda
47. Turkish titles
48. Character in "Peter Pan"
49. Hooter
50. Like some fruits at times
54. Man —— (entre nous)
55. Nursery item
57. Eyes: Slang
58. Hall of ——
59. Gaffe
60. Pay
61. Glove man
62. Whitens
64. Turnstile item
65. Pastry
68. Competitions
69. Gymnastic feats
71. —— shoe-string
72. Signs, informally
73. ——-Coburg
74. Gatherings
75. Qualifying words
76. Farm sound
77. City on the Sangamon
81. Bullish times
82. Irregular ode
84. Fissures
85. Salad item
86. "Dear me!"
87. Hacienda features
88. Punch: Colloq.
89. Storied ship
92. Attack
93. Blue-green
94. Bleacherite
97. Small amount
98. Do the unexpected
101. Simulated
102. Greensward
103. Clerical leave
104. W.W. II powers
105. Jefferson
106. Two-—— (in theater)
107. Cons
108. Witticism

DOWN

1. Escort
2. Amu Darya
3. Attendance
4. Dallas campus
5. French resort
6. Some tests
7. Flower
8. Adjective ending
9. Application
10. Whence's companion
11. Eastern VIPs
12. Amaryllis's cousin
13. Small, for one
14. Adjust
15. Appear
16. One or goose
17. Williams and Kennedy
21. To the rear
23. Wastelands
24. Family member
29. Vaults
30. Halo
31. —— letters
32. Do house-work
33. Skewer item
34. Town south of Asmara
35. Resorts to
36. Narrow-minded one
37. Greek city
38. Vacation place
39. Unclouded
40. Straws in the wind
42. Oasis feature
43. Shows
46. Crescents
48. Endings with three and four
50. Sty noises
51. Assuage
52. Zealous
53. Closing words
54. Prepares to take off
56. Shoe parts
58. Typesetter's concerns
60. Some voters
61. Packaged
62. Pleat
63. City of Vietnam
64. Virulent
65. Contests
66. Put down
67. Talking back
69. Lucknow wear
70. Aids'
companion
73. Sprinkle
75. Bamboozle
77. Seasoned
78. Delight
79. Lawbreaker
80. Heatedly
81. Digest
83. Habaneras
85. Woos
87. Sawlike part
88. Military group
89. Vessel
90. Painful word
91. Preposition
92. Idaho
93. Sailing
94. Prix ——
95. In present condition
96. Hotbed
98. Location: Abbr.
99. Tool
100. Reign, in India

Literally Speaking
by Anthony Morse

ACROSS

1. Gold or copper
6. Rib
11. Hold up
16. Mme. de ——
21. Fresh air
22. Chose
23. Uneven
24. Fenetre's relative
25. Applause in Yankee Stadium
27. Irritated archer
29. Conn. name
30. Red Square name
31. Embed
32. Stays in place, as a ship
33. Peer
34. Labor name
35. Alhambra room
36. Clasp
40. Minimum
41. Noted contralto
45. City on the Somme
46. Misstaters
47. Gray color
48. Girl's name
49. Parts of insects' jaws
50. Warning signal conks out
53. Cards
54. Latin phrase
55. Hot spots
56. Slips
57. French numeral
58. Largest digit
59. Sheer linen
60. Thin disk
62. Miss Starr
63. Clock setting: Abbr.
64. Certain Roman ruins
66. Clarence's cousin
67. Radar spot
69. Light-Horse Harry
70. Hero in Greek legend
71. Horse
73. Flexible span
80. Oriental pagoda
83. '49 gold rush name
84. Type of flu
85. Sudden move
86. Blanc
87. Warsaw people
88. Asian VIPs
89. Central
90. Andrea del ——
91. Brain passage
92. Drama school teachers
95. Fibers
96. Poetic word
97. Intervening: Law
98. Duplicate
99. Polynesian skirts
100. Scorned
102. Mixes
103. Personality plus
105. Former dog star
106. Western resort
107. Refuse
108. Malevolence
111. Greek island
112. Reluctant
113. Photo of a kind
117. Where to find an almond
119. Mute domestics
121. C'est ——
122. Evangelist McPherson
123. Island west of Curacao
124. Radio's Baby Snooks
125. Put right
126. Reuners
127. Bremen's river
128. Low point

DOWN

1. A Dick
2. Pound
3. Dupe
4. English queen
5. Word book: Abbr.
6. Stick
7. —— shut
8. Author Gertrude
9. Bird
10. Commercials
11. Not comme il faut
12. Wandering
13. Goofy
14. Aide: Abbr.
15. Favorable word
16. Fly in the ointment
17. "I haven't got a thing ——"
18. Weapons
19. French political unit
20. Fabric
26. Groups
28. Men about town
31. Buck or Bailey
33. Pulitzer Prize poet, 1929.
34. Grocery sign
35. Cuts
36. One of the Four Horsemen
37. —— of Gaul
38. Mute domestics
39. Kid
40. Attend a lecture
41. Seeds
42. Sequels
43. New York lake
44. Winter resort
46. Thread
47. Up ——
50. Australian export
51. Salute
52. Clockmaker Thomas
53. Field of activity
57. England's lifeblood
59. Candle
60. Doll up
61. Tree genus
62. Bounty man
64. Penalties
65. Spanish duke
68. About 61 cubic inches
71. Spotted
72. Shakespeare, very often
73. "...to a —— a bone..."
74. Custom
75. Alpine wind
76. City map areas
77. Lace trimming
78. Rages: Latin
79. Legal degrees: Abbr.
81. Sinus cavity
82. Mother of Xerxes
86. Polynesian
88. Mixed up
89. Make: Fr.
90. Marks
92. Sonnet part
93. Opening for pets
94. Mixtures
97. Botched a pool shot
99. Turkish title
101. ——
102. Departed
103. An early Tarzan
104. Shooting affair
106. Topic of discourse
107. Home, in old Rome
108. Ryun's distance
109. Former Asian kingdom
110. Wash
111. Type of pine
112. Fly or feather
113. Code word for a letter
114. Whitelaw ——, journalist
115. Bow: Prefix
116. Belgian river
118. Long Island harbor
119. Blackbird
120. —— Saud

55 Word Weaving by Jack Luzzatto

ACROSS

1. Let off
7. Short of
13. Italian foods
19. From office boy to boss
20. Expert teaser
22. Eastern Christian
23. Philosophic doctrines
24. Cupboard
25. Surveyor's helpers
26. Wander
27. Creator of Hans Castorp
29. Finery
31. Degrees
32. Old measure
33. Less taxing
35. Fastener
36. Eleonora
37. Condescend
39. Capek
41. Corrupts
43. Peaks
45. Wrap in waxed cloth
47. Tidy
48. Flew in a way
50. Purvey
51. Finishing touches
55. Settled up
56. Computer word
59. Girl's name
60. —— tenens (stand-in)
62. "Make thee —— of gopher wood"
63. Mother-of-pearl
64. Farewell: Lat.
66. Common effort
69. Box of a kind
70. Off center
72. With: Scot.
73. Column style
75. Associate of Phiz
76. Top men
79. Plane wing support
81. Of deserts
82. Girl's name
83. Opera heroes
84. Large birds
86. Vegetable
87. Given by word
88. Restore
92. U.S.

violinist
94. Axe mark
98. "Go Tell —— Rhody"
99. An Allen
101. Brings to mind
103. Arctic explorer
104. Man's name
105. Expressed contempt
107. Gone
108. Bean
109. Gossip, down South
111. "The —— Worker"
113. Lawless one
115. Patterns for tracing
116. Grudging
117. Interpolate
118. Gives pause

119. Deeds
120. Lost sheep

DOWN

1. Made points
2. Release, in a way
3. Wild sheep
4. 500 sheets
5. Poetic dusk
6. Tense state
7. Deceitful one
8. "Camelot" librettist
9. —— sahib
10. Repute
11. More crafty
12. Equivo-cation
13. Strict
14. Buffalo's cousin
15. A Caesar
16. Jewish month
17. Relaxed
18. Five ——
21. Plunder, old style
28. Questioned
30. Eye part
33. Wind
34. News sum-mary
36. Type of computer
38. Festivity
40. Makes dull
42. Roman poet
44. French claret
46. Queen: Sp.
48. More dignified
49. Iridescent
50. Pilot's concern
52. Islands in

Bay of Bengal
53. Stheno et al.
54. Pepper effect
55. Devastate
56. Finland, to the Finns
57. Musketeers and others
58. Image
61. Form of carbon
65. In one's ——
67. Follow
68. More fussy
71. Adjusts sails
74. Church laws
77. Perspicacity
78. Having a dull finish
80. Machete

83. Japanese verse form
85. Overstuff
87. Ability
88. Poured
89. Gibraltar to Lapland
90. Getting nowhere
91. Topic
93. Appraise
95. Not so fresh
96. Steichen's eye
97. Sincere
100. Audacity
102. High perch
105. Suffix with gang or mob
106. Platform
108. Asea
110. Exist
112. Small house
114. Political winners

56 Quotations by Hume R. Craft

ACROSS

1. Eight English kings
8. Scored at tennis
12. Dread
16. Culture mediums
20. More wary
21. Nostalgic theme of poets
23. Laugh
25. Shelley's lament for Keats
28. Haciendas
29. Not on ——
30. Mounts
31. Shaw subject
32. A kind of wind
33. Leases
36. Chemical compound
38. Hammock cords
41. Clean a pipe
45. Crossover
48. Practicality
52. Forerunner
54. "—— alive"
56. Voice
57. Silvery hair of song
59. Magot
60. Seed coat
61. Point in an orbit
63. Biblical king
66. Rent
67. Goes to court
70. Quixote, et al.
75. Gels
78. Warning signals
80. Hipsters
82. Patsy
83. Kentucky school
84. Certain growths
86. Censured
88. Sounding made by radar
89. Medley
90. French painter
91. Bode
92. Suiting
93. Large basket
95. Lee's men
96. Indian reed
97. It —— laugh
99. Finger lake
102. Staple
103. Bristle
105. Exported
110. Military headwear
112. Famous players
113. Oedipus and others
116. Certain craving
119. Attempts
120. Legendary ivory statue
122. Lover of beauty
125. Lucifer
127. Ring men, familiarly
131. Rodent
132. Spin: Scot.
134. Command
138. Beginning golfer
139. —— as a fiddle
141. Tennyson title
146. Leads
147. Lords it over
148. Sentimental talk
149. East: Sp.
150. N.C. college
151. Or ——
152. Sioux

DOWN

1. Call forth
2. Hindu festival
3. Burns's words for a beastie
4. Field
5. Rough waters
6. Crossword clue: Abbr.
7. Broadway sign
8. Whaling man and others
9. Electronic device
10. Ham actors
11. TV room
12. Verb for Tinkerbell
13. Comfort
14. Pine
15. Double-checked mss.
16. Prepositions
17. Insects
18. Campion title
19. Coal deposit
22. Italian food
24. Sullivan and Begley
26. Beta or gamma
27. Theory
33. Kind of peeve
34. Tennis star
35. Squatters
37. Verb ending
39. Eastern weight
40. Tax bureau: Abbr.
42. Damage
43. Digit
44. Hagen
46. Droop
47. Poet's word
49. "—— giddy as..."
50. Small drink
51. W. W. II area
53. Civil War initials
54. Users of cellars
55. Small spaces
58. Pronoun
62. Organizes (with up)
64. Zoro-astrians
65. Spy
67. Small seal
68. —— corda (soft pedal)
69. Bar
71. Field: Lat.
72. Slangy negative
73. Road surface
74. Petiole
76. Perform again
77. Cowboy gear
79. Drags: Colloq.
80. Quarter
81. Shortly
85. Pier union: Abbr.
86. Actor Calhoun
87. Unruly group
90. Lacus Asphaltites
94. Bartender's rocks
95. Engrossed
98. Vibrate: Abbr.
100. Musical instrument
101. Horse talk
102. Baseball name
103. Quick-witted
104. Price ——
106. Climax
107. Lupino
108. Clay: Prefix
109. Biblical song: Abbr.
111. Appian Way
112. Hollywood area
114. Soaking, and no kidding
115. Adherent: Suffix
117. Ne'er-do-well
118. Wartime agency
121. Made of wood
123. Cutting: Fr.
124. Scotsman's aims
126. Word after hand or horse
128. Chars
129. Camera glass: Var.
130. Bird
132. Army man: Abbr.
133. "Winnie —— Pu"
135. Organic compound
136. Earth's envelope: Abbr.
137. Climb
139. Middle East port
140. Triple or homer
142. Noun suffix
143. Before dee
144. "—— a deal!"
145. Time period

57 Guess Who by Betty Leary

ACROSS

1. Renounce
7. Actress Elsie
12. Egyptian goddess
16. Beak
19. Smallest ones
20. Turn outward
21. Easily done
23. Biblical name
24. Presiders
25. Toy
27. Folios: Abbr.
28. Fuel
29. Shell
30. Place
31. Purposeful
33. Appendage
34. To the ——
36. Constructed: Abbr.
37. Nonsense!
38. Pearl Buck heroine
39. Second-rate
41. Elm fruit
43. "Come —— faithful"
44. Halo
45. Style of fiction
48. Iowa town
50. Tasted, in a way
52. Any of the Furies
53. Hair style
55. Constellation
56. Desk item
57. Pedestal parts
59. Poison tree
61. Cooked
63. Bower
65. Waterfall: Scot.
66. Packaged, in a way
68. Like Prospero and Miranda
69. Adjective suffix
70. Old Dutch measures
72. Long-legged birds
74. Pawns
75. Huckster
78. Business abbreviation
79. Cut
83. Glossy lacquer
84. People of rank
87. Algerian city
88. Suffix with block and brig
89. Bounce
90. Archeology finds
91. Pronoun
93. Fenced areas: Abbr.
95. Race horse
96. Vehicle
97. Sounds from the gallery
99. Turkish weights
100. Haven
101. Frenchman's roof
103. Basket material
106. Texas city
108. Garment
110. Cornbread
112. Couple
113. Informal wear
115. Canadian physician and others
116. Busybody
120. Math abbreviation
121. French adjective
123. Orchestra section: Abbr.
124. Walls in
125. Etruscan title
126. Occupied
127. Rome, to Caesar
129. Signify
130. Can. province
131. 1002
132. All
135. Opening in a game
137. Half boot
138. Staves off
139. Slow learner
140. Eliminate
141. Sign, informally
142. Shaggy dog
143. Advantage
144. Stopped over

DOWN

1. One of the Furies
2. Lament
3. Advice from Mother Goose
4. Recipient
5. Road map entry
6. Letter
7. Flat
8. Sailor's call
9. Connecting part
10. Annoy
11. Refinery worker
12. Arid wastes
13. Acid prefix
14. Lhasa's site
15. Workers' group: Abbr.
16. Part of an adage
17. Maneuvered
18. Pear
21. U.S. agency
22. Laud
26. Public officer
29. Pronoun
32. Fitzgerald
34. Splendor
35. Round
36. Bull form of Ra
40. Congo animal
41. Warning devices
42. Consequence
43. College title: Abbr.
45. Laborer
46. Campus area
47. Good times
49. Woeful
50. Biblical wife
51. German philosopher (1855-1941)
54. Disgusting
56. Not clerical
58. Price cut: Abbr.
60. 100 centavos
62. Turpentine resins
64. Harmony
66. Chits
67. Der ——
68. Eastern college
71. In ——
73. British subway
74. —— around
76. Swiss river
77. Fort in Kentucky
80. Pros
81. Just sits
82. Good queen
85. Steak garnish
86. Goldbricks
89. Palmetto State native
90. English spa
92. To be: Lat.
94. Hale's Philip ——
95. Golf term
96. Spanish uncle
97. Sits in judgment
98. First name in Dogpatch
102. Football's Simpson et al.
104. Girl of song
105. Shaggy dogs
107. Legendary king and others
109. Times of day
111. Words for a poor dresser
114. Notions in Paris
116. Trembled
117. Container
118. Indian in America
119. Boxed
121. Make oneself heard
122. In good time
124. Goal
126. Kaffir warriors
128. Abbreviation in rental ads
129. Teenage hairdo
130. Abbess
133. Certain verbs: Abbr.
134. Project
135. Weight units: Abbr.
136. Of age: Lat.

In the Old Sod   by A.J. Santora

ACROSS

1. Town near Salerno
6. In cipher
11. Years
15. Kneehole
19. Nikolai
20. Knowing
21. Extinguish
22. Matrimony
23. "—— look at it"
24. 1835 novel
26. ——prinz (Ger. title)
27. Feel pity
28. Zigzag
29. Knowing
31. Nobel physicist, 1925
33. —— majesty
34. Children's writer
36. Halberd and battle-ax
39. Cables
41. I hate: Lat.
42. Spells
44. Parhelion
45. Flamboyance
49. Journey
50. Belgian town
51. Urey, for one
53. Streaked, as wood
54. That is: Lat.
56. Iconoclast's opposite
58. Go-go dancer of myth
60. Reagan, for short
61. Item
63. With
64. Belgian shoe
66. Foxy
67. Dairy case item
70. Japanese apricot
73. ——-brac
74. Poetic start
75. Prepositions
76. Easily shifted: Abbr.
79. Jitters
81. Pears' cousins
84. Crown
86. Federal group: Abbr.
87. Sets in an order
89. Warsaw for one: Abbr.
91. Kosygin's no
92. Like some satellites
94. Home: Abbr.
95. Big leagues
97. Month: Abbr.
98. Northern
100. Autocratic
101. Freely, in music
103. End of the loaf
105. Rule: Fr.
107. Record player
108. Nun of an order
112. Color
114. Arabian Nights' total
115. Light overcoat
117. Shore
118. Composition
119. Good taste
120. —— water
121. —— curiae
122. Verse man
123. Injection, familiarly
124. Prows
125. Followings

DOWN

1. Raines
2. Nut tree
3. Ready to putt
4. Some poems
5. Like: Suffix
6. Rome's "censor"
7. Man ——
8. Beclouds
9. Clears a tape
10. Blood rels
11. Together, in music
12. Bay of song
13. Envoy's home: Abbr.
14. Burst
15. Medic of films
16. Reconciliations
17. Blarney ——
18. U.S. artist
25. Type of watch spring
28. Bosses
30. Shoot
32. Part of Mao's name
35. Cobras
37. Extras, in music
38. Honey drink
40. Disentangled
42. To-do
43. Church listing
44. White clovers
46. To an extreme
47. Restore
48. Whirlpool
51. Hint
52. Dies ——
55. Ballet movement
57. Church service book
59. —— of strength
62. Cultivated
65. —— ahead (lead)
68. Cliff
69. Auditors
70. E Pluribus ——
71. Arizona sight
72. Prickly
76. Medical center
77. A rabbit
78. Atlas lines: Abbr.
80. Ghoul-like
82. John's problem, off and on
83. Newspaper pioneer
85. Rapidly
88. Settle down
90. Rory —— Irish rebel
93. Spiny lily
95. "To —— truth"
96. Corroded
99. Appears suddenly
100. Obliging
101. —— punch
102. Lake, in Ireland
104. "To —— human"
106. Put into law
107. Biblical land: Var.
109. Bismarck
110. Speck
111. Soaks
113. Pronoun
116. Myrna
117. Prosecutors

59 Fit to be Dyed by Mary Murdoch

ACROSS

1. Meld
6. Variety bit
9. Black Sea arm
13. Signature of a playwright
19. Indian timber tree
20. Shout
21. Appoint
22. Record
23. Outer layer
25. Sea birds
28. Missile
29. —— de vie
31. Chemical prefix
32. Coin-tossing routine
33. Asparagus sprengeri
37. —— of dishes
38. Writings: Abbr.
39. Fare
40. Recent: Pref.
41. Adjective suffix
43. Corrupt
48. Brief biography
49. Méditer-ranée, for one
50. Coins
52. Girl's name
53. Cuts of meat
55. Witticism
56. Goodbyes in Roma
58. Droop
59. Time period
60. Mme. ——
63. Rats
65. Suffix for top or typ
66. Wine
67. Jane Fonda film
69. Mischie-vous: Sp.
70. Poet Walter et al.
72. Lozenge
73. Terry
75. Channel
76. Hairlike structure
77. Mountain passes
81. Observing
83. Landing vessels
84. Pales
86. Euryale, for instance
89. Italian man's name
91. Cassini
92. Mellow
93. Regards too highly
95. Theater tests
97. Springs
98. Cockney dwelling
99. Stew
101. Wife
102. Literary works
103. Carried on
105. Golf great
106. Ballet step
107. Sally ——
108. Trumpet call
110. Under war-ranty: Abbr.
111. Civic: Abbr.
112. Mass of ice
113. Sawlike: Prefix
116. Ohio city
118. English primrose
122. I.O.U. holders
127. Chemistry degree
128. Bear: Sp.
129. Moon valley
130. Smollett's spendthrift
133. Go back in
135. Indian
136. Exude
137. Be troubled
138. Sovereign's stand-in
139. Chair parts
140. Prong
141. Aves.
142. Horse sound

DOWN

1. Sayings
2. Holds forth
3. Air-tower gear
4. Drink flavoring
5. Goddess of healing
6. Debate
7. Sedan
8. Globe, for instance
9. Gun girl
10. Ibex
11. Melville novel
12. Kind of marble
13. Inhabited by gremlins
14. Salts
15. Comedian Laurel
16. Arizona tribe
17. Aleutian island
18. —— Indies
19. "Go —— Rover!"
24. Judith Anderson role
26. Ape
27. Docs
30. Fore's partner
34. Wagons-——
35. Concerning
36. Kind of instrument
42. So ——
44. Sporting place
45. Flavoring
46. Missile places
47. "... could —— lean"
48. Common
49. Obligations
50. Unfeelingly
51. French coin
53. French school
54. Florida city
55. Dumas ——
57. Kind of wax
59. Spanish hero et al.
60. Carl Van
61. Renounced
62. Sooner
64. Asserts
66. Films
68. Certain discs
71. City official
74. Household gods
76. Litigant: Abbr.
78. Melodies
79. A Yokum
80. Scottish tools
82. Demantoid
84. Takes a trip
85. Business abbrevi-ations
86. Burgess's boors
87. Immature seed
88. Varnish ingredient
90. Flower
94. Thine: Fr.
96. Some Arabians
97. Bills: Slang
100. Pilgrimage to Mecca
102. Simple's partner
104. Elation
106. Australian birds
107. Operetta composer
109. Headings: Fr.
111. Twice DCL
112. Certain noblemen: Abbr.
113. Fur worker
114. Give in
115. Passive
117. French pronoun
119. —— to eat
120. Carols
121. A Beatle
122. Accoun-tants: Abbr.
123. Corded fabric
124. Of an age
125. Ten: Prefix
126. Kind of truck, for short
131. Fasten
132. Sat down
134. Pause fillers

ACROSS

1. Sufficient
6. Fabric
10. Uriah's family
15. Carpenter's tool
21. Sacred text of Islam
22. Prepare
23. Available
24. Ham actor
25. Dance
28. III, in France
29. Director
30. "L' ——, c'est moi"
31. Disparages
33. Cheers
36. Tranquility, for one
38. Seven: Prefix
41. High peak
42. Direction: Abbr.
43. Tumult
46. Marienbad and others
47. Miss Street and others
49. By: Sp.
50. Attraction
52. A science: Abbr.
56. Swift's forte
57. Assuming airs
60. Garden workers
61. Go over with a dry mop
63. Born
64. Pensacola, for one: Abbr.
65. Eye parts
66. Kind of novel: Abbr.
67. Jumble
72. Boxing champ of the '20s
73. Crew chiefs, for short
75. Be in the red
76. Rialto sign
77. Hitchcock movie
80. Hard wood
81. In opposition
85. Ralph
88. Two or more eras
89. Tools for cutting holes
91. Word of disgust
93. Fleming
94. Certain beans: Var.
96. Entice
97. Mischief

101. A kind of stick
102. Quemoy's neighbor
104. Crag
105. Muslim saint
106. Maltreats
109. Nautical term
110. Deceit
115. Mythical darkness
117. Set of three
118. Stadium call
119. Royal initials
120. Actress Judge
121. Hesitates
122. Informal greeting
126. Ger., Neth., etc.
127. Sweet potato
131. —— saying goes
132. Ivy Leaguer
133. Serpents
134. Part of the South
136. "... —— a man with ..."
139. Carbon compound
141. —— Fideles
142. Jumbled
149. School task
150. Like a lot informally
151. Tabriz's land
152. Cleanse
153. Heedful, old style
154. King of Judea
155. Pulls
156. Pass

DOWN

1. Egyptian spirit
2. Farm sound
3. Golf tour member
4. Strips
5. Noun suffix
6. Black widow
7. St. Pierre, for one
8. Shoe part
9. Sea speed unit
10. More piquant
11. Ref. book
12. An anesthetic: Abbr.
13. —— call on
14. German count
15. Erasure
16. Visions
17. Pivotal
18. Condition
19. Mosquito genus
20. Take by force
26. Serves a purpose
27. Part of the island state
32. Makes return
33. Roulette plays
34. Lend ——
35. Every which way
37. Xanadu's river
39. Map
40. Printing error, for short
43. Wildly
44. —— -hoo
45. Attract
46. Bristles
48. Put the ——

(shut)
51. Metallic sound
52. Desire strongly
53. Willies
54. Period of history
55. Writings: Abbr.
58. Letter
59. Slangy answers
60. Confusedly
62. Biblical pronouns
68. Have
69. Army unit: Abbr.
70. Ganymede, for one
71. Female rabbit
72. Muffin
73. Plant study: Abbr.
74. Crew member
77. Uncle ——
78. Tibetan animal
79. Cricket sides

82. Person
83. Sea eagle
84. Korean soldier
86. Yutang
87. "Mighty —— a rose ..."
90. Korean port
92. Yarn measure
95. Black Bird
97. Derisive cries
98. Curved lines
99. Godly: It.
100. " —— and Mehitabel"
102. Rug
103. Fortas
104. "Arms and ——"
107. Fancywork
108. Dawn
111. Expressions of disgust
112. Chimney dirt
113. Bean of India
114. Pump
116. Sunday talks: Abbr.

118. Tolerant
121. Creator of Shangri-La
123. Passed, as time
124. Greek district
125. Fatty acids
127. City in Florida
128. Youngest son
129. Take —— (pause)
130. Moon crater
131. In reserve
133. Exhausted
135. Exclamation of surprise
137. Do a newsroom job
138. Learner
140. Monster
143. British oath
144. 12 dozen: Abbr.
145. Handle rudely
146. A Spanish queen
147. Medal: Abbr.
148. Again

61 Variety Package by Peter E. Price

ACROSS

1. Children's game
11. Priest's vestment
14. "Pease porridge —— ..."
20. Circum-spect monkey
21. Aces
23. Washrooms of a sort: Var.
24. Anybody's guess
25. Dutch pottery
26. Shelley's elegy for Keats
28. Wire: Abbr.
29. Mustard, laughing, etc.
30. Tartu's river
31. High: Music
33. Word for bad liquor
35. —— bad example
37. Henry and Jane
39. "Mona Lisa," et al.
41. Capital of Spain under Moors
46. Certain starlets
48. —— and ahed
49. Mobile home
50. Song of French Revolution
51. Make a move
54. Red Sea land
56. Wroclaw's river
57. Champion filly, 1957-8
58. Calliope et al.
59. Indian tourist attraction
61. Pro ——
62. Repair
63. —— Douglas, novelist
65. Rebel
66. —— stand-still
67. Chaney
68. Scared out ——
70. Kind of poet
72. Chinese river
74. Teutonic god
75. Tried
77. Famed New York boss
79. Smallest state capital
82. Before Sept.
83. Western group: Abbr.
84. Alias the Cowardly Lion
86. Lap robe
87. Railroad network: Abbr.
88. Gullet
91. Society founded in 1776
94. Ness and others
96. Honey-combs: Lat.
97. Type size
98. Cafe
99. It —— much to ask
100. W.H. —— poet
101. Where the wise old owl sat
103. Clock sounds
105. Pension plan of the '30s
107. Prudent: It.
108. Tomb of the ——
111. N.Y. lake
112. Invitation P.S.
114. Korean city
115. Brave talk
116. Evergreen
117. Put-ons
121. Pronoun
123. Testing devices
125. Hebrew measures
127. Musical based on "Shrew"
130. Child's behavior at times
132. Yore
133. Alms: Lat.
134. Opera by Verdi
135. Music to torero's ears
136. Radio transmitter

DOWN

1. Daddy long-legs genus
2. Egg, in Paris
3. City in S. Calif.
4. Shifted: Abbr.
5. —— a time
6. Detroit name
7. Thighbones
8. Chekhov's first play
9. Formal award
10. The sign, to a Spaniard
11. Nootka Indian
12. Booty
13. Monday ail-ment
14. Somewhat: Suffix
15. Falls for a married woman
16. King of Siam's friend
17. Jet housings
18. Andaman people
19. Birthplace of Anacreon
22. Selective philosophy
23. Tom Collins
25. Fiscal problem
27. Unspecified quantity
32. Rival of Tulane
34. Closet bar
36. Jewish scriptures
38. Member of F.D.R. Cabinet
39. Medals
40. Neighbor of la.
42. Fashion name
43. Card game
44. French headgear
45. Famous mountain
47. French waters
52. Author of "The Care-takers"
53. Northern capital
55. Town in N.W. France
58. Big name in vases
59. Mock orange
60. God of the without the kick
62. Caress
64. At a loss, financially
67. New Guinea port
68. Missouri mountains
69. Isn't it, Shake-speare style
71. Thermo-meter abbreviation
72. Book by Sammy Davis
73. Russian composer
76. Reimburses
77. Venetian fishing boats
78. Woman, in Hawaii
80. Ptomaines found in meat
81. Adjective suffixes
85. Part of a box score
87. Scat!
88. Ogled
89. Persons exacting retribution
90. Casements
92. Injunctions
93. Aleutian isl.
95. Small beds
96. Brouhaha
99. Kind of triangle: Var.
100. Quinn and Newley
102. Scullers
104. Jewish delicacies
106. Suffix for polli
109. Onetime N.Y. greeter Grover ——
110. Voided
113. Dun-color-ed: Prefix
115. —— -les-Bains, France
117. Terrier
118. Yesterday: Fr.
119. Org.'s cousin
120. Russian river
122. Latin abbr.
124. Book by E.E. Cummings
126. Handwriting on the wall
128. Silkworm
129. Prior to
131. Slum area need: Abbr.

winds

Words to the Wise
by A.J. Santora

ACROSS

1. Assemble
5. Victor's due
9. Hebrew letter
13. Dennis of tennis
20. Indigo
21. Prefix with distant
22. Stevenson's retreat
23. Factor
24. Taro
25. Discovers
27. Limits
28. Benét play, with "The"
31. Lead a horse
32. —— Nagy of Hungary
33. Strange
34. Alert
35. Type of ink
37. Bizarre
39. Rebozo
44. Hosp. people
45. Goad
47. Parts of ski lifts
49. Ref. book
51. Square
52. Arthur of tennis
54. Silvery salmon
56. Flabella
58. Management's concern
60. Rent
62. With 79 Across, an old "Laugh In" phrase
64. Misuses the thermostat
66. Gems
69. Hong Kong or Asian
70. Direction
71. Split
72. West Indian music
74. Spelling ——
75. Farm tool inventor
76. —— disant
79. See 62 Across
85. Map abbreviation
86. Hunter of the sky
87. Oahu town
88. Spiteful ones: Colloq.
89. Payment
91. —— Anne
92. College at Cedar Rapids
94. Fat
95. Dredging bucket
98. Nuclear experiments
100. Predatory fish
101. Young hare
102. Nobleman
104. Urban problem
106. —— pinch of salt
110. Sobeit
111. Symington, familiarly
113. Brisk
115. Gulpers
117. Fleming
118. Pari —— (equally)
120. Writing fluid: Fr.
122. Approaches
124. Style of painting
126. Hilum
128. Yastrzemski
129. Comedians of a sort
131. Forgotten names are left to them, said Preston
137. Alpaca's cousin
138. Flattened: Sl.
139. Without: Fr.
141. Ring-shaped
142. Eared seal
143. Prefix with plasm
144. N. Z. pine
145. Roof style
146. Dogs, for short
147. "—— in the course of . . ."
148. Italian family

DOWN

1. West
2. Ups ——
3. Lateral air-flow
4. Czech neighbor
5. Mesta
6. Zoo's counterpart
7. Sally ——
8. Flubbed
9. Chili con ——
10. To me: Fr.
11. Model
12. Meat dish
13. Viewpoint
14. Excuse
15. Glasses
16. Struck
17. Head, in Paris
18. Unique person
19. P.M. times
22. Beetle gem
26. Confess
29. Adherents: Abbr.
30. "If I —— king"
31. Scarlett's estate
36. Rock ——
37. Speak
38. Initials on a skivvy
40. Despised
41. Song
42. Departed
43. Falls back
46. L.A. time
48. —— of fish
50. Procession
53. Glen ——, Ill.
55. Costello
57. "—— the rose"
59. Pronoun
61. Detect
63. Sharp
65. Panorama
66. Eye: Prefix
67. Dad
68. Got down
69. Crossword puzzle standby
73. Placates
74. Savarin
75. The double helix
76. Skated
77. Fashion first name
78. Paris suburb
80. Coin of Iran
81. Kitty of novel
82. Bide ——
83. California wine area
84. Order of frogs
89. Signs
90. Guard unit: Abbr.
91. European river: Fr. sp.
92. Football player: Abbr.
93. Willow
95. Applaud
96. Late golf pro
97. Sts.
99. Lively music
100. Take form
103. Continent: Abbr.
105. Eating pal
107. Graphs
108. Chickens out
109. Termites
112. Preposition
114. Flashy: Informal
116. Call for cattle
119. College in East Orange, N.J.
121. Drive-in girl
123. Fully renovated
125. Verse
127. Movie award
128. Shades of brown
130. Undealt cards
131. Panama Indian
132. —— of Cutch
133. Burden
134. —— a turn
135. Stroller
136. Engrave
137. Group of whales
140. Prosecute

63 Point of View by William Lutwiniak

ACROSS

1. Flavorful seed
6. Turkish V.I.P.
11. Potter's adjunct
15. Hymenopteron
19. Oil color vehicle
21. Hearing defect of sorts
22. Federal org.
23. Corn lily
24. Time of the week
26. They know everything
28. Musical passages
29. Give-and-take affairs
31. Teachers' org.
32. Stomach
35. Peerage members
36. Honshu volcano
37. Layers
41. Chemical endings
43. Family members
44. Boors
45. Like some tomatoes
47. Be social
49. Halloween costume
50. Irish darling
51. Pre- ——
52. Outdoor people
53. With 24 Across, a know-it-all
55. Entr' ——
56. Proxy
57. Malayan sirs
58. Barnyard sound
59. Different
60. Football play
61. Garment
62. Eased off
64. Scuba fishing gear
65. Depressing
66. Words from a "friend"
68. Mother of Achilles
69. European bison
71. Numerical prefix
72. Wood finisher
74. Accumulating
75. Certain
77. Motorist's need
80. Fine wool
81. Name in Broadway fame
83. Embellish
84. Dream: Fr.
85. Kind of verb: Abbr.
86. By hand: Prefix
87. Irish spade
88. French painter
89. Incursion
90. Bridge-table encores
93. Go back
94. G.I. address
95. Very: Music
96. Disseminates, as tales
97. Distinct
98. Desert rodent
100. Takes five
101. Ruler: Abbr.
102. Wise
103. Early ascetic
104. Contradict
105. Hussar's gear
107. Had charge
108. Object
109. Valentine figure
110. Salty one
112. It's always 20-20
116. Unerring appraisals
121. By word
122. Cover fully
123. Cutlery
124. Young eels
125. Terrier
126. Weakens
127. Longhorn
128. Servicewomen

DOWN

1. Sand: Prefix
2. Modern: Prefix
3. Auto system: Abbr.
4. Caesar et al.
5. Lift up
6. Reels: Scot.
7. Harding et al.
8. Six in Italy
9. Distributes
10. Moot
11. Ollie's friend
12. Oxford's river
13. Place for books: Abbr.
14. Soft muslin
15. Sorceror
16. Fireman's gear
17. Title
18. Family members
20. Ill-starred lover
21. Works hard
25. Corday's victim
27. Grand ——
30. German river
32. Accidents
33. Leeward island
34. Part-timers
36. Then: Fr.
38. Fighter of a kind
39. Lacks stability
40. Math aces
42. Disbursed
44. Crude shelter
45. Mark
46. Fasten
48. Scrap for Fido
49. Protects
50. Rose's love
53. Coverlet
54. Newspaper part, for short
55. Tete- ——
57. Leather strip
59. Certain sports tourneys
61. Office help
62. Engraving tool
63. —— were
64. Leveling wedges
66. "Of thee ——"
67. Other: Sp.
68. Cup: Fr.
70. Venerably traditional
72. Skedaddles
73. French exclamation
74. Ponchos
75. Fish bait
76. Unproductive ones
78. Mean
79. Orderly
80. Delusion
81. Social class
82. Knowledgeable
84. Ecstatic reviews
86. Girl's name
87. Condition
88. Cyclotron abbreviation
90. Art of disputation
91. Certain monuments
92. Not migratory
93. Income
95. Some skirts
97. Ferber novel
99. Parish official
100. Congressman: Abbr.
101. Carnelians
104. Tag ends
105. More reasoned
106. Fishing gear
109. Fellow
110. Action
111. Initials on a card
112. Exclamations
113. Nettle
114. Vote against
115. Area of India
117. French co.
118. Multitude
119. Misdo
120. Draft initials

64 Passing the Word by Cornelia Warriner

64

ACROSS

1. Hanger-on
5. Rascal
10. Metal beam
14. Hobo's vegetable
18. Tennis star
19. Light craft
20. Uncanny
21. Chicago name
22. TV fare of sorts
25. Noted jockey
26. Nautical chain
27. Yew
28. Roundup gear
29. Prepares to swim the Channel
30. Sea birds
31. French psychologist
32. Short
33. Baldwins
36. Dancer Pauline
37. Workmanship
41. Restrain
42. Computer workers
44. Form of Rachel
45. Lips
46. Silk, in Paris
47. River to the Seine
48. Sea-story writer
49. Elec. unit
50. Press items
54. Ship
55. Is worthwhile
57. Like a child's nose
58. Hair tints
59. Anon
60. Eye cell parts
61. Once, in a prescription
62. Slender probe
64. Emphatic words
65. Some news items
68. Shrew and others
69. Brinkley, Wallace et al.
71. Spinner
72. Solar deity
73. Prefix for an antiseptic
74. Former diva
75. Places: Lat.
76. Three-way joint
77. Without words
81. Sea off Australia
82. "—— its martyrs"
84. And —— grow on
85. Scuffle
86. Rabbit
87. Ship parts
88. Positive
89. British party
92. Add
93. Both: Prefix
94. Old French coin
97. Rig out
98. Cramped quarters
101. Sausage
102. Roman road
103. Fiber for rugs
104. Baseball team
105. Soil
106. Disorder
107. Heat, as milk
108. Stepped

DOWN

1. Tense
2. Catch sight of
3. Loafer
4. Lacrosse team
5. Mocks
6. Concerns
7. Handle: Fr.
8. Family member
9. Shedding
10. Mosaic piece
11. Animal
12. Jason's ship
13. Ham on ——
14. Biblical words
15. Criticizes: Colloq.
16. Muslim tongue
17. Ocean, to poets
21. Egyptian god
23. Infection for short
24. Sounder
29. Way out: Fr.
30. Trees
31. One kind of fan
32. A garnish
33. Catch ——
34. Some TV time
35. Publicity agent of yore
36. Name for Santa
37. Concord
38. U.N. workers
39. Indian title
40. Leap and light
42. T.V.A. output
43. A.M.'s to poets
46. Divide
48. Entertained
50. Memos
51. Notched: Bot.
52. Roman wars, 264-146 B.C.
53. Burdens: Lat.
54. Delineates
56. Certain bucket
58. Brings up
60. Punctuation mark
61. Location
62. Marine ray
63. Fire ——
64. River nymphs of Greek myth
65. Mouth: Prefix
66. Kind of train
67. Heavy stake
69. Not up ——
70. Roasting rods
73. The men —— life
75. Mislay
77. Intrude suddenly
78. Wavers
79. Golfing words
80. Old capital of Egypt
81. Item for a whatnot
83. Orchestra man
85. Took a bath
87. Shoe parts
88. —— a rat
89. Obscene
90. Water: Prefix
91. Famous duelist
92. Mal de ——
93. Theater org.
94. Recipe word
95. Words of disbelief
96. Kind of car
98. Dickens boy
99. Vibrate: Abbr.
100. Can. province

65 Stepquote
by Eugene T. Maleska

ACROSS

1. Start of an eleven-word quote descending in stairstep fashion to 143 Across
7. Misfit of W.W. II
14. Lorraine's partner
20. White's "—— from the Fortieth Floor"
21. Interstices
22. Peter made three
24. Encore for boxers
25. Argentine seaport
26. Stepquote source
27. Words of confidence
28. What debeo means
30. Indian weight
31. Tam-tam
32. Prefix for gram or logue
33. Boone
34. Type of bigot
36. False
38. Two cups
39. Sheep
41. Stepquote part
44. Style name
45. Flood and spring
46. Flee
48. Vaughan et al.
50. TV cabinets
52. Barkley
54. Write a music score
56. Paris subway
57. Lone
61. Heel over
63. Terminal
66. Cap- ——
67. Funny fellows
69. Isle of the oracle
71. Cognition
73. Tennis terms
74. Theater section
75. Scattering
77. Moist
78. Nobel product
79. Goes out on a limb
81. Indiana Indians
82. No longer new
84. Emergency care
85. Where Zeno taught
87. Hoover Dam's lake
88. Calm
90. Not for all the —— China
91. Staggers
92. Ye —— tea shoppe
93. Estimate
95. See 57 Across
97. Summoned back
99. For —— sake!
101. Mend the oxfords
103. Ruined city in Iran
104. Fish spears
107. Logomachy
109. Be frugal
113. The mating game
114. Layer
116. Stepquote part
118. Levant or Hammerstein
119. Zola's "Le ——" (1888)
120. Military lodging
122. With the result
124. —— pro nobis
125. St. Pierre
126. Buffoon
127. Yemeni
130. Sediment
131. Struck
132. Citizens of Valletta
134. Bohemian composer
136. Flaccid
138. Stepquote author
139. Baby hare
140. Expanded
141. "Thanatopsis" poet
142. Cuban province
143. End of Stepquote

DOWN

1. Novel by R.P. Warren (1959)
2. Sanguineous
3. Author Hunter
4. Mass. campus
5. Spore clusters of rust fungi
6. Stepquote part
7. Willy Loman, for one
8. Coach Parseghian
9. Gov't. branch
10. Concert rendition
11. Babylonian deity
12. —— mouse game
13. Large parrot
14. Recessed
15. Sierra ——
16. Close-fitting
17. Publicize
18. Voltaire hero
19. Malbin, Stritch, etc.
20. Camera support
23. Jalousie
29. Comes in first
31. Make neat
34. Convened again
35. Old card games
37. Twitch
38. Guided
40. Blues
42. Judo exercises
43. Stepquote part
45. Body part
47. Brilliant gray
49. See 38 Down
51. Goad
53. A —— (presumptive)
55. Sniggler
57. Break of continuity
58. Bounding main
59. Scatters trash
60. Dieter's dish
62. Not at all
64. "Not so deep ——..."
65. Citrus drink
68. Makes taut
70. Carrie or Kenny
72. Dug
75. Type of glass
76. Uganda group: Var.
80. Elevator's neighbor
83. Scorn
84. Olivia's clown
86. Spore sac
87. Teeth
89. Obligations
91. Passes on
94. Opinion
96. Tennis strokes
98. Neckcloth
100. Fence stairs
102. Bleach
104. "Behold —— of God ..."
105. Convivial one
106. Salt: Fr.
108. This, in Spain
110. "—— bury Caesar..."
111. Seaman
112. Babbled
113. Malfeasant's act
115. Fruit-juice gadget
117. Stepquote part
120. Wisent
121. "Three Coins" fountain
123. Savory jelly
126. Pueblo site
128. Fit to ——
129. Bossy's home
131. Skiddoo
133. Essay
134. Road sign
135. Trampoline
137. Bantu language

66 Miscellany
by Jack Luzzatto

ACROSS

1. Spotting systems
7. Certain storage places
14. Pause in verse: Var.
20. Vinegary
21. Drowsing
22. Legal claimant
23. Bee's goal
24. Swimmer
25. Way out
26. Verse
27. Tries the bait
29. Tin Pan Alley girl
31. Used up
32. Initial score
34. Especially gifted one
36. Temple, old style
37. Small town
38. Paint tester
39. Fattened steer
40. Martinique volcano
42. Causerie
43. Sacred mountain in Szechwan
45. Merchant to an army
47. Desert hazard
49. Cicero topic
53. Pushes on
54. Closes the gap
55. Rope-ladder rungs
57. Shopping centers
58. Savory
59. Sets a tempo
60. Hymenopter
61. People for
62. Clairvoyance
64. Chaser for tequila
65. Large lizard
66. Less
67. Silas Marner's golden girl
68. Worthwhile quality
69. Regions
71. Of an Eastern people
72. Capital of Albania: Var.
73. Artificial
74. Harness ring
76. Turned into
77. Name for a field dog
79. Awry
80. Sublease
81. Vilify
84. Get along well
86. —— noire
87. Sum, ——, fui
91. Newsprint plants
93. John 1:1-14 as part of a mass
95. Shooting match: Fr.
96. Tropical sunhat
97. Small-horse drivers
98. Clear
99. Draw forth
101. Iatric
103. Bring into accord
105. Opening word
106. Cut off
107. Patcher
108. Wobble
109. Braced for shock
110. Virulent ones

DOWN

1. Decamped
2. Sin of sloth
3. Decree in Scotland
4. Lawyer: Abbr.
5. Laughing
6. Jots down
7. Caliber
8. Kind of computer
9. Ranked
10. Dolorous word
11. Achieve
12. Abrasives
13. Try
14. Do housework
15. Teatime at sea
16. Discourse: Abbr.
17. Discomfort
18. Seaport on the Don
19. Leblanc thief Lupin
28. Not so gay
30. Classic roué
33. Singing groups
34. Gains altitude
35. Swiss miss
38. Grilling
41. Right-angle extensions
42. Linked set
44. Religious music
45. More chic
46. Hullabaloos
47. Lukewarmness
48. Lamentable
50. Word switch
51. Real
52. Fourth ——
53. Ascribe
54. Most precise
56. Athletic aftermath
58. In stitches
59. Songbird
62. Usurp
63. Binge
64. Ventilates
66. Image of eternity
68. Cheese fanciers
70. Small civet
71. Impels
72. Signal one's punches
75. Most betimes
76. Davis
78. Jackpot starter
80. Rebounded
81. Best, as a pupil
82. Receiver of goods
83. Rebel
85. A thanedom for Macbeth
86. District in Yugoslavia
88. Neat
89. Fisherman
90. Churchmen
92. Measurer
93. Union unit
94. Port of old Rome
97. Heap
100. Small boat
102. Female hare
104. Oriental New Year

67 Literal World by Anthony Morse

ACROSS

1. Anaconda's relative
6. Prankster
11. Spectral type in the sky
16. City near Bombay
21. Type of architecture
22. Yellowish-red color
23. High spot
24. Ration
25. Relatives in Haarlem
27. Poilus march off
29. Stub ——
30. Carol
31. Candy
33. Father of Ajax
34. Row
35. African antelopes
36. Lancelot's uncle
37. Satellites
41. Modern name for Lutetia
42. Without pity
43. Exclamation
47. Doctrinal rejection
48. Rascals in Havana
50. Court decree
51. Fads
52. Venetian feature
53. Bad
54. Buck
55. Matured
56. Suffix for some acids
57. Aquatic mammal
61. Relative of 1 Across
62. Star
63. A locale in "My Fair Lady"
65. Whole
66. Rests upon
68. "...the end is not ——"
69. Weapon for a soldado
73. World area
74. Ancient road
76. Man: Latin
77. Specially-shaped clock
78. Scottish resort
80. Compos mentis
82. Young man got mad
88. Drink
91. Invention
93. Dutch cupboard
94. Auriculate
95. Choler
96. —— Roy
97. Establishes
100. Heel over
101. Anti, out west
102. —— la Cité
104. Period
105. "To —— human"
106. Celestial fluid
107. Entreat
108. Bahians off the beam
111. Pin used in ceramics
112. Former Chief Justice
113. Prune
114. Certain paintings
115. Supports
116. Carriage
117. Doesn't exist
118. Old Brazilian money
119. Navy men
123. More depressed
124. English poet
125. Nautical word
129. Cockneys take a close look
131. Gossips in Lampang
134. Shepherd in "As You Like It"
135. Tarzan's rope
136. Talk-show host
137. Thin mortar
138. Filch: Slang
139. Joined
140. Ancient tomb
141. Islamic spirit

DOWN

1. Opera girl
2. Set-to
3. Preposition
4. Trio of rhyme
5. Berliner's alas
6. Craft
7. Result of high-pressure living
8. A kind of road
9. Japanese apricot
10. Rural poem
11. Disreputable
12. Feudal people
13. Card
14. River to the Rhone
15. College officials
16. Cloys
17. Tree genus
18. Spatial infinity
19. New: Prefix
20. Egyptian disk
26. Concord
28. Drove
32. Neat as ——
34. Heroine of 1891 novel
35. French smoker's need
36. Circus purchase
37. Full of sayings
38. Three miles
39. Squawk from Peron
40. Requirement
41. Penal
42. Tutoring
43. Charlemagne's domain: Abbr.
44. Dark periods in Riyadh
45. Lead-part players
46. Finally
48. Religious law
49. Norse goddess
50. Mime
52. Early associate of Caesar
57. Ale server
58. Arabs
59. Common contraction
60. Bristly
63. Enzyme suffix
64. Wrench
65. 1952 Pulitzer play with "The"
67. Shoe material: Abbr.
70. Bro's opposite
71. O.K.
72. Ace ——
75. Refreshment
79. River bottom
80. Director's guide
81. Swiss pine
83. Cattle genus
84. Meantime
85. Headland
86. Eastern women
87. Bits
89. Baltimore man
90. Styles
92. Even
98. Ancient Syria
99. Siberian river
100. Vial
101. Feigns
103. Grammar case: Abbr.
105. Approves
106. Notes
108. Without restraint
109. Covered in a way
110. Moon figure
111. Evaporates
113. Spanish numeral
115. Early U.S. homes
116. Penalty, in France
117. Form of Helen
118. A Montague
119. Less than mins.
120. Omar word
121. Old Roman fields
122. Radar dot
123. Bill
124. Gait
125. Israeli port
126. Capital of Aisne
127. Case
128. Italian family
130. Godly: It.
132. Rascal
133. Embryonic fowl

68 Music Lesson
by John Owens

ACROSS

1. Gil ——
5. Stunted tree
10. Doze
15. Some radio men
19. Hindu scale
20. Record player: Abbr.
21. Anathema
22. Thanks ——
23. Borodin hero
24. Beethoven Quartets Opus 59
26. Part of N.B.
27. Musical quality
29. A kind of ear
30. Quadrangle
32. Prohibits
33. Kind of pie
35. Reddish brown
36. Song: Ger.
39. Following
41. Decoration on metal
45. Imitating
46. Disease germ
47. Breach
49. Dehydrated
50. Reward, old style
51. Spanish cleric
52. Noted columnist
54. Flying prefix
55. Plead
56. Passageway
57. "Turn of the Screw" composer
59. —— jour
60. Evil Jewish spirit
62. Do a grammar chore
63. Amen
65. Uneven
66. Pentateuch
67. Passengers
68. Monks
70. Indian soldier
71. Choral works
74. —— Alamos
75. Danish composer (1865-1931)
77. —— organ
78. Irving character
79. French opera section
81. Soot marks
82. Lowland: Scot.
83. Sheath
84. Perfume
86. Paleolithic, for one
87. French painter
88. Greenland base
89. U.S. composer
91. Composer of symphonic poems
93. Rang a bell
94. Lawyers: Abbr.
96. Tidal flood
97. Connery
98. Italian opera, with "La"
102. Large bird
103. One kind of partner
107. —— soit . . .
108. Baroque forms of composition
111. College course: Abbr.
112. Greek letters
113. U.S. emblem
114. Stale
115. Bristle
116. System: Abbr.
117. Taters
118. Misplayed
119. Waste allowance

DOWN

1. Small herring
2. Como
3. Greek contest
4. Spanish dance
5. Schumann's first symphony
6. Talks
7. Optimistic
8. One: It.
9. Small shop
10. Wall bracket
11. Former Broadway play
12. Formerly, old style
13. Glacial ridge
14. TV place
15. Carmen specialty
16. Shake ——
17. Prefix for gram or lith
18. British gun
25. Without
28. Eng. or Lat.
31. Police activity
33. Lehar's widow
34. Title of six Bach suites
36. Viola da ——
37. Swords
38. Composer of "Ozark Set"
39. Teams
40. Experience
42. Liszt opus
43. Vive ——
44. Tooth: Prefix
46. Worth
48. Kitty
51. South African composer
52. Finery
53. Heavily: Music
56. Ornament
57. Nobleman
58. Direction
61. —— pro nobis
62. Gregory et al.
64. Miss Lillie
66. Having left a will
67. Opera
68. Gordon of the comics
69. Composer of the "Dyb-buk"
70. Legatos
71. Centers
72. Passageway
73. Tempo
76. Uncle: Dialect
77. Pastor's home
80. Throw into ecstasy
82. Old French dance
83. Violin part
85. S.A. monkey
87. Myopic cartoon Mister
88. —— she blows!
90. Conditions
92. Egyptian king
93. Stopped
95. Subway fixture
97. Outpouring
98. Pronoun
99. Routine
100. Med. course
101. Pointed: Fr.
103. Recipe word
104. Cooler
105. Half or quarter, for instance
106. Pest
109. King Cole
110. Timetable abbreviation

69 Space Madness — by Eileen Bush

ACROSS

1. Early astronaut program
7. Particular: Abbr.
11. Truman's birthplace
16. Universe: Prefix
21. One of a meteor swarm
22. Cinema, in Europe
23. —— in arms
24. Hollywood name
25. Suffers attrition
26. Name of a planet's transit, perhaps
28. Chic
29. Forty ——
30. Rejects
31. Old and New
33. Kind of sign
34. Silly
35. Paw: Fr.
37. Like a julep
38. "The groves were God's first ——"
40. Spells
41. Numerical prefix
42. —— Magnon
44. Light ——
45. Drilled
46. Look of sorts
47. Chinese name
50. Round figure
52. Shore birds
53. Fighter planes
55. Conductor's word
56. River to the Colorado
57. Inform
58. Soviet moon rocket
59. Warm glow
60. Docking
63. Early dulcimer
64. Band, in heraldry
65. Humid
66. Art works
67. Fan
68. Seep
69. Artist's wear
71. —— d'oeuvre
72. Oct. 31 wear
76. Juncture
77. Ruth's husband
78. U.S. satellite
82. Narcotic
83. Dive, astronaut style
86. Upper space
87. Stroke on a letter
88. Twofold
89. Pronoun
90. Rise
91. Pendants on watch chains
93. Water bird
95. Absent
96. Desire
97. Reddish color
98. Employes
99. Part of N.B.
100. "To —— With Love"
101. Descended
102. Face for 72 Across
103. Organ stop
105. Kiel or Suez
107. Legal plea
108. Shopping areas
109. Color
112. Computing machine
114. Substantial
116. Overeats
117. Illinois city
118. Lunar blues, so to speak
120. Catch one's ——
121. Alpine peak
122. Mountain chain
123. Attracted
124. Kind of bean soup
125. A Churchill
126. Seed coating
127. Indian weights
128. Direction on a ship

DOWN

1. Early astronaut
2. Uncanny
3. Like lunar living?
4. Oily hydrocarbon
5. Deny: Fr.
6. Libidos
7. Master of a vessel
8. G.I.-locker photos
9. Access
10. Bathos: Slang
11. Wash basin: Abbr.
12. Backed in a way
13. Certain art works
14. Malign
15. Balance
16. Humor for serious astronauts
17. Former Philippine President
18. Meager
19. Borgnine role
20. Scraps
27. Ad astra per ——
30. Chef's creation
32. Mohammedan noble
34. Moonship's forte
36. Implements
39. Perfume ingredient
40. Greek goddesses
41. U.S. problem
42. Poke fun at
43. 100 kopecks
45. Forward
46. Maid
47. Helden- ——
48. Fence passage
49. Glacial ridge
51. That: Ger.
52. Retrogress
53. Under: Fr.
54. Burlap fiber
56. Part of a chromosome
57. U.S. President
60. Level
61. Goes like a spaceship
62. London's Old ——
63. French preposition
65. Type of roof
67. Fictional detective
68. Sign on astronaut's door
69. Convince: Colloq.
70. Pasture sound
71. Intimidates
72. TV star Bill
73. —— citato
74. Tempter of Ulysses
75. Part of a comet
76. Hot Springs et al.
77. Biography word
78. Do art work
79. Moon eruption, perhaps
80. Frenchman's name
81. Fraternal group
83. Fat
84. Host
85. Music pieces
86. Colorado park
88. Do housework
90. Top- ——
92. Old pen
93. Half: Ger.
94. Navy man
95. Form of Helen
98. Snood
99. U.S. painter
101. Seaport of Italy
102. Inundates
103. One who sponges
104. Aid to success
105. Type of lily
106. Church area
107. In harmony
108. Watered silk
110. Type of nonsense
111. Pale
112. Hacks
113. Common Latin verb
115. Tote board listings
116. Mardi ——
119. Bible book: Abbr.
120. Win —— mile

70 Birth of a Nation by Bert Beaman

ACROSS

1. Varnish ingredient
6. Basket fiber
11. U.S. author
16. Time and
21. —— Home
22. Godunov
23. Architecture style
24. —— Khali (Arabian desert)
25. "...be-comes —— dissolve..." (from 111 Across)
29. Certain Alaskans: Abbr.
30. Rely on
31. Town in Maine
32. —— Forge
33. —— light
35. Oilskin hat
37. Asian civet
39. Forward
40. Rips
42. Store
44. Rage
46. Stationery item: Abbr.
48. Shakespearean character
50. Chemical suffixes
52. Bovary
53. Kind of dirt
56. With 111 Across, a document
59. "...us beyond —— tried..."
61. Networks
62. Resting
63. Asian river
65. Items on pirate flags
66. W.W. II vessels
68. Action: Suffix
70. Range
73. Golfer's concerns
74. Fat: Prefix
76. Smorgasbord items
79. Fabric finish
80. Being: Lat.
81. "—— Governments are instituted ..."
87. Make over
88. Laugh: Fr.
89. Flying prefix
90. Shorthander
91. Soon
92. Experience
94. Speed
96. Czech composer
100. Removes stitches
102. Mild oath
105. Concert offering: Abbr.
107. "—— mind in..."
108. Boston ——
111. See 56 Across
114. Peer Gynt's mother
115. Word with drop or fall
116. French town
117. Rock shelf
118. Message: Abbr.
119. Spectral type
121. Actress Vivienne
123. Give —— (heed)
125. Men's party
129. Breaks
131. Showed gloom
133. "Life ——"
136. Hindu poet
138. Kind of ion: Suffix
140. "—— the West Wind"
142. River to the Rhine
143. "Our Lives, —— Honor"
147. Spaces
148. Alla —— in music
149. Remoulade
150. Reach
151. Layers
152. Beasts
153. —— Testament: Ger.
154. Gray

DOWN

1. Sticks
2. Portly
3. President's stratagem
4. —— Fideles
5. French article
6. Construction piece
7. Spore cluster
8. Carpenters' gauges
9. Erect
10. Inner: Prefix
11. Scent
12. Revere
13. Scenes of action
14. Counterstrokes
15. King conqueror
16. Harp: It.
17. Prepares peas
18. Poplar
19. Approach midnight
20. A signer of 56 Across
26. Spatial
27. Balkan state
28. Subdued
34. Attack
36. Came down
38. Certain
41. Stage direction
43. British cavalry force: Abbr.
45. Cover
46. Common French verb
47. Pacific islands: Abbr.
49. Union members
51. Close
53. Kosciuszko, for one
54. Most qualified
55. Words of assent
57. Phone sounds
58. Au revoir
60. Large fowl of West
64. Track event
67. One at a stadium mike
69. Antitoxins
71. Deform
72. Combine with: Suffix
75. Global area
77. Richard Henry ——
78. Rope part: Abbr.
81. Shock
82. Certain rinses
83. With one's back to: Fr.
84. Whale
85. Accumulate
86. Normans, for example
93. Psychiatrist's problems
95. Paid: Slang
97. Tracked down
98. Noun ending
99. Ship part
101. Admonish
103. Times of day: Abbr.
104. Quandary
106. —— cloth
109. Hayworth
110. Charms, in London
112. Kind of gage
113. Writer Marsh and others
120. Old capital of Brittany
122. Footless
124. Copies
125. Ermine in summer
126. Bull: Prefix
127. Coincide
128. Succeed
130. Symbol of leakiness
132. Look like the ——
134. Ridge
135. Influenced
137. Betsy
139. Employs
141. —— bien
144. Auto dealer's abbreviation
145. Shipper's group: Abbr.
146. Titled Turk

71 Up and Away by Cornelia Warriner

ACROSS

1. Le Mans entry
6. Tattle
10. Theda et al.
15. Down with: Fr.
19. Soap plant
20. Opera
21. Roman official
22. Bridge: Fr.
23. Subject of a Verne novel
26. Church booklet
27. Rule the ——
28. Permeate
29. Navy specialists
31. Like falling off a log
33. Article
35. Take again
38. "—— Not Alone"
39. Poetic form
40. Name for early moon-bound spider's home
43. —— weensy
44. Billiard stroke
46. Lisa and others
47. Brazilian Indians
49. Preference
51. Month
52. Confound!
56. "—— had a million"
57. Party man
58. Ingredient of a satellite
60. Former V.I.P. at U.N.
62. Unpolished
63. Gladden
64. Taker
67. Footwear
68. Plays
69. Dog-tired
70. Leisured
72. Song
74. Mariner's job
76. Sped
77. Shoshonean
80. Soft-drink quality
81. Lariat
82. Separated
84. English dramatist
85. —— worms
86. Pine substance
88. First baseball czar
92. Certain V.I.P.'s
95. Blaster's need
96. New York city
97. "—— twig is..."
98. Shrewd
99. Grasslands
100. Glass, in pharmacy
102. Saarinen
105. Did dishes
107. Increase, old style
108. Assignment for the Apollo 11 men
114. One in ambush
115. Missouri tributary
116. Black: It.
117. Asian sorghum: Var.
118. Porsena
119. Salamanders
120. Coffee grind
121. Successful

DOWN

1. Rule, in India
2. I love: Lat.
3. "... —— the stars"
4. Man's name
5. Western city
6. "... be a dog and ——"
7. Eng. course
8. Flurries
9. Lessen
10. Phone sound device
11. Navy man: Abbr.
12. —— de Oro
13. In space
14. Classman: Abbr.
15. Point in orbit
16. One of trio on first moon orbit
17. Companion of 16 Down
18. Obdurate
24. Baltic state: Abbr.
25. Assembles
30. Has an obligation
31. July 31, for example: Abbr.
32. Cotton from Bengal
34. Selfish one
36. Labor pioneer
37. Architects' patterns
40. Private eye
41. Relatives, familiarly
42. West
43. Soft mineral
45. —— fire
48. Russian hemp
50. Flanged beam
51. Set —— of interest
52. "Au Clair ——"
53. Paper measure
54. Movie dog
55. Pipe joints
58. Brant
59. Man of the hour
61. Whetstone
62. Australian shrub
64. Bligh: Abbr.
65. —— breve
66. Flight ——
67. Medical assay
68. Three: Ger.
70. English painter
71. Musical syllables
72. Brown colors
73. Words for a good splashdown
75. Very: Fr.
76. State: Abbr.
78. Put through a dry run
79. Scottish city, to poets
82. —— Paulo
83. Alternatives
84. Evergreen
85. Inch along
87. Certain times: Abbr.
88. Gemini spaceman
89. Girl's name
90. Infernal
91. Brave ones
93. College chores
94. Beginner
97. Divert
99. Fruit
101. Preposition
103. Covering
104. River to the Baltic
106. Prefix for a country
109. Shooter
110. Deputy: Abbr.
111. Silkworm
112. Gold: Sp.
113. Fuzz

72 Wherewithal
by H.L. Risteen

ACROSS

1. Slight
5. Harbor sight
9. Carthage foe
13. Some doorbells
19. Olympian
21. Editor of a kind
23. Burger ballad
24. Plea of the '30s
27. Trades
28. Nobleman
29. Old-time reporter's goal
30. Edge
31. An Astaire
32. Prizes
35. Assemblage
36. Prefix for fit or factor
37. Old English letter
39. Makes turbid
40. Indian V.I.P.
41. Reduced
42. Common abbreviations
45. Mine passages
47. Hitler predecessor
48. Mark
50. An apostle: Abbr.
51. Old ——
52. Solicitudes
53. Dumas hero
57. "Exodus" hero
58. Portuguese money
59. French city
60. Aaron
62. Parseghian
63. Most rigid
65. French keys
66. Artery
67. Young animal
68. Bristles
69. Paired
70. Onward
71. —— majesty
72. Inconsistent
77. Monterrey money
78. Ventilator
79. —— of thought
80. Confuse
82. Insect
83. Fishing equipment
84. Of an arm bone
85. Salutation in Soissons
87. Dessert
88. Zoo attractions
89. Undergrad clubs
90. Moved, at sea
91. Merkel
92. Infer
94. Santa ——
95. Cobbler supplies
96. Fetch
97. Obscure
99. Troubles
100. Report
101. Exclamation
102. Farm areas
105. Flirts
107. Cross out
108. Folding money
110. Water birds
111. Crosscut saw
112. Doctor's needlework
114. Palm genus
118. Unburden
119. Frisky
120. Persian sprite
121. Pastry item
123. Words prior to being parted
128. Shore bird
129. Freckle
130. Grieg girl
131. Oriental rugs
132. U.S. engineer
133. Coal layer
134. Promontory

DOWN

1. Strand
2. Annoys
3. Disregard
4. Beverage
5. Ocean: Abbr.
6. Leave —— huff
7. Groups of nine
8. Old English coins
9. Stem: Prefix
10. Siamese coins
11. Rigging
12. Person of great wisdom
13. Athenian foe of Sparta
14. Bestow, as praise
15. Neither Dem. nor Rep.
16. Drudge
17. Small animal
18. Oozed
19. Eastern church title
20. Rooted custom: Abbr.
22. Rock pinnacles
25. Army man: Abbr.
26. Urban sunbath areas
33. Eastern notables
34. Obligation
35. Throws
36. Vamp of silents
38. Summons
40. Roman goddess
41. Alaskan attire
42. French political units
43. Middlesex money
44. Mint worker
46. Dutch coin
47. Kennedy items
49. "We —— on like this"
51. Long —— (money)
52. Grow, as a vine
54. Earns, informally
55. Fabric
56. Marquis de ——
59. Fix a dress
60. Does a vaudeville turn
61. European river
64. Healthy: Sp.
65. Lawyers' staple
66. Tree
69. Gets stuck
70. Coins of India
71. Headwear: Slang
73. Noisy canine
74. Message
75. Western range
76. Byways
77. Cashier's stamp
81. Muse
83. Molten outpourings
84. Soviet range
85. Heavy knife
86. Public
89. Business gamble: Colloq.
90. Big hit
93. Roman period
94. Tropical plant
95. Pacific sea
98. Islamic text
100. Suite
101. Well-known Greek
102. Heavenly being
103. Toy
104. —— pools
106. Nondieter's friend
107. Farm animals
109. Holy Land man
111. Chicago team
112. Numerical prefix
113. Period
115. Kicks
116. Indonesian isle
117. Russian river
119. Russian whip
120. Sibilant signals
122. Asian land
124. Cells
125. State: Abbr.
126. High note
127. Vegetable

ACROSS

1. Glacial epoch
7. Quality
12. Setting for "Kate"
17. Well-excavated city of Egypt
18. —— mark
20. —— phrase
22. Paris subways
23. Experts in looking back
25. Belonging to: Suffix
26. Formerly, old style
27. Comes in last
28. Then, in France
29. Furnace man: Abbr.
30. Roistering
33. Theater area
34. Rain in Paris
35. "—— bug in . . .
37. Up
39. Amundsen and others
40. Shrewish ones
42. Shoe width: Abbr.
43. Eject
44. Mexican coins
45. Materials for a dig
51. French revolutionary family
53. Caravansary
54. Sullivan and others
55. —— machine
56. Gums: Prefix
57. Alpine tunnel
59. Endure: Scot.
60. Stratagem
61. Marionette maker
63. Man's name
64. Denials
65. Dwellings of a kind
66. Building beam
67. Potpourri
68. Really?
71. Grasp
72. Part of N.B.
73. Settled down
74. Stared
75. Overage
77. Moraine
80. Mountain in Greece
81. Le Gallienne and others
82. Boater
83. Clog in a way
85. Lorna and family
88. Watched the late show
90. "Beneath the —— frown he stands..."
93. Fragrant root
94. —— de deux
95. A geological age, for short
97. Famous Giant
99. 500 sheets
100. Confused skirmish
102. Golf positions
103. Earth
105. Locale for Schliemann
108. Ancient Cretan
109. Antelope of India
110. Dessert
111. Settle
112. Blinds, as a hawk
113. Rigid
114. Imminent

DOWN

1. Betels
2. Dark rocks
3. King in "Iliad"
4. —— cadabra
5. Certain scientists
6. Feminine suffix
7. Sculptured form
8. Clergyman
9. Residue
10. Sloping type: Abbr.
11. Locale of a Marx movie
12. Directions for readers: Abbr.
13. Before Sept.
14. Excavate in a special way
15. Destroy the spirit
16. Former Belgian queen
18. Clan identity
19. Rose-red dye
21. Blockheads
24. Tennis term
26. Mitigates
31. Aegean sight: Abbr.
32. Trash item
34. Elegant: Slang
36. Eye part
38. H.H. Munro
39. Charlotte ——
41. Word form for cave
43. Most peculiar
44. Proportionately
46. Ore deposit
47. Sea nymph
48. Germs
49. Gladdens
50. Slips
51. Pondering
52. —— of love
53. Elf
58. Marine fishes
59. Russ. river
62. Idol
64. Hitler
67. Spanish jars
68. Compute
69. Improved
70. Archaeologist's work
74. Fall guy
76. Rio's beach
78. Times of day
79. End slowly
80. Lily plants
84. —— be (in case)
85. Mark Van ——
86. Appetite, in psychology
87. Divine revelation
88. Of a Frankish people
89. Son of Poseidon
91. Impassable
92. Layers
94. Cosset
96. Saltpeter
98. Former Chief Justice
100. But, in Paris
101. Word in Mass. motto
104. Ref. work
106. Lace
107. Post: Abbr.
108. English teachers' group: Abbr.

74 Riddles by Frances Hansen

ACROSS

1. Moved like a snail
6. Remove a cartridge primer
11. Wets down
16. "My Lord, —— Morning!"
21. Actress's helper
22. African antelope
23. —— of the finger
24. Took to court
25. Greek market
26. Enlarge
27. N.Z. native
28. Allow as how
29. Down-in-the-dumps lama?
31. Whirlybird hitchhiker?
34. Informal greetings
35. Thos. and others
36. Malaysian sir
37. Uneasy
38. —— date
40. Small plant leaf
42. Fatty
46. Unadorned convent headgear?
50. Constellation
53. Strong ——
54. Chemical suffix
55. Italian poet: 1754-1828
56. —— Mater
58. Persian fairy
59. Aim
61. Wee one
63. Becomes winterbound
64. Footless animals
65. Cousin of a sari
66. Constant
67. Long distance, figuratively
68. Bit ——
69. Nimble
72. "Young Man of Caracas" author
74. José's aunt
76. Individual
77. Jaunty bird?
81. Tasteless

84. Corrida cry
85. Musical notes
86. Almond drink
88. City near Boys Town
89. Cup: Fr.
91. Hobo song words
93. First name in whodunits
95. Asian nurse
99. Organ parts
100. Bulk
101. Hugh Capet, for one
102. A Borgia
104. Type of billy
105. Makes fast a rope
106. Endured
108. Like Abner
109. New York Indian
111. Compass point
112. Excusable servant?
116. Certain beds
118. Dorm buddy
120. —— Mare
121. Makes tea
124. Chassé
125. —— Darya
126. Likely: Abbr.
130. Breakfast fish exporter
134. Brooding Indian
136. Jewish months
137. Lugger
138. Loup ——
141. Fragrant oil
142. Vocal style: Abbr.
143. Musical work
144. Confederate general
145. Fingerprint feature
146. Baltic people
147. She just growed
148. Hit a high fly ball
149. Roles

side dish?

DOWN

1. Coarse fabric
2. Scoundrel
3. Hard wood
4. Brightens
5. Mine car
6. Petula Clark hit
7. Norse boys' names
8. El ——
9. Honest one
10. Hairnet's companion
11. Vic
12. Don't be ——!
13. Between l and r
14. Polynesian skirt
15. Flowering shrub
16. Unidentified one
17. Cheerful dad?
18. Take ——
19. Adjust
20. Mime
30. Bone: Greek
32. In the pink
33. Attacked
36. Kind of dance
39. Faucets and pipes: Abbr.
40. Zola
41. Spud grader
43. Small change in 25 Across
44. Piano mute: Sp.
45. Lived
46. Muslim title of respect
47. Don Juan's mother
48. Plateau
49. "Be —— so humble..."
51. See 2 Down
52. Red powder of India
56. Shoe, in Italy
57. Whensoever
60. Oil country: Var.
62. Chicken purchaser
63. —— man answers
64. Embarrass
66. Hard to pin down
70. Revolves
71. Native: Suffix
73. Mild rural expletives
75. Lupino
77. Saucepan ammunition?
78. Herb genus
79. Does a cobbler's job
80. Live teddy bears
82. Nymphette of fiction
83. Shoe widths
87. Scotch uncle
90. Cracked spar
92. Beauty spot
94. O'Grady
96. Bamako's country
97. "Questa o quella," for one
98. State of misery
102. Arise
103. Noble: Ger.
105. More plain
107. Ancient cast
110. Loathes
112. Yea or nay
113. Comes forth
114. Tuck's partner
115. Dry-cleaner
117. Sonnet part
119. Fish hawk
122. Snap
123. Watch the late show
125. Soap plant
127. Machine part
128. Modern paintings
129. Rolls a log
130. Poet Shapiro
131. French notion
132. Agreement
133. Jaywalkers: Abbr.
135. Bawl
139. Bird of prey, Cockney style
140. Ferdinand V

75 Capital Ideas by Kirk Dodd

ACROSS

1. Hails
8. Cavies
13. Coin of Mid-East
20. Address loudly
21. People of Teheran
22. Plunge into a fluid
23. City in Granada
24. N.A. geological era
26. Grampus
27. Early Brazos settler
29. Moslem saint
30. Nobel physicist: 1952
32. Set a course
33. Heads
34. Middling
35. Hibernia
36. Styptic
37. Sheepfolds
38. Fountain orders
39. Children's game
41. City in West Germany
42. Satchel
43. Mean sea-level line
44. Interweave
45. Summon
46. Oddments
48. Beverages
49. One-time caller at Trinidad
53. Pea and nut
54. Erie, for one
55. Cracow people
56. Number
57. Strikes
58. Pebbles
60. Burma, Pakistan, etc.
61. Indian
62. Lemur
63. Aegean island
64. Perfume
65. Archipelago of Pacific
67. Grass genus
68. Ones at the helm
69. Elder: Fr.
70. Opted
71. American family of painters
72. Thin layer
75. Teen-agers' monopoly
76. Bewailed
79. Poplar
80. Opinions
81. Restrain
82. —— clock scholar
83. Soviet press agency
84. See eye ——
85. Productive
86. Hauls
87. High note
88. English essayist (1861-1922)
91. Agency of the 30s: Abbr.
92. Sec. of State under Wilson
94. Idle
96. Enliven: Lat.
97. Jog
98. Drain
99. Result of a salary cut
100. Rapiers
101. Encourages

DOWN

1. —— as a judge
2. Chaplin
3. Fruit
4. Inoperative
5. Cache
6. U.S. sculptor
7. Like some churches
8. Biblical treasure city
9. Court decree: Fr.
10. French city
11. Nova Scotia's —— Royal
12. Located
13. Liquid measures: Fr.
14. Kaffir fighters
15. Word of concurrence
16. Indian weight
17. Locale in Marine song
18. Peacocks
19. Emblem of 15th century
25. "Drang nach ——"
28. Rel. of sing.
31. Barley and rye
34. Oregon city
36. Vis- ——
37. Dances
38. Sorcerer
40. "——, sorry"
41. Of a space
42. Dells
44. Inclinations
45. Presidential family
46. Second-stringer
47. Tropical raccoon
48. Dyeing technique
49. Beverage
50. Dog
51. Eastern Christian
52. Torrefies
54. Siren of "Odyssey"
55. Ceremony: Fr.
58. Novel heroine
59. Poker move
60. Mollusk genus
62. Singer Frankie
64. Leeds's river
66. Postal system
67. Does an after-sports routine
68. Quince, for example
70. Indian
71. Girl's name
72. Pitchout, in football
73. Ear shell
74. Ore range
75. Famous sculpture
76. Guipure
77. Understanding
78. Prescription units
80. Kind of ball
81. Low parts of ships
84. Czech range
85. Meander
86. Western attire
88. Garment
89. Lie at anchor
90. Leaves
93. Type measures
95. Winter topic of talk

76 Colorful Airs · by Anne Fox

ACROSS

1. Skirt
7. Indian weight
11. Greatest
15. Man with a sword
16. Arithmetic device
19. Nonentity
21. Well-known Cockney
23. Bird
24. Canals on U.S. border
25. Mean abode
26. Track
27. Evergreen
28. Helper: Abbr.
30. Forbearance
32. Place for a barbecue
34. Home buyer's concern: Abbr.
35. Luster
37. Give the go-by
39. Meaning
41. Buddhist temple
42. Plumber's concern
45. "—— corny as..."
47. Role in "Barber of Seville"
49. On the loose
52. Planet
54. Word in a Hardy title
56. Greek letter
57. "...we all do fade as ——"
59. Disturb
61. Embankments
63. Recent: Prefix
64. Kingfish
65. Fastened
67. One of the Three Stooges
68. Groups: Abbr.
70. Town on the Hudson
73. Secular
74. Girl's name
76. Swelling disease of fish
77. Early age
79. English river
80. Postulate
82. Slack part of a sail
83. Minor
84. Noun suffix
85. Writ against a debtor
87. Nickname for Miss Ederle
89. Fabrics
91. One who makes up
93. State: Abbr.
94. Hostess's request
95. Container
97. Flint: Prefix
99. Swedish chemist
101. Gladden
105. Word element for a country
107. Silent star
109. Plants of a region
112. Caledonian
113. Charge
115. Scratchers
117. Dunne
119. Chem. prefix
120. Bridge moves
121. Broadway play of 1953
124. Flowers
125. Design
126. Bull-like
127. Tree toad
128. Modern concern
129. People of a world area

DOWN

1. Winter footwear
2. Indolent
3. Bolivia's La ——
4. Esau's wife
5. Biblical locale
6. Treasure ——
7. Ballerina Maria
8. Sash
9. Plaster backing
10. Misbehave
11. Star in Cetus
12. A kind of den
13. Gear for hams
14. Russian cart
15. Flat-topped hills
17. Bones
18. Dog
19. Vast
20. Lease again
22. Poetic words
29. Tissue: Anat.
31. Arizona city
33. Privy to
36. Chemical liquid
38. Village in New York
40. Vain: Ger.
43. Shining
44. Wailed
46. Thick-set
48. Of snow
49. City in Illinois
50. French saint
51. Area of Queens, N.Y.
53. Scout activity
55. Strangest
58. Dye workers
60. Slow, in music
62. Chinese mediums of exchange
65. Abdomen: Prefix
66. River of Ukraine
69. Weather word
71. Ex-film star Jack
72. Taunts
75. Ancient Greek city
78. Unworldly
81. Tim's quality
83. Feature
86. End: Pref.
88. Unhearing
90. Army men: Abbr.
92. Boxing jabs
95. Headpiece
96. Not on credit
98. Sound like an old door
100. Japanese seaweed
102. Colorless liquid
103. Subway items
104. Storehouse
106. European thrush
108. Signed in a way
110. Lariat
111. Indian coins
114. Fluids
116. Bristle: Prefix
118. Small case
122. Richthofen, for one
123. Relative of Mme.

ACROSS

1. Sailors' drink
5. Monkey
10. Half of a magic formula
15. Wheedle
21. San ——
22. Oriental rug
23. Man of Meshed
24. Cut out
25. Hindu god
26. Music by Cole Porter
29. Moves furtively
31. Apiece
32. Levee
33. Up ——
34. Pacific org.
35. Bone
38. Meet
39. Piano piece
41. Card game
43. Sew up
45. Mogul
49. Music by Gershwin
54. Dance
55. Irish exclamation: Var.
56. "Conning Tower" man
57. British marshal of W.W.I.
58. Gelid
59. Barrier of physics
60. Keepsake
62. Apocrypha books: Abbr.
63. Half of a musical
64. Capers
65. Somewhat
66. Capuchins
68. Theater ticket bargains
70. Cliff dwelling
71. Clash
72. S.A. weapon
74. Runabout
75. Fur
76. Song of 1862
80. Defense group
84. Baleful
86. Old pottery pail
87. Clumsy fellow
88. U.S.A. rank
89. Nonsense!
92. Recanted, in a way
95. Gypsy: Fr.
96. Art form
97. Exclamation of disgust
99. Fall guy
100. Musical of 1933
101. Tête-à-tête
102. Musical syllable
103. White House tenant
104. Gas: Prefix
105. Family members: Abbr.
106. Dub
107. Lyrics by Mitchell Parish
111. Zinc
113. Sea birds
114. Punk
115. A Chaplin
116. Zip
117. Lowlander
119. Mediterranean ship
123. War ——
126. Cartoonist Addams
128. Gumbo
129. State of India
130. Part of "Annie Laurie"
136. An age
137. —— middle course
138. Golden
139. Manifest
140. Dare, old style
141. Residue
142. American poetess
143. Spanish port
144. Letters

DOWN

1. Shade of green
2. Rule: Fr.
3. Vincit —— veritas
4. Part of an academy song
5. Bulges
6. Kirghiz city
7. Guevara
8. Round Table knight
9. Giraffe's cousin
10. Wharf
11. Sphere
12. —— Forks (B.C. battle)
13. Dark
14. Material
15. Navy initials
16. Wild sheep
17. Music by Hoagy Carmichael
18. —— about
19. Unaspirated
20. Arctic island
27. Return partner's suit
28. Tenfold
30. Eyelid darkener
35. Allegro, for one
36. Pelvic bones
37. Containers: Abbr.
38. Dance
40. Kind of ball
42. Strapping
44. Town wear of song
45. Edging
46. Mood
47. Agalloch
48. Turns left
49. Witches
50. One of the Du Ponts
51. Italian condiment
52. Thai language
53. Offer
59. Talent
61. Scotch refusal
62. Poetic times
63. Holm
64. Fairbanks
66. Fortify
67. Pronoun
69. W.W. II initials
71. Guys
73. Under way
76. Ency. ——
77. Uh-huh
78. Swat
79. Principle
81. Incense holder of old Rome
82. Drum
83. An enzyme
85. Wild goat
88. Game shot
89. Position tracker
90. Group of Islamic savants
91. Iroquoian
93. Old Rhodes sight
94. Japanese ware
95. Not with it
96. Slam
98. Chin
100. Actress Ada
102. Wallop
103. Salon item, for short
104. Vapor: Prefix
107. Languid
108. Ease
109. Duty
110. Cunning
112. Old fogy
116. Prize
118. For this: Lat.
120. Cheap merchandise
121. Worn at the edges
122. Coins
123. Go by
124. Flower: Prefix
125. Item sometimes big
127. Piece of metal
128. Mickey and family
129. Capital of Moselle
131. Cape
132. German dessert
133. Girl's name
134. Florid
135. Son of Gad

78 Working People

by Thomas W. Schier

ACROSS

1. Smooth off
7. Lugosi
11. Marlowe, for one
15. Living quarters: Abbr.
19. Minnesota Fats, for one
20. Michigan's waterfront
21. Pack animal
22. Kind of hog
23. Offer a legal excuse
24. Heath genus
25. Faust
27. Memorable play of 1946
30. Brand of figs
31. Attach firmly
32. Staff officers
33. Sets ——
37. Neck wrap
38. Glacial ridges
40. Luminous circles
43. Mediocre
44. Campus building
45. Kind of jacket
48. Door-to-door lads
51. Overly bland
55. Hip bones
56. Word of mouth
57. Bristle
58. Elevation: Abbr.
59. Doing: Suffix
61. Collaborator
63. Slope, in fortification
67. Merry-andrew
69. Exclamation
70. Teachers' org.
71. African javelin
72. From —— Z
73. Makes a scene
75. Foggy
77. Danish coin
78. Bell sound
81. Well-known Russian
85. Ripened
86. Prefix with corn or form
87. Illinois first name
88. Hercules's captive and others
89. Jack in

91. "—— du Printemps"
93. Navy man: Abbr.
96. Peas or beans: Abbr.
97. Musical composition
101. African fetish
102. Glad, to poets
103. Swedish town
104. Stake
105. Pronoun
106. Item in a bibliothèque
108. Cordelia's father
110. Onlooker
113. Cooper man
117. Find by chance
118. Raceway event
119. City in West
120. Candy
122. Lawyers: Abbr.
126. Wheel part
127. Petitions
129. Town of Asia Minor (Latin sp.)
131. This, in old Rome
132. Metal piece
134. John Gay opus
139. Hothouse workers
143. Negative contraction
144. Type of decoration
145. In —— shell
146. Bell town
147. Yes ——
148. ——-camp
149. Fabric
150. Sounds for attention
151. Kind of tube
152. Coin user of a sort

DOWN

1. Cards in a low straight
2. Garden features
3. Grayish-green
4. Mine: Fr.
5. Eastern ketch
6. Nine: Prefix
7. Stove part
8. Discoverer of Vinland
9. Part of a train, for short
10. P.I. sumac
11. —— pencil
12. Fragment
13. Offend
14. Extremely
15. Military acronym
16. Hairdo
17. Quivering motions
18. Rivulet
20. Leave port
21. English spa
26. Calm area
28. Unit of metric length
29. Word for annual winds
34. Flanders Field symbol
35. Sailing
36. Newsman
39. Helpers of Drs.
41. Excluding both
42. Piercing tool
44. Sweet: It.
46. Pismire
47. Chauffeurs of a sort
49. Fence part
50. Domineering
51. —— Mahal
52. Be obligated
53. Cricket sides
54. Spring wild flower
60. Impossible
62. Gambler's mecca
64. Excited
65. Like Ben Jonson
66. Variegated
68. Child's game
71. Month: Abbr.
73. Electronics initials
74. Member of a Burmese people
76. Western group: Abbr.
78. Sofian: Abbr.
79. Unique person
80. Unless: Lat.
82. Cheer
83. Copter, at times
84. "—— Three Lives"
85. Man's nickname
87. Pungent
90. Surpass
92. Metal point
94. Sourpuss
95. 4,840 square yards
98. Jutting rock
99. Clumsy boat
100. Noun suffix
102. Household plants
104. Item for a leaky boat
107. Steam
109. Consort of Shamash
111. Sheathed
112. Spanish queen
113. Champion of the people
114. Batter's quest
115. Palliates
116. Forest group
118. Threefold
121. French historian
123. "... —— a way"
124. Harangue
125. Alpine figure
127. Soul: Fr.
128. Surprised exclamation
130. —— as a pig
133. Concerning
135. Rope fiber
136. Wyandot's cousin
137. Miscellany
138. Siliques
140. Beat the ——
141. Prison areas: Abbr.
142. Interweave

79 Taking a Position
by Threba Johnson

ACROSS

1. Hero of Greek legend
5. Shakespearean shepherdess
10. Himalayan animal
17. Alaskan city
18. Order: Fr.
20. Madison Ave. thinkers
21. Author O'Connor
22. Goodman book
25. Making a thrust
27. Cassia plants
28. Wrong: Prefix
29. —— cantorum
30. Like: Suffix
31. Welsh name
33. Racetrack pests
37. Negrito
38. Theologian of 16th cent.
41. Alike: Fr.
43. Old weapon
44. Choices: Abbr.
46. Conditions
47. Gounod's "—— et Baucis"
50. Army medal
51. Means of transportation
54. French season
55. Skilled interpreter
57. Marquis de ——
58. Initials on an airline board
59. Backed a cause
61. S.A. catfish
62. Kind of eclipse
64. 1949 treaty
66. Word of respect in India
68. Feminine suffix
69. Epitaph for a movie palace
74. Preposition
75. Divinity degree
76. Majority
77. Do a grammar chore
78. Mexican Indian
80. Hinder legally
82. Sit-down result
84. Vestments
86. On the —— a wave
88. Letter
89. Slight
91. U.S. dept.
92. Devices for catching fish
95. Pique
96. Homeless tot
98. Rat- ——
100. Nautical term
101. "No" voter
104. Road: Abbr.
105. —— the land
107. Testing places
109. Long time
110. Sell: Fr.
112. Young seal
114. Rattle on a harness
116. Subscription affair
117. On Cloud 9
122. Part of to have: Fr.
123. Without means of rowing
124. One-up word
125. Bow man
126. Circuses
127. Momentum
128. Places of refuge

DOWN

1. Ones called for service
2. Leonard Woolf book
3. Mexican friend
4. Of old age
5. Steal, in Scotland
6. 1949 peace Nobelist
7. Toast
8. Cinched
9. Have —— ear
10. Sleeper
11. Dutch cheese
12. Ledger entry
13. Singers
14. Large bird
15. Gas: Prefix
16. 3 mins. of boxing: Abbr.
19. Nine: Prefix
21. Maxwell and others
23. Called to order
24. Treatment
26. Village of East Bengal
30. Caucasus native
32. Some social climbers
34. Rostin book
35. With a will
36. One who quits
39. Miller play
40. Part of a Goldsmith title
42. Smoked salmon
45. Diligent
48. Adjective suffix
49. Composer Rorem
52. Medical prefix
53. Borge
56. Obeys a street sign
60. Compass reading
63. Sternward
65. A king of Egypt
67. "—— body meet..."
69. Madeira port
70. Inimical planet
71. Pinafore
72. French town
73. Soviet range
79. Lawyer: Abbr.
81. Darkness
83. Par ——
85. Sports areas
87. Danish money
90. Pass a rope through
93. Fruit
94. Make oneself heard
97. Senses
99. Formal wear
102. Regulate
103. Tebaldi
106. Code, in Spanish law
108. Are: Fr.
111. To no extent
113. Kind of school
115. N.M. colony
116. Marsh grass
117. Central area
118. Zoology suffix
119. Biblical prince
120. Football scores: Abbr.
121. Article

No Extra Charge
by W.E. Jones

ACROSS

1. Character in "Faerie Queene"
7. Lombardy lake
11. Iceland epic
15. Concentrates
20. Layer
21. States
23. Money's off-shoot
24. Yoga posture
25. Acrobatic bookkeeping
27. Wall St. prefix
29. Calendar abbr.
30. Sell —— of goods
31. The's, e.g.
33. During
34. Head areas
36. The —— of Tempe
37. Spire ornament
39. Direction
40. Pulitzer author, 1958
41. Advisory groups
45. Finished the laundry
47. Relatives
50. Of melody
51. Graduation guests
53. Hogarth men
54. Buck
57. That is: Lat.
58. Defeats at bridge
59. Moon goddess
60. 40,000- —— (big ship)
62. Genus of bees
66. —— bonne heure
67. Mailed
68. Makes a stab at
69. Belief
70. Slow as ——
74. Grants
75. Shed copiously
76. Inspire
78. Of heat
80. Costa Rica export
81. Takes a new tenant
82. Tunneled
83. Formality
85. Cooking byproducts
86. Panama port
87. Roman jug
88. Dock: Abbr.
91. —— everything
92. Flair
93. ". . . —— trash"
96. Relative of zool.
97. Special drink
99. Symbol of wealth
101. Cavity: Anat.
102. Stars, for Cicero
104. Port where Greeks sailed for Troy
105. Most feeble
106. Of the wrist
107. Poured
111. Town in Hungary
112. Wine vessel
113. His: Fr.
115. Chinese dynasty
116. Student's emblem
120. Wash: Lat.
122. Mozart opus
125. Contradict
126. City in Korea
127. Modern Aladdin's lamp
129. Has it made
132. Publicized
133. Batting backstop
134. Water wheel
135. Long time for poets
136. Eastern civet
137. Stettin's river
138. Tiresias was one
139. Large basket

DOWN

1. Illinois city
2. Polo
3. Leaves undone
4. Inlet
5. Blows up
6. Cats
7. Puts and ——
8. Athletic field
9. "Testimony of Two ——"
10. Killer whale
11. Chancel
12. Shore bird
13. A type of net
14. Lane: Fr.
15. Golf goal
16. Mountain in Thessaly
17. Garb
18. Jets, e.g.
19. Worked on floors
22. Sycophantic
26. Wing: Fr.
28. Ambitious one
32. Color
35. Extra jurors
38. Angers
41. —— about
42. Presently
43. Bundle
44. Quills
46. Toronto man
47. —— Major
48. A season
49. Provide a treat of sorts
50. Jousts
52. Drinks
54. That makes
55. Mink's relative
56. Eric, for one
59. Landed estates
61. Relative
63. Smart to a point
64. Concept
65. Fixes a lawn
67. Flaps violently
69. Boat
71. Go too far
72. Elève's school
73. Wraparound
74. Cape
75. Grand Central feature
76. Cupid
77. Mother of Castor
79. Slowly: Music
80. Pretty one, in Rome
82. Fled
84. Passages
86. —— Grande
89. Cowpoke's mount
90. Level
92. Most improbable
93. Rabbit's tail
94. Lacquered ware
95. Writer Bagnold
96. Machetes
98. Waves: Sp.
100. Comedian of silent films
101. Tiny Tim's voice
102. Biblical city of Palestine
103. Name in golf Hall of Fame
105. Extolled
106. Spur: Biol.
108. Develop
109. Live coal
110. Noun suffix
111. Friend
114. Dry: It.
116. Romero
117. Landing places
118. Goddess of peace
119. Saltpeter
121. Horace's metier
123. South African assembly
124. Son of Seth
125. Biscay, to the French
128. Chemical suffix
130. Before
131. —— publica

81 Looking Sharp   by A.J. Santora

ACROSS

1. Señor's talk
6. Throwback
13. The —— luxury
18. Bargains
19. Suite
20. Type of ether
21. Broadway name
23. Collier
24. In trouble
25. Bit of reading
27. Compass point
28. Great miler
29. Impudence
31. Slithery
32. Mineo and namesakes
33. Credibility
34. Stitch for samplers
38. Plains Indian
40. Senior member
41. Part of R.B.I.
42. Bedrock
43. Quenched
45. Kind of rug
47. Heraldic fur
48. Fearful
49. Recoil
50. Neapolitan, for one
54. Pitch pipe
55. Glances of a kind
57. Holiday time
58. Floodlights
59. Mexican mullet
60. Fit to ——
61. Entrance
62. "—— Got Rhythm"
63. Led the attack
67. Threadlike
68. Tints over
70. Paid up
71. Winner of olés
72. Siouan
73. Grand and others
75. Dissenting view
76. Book section
78. Carry: Lat.
79. Bridge seats
80. Hang fire
82. 1926 Pulitzer novel
84. Cheer
87. Cupid
88. Philippine tree
90. Suffix for gang or trick
91. Irritate: Colloq.
92. Word connector
93. Library worker
96. "—— tennis?"
99. Foolish
101. Overhead liability
103. Ground quartz
104. Reprimand
105. Commiserates
106. Delicious
107. Certifies
108. Word on a French map

DOWN

1. Out at the elbows
2. The Veep
3. Ironside of TV
4. Table extender
5. Pitched in
6. Custody
7. Ball holder
8. "Take —— from me"
9. Passport entry
10. Approximately
11. Boulevard of note
12. Decoration
13. Court marker
14. Mon ——
15. Support for edgy people
16. Pull (tease)
17. Anticipate
18. Chekhov Uncle
21. Small town
22. Instruct
26. —— joint
30. Released: Colloq.
32. Affirm
34. Stud or draw
35. Seen
36. Weight
37. Circle or sanctum
39. Guinness et al.
40. Defies
43. Road turn
44. Army men
45. Severity
46. Disturbed the peace
47. Dog, for short
48. Step
49. River of a blues song
51. Campus girl
52. Zoo adjunct
53. Paris version of IRT
55. Active one
56. Takes aboard
59. Elks
61. Buenos ——
63. U.S. painter and illustrator
64. Inimical one
65. Don's January
66. Stocks selling —— (bear market)
67. Onward
69. Mink's cousin
71. Tryout
74. Pertaining to uprising
75. Figure in O'Neill play
76. Rubinstein
77. Cleaning aid
79. Correct
81. Dit's companion
82. Way off beam
83. Groups of aides
84. M-16's
85. Pale green
86. Possessive
89. Jai-alai gear
91. Brief novel
93. Relative of sultry
94. Gardner
95. Relatives of TV's: Abbr.
97. Skip
98. —— chance
100. Profit
102. Poetic word

82 Rhymes from Way Out by Edward J. O'Brie

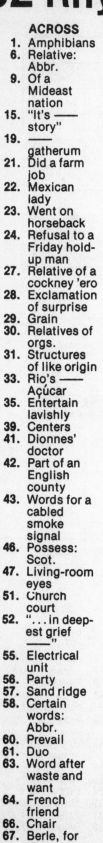

ACROSS

1. Amphibians
6. Relative: Abbr.
9. Of a Mideast nation
15. "It's —— story"
19. —— gatherum
21. Did a farm job
22. Mexican lady
23. Went on horseback
24. Refusal to a Friday hold-up man
27. Relative of a cockney 'ero
28. Exclamation of surprise
29. Grain
30. Relatives of orgs.
31. Structures of like origin
33. Rio's —— Açúcar
35. Entertain lavishly
39. Centers
41. Dionnes' doctor
42. Part of an English county
43. Words for a cabled smoke signal
46. Possess: Scot.
47. Living-room eyes
51. Church court
52. "...in deepest grief ——"
55. Electrical unit
56. Party
57. Sand ridge
58. Certain words: Abbr.
60. Prevail
61. Duo
63. Word after waste and want
64. French friend
66. Chair
67. Berle, for short
68. Novel
70. Scot's denial
72. Life ins. man
74. Energy: Abbr.
75. Throat, in England
76. Clerical union's demand for a raise
82. One who keeps 64th notes
83. Words for a navigator's role
84. Now
85. Against
86. Three, in Rome
87. Fast plane: Abbr.
88. She: Ger.
89. Speeds
90. Wan
91. "A rose —— rose"
93. Fireproof material: Abbr.
95. Plant beards
98. Balaam's transport
99. Whitney
100. Droop
102. Consecrate
105. Misfortune
106. Earthquake: Prefix
109. Extracted
111. Ridicule (with "of")
112. Charlemagne domain: Abbr.
113. No. 1 airport runway
116. Do —— turn
118. Paints
120. Poetic adverbs
121. Took out
124. New Deal name
125. One more
127. Points
129. Shoe size
131. "When I was ——"
132. Aqua ——
133. Forecast for a poor shoe repair
139. Flying initials
140. Excite
141. Roman date
142. Tuneful
143. Soccer star
144. Couch
145. Receive
146. Suffered

DOWN

1. Leading mod art store
2. Laughter in Nebraska
3. Dictum of a prudish girl watcher
4. Nursery words
5. Latin possessive
6. Lad
7. Kind of pronoun: Abbr.
8. Harem room
9. "There —— answer"
10. Try to attain
11. Hearts, clubs, or whatever
12. Digits: Abbr.
13. Poker player's words
14. Coral islets
15. Have —— for (esteem)
16. Comment on how part of an audience will react
17. Bell town
18. Slow-witted
20. Muscle: Prefix
21. Despise
25. Conflict
26. French river
32. Norse god
34. Corporation levies: Abbr.
36. Earth goddess
37. Girl's name
38. Fleur-de-
40. Heroic sea rescue
44. Time period
45. Old form of be
48. Long time
49. Thrifty
50. Words for a star at liberty
53. Castor bean
54. In the earth: Fr.
57. Large steam shovel
59. "—— Wimpole Street"
62. Eye parts
65. Woodchuck
66. Chair backs: Var.
67. Fever disease
69. Like a V-shaped object
71. Flemish name of Ixelles
73. Brimless hats
75. Waters
76. Start of some riddles
77. Abelard's beloved
78. These: Fr.
79. Of age: Abbr.
80. French pronoun
81. Royal initials
90. Laborer
92. City in Turkey
94. Heat measure: Abbr.
96. Out of fish eggs, too
97. Shabby feat
100. Rational
101. Reverence
103. —— out
104. Hindu grant
107. N.M. capital
108. Before mash
110. Jogged some
111. Damage
114. Region of France
115. —— majesty
117. Travel briefly
118. Slurp
119. Occupied
122. Lampreys
123. State: Abbr.
126. Food: Slang
128. Fr. miss
130. Oahu town
134. Scrap
135. Lively dance
136. Poem
137. Wager
138. Conjunctions

83 Around the House
by Emanuel Berg

ACROSS

1. Projects
5. Went hot-rodding
10. Investment item
15. Merganser
19. Biblical giant
20. Allen
21. Lombardi
22. Greek liqueur
23. —— et orbi
24. "—— human hopes"
26. Sinn ——
27. Not any, in law
28. "—— were the days"
29. Holm oak
30. S.A. plains
32. It's yet to come
34. Tennis points
35. Matches up
36. Starchy plant
37. Beaverlike
39. Tasteful
42. Do-nothing
45. Arctic sight
46. Wine: Prefix
47. Sheol and others
48. Silver: Abbr.
49. Droplet
50. Soil science: Abbr.
51. Havens
52. Pairs
53. Nearer
55. Bishopric
56. Shofar
57. Nandus
58. Pacific isles
62. Fit to drink
64. Pass off (with "on")
65. Disappeared
66. Guarantee
67. Gay
68. European capital
69. Writer Victor, to cockneys
70. Reaction
72. Roric
73. Cinch
74. Surveyed the joint
77. Track
78. —— with (favor)
79. Wood: Prefix
80. Gluck
81. Drum staves
82. Unpopular bird
84. Lung ailment

86. Boa
87. Vex
88. Poignant
89. Clever move
90. Resembling the Acropolis
94. Artist's pad
96. Auction word
97. Field mice
98. Dirigible, for short
99. Bowfin genus
100. Pasqui-naders
103. Hand: Sp.
104. Type of etching
105. Irregular
106. Siren signal
107. African antelope
108. Nervous
109. Stormed
110. Western sights
111. June 6, 1944

DOWN

1. Brief trip
2. California's Jesse ——
3. Deipnoso-phists
4. Sports gear
5. Hurl again
6. Musketeer
7. Father Brown's creator
8. Roof part
9. Life-essen-tial acid
10. More sinister
11. Takes the hook
12. Chalcedony
13. Army grade: Abbr.
14. Collapse
15. Fine till now
16. Kind of cheese

17. Pinza
18. Tony of early radio
25. More subtle
28. Pressure units
31. First-cen-tury date
33. Keens
34. Field: Lat.
35. Search into
38. Iowa city
39. At —— for words
40. Daughter of Cadmus
41. Against
42. Dance step
43. From —— in
44. —— thing
45. Fishing bob
49. Hallowed
50. When the scholar used to come
52. Handouts

53. Animal's spine
54. Pluvial
56. Engaged
57. Dinner course
59. Parlor Romeo
60. Lake near Como
61. Visit
63. Rule of too many thumbs
64. Suomi people
65. Wooden pin
67. Covered with a cosmetic
68. Garden plot
71. Aspect
72. Fashion name
73. Seal
74. Mushroom part
75. Word with

out or aboard
76. Vilifying
78. Cask part: Scot.
79. Columbia team
81. Golfer Gene
82. Italian coin
83. Churchmen
85. Herb
86. Flew, in a way
89. Small wood
91. Extreme
92. African country
93. Kind of resin
94. Stare
95. Surrounded by
96. City problem
97. Mean
101. Sky Altar
102. Business org.
103. Up-to-date

84 Executive Suite
by Ross L. Jamison Jr.

ACROSS

1. Nestors
6. Latin dance
11. Cut over
16. Prickly pears
21. Lambeau of football fame
22. Lag behind
23. Venetian medal
24. French city
25. Yucca
27. Hard-times token
29. Yutang
30. Throat feature
31. French drink
32. Charlie Chan exclamation
33. Tennessee player
34. Elixirs
36. Tournament rounds
38. Baba and others
39. Simple
40. Unemployed
41. Water lily
42. Coldly analytic
44. Year, in Paris
46. Five-spot
47. Changing the decor
49. San Antonio attraction
52. Lament
53. Monitor lizard
55. Prospector's find
56. Grant an extension
57. Enterprise
59. Danube tributary
60. Townsman
62. Root
63. Limestone formation
65. Complete costume
66. Windy City, for short
67. Household member
68. Scandinavian
70. Duo
71. U.S. time zone: Abbr.
74. Spider monkey
76. Precious stone
78. Bring upon
80. Word of assent
81. Italian city
83. Old Roman day
85. Answer
87. Pat gently
89. Decorative braid
91. Parliament of Mideast
93. Variety of cherry
97. Spanish mining city
98. Money on the Corso
99. Drive
101. Memphis street
102. Spatial
104. Ekberg
105. Metal fastener
106. Oakley
107. Relative of a flapjack
109. Crafty
110. Opposite of verso
111. Approached, poetically
113. Storehouse
115. Kingfish
116. Galway Bay islands
118. Czech town
119. Old
120. Fought roughly
123. Bribe
124. Possessive
125. Footlike part
126. Confederate general
128. Sea union: Abbr.
129. Woman's coverall
132. Chinese vermilion
134. Chemical compound
135. Cavity
136. Immense expanse
137. Singer Della
138. Courser
139. Kind of drum
140. One of the strings
141. Skaldic poetry

DOWN

1. Brave's trophy
2. TV section
3. Subsidy
4. Shade maker
5. Cardiologist's concern
6. British guns
7. Bellicose god
8. Huckster's milieu
9. Lodging place
10. Tankard contents
11. Cookie of baseball
12. Son of Isaac
13. Moment, for short
14. Former Detroit slugger
15. Site of Statuary Hall
16. Third word of "Aeneid"
17. Kind of lamp
18. Carriage horse
19. Quartet member
20. Cordage
26. "—— but the brave"
28. Bone: Prefix
31. Outer garments
35. Similar in action
37. Graz's river
38. Set straight
39. He-devil
41. River to Gulf of Gaeta
42. Thatch grasses
43. —— diem
44. Moslem V.I.P.
45. One of the Parcae
46. Kismet
48. Spanish peso
50. Ear of corn, in Africa
51. Proprietors
53. Bravery
54. New word: Abbr.
58. Fish afflictions
61. Parthenogenetic fiber
64. Zig's partner
65. Counting-out word
67. Town near Sacramento
69. Atlantic sea bird
71. Winter melon
72. Filched
73. "Grass Harp" author
75. Forage plant
77. Singer Torme
79. —— avis
82. Fermi's nationality
84. Sully
86. Variety of cotton
88. Superiors
90. Revoke a legacy
92. Operatic piece
93. Infested with tiny insects
94. English breed of eggs
95. Yokel
96. Aware of
98. Release
100. Mah-jongg piece
103. Sudden collapse
108. Greek letter
110. Put back
112. Eggs: Ger.
114. Region of France
115. Mutts
116. Residue
117. Resting place
119. Awareness
120. Early Haitian Indian
121. Ancient city of Syria
122. Certain ranchers
124. Flock
125. Rain hard
127. Soviet range
130. Victory sign
131. Cell constituent
132. Ad ——
133. Man's nickname

Showing the Way
by Nancy Schuster

ACROSS

1. Add more stickum
8. Recital pieces
14. Ivan's villa
19. In
20. More annoyed
22. Chills
23. Prisoners of a kind
25. —— Bulba
26. Prayer form
27. Tie up
28. Brontë heroine
30. Number prefix
31. Collection of sayings
32. Beaux ——
34. —— sack
36. Substitute
38. Canasta play
40. Fine fur
41. Entree
43. Manner
44. Sandy ridge
46. Latticework
48. Of a grain
50. Wire measures
52. Paris name
53. Losing money
56. Sink fixtures
59. Nervous walking
61. Signore's land
62. Try to outdo
63. Pale
65. Part of the forest scene
66. Branch of peace
67. "—— corny as . . ."
69. Wire: Abbr.
71. African antelope
73. River to North Sea
74. Baseball hit
76. Long-beaked Atlantic fish
78. Passion
80. Sounds of hesitation
81. Color
82. Bears, mice and pigs
84. Elicitors
86. Skyline sights
88. Drooping
90. Pseudo-esthetic
91. Composer
92. Popular dosage
94. Radical in famed 1921 trial
98. Wings
100. Pants
102. Whale
104. Splash over
105. Briefcase item
107. Weaken
108. Some poultry
110. Cockney's distress cry
111. Tending to: Suffix
112. Lancaster
114. Waters: Sp.
116. Ethiopian town
118. "—— the West Wind"
120. Covert
123. TV fare
124. Early epoch
125. Retinue
126. Wood nymph
127. Caught
128. Frightened, hillbilly style

DOWN

1. Publicity
2. Lancelot's love et al.
3. Part of a coach's job
4. Official deeds
5. Goad
6. Zero and successors in "Fiddler"
7. Dutch commune
8. Crowned a certain way
9. 1900-mile Asian river
10. Protection
11. Polka dot on a garment, in a way
12. Article in Bonn
13. Move back
14. Office stamp
15. Moslem title
16. Animal act, usually
17. Beating items
18. Official edict
21. Alfonso, for one
24. Perfume
29. Met again
33. Prepares
35. Scientific group: Abbr.
37. Agreeably
39. John's predecessor
41. "Half ——"
42. Involved explanation
45. Baltic gulf
47. Back talk
49. Chemical prefix
51. At sea
53. —— form
54. Young eels
55. Textile workers
56. Apish
57. "Louder-and funnier" area
58. Biblical pauses
60. Kansas college
62. Early movie name
64. Prefix for a body net-work
68. Cut off
70. Stage cover
72. Gloomy
75. Italian painter
77. Barks
79. Enlistees: Abbr.
83. —— -disant
85. Nestling
87. Former Indian leader
89. Charged a certain way
92. Gardner
93. Kind of potato
95. Detergent
96. University unit
97. Resisting
98. Furnish
99. More clashing
101. Nautical direction
103. "—— Krupp"
106. Popular investment
108. Soft candy
109. —— Coeur
113. Baseball data: Abbr.
115. Pesty bug
117. "—— horse!"
119. Philippine tree: Var.
121. Garden tool
122. Old Gov't. agency

86 Out Yonder by Mary M. Murdoch

ACROSS

1. Shuns
7. Showers
12. "...falling —— log"
16. Solidifies
21. Mint plant
22. Being led
23. Fasten
24. —— in the dark
25. Song for Pierre
27. Headgear
29. Highest note
30. Mine passages
31. Correct
33. Wartime raider
34. Loose
35. Printer's marks
36. Textile degrees
37. Veterans' org.
40. Diagonal
41. Works
42. Subject of a pop-song ode
46. A chicken —— pot
48. Pouch
49. "—— Now"
50. —— tree
51. Akin
52. Pottery
54. Barbecue rod
55. Hindu temples
56. Bancroft and others
57. Top-notch
58. Pule
59. Otherwise
60. Babble
61. Goes by plane, old style
63. Go pale
64. More: Sp.
65. Large sponge
67. Common contraction
68. Plants of regions
70. Gob
71. Water tank
72. Related
73. Electrical device
77. Physics and others: Abbr.
80. City officials
81. Old-World sandpiper
82. Leaders
83. Black
84. Wells's Mr. Kipps et al.
85. Part of a Kipling trio
86. Coin
87. View
88. Direction: Fr.
89. Rich and strong
92. Hartebeest
93. Scot's snow
94. Cleaving tools
95. News sections, for short
96. Joined in a way
97. Trellis
99. More plucky
100. Elan
101. First, etc., in football: Abbr.
102. Throw
103. Church part
104. Church season
105. Popular refrain of tots
107. Show off
108. Careened
110. Tangled mass
113. Period of revelry
115. Collins mystery
118. Lop off
119. 20 quires
120. "—— give you..."
121. Two-seated wagons
122. Like a fork
123. State: Abbr.
124. Nova Scotian cape
125. U.S. Indians

DOWN

1. Summit
2. African river
3. Other: Sp.
4. Partner of ft.
5. —— Irae
6. Hot-tempered one
7. Moon valleys
8. "What's in ——?"
9. Obsession: Suffix
10. One, two, etc.: Abbr.
11. Like sugar
12. Attacks
13. Mythical deities
14. Discovery
15. Priest's robe
16. Auto-drive part
17. Snoops
18. Mother of Zeus
19. Peace Nobelist in 1946
20. State and Main: Abbr.
26. Southern caverns
28. Be away, as a suburb
32. Turmoil
35. Classifies
36. French drink
37. Crown
38. Writer Thirkell
39. Odd plant
40. $2-window fodder
41. Serving piece
42. Vegetables
43. Houseleek
44. Deems
45. Corroded
47. Farewell: Lat.
48. African people
49. Word after one fell
52. Growing out
53. Japanese island
54. Devon, for one
56. Hungarian hero
58. Pup
60. French dads
61. —— of potatoes
62. Color
63. Caprices
65. Roulette colors
66. Exist: Fr.
67. Sycophant
69. Harold of silents
71. Mont ——
72. Lawrence's "—— Rod"
73. Market sign
74. Therefore
75. Orator
76. S.A. tanagers
78. Swindlers
79. Sam and others
80. Parsonage
81. Planing tool
83. Behold: Lat.
85. Lily plants
86. Parent in London
87. Abel's brother
89. San Quentin
90. Jalopy
91. Fanciful
92. Give ear
94. Nonplused
96. —— -man
98. Adjust
99. Flashes
100. Early explorer of America
103. Opera parts
104. Delineates
105. French mate
106. Vingt- ——
107. Entreaty
108. Scant
109. Certain medals
110. Polish measure
111. Pay up
112. Hardy girl
113. N.Y., for one
114. Chair part
116. Initials of fairy-tale author
117. Chinese pagoda

Word Assortment by William A. Lewis Jr.

ACROSS

1. Salad plant
6. Interlock
10. Tops
15. Confine
16. Russian country house
17. Up and around
19. Office worker
21. Companionably
23. Vessel
24. Gobs
25. The past
27. Shell-gamer's need
28. Leak
30. Adds up
32. Brother
33. Spoiled one
34. Council
36. Confines
38. Accessible
39. Corresponded
40. Midge
42. Out of shape
44. Prepares vichyssoise
45. Filler material
48. Certain mail
49. At will
50. State: Abbr.
51. Tease
53. Word in L.A.
54. Good word for Charlie Brown
55. Military group: Abbr.
57. Like some containers
59. Redistilled liquor
63. To the good
65. Hope and
66. Roast: Fr.
67. Catch
68. Very unpleasant
70. Marina sights
72. Wax
73. Actor Claude
74. Certain room
75. One's nature
77. Form of Rachel
78. Guzzles
80. Take it easy
82. Kohinoor, e.g.
84. Defend
85. Harbor sound
87. Snow vehicle
88. Car co-ops
89. Livid
90. Catty sound
92. Easy prey
95. Ill temper
96. Skillet
98. Bit of liquor
100. Blue or green
101. Bravo!
102. Academic elite, informally
104. "There —— any more"
106. Hebrew letter
107. Prosperous
109. Military to-dos
112. In a grand manner
113. Roundish
114. French relative of F.B.I.
115. Giggle
116. Indiana port
117. Gambling choice

DOWN

1. Flavor
2. Modern convenience
3. Lazy writer's abbreviation
4. Please
5. Chair part
6. Degrees: Abbr.
7. Nymph of myth
8. Place for things
9. Breadstuff
10. Tavern workers
11. Rice
12. Runners
13. Kind of ear
14. Aerial maneuver
15. Digging tools
16. Housecoat
17. Held back
18. Very
20. Support
22. Ship men
26. Reruns
29. Place to fish
31. Rebuff
33. Oral summary
35. Smear
37. Cheerful
39. Companion of deals
41. Former Russian
43. Move heavily
44. Bin
45. Biblical wife
46. Word of greeting
47. Men's-wear items
49. "Across the —— plain"
52. Variety acts
54. Early invaders
56. Light covered cart: Var.
58. Feature of an old floor
59. Informal title
60. Provincial
61. Deep sound
62. Joined, in a way
64. Factotums, old style
66. Pay, in a way
69. Uncontrollable
70. Relative of uh-huh
71. Earth fault
74. Ruthless
76. Season
78. Team that scores upsets
79. Scads
80. Car
81. —— bien
83. See 61 Down
84. Violin stroke
85. Word for a pilot
86. Not at all
89. Take offense
91. Tenuous strip
93. Quaker-ladies
94. Meaning
96. Violin item
97. Roman emperor
99. Grind, as teeth
102. Memphian deity
103. Burn
105. Straight
108. Caustic
110. Pen
111. Altar: Lat.

88 Punny Girls by John Willig

ACROSS

1. Scheme
6. Gaucho gear
11. Where the Acheron flows
16. Saw
21. Raid
22. "Stop ——"
23. Grownup
24. Parlor piece
25. Gateway to U.S. wonderland?
27. Invalid, in a girlish way
29. Have status
30. Chinese weight
31. Without spirit
33. Eases
34. Seam
35. Catch-all for some
36. "—— forgive..."
37. With venom
41. Film director
42. Bird: Lat.
43. Shield knob
47. Somewhat
48. Police conveyance?
50. Scottish terrier
51. Atoll ingredient
52. Too much: Music
53. —— jacet
54. Golf nickname
55. Periods
56. —— over lightly
57. Father of Boys Town
61. Relative of a plater
62. Rude refusal
63. Entertain
65. Dessert
66. Moving back and forth
68. Just manage, with "out"
69. Going at a good clip?
73. Tax, in Dublin
74. At hand
76. Electric ——
77. Ring name
78. Some lotions
80. Girlish tantrums
82. Fuller explanations?
88. Kipling's O'Hara
91. Former Italian colonial
93. Bishop in "Henry V"
94. Mistreat
95. Feminine suffix
96. Drop bait lightly
97. Small covered passage
100. Annoyer
101. Formerly, of old
102. Part of long-run play title
104. Dawn goddess
105. Split ——
106. Play part
107. Illuminated
108. Settles anew?
111. Withdraw
112. "Simon ——"
113. V.I.P. place
114. Hawk leashes
115. Chiding mother, for one
116. Odd: Scot.
117. Links
118. Kind of collar
119. Basic items
123. Stale
124. Assert
125. Sumptuous
129. Tag for a hot rodder?
131. Name for an eloper?
134. "—— at last!"
135. Siouan
136. Old word of regret
137. Kind of crime
138. Smartly dressed
139. Carried
140. Retreats
141. Stage devices

DOWN

1. Distant
2. Piano hit of 1920's
3. Pluck
4. Duchesse, for one
5. Observe
6. Kind of garden
7. What Buzzards Bay is
8. Asian sea
9. Hamilton bill
10. Signifies
11. Cutting tool
12. Astaire
13. In a proper way
14. Building wing
15. Has top billing
16. Confuse
17. Low place
18. English river
19. Trot or gallop
20. Butts
26. Saragat's country
28. Tidings
32. Lauder, to cockneys
34. Certain tone
35. Paw, in Paris
36. Salad ingredient
37. Creed set up in 325 A.D.
38. Hooded jacket
39. Girl's gift for finding goodies?
40. Start of Clement Moore poem
41. Postal device
42. Hillbilly's anti
43. Mideast initials
44. Attired like a mouse
45. Some Irishmen
46. Walk ——
48. Heartsease
49. Eureka's relative
50. Jargon
52. Barnstorm
57. Newspaper section: Abbr.
58. One kind of gift
59. Started, to poets
60. Inert gases
63. Camel's-hair cloth
64. Textile dealer, in London
65. Filch
67. Kind of train: Abbr.
70. Pasture
71. Winglike part
72. Liturgical prayers
75. Reckoned: Abbr.
79. Noun suffix
80. Awards
81. Yemen's land
83. Resinous substance
84. Lack of vigor: Var.
85. —— du Diable
86. Building beams
87. Inning units
89. Where to be on a rainy day
90. One's own thing
92. Grate upon
98. Some turkeys
99. Group of fifty
100. Revolutionary general
101. Of the church: Abbr.
103. Muscle: Suffix
105. Super's helper
106. Long time
108. Sound range
109. Polished
110. Smallest one
111. Disdain
113. Attracted
115. Swiss ——
116. Sec. of State under Cleveland
117. Swell
118. Oust
119. Thai language
120. Honduran port
121. "Thanks ——!"
122. Confined (with "up")
123. —— and potatoes
124. Macaws
125. Young salmon
126. Bone: It.
127. Organ part
128. Gossipy women
130. Inner: Prefix
132. Drink
133. Owned

ACROSS

1. Russian agency
5. Hawaiian shrub
10. Ship of ——
15. Like: Prefix
19. Oriental babysitter
20. Records
21. Ocean routes
22. Pal of void
23. Kind of skirt
24. First ocean steamer
26. Duck
27. Crucial time in tennis
29. Stake
30. Leather workers
32. Armadillos
33. Experience
35. Polish city
36. Reproductive cell
38. Captain's role, at his table
39. Hags
42. Jewish months
43. Famed clipper
46. —— cost
47. Kind of pronoun: Abbr.
48. Hall of ——
49. Blockhead
51. Broadway signs
52. Roof ornament
53. Constitution
55. Least in age: Abbr.
56. Flag
58. German river
59. Macaw
62. Church area
63. One kind of man
65. Auricular
66. New Havenite
67. Socrates, for one
68. Buffoon
72. Fleming
75. Liner holding Atlantic record
79. French article
80. Group
82. Emphatic word after yes or no
83. Attention-calling words
84. Building beam
85. U.S. admiral (1874-1939)
87. Some ads
89. Jewish liturgy
90. Definite period
92. Sugar source
93. Toolbox item
94. Part of a poetic foot
95. Take part in
97. Bake eggs
98. Thugs
100. Town on Thames
101. One who makes trades
104. Within: Prefix
105. Genoese admiral
109. Lion's trademark
110. Sea, to poets
111. Radioman's O.K.
112. Certain exams
113. Tritons
114. Fat
115. Famed acting family
116. Outdated
117. Printer's term

DOWN

1. Perth wear
2. Gallic companion
3. Chris craft
4. Clipper owners
5. Clothes
6. Otto and E.J.
7. In —— (peeved)
8. French article
9. King of Judah
10. Point of view
11. Owner of la plume
12. Bancroft
13. Crumpets' companion
14. Biblical valley
15. Pleads
16. Historic troopship
17. Relating to: Suffix
18. Reverses
25. Shakespeare's "—— deep"
28. Horse fare
31. U.S. bureau
33. One who lugs
34. Houston player
35. Tea
36. Stares
37. Proficient
38. Like N.Y. in summer
39. Aisle walker
40. Genesis name
41. Method: Abbr.
43. Framework
44. Pantywaist
45. Accesses
48. Roman historian
50. Chinese silk
53. Eastern vine
54. Knobby
57. Direction
60. Creeks
61. Do Hamlet
63. Procrastinator's word
64. Writer James and family
65. English Impostor
67. Lorelei, for one
68. Swiss city
69. Type of lifeboat
70. Walking ——
71. Slangy word of derision
72. "—— I can do it"
73. Asian range
74. Ill-fated ocean
76. Palms
77. Detection device
78. A title for Macbeth
81. Fulton's Folly
84. Ancient vessels
86. Being, in philosophy
88. Colombian town
89. Came down
91. French wine
93. Group of words
95. Scatter
96. Gardeners
97. Canvas
98. Diamonds
99. Two-toed sloth
100. Keenness
101. Bikini parts
102. ——en point
103. What's left
106. Alternative
107. Afr. brandy
108. Hour: It.

Thanksgiving Fare
by W.W.

ACROSS

1. Designation: Abbr.
5. Between sum and fui
9. Tricks
14. Lion
19. Whimpers
21. —— a million
22. Creators of jams
23. Shape in a way
24. Holiday dining décor
27. Plant fiber
28. Columbus campus
29. Get the air
30. Of a body fiber: Prefix
31. Begins to work
32. Limousines
34. Ventured
36. Girl's name
38. Controversial
40. Mom's baking standby
44. Words of disavowal
48. Officer of ——
50. Keen qualities of sense
51. Supporting bar
52. Coty
53. Of a volcano
54. Frolics
55. Young one
58. Airstrips: Abbr.
61. Day times: Abbr.
62. Sandwich filler
63. Football platoon
65. Atelier items
68. C.P.A. job
69. U.S. composer
70. Yearly pay for a few
72. Foulard items
75. Derisive sound
76. Table décor
80. Roman halls
82. Western smokes
84. Social bore
85. Fawn
86. Moslem prayer
87. Dark rock
89. Late-flowering tulip
91. Soup seeds
94. Man's nickname
95. Bone: Prefix
97. Caesar's but
98. City in Picardy
99. Cubes and spheres
102. Hindu deity
104. Behaves well
105. Road menaces
107. Parallel
110. Novelist's problem
111. Sleigh for today's grandma
113. Shooting, in a way
116. Bare the head, old style
118. "It's —— thing"
120. Scourge
121. Scott hero
124. Some dogs
128. Certain Italian, to French
130. Peer Gynt's mother
131. Alert
132. Repast topper
135. Nonconformist
136. Skin: Prefix
137. Ten: Lat.
138. Obtain repairs
139. —— work
140. Tree secretion
141. Biblical tower
142. Scout groups

DOWN

1. Place in proximity
2. Heartbeat control device
3. Strong approval
4. Your: Fr.
5. Inward: Anat.
6. Ocean-research unit
7. One source of salt
8. Kind of serviceman: Abbr.
9. Prestige
10. Standout
11. Doer: Suffix
12. Subway workers
13. Silence!
14. Hit a high fly
15. Holiday menu item
16. 1969 champs
17. Famed island
18. Arabian Sea gulf
20. Frugal one
21. Scot's alas
25. Privileged people
26. Well-done part of a roast
31. Red or White
33. Residue
35. Verb suffix
37. Possessive
39. Vegetable for mom's table
41. Mayan month
42. News pieces
43. Spanish relatives
45. State: Abbr.
46. Slue
47. "—— deal!"
49. Evergreen
51. Drool
54. Musical ending
55. Sea birds
56. In progress
57. Crux of a holiday meal
59. Kennel sound
60. Ad subject
62. Home-cooked item
63. Metric units: Abbr.
64. Tennis scores, in a way
66. Medit. island
67. Eagles
68. Galatea's beloved
71. Kiln
73. Craft
74. Agreed with
77. Khan
78. Well-known Italian
79. Small violins
81. Scottish county
83. Misfortunes
87. City of Brazil
88. Of an acid
90. Like a moonlit night
91. Bedside item
92. Ludwig
93. Spanish lad
94. Name in movies
96. Refrain syllable
99. Like a freshly cleaned suit
100. Lower
101. Indian titles of respect
103. One who transfers property
105. Scottish precipitation
106. Slipped over
108. Girl with a headset: Abbr.
109. Veld animal
111. Short of
112. Third of a famous nine
114. Stick one's ——
115. Welcomes
117. Songs
119. Eastern V.I.P.
121. —— avis
122. Was beholden to
123. Cake
125. Comparative suffixes
126. Prefix for god or john
127. Oxygen prefix
129. Navy V.I.P.: Abbr.
132. New Deal man
133. Presidential initials
134. G-man

ACROSS

1. Dog-sled driver
7. Hard feelings
13. Takes it easy
19. Bird with hanging nest
20. Watcher over me?
21. Specialized ornament
22. Site of S.M.U.
23. Wings of buildings
24. Minimal beach wear
25. Like printers' hands
26. Customarily
28. Wool fabric from Asia
30. Sholokhov's quiet river
31. You: Ger.
32. Woodworkers' aids
33. Dostoevski
34. Glacial offshoot
35. Spoiled-child specialties
37. Waterproofed, as ropes
38. Meticulous
39. Estimate
40. Furthers
41. Place for rolling stock
43. Draw from
46. Deprives of energy
48. System of beliefs
51. Adversary
52. Morose
53. Rage and elation
56. Heels
57. Seafood treat
58. Telling of tomorrow
59. Brief mornings
60. Models of cold perfection
62. Music to a matador
63. Comic's routine
65. Acclaims
66. Amused expression
67. Slipping, as of a disk
68. Slick
69. Vogue
70. Circe's product
71. Movie pioneer
73. Mrs. Grundy and others
74. Hindu scriptures
76. Bungle
77. Blueprint
78. Younger son
81. Crafty qualities
83. Sudden city
87. Hebrew measure
88. Game for anyone
89. Revivers for swooning ladies
90. Tramp, for short
91. Take forcibly
92. Rouse to fury
93. Disconcert
94. Nautical place
95. Numeral system
97. Role for wide-eyed girl
99. Out of the weather
101. Undeveloped
102. Desserts
103. Snows: Fr.
104. Grooms
105. Officer to Macbeth
106. One who manages

DOWN

1. Follower of fashion
2. Muse of astronomy
3. Lustrous
4. Pious
5. High note
6. Strong of purpose
7. Characterizations
8. Encouraging word
9. Trawl
10. Metal fastener
11. Adjective for Podunk
12. Live
13. Pole tossed by Scots
14. Overlook
15. Arctic diver
16. Projector inserts
17. Vocalists
18. Meager
20. Surfeits
27. Show rage
29. Physical entity
32. Slang for easy money
33. Mistaken suppositions
34. Cage bird, for short
36. Crops
37. "—— the tales . . ."
38. Beer heads
40. Rock salt
42. Takes as one's own
43. Vamoose
44. Charms
45. Colorful Arctic fall
46. Followed
47. Successive
49. Drove
50. Chemical dye
52. Mops of hair
54. Time period
55. Rises on a wave
57. Inclined
58. Edible South Sea worm
60. Earth
61. Berates
64. Twist
66. Wordless sound
68. Cheerfully
69. Mine vehicles
72. Height
73. Novelist's concern
75. Ripe
77. End of the earth
78. Island makers
79. Unaware of right or wrong
80. Douglas forte
82. Some wear, familiarly
83. Military centers
84. Accommodate
85. Expressionless
86. Most recent
88. Diplomatic assets
89. Reject rudely
92. Fur
93. Pearly mussel
94. Saudi Arabian area
96. Nectar collector
98. Dine
100. Born

92 Gift Suggestions

by Frances Hansen

ACROSS

1. Betty of song et al.
6. Resort in West
11. Makes passes at a fly
18. Wayne and Dix: Abbr.
21. Handy
22. Nasty
23. Narcotic
24. Exclamation
25. Prisoner's castle, in fiction
26. Ice-cream holders
27. Equally taut
28. Ring: Abbr.
29. Words after "Hey" in old song
33. Old British middle class: Abbr.
34. Not public: Abbr.
35. Dickens girl
36. Reddish brown
37. Popular play and movie
44. Razor-blade features
45. "I —— gay musician"
46. Nigerian people
47. Coffee maker
48. Cut off
50. Columbo
51. After Santa
54. "Now, Jonah, he lived in ——"
57. White poplar
59. Eye: Prefix
60. Most like Daddy Warbucks
62. New York town
65. Came onstage
67. Sternward
68. Item for the press
72. In style
75. Nabokov book
76. Superlative endings
79. German spa
81. Raleigh's rival
82. Greatly
84. Something fur me?
87. Specify
88. River to Tiber
89. Quick to learn
90. Summit
91. Cameroon tribe
93. Farm crop
94. Bewildered
96. My gal
98. "—— was worth while..."
101. Start of Nash verse
105. —— orchard (Western grove)
109. Beluga
112. United
113. Smile lasciviously
115. Prepare
116. Italian wine town
117. Upon: Fr.
118. Asian or swine
119. Guevara
121. Bill
122. Iranian money
124. Singer Bailey?
131. Fisherman
133. Peacock blue
134. Islet
135. In addition
136. Familiar Dickens phrase
143. Purpose
144. In fashion
145. Lend ——
146. Mennonite
148. Vital cell acid: Abbr.
149. Ancient one
150. Hawaiian chants
151. Slow to catch on
152. "—— lords aleaping..."
153. Old and New England towns
154. Rub out
155. "King Lear" role

DOWN

1. Kissing kin, familiarly
2. Baby's shoe size
3. Lab burner
4. "—— want a brand-new car?"
5. Did a garden job
6. Spore sacs
7. Part of the winter scene
8. Poilu's wine
9. Like Adam's abode
10. —— -ce pas?
11. Tint delicately
12. Felt indisposed
13. Equally high
14. Pronoun
15. Prefix for an Asian
16. Orgs.
17. "—— is cast"
18. Confronting, with "to"
19. Most like Twiggy
20. Sea N.E. of West Indies
30. Squatter's cult
31. Del Sarto
32. O'Casey
37. River to Moselle
38. All: Prefix
39. Secular
40. Emulated Webster
41. Asian tents
42. Hebrew letter
43. Ruby and emerald
49. Marquette
52. "I'll take ——" (coat choice)
53. Of bronze: Abbr.
55. "Scots Wha ——"
56. English poet
57. Landon
58. Kind of nut
61. Corset part
63. Tack
64. Swiss painter
66. Turnpike exit
69. Land mass
70. Delighted
71. Letters
72. Dickens, for short
73. Symbol of satiety
74. Place to wear furs
77. Nordic bard
78. Recipe abbreviation
80. Miserly
83. Turner
85. "—— the bag"
86. Chemical compound
87. Word with cote or tail
89. Totals
92. Wide collar
95. Namesakes of a Spanish queen
97. Ibsen role
99. Son of Odin
100. Ms. men
102. After "days of"
103. "—— summer's day"
104. Between huit and dix
106. To thee: Fr.
107. Now: Lat.
108. Graf ——
109. Widely separated
110. —— with (conforms)
111. Set arranger
114. Solvents
118. Matures
120. Diminutive suffix
123. Opening word
125. In —— position (resting)
126. Armed ship
127. Infer
128. Anglo-Indian troop
129. Hair dressing
130. Lodged
132. Take it easy
137. Tender, Scotch style
138. Fake: Abbr.
139. Specify
140. Gds.
141. Tweed's group
142. She: It.
147. Part of H.R.H.

93 On Location by Hume R. Craft

ACROSS

1. Upstairs and downstairs
6. California wine valley
10. Drooping
14. Change lines in music
19. Map addition
20. Civil War combatants
22. U.S. textile inventor
23. Cobbler
24. Air terminal of sorts
26. Plow soles
28. Word of obligation
29. Mythical place of darkness
30. Hankering
31. Basilica area
33. Periodical, for short
34. Minuscule
35. Compass reading
36. Resign
38. Mischief-maker
40. McGuffey's output
43. Gyrated
45. Coated iron plates
47. "—— blue?"
48. Where Ybor City is
52. Look after
53. Locations
54. Business-letter abbreviation
55. Wind around
56. "...can you spare ——?"
58. Recipients
61. Bulrush
62. Went on about
63. Sunday talk: Abbr.
64. Butterfly
66. Home of the IRT
67. Weak consonants
69. Belief
71. Some jewelry
73. Expose
74. Fur animal
77. Mauna ——
80. Restraint
82. "Recessional" word
84. Nickname for Australians
86. Couple
87. Kilmer title
89. Relatives of rabbits
90. TV name
92. Precipitated, old style
93. Item in the black
94. "—— was saying"
95. Worthless
96. Gets off the track
97. Dour
99. Before
100. ——-terre
102. Dull noise
105. German article
106. High note
108. Insulative material
109. Freudian concepts
112. Hill nymphs
114. Orange oil
117. Tragus
119. Certain go-between
123. Flycatcher
124. Drew, for one
125. Palmist's reading
126. Equip for battle, old style
127. River to Hudson Bay
128. Paris airport
129. Whilom
130. Eye swellings: Var.

DOWN

1. Little girl
2. Lizard genus
3. Galaxies
4. Scout doing
5. Rill
6. Filch
7. Stein's repetition
8. Robin's pal
9. —— Domini
10. Old Greek war cry
11. Certain U.S. campus
12. Like three
13. Before omega
14. Welcomes again
15. Let up
16. Payola
17. High male voice
18. Dodger name
21. Masses
25. Urgency
27. Barbecue parts
32. Escarpments
34. Professional mourner
37. Bones et al.
38. Kind of flight
39. Hodge-podge
41. Mike man
42. In a brown study
43. Movie biggie
44. Foot keyboards
46. Kind of book
49. Funicular
50. Synthetic fiber base
51. Man's nickname
54. Arthurian lady
57. German river
59. Happening
60. Singing voice: Abbr.
65. Asian boundary river
68. Cul-de-——
70. Singer Diana
72. Got the import
73. Can. province
75. Pinkish colors
76. Oil jar
78. Soup pods: Var.
79. Slanting
81. Axes
83. Starting places
85. People of Assam
88. Certain watchmakers
91. Roman official
95. ——-hand
98. Girl
101. Storehouses
102. Famed Idaho name
103. Tropical palm
104. Thought-provoking
107. Skeptical
108. Mickey et al.
110. U.S. industrialist: 1804-1886
111. Banana bunches
113. Lily plant
115. Eye
116. Learning: Scot.
118. Let out
120. Even if, for short
121. Chalice veil
122. Asian holiday

94 Yuletide Thoughts by Anne Fox

ACROSS

1. —— Flow
6. Give up
10. Erst
16. Kind of tree
20. Cry ——
21. "Render therefore —— Caesar . . ."
22. Greek goddess
23. U.S. statesman
25. Of a bone
26. Nobility: Ger.
27. Type of patch
28. Exciting edition
29. State: Abbr.
30. Give the once-over
32. Go up
34. Pourboire
36. Gen. Arnold
37. Conniption
39. A lot
40. Marrow
41. Saison
42. Fatima slept here
43. Savor
45. Panegyric
46. Gloomy one
47. Words by John Donne
53. Famous hunter
54. Egg: Prefix
55. Plain of southwest U.S.
56. Old English letter
57. Soak
58. Mudskippers
61. —— majesty
62. Categorizes
66. Aleutian island
68. Whimsical
70. One of a Latin trio
72. Spelt
73. Sub follower
75. L.B.J. in-law
77. Kind of coffee
79. Wing
80. Words by Walter de la Mare
87. —— polloi
88. Out of the way
89. Relative of esse
90. Outer: Prefix
91. Old Greek coins
93. Duration
95. Harangue
98. Foil
102. Might
104. Passport entry
106. Asian area
108. Tiergarten sight
109. A degree
110. Capricious
112. Smidgen
113. Dutch wife
115. Words by Esther S. Buckwalter
121. Widely
122. Waters: Lat.
123. Christmas ——
124. Writer Rand
125. Relative of st.
126. Chinese tree
127. English age: Abbr.
128. Alsatian brandy
132. Marble
133. Drink
134. Ruled out
137. Channels
138. Live
139. Yeah
141. Links
143. Approach
145. Ruy Diaz de Bivar
147. American pioneer
148. Republic created in 1948
149. System of exercises
150. Like some seals
151. Weather word
152. Hoss
153. Bustle
154. African lake

DOWN

1. Work group
2. Arum lily
3. Birdlike
4. Grass genus
5. Following "The Gospel"
6. Scruple
7. Wavy, in heraldry
8. Native: Suffix
9. See 62
10. Words from St. Luke
11. Living
12. Holy picture
13. Come to earth
14. Siouan
15. Speak of
16. Words by William Morris
17. Relative of a whammy
18. Busy
19. Corrigendum
24. Micronesian native
31. Pacific island
33. Rabbit tails
35. "It grows as ——" (N. Mex. motto)
38. Call to hunting dogs
39. Forte
40. Defendant's answer
43. French painter
44. Game piece
45. Native
47. Roman public areas
48. State: Abbr.
49. Hayworth
50. Raise ——
51. U.S. agency
52. Exclamation of surprise
59. Puts out
60. ". . .and they were —— afraid"
62. With 9 Down, words from Ecclesiastes
63. Pipe
64. High
65. Manche capital
67. Prefix with corn or cycle
69. Letter sign-off
71. African people
74. Friendliness
76. Impetus
78. Board member: Abbr.
80. Cut up
81. Tramp
82. Kind of act
83. Drink
84. Canadian writer
85. Sew together
86. In our time
92. Focusing medium
94. State: Abbr.
96. Persian rug
97. Literature Nobelist in 1948
99. Sea of Russia
100. Rounder
101. Go to ——
103. Each: Fr.
105. Sports gear
107. Air: Abbr.
110. Part of a taxi meter
111. Caesar, at one time
114. Bombast
115. Swift's "Tale ——"
116. Blankets
117. Samuel Butler novel
118. Kind of fringe
119. "—— child is loving . . ."
120. —— monde
128. Sheikdom of Arabia
129. Holy: Lat.
130. Blubbers
131. Gabler
134. Exceedingly
135. Son of Isaac
136. Calendar abbreviation
137. Academy Award film: 1958
140. Spanish number
142. "A rose —— . . ."
144. Dash's partner
146. Put down

95 Gadget Counter
by William Lutwiniak

ACROSS

1. Rebuff
5. Complies
10. Ululates
14. —— song
18. Girl who wants, and gets
19. Musical piece
20. Lively dance
21. Porthos et Aramis
22. Surprise
25. Platform
26. Caprices
27. Points
28. Clefts
30. Neighbor of Ala.
31. Cocktail garnishes
32. Noun ending
33. Calling by name
36. Tonsorial service
37. Self-inflated one
41. Have —— to
42. Manicurist's concern
44. ——-disant
45. Italian numeral
46. Bearish times
47. Coffee-makers
48. Esteemed panfish
49. Numerical prefix
50. Honestly
54. Folkways
55. Guards
57. Fencing move
58. Of a cereal
59. Incites
60. Small cabaret
61. Toxophilite gear
62. Wrap
63. Land of Minos
64. Encircled, of old
67. Money of Thailand
68. Contributes
70. Galena
71. Wishes undone
72. Reward, old style
73. Have a go
74. Silk, in Paris
75. Neighbor of Oreg.
76. Approached a solution
80. Traveled, in a way
81. Combina-tions
83. Staff men
84. Compulsion
85. Over-eager
86. Villain's forte
87. The McCoy: Abbr.
88. New York
91. City of Peru
92. Certain writers
96. His: Fr.
97. Performs obsequies of a kind
100. Popular garnish
101. —— price
102. Kind of seal
103. Topnotch
104. Berra
105. Social group
106. Service-women
107. For fear that

DOWN

1. European
2. She-wolf: Sp.
3. Sleep like ——
4. Hill of Rome
5. Near future
6. Part of a White House name
7. Individuals
8. Sound of gusto
9. Background
10. Inexperi-enced ones
11. "—— well"
12. Pronoun
13. TV offerings
14. Withering
15. Straw in the wind
16. Haystack
17. Invites
20. Term in grammar
23. Vogue
24. Turning point
29. Farm animals
31. Washer cycle
32. Group of three
33. What Sam made too long
34. Con ——, in music
35. Firing
36. Sounds of dolor
37. Granite center
38. Daft
39. City on the Seine
40. Pointers
42. Atropos et al.
43. Cloud: Fr.
46. Nasty
48. Relative of tequila
50. Exams
51. Blackthorn fruit
52. S.A. capital
53. Below: Ger.
54. Corday's victim
56. Street sounds
58. One lap, for Armstrong
60. City on the Mark
61. Boundary
62. —— Arabia
63. Collegians
64. Men of Tartu: Abbr.
65. Iroquoians
66. Realty papers
67. Hat feature
68. Covered with moisture
69. Athirst
72. Musical instruments
74. Of a branch of medicine
76. Fiji's capital
77. Bert of golf
78. Mortgages
79. Conceives
80. What Jack did
82. Papeete's island
84. Wood nymphs
86. Revered one
87. Different
88. Like last week's meat
89. Melange
90. Oil used in varnish
91. Igneous rock
92. Immunol-ogist's con-cerns
93. Oxford
94. Sawbucks
95. Opposite of dele
98. Shosho-nean
99. Fortune

96 Word Collection
by Lewis C. Breaker

ACROSS

1. Note holders: Abbr.
4. Libations
8. Bring bad luck
12. French soul
15. Mortar ingredient
17. Two
20. Comminuted
21. Inducting
23. Eats greedily
24. Light-bulb filler
26. Kind of ale
27. Prevent
28. Silvery
32. Former Indian state
33. Towel lettering
34. Excursion
35. Beauty of myth
37. Shreds
38. "Wherefore —— thou?"
39. Grates
40. Scattering
42. Method: Abbr.
43. Ferment
44. Handled rudely
45. Weaving frame
47. Hetty and Lorne
50. Machetes
51. Green gem minerals
55. Take it easy
56. Spartan serf
57. Origination
58. Son of Adam
59. Surrounding spaces
61. Asiatic river
62. Donkey disciples
64. Certain stocks
65. Belief
66. Slides
67. Learns, old style
68. Propositions
69. Examine critically
70. Turns over
71. Japanese assembly
72. U.S. air group: Abbr.
75. Mean persons
77. Middle East waterway
78. German article
81. Moslem holy man
83. —— the punch
84. Raced
85. Spanish muralist
86. Edible roots
88. Assets
90. Legal thing
91. Bouquet de Flore
93. Channel seaweed
94. Stock exchange man
95. Payment
99. Place of suffering
101. A judge, at times
102. Put in ecstasy
103. Astral sign
104. Throw
105. Bunch of bananas
106. Road curve

DOWN

1. Conduit under a road
2. New York's North and East
3. Inkling
4. —— Baba
5. Skink, gecko, et al.
6. Issue
7. Grasslike plant
8. Estate tenures for wives
9. Cheshire Cheese, for one
10. Steel town in Norway
11. Indian memorial
12. Extemporize
13. Liliom's creator
14. Posers
15. Trill
16. European coins: Abbr.
18. Shrew
19. Vitality
20. City on Vltava River
22. German author
25. Sergeant's words
28. Yorkshire river
29. Angered
30. "—— or never!"
31. Removes hair
34. L.A. team
36. Electrodes
39. Wryneck genus
40. Name for Shropshire
41. One using an exit
43. Intense ones
44. Greek state
46. Muezzin's perch
47. Alumni, for short
48. Establishment opposer
49. Varnish ingredient
50. Lahr and others
51. Locks up
52. Eras
53. Musical work
54. Aegean island
56. Warmer
57. Snoops
59. Modern home construction
60. Nobles
63. Smart
65. In the home of: Fr.
67. Post-Thanksgiving menu
68. One-all
70. Small violins
71. Union obligation
72. Hindu guitar
73. Bewilders
74. Kind of sundae
76. Menlo Park monogram
77. Apparition
78. Eastern cedars
79. M. Lupin
80. Metric measure
82. Illinois city
84. Knowing, old style
85. Private eye
87. Free-for-all
89. Fads
90. Minotaur's home
92. Greek goddess of vengeance
94. Recipe abbreviation
96. Opposite of syn.
97. Army man: Abbr.
98. French adjective
100. Actor of sorts

ACROSS

1. Order to torpedoman
6. Present
11. "—— are about to die..."
16. Architect Jones
21. Word games: Abbr.
22. Of an acid group
23. French airmail word
24. "Sing —— songs..."
25. —— bell
26. All set
27. Loud cries
28. Hartebeest
29. Broadway phrase
32. "—— fairer than the day"
33. Start of Keats poem
34. Writer Rand
35. Times of day, for short
36. Fervent plea, with "us"
38. Gray: Fr.
40. Collected writings
41. Overseas address
42. Mouth: Slang
43. Sandburg words, after "I am"
52. Sound: Prefix
53. Clement and Marianne
54. Eastern nurse
55. —— good turn
56. The Bulbul Amir
58. Chinese dynasty
59. Nevada bandit
61. Talking bird
65. Decorate again
67. Frown
69. Moves furtively
71. Unit of loudness
72. Zambales people
74. Showy perennials
76. Malay hysteria
78. Sympathy's partner
79. Poe's lament
85. Presidential nickname
86. Famous fiddler
87. Israeli dances
88. Man for introductions
89. Combine: Suffix
91. Fiber plant
94. Xmas V.I.P.
96. Poem part
99. Mustapha Kemal
101. Latecomer's penalty
103. Holiday months: Abbr.
105. Kills
106. Corrode
108. Garish sign
109. Ascended rapidly
111. Intentions
112. What "no man lives without"
118. Bread: Prefix
119. Greek letters
120. "Ain't We Got ——?"
121. Savvy remark
122. Part of winter lawn scene
124. Hair job, for short
126. Between sine and non
129. Start of Xmas carol
133. Swords
134. Biblical quotation
137. Alentejo's capital
138. Writer Jones
139. Devil
140. "—— ears," said the rabbit
141. Mortise partner
142. Voter
143. Churchill gesture
144. Titter
145. Cunning
146. Sits
147. Heaps
148. U.S. Indians

DOWN

1. Native of area of Iran
2. J.F.K. and L.B.J.: Abbr.
3. —— check (hunting term)
4. Party worker of a kind
5. Man's name
6. Mountain lake
7. Last in a series
8. Pepys' pride
9. Append
10. Toy
11. "—— with a maid"
12. Consequence
13. Rogers and others
14. One kind of smoke
15. Cricket sides
16. Signed in a way
17. Hostess's oversight
18. "No man —— to his valet"
19. Hunting code
20. Harem room
30. Dialect
31. Heavy hair
32. Shouted down
36. Unit of fuel use: Abbr.
37. Shipping term: Abbr.
39. Catch sight of
40. Pleased sounds
41. Excited
43. Ivan, for one
44. —— Sound, Fla.
45. Tippy furniture
46. Profit's partner
47. Norse king
48. Voice parts
49. Cockney flats
50. False god
51. Funny show: Abbr.
57. Discovered by chance
59. "...—— that I know is damn'd"
60. Union general
62. Result of being trod on
63. "—— Year's gift..."
64. Cure
66. Creates
68. Accompanying
70. Flower stalks
73. Canary's cousin
75. Body fluids
77. Old ones: Abbr.
79. "—— o' kindness"
80. —— -kiri
81. Party disappointment
82. Mahatma
83. Bone: Suffix
84. "Don't ——" (plea of hostess)
90. Label for a gay party, with "Babel"
92. On the ocean
93. Uris
95. Emoting: Abbr.
97. Ferment
98. Set a value on: Abbr.
100. Indian dye
102. "The flowers —— ..."
104. Wheat of India
107. Actress Louise et al.
109. Japanese coin
110. Place firmly
112. An Apostle: Abbr.
113. After "now"
114. —— dime
115. Hebrew letter
116. Demote: Colloq.
117. Descendant of Adam's son
123. Intended
124. Tree genus
125. French school
126. Seemingly
127. Up to
128. Equally old, with "of"
130. Madagascan lemur
131. Free-for-all
132. Gardner's namesakes
134. "...see my stuff"
135. Hostess initials
136. Danube tributary
137. King of Siam's word: Abbr.
138. Seat of a sort

98 Word Parade
by Joseph LaFauci

ACROSS

1. Light gray
9. Slovenly chap
13. Brown, rainbow, etc.
19. Italian cheese
20. Etna's output
21. Greet, as a villain
22. Honor
23. Caused to see red
24. Belong
25. Rhone tributary
26. Unkempt hair
27. Housewifely chore
29. Sourdough's find
30. Yard and boom support
31. Fundamental
33. Girl Friday's station
34. Biblical city
35. Generation
36. With: It.
37. Intolerantly petty
41. Pretends
43. Disapproving sounds
44. Track supports
45. Yesterday, in Rheims
47. Run on
48. Sindbad's bird
49. Never: Ger.
52. Role in "Private Lives"
54. Mechlin or Honiton
55. Serenade, for one
57. Football fields, for short
58. Blackbeard
60. Blend
61. Hollow sound
62. Buffalo of India
63. Epithet for a kettle
64. Gradual decrease
65. —— fixe
66. —— one's time
67. Origin
68. Manservant
69. Crossed out
70. Seize
72. Masonry creation
73. Shopped
75. Name for a dog
76. Hasten
77. Orchestra strings
78. Flying prefix
79. Heraldic fur
81. Big name in Pittsburgh
82. Printed matter
86. Resourceful
88. Face: Slang
89. Hindu deity
90. France's Le ——
91. Cure of a kind
92. Attempt
94. Destiny
95. Days of yore
96. TV comedy star
99. Drone
100. Novarro
101. Wild golf strokes
103. Ancient Syria
104. Working
106. Lease signer
107. Bare
108. Consigned to obscurity
109. Aspects
110. Garden
111. Lee's horse

DOWN

1. Foreshadow
2. Tennis term
3. Ward off
4. Lacerated
5. Corse, for one
6. Ungentlemanly one
7. Cooper Indian
8. Town hall, for one
9. Drifted
10. Byron poem
11. Exaggerated
12. Fast traveler
13. Mull
14. Sonority
15. Kirghiz city
16. Make a wise judgment
17. Defiled
18. Bullock
19. Original
28. Doctrine
31. Filleted
32. Galleon
34. "Fables in Slang" author
36. Numismatist's goodies
38. Freshwater fish
39. Consider
40. Pleasing
42. Like some fast deals
46. Resembling a pest
48. Egyptian city
50. Poor
51. Incited, with "on"
52. Succeed
53. Quality of some psychedelic drugs
55. Actress Velez
56. Watched jealously
57. Eva
59. Alleviate
60. Not making the grade
63. Expert advisers
64. Words for a summer drink
68. Italian actress
69. Singer Bobby
71. Pronoun
72. TV maestro
74. Kind of race
77. Concentrated
80. Feminine suffix
81. Entitle improperly
83. Human being
84. Recover from
85. Tied
86. Degraded
87. "Leave —— to Heaven"
88. Girl's name
90. D.C. hostess
93. Dandy
94. Ruinous
96. Part of N.B.
97. Counterweight
98. Govt. agents
100. Frenzy
102. Coolidge
105. Gun an engine

99 Centerpieces

by Thomas W. Schier

ACROSS

1. Dolmans
6. Bridge over Moslem hell
11. Climb
16. One at ——
21. Style of painting
22. Employed
23. Ambitious
24. Boo-boo
25. Statesman and author
28. Alpaca's cousin
29. Vaudeville turns
30. Long-billed bird
31. Wide-awake
32. Bullets, in France
33. French marshal
34. More reasonable
35. —— barrel
36. Small antelope
37. Arias
38. Actor
39. Boring tool
40. Orator and novelist
46. L.P., for one
49. New World capital
50. Lear's daughter
51. Greek region
52. Barton
54. Inter ——
55. Darling: It.
56. Military groups
57. Man of parts
58. Bad guy and film bad guy
63. Red
64. Carney
65. Transports
66. Man's name
67. More gentle
68. Antisocial one
69. —— polloi
70. Flower, in Berlin
71. Hallows
74. All rose —— man
76. Use one's neck
77. Houston
80. Canadian city
81. Former quarterback and novelist
84. Cay
85. Sudden reaction
86. Bowling alley
87. River to Baltic
88. Electron tube
89. Song refrain
90. Juvenile writer Oliver
92. Doctor's allotment
94. Telepathy's relative
95. Justice and Ohio man
98. African tribe
100. Effects
101. Highest point
102. Able, Baker, —
105. Like a swamp
107. —— de lune
109. Cry of contempt
112. Stassen
113. Prospector's companion
114. Dissertation
115. —— War
116. Range areas
117. Socialist and novelist
120. Wrathful
121. Endeavored
122. Kitchen implement
123. Play backer
124. Lease anew
125. Scowl
126. Bergen's Mortimer
127. Solan and gannet

DOWN

1. Broadway name
2. Swiftly
3. —— line
4. Slips
5. Augean stable, for one
6. Alluring
7. Accustom
8. Kind of monger
9. Slippery —— eel
10. Lacrosse team
11. Fur-hunting
12. Frisk
13. Athens sight
14. Baltic native
15. Poetic word
16. Excited
17. German dramatist
18. Wholly
19. Baltic port
20. Take out
26. Muse of comedy
27. Grotto
32. Purses
34. Arrange
35. O'Neill
36. Surmise
37. Old porticoes
38. French painter
39. Understanding
40. Boatman
41. Assess for a purpose
42. "Instant Replay" author
43. —— how
44. Lind or wren
45. Hostile
46. Furious
47. Uneven
48. Do a banquet job
49. —— California
52. Part of a table setting
53. Greene of TV
55. Examples
56. More hostile
59. Hard rubber
60. Small ruling group
61. Collusion
62. Accompanying
63. Stuck to
67. Censure
68. Organized, with "up"
70. Tributary
71. Digression
72. Patriarchs
73. Ship's deck
74. To any degree
75. Kind of poll
76. Kind of gang
77. Type of car
78. Lay ——
79. Bare
81. City in Japan
82. —— ego
83. Red dye
85. Grayish color
90. Famous trail
91. Implore
92. Legal rights
93. Repute
95. Bagnold
96. Build up
97. Sumac plant
98. "Jane Eyre" creator
99. Ready
102. Church area
103. French port
104. Of a surface
105. Mandalay's land
106. Abalone
107. Italian philosopher
108. Like some excuses
109. Harbor sight
110. 4,500-mile range
111. Games man
113. Do eggs
114. Unconvincing
115. Long hair
117. Badger
118. Corp. officers
119. Witch

100 The Face Is Familiar by Eugene T. Maleska

ACROSS

1. Termagant
6. Cleft
12. Epithet for Samuel Johnson
16. Relative of hi-fi
17. Panay port
18. Papa Bear of football
20. Patti Page
22. Wards off
24. Bittern
25. Eating places
26. Bishop's headdress
28. Novelist Levin
29. Grub
30. Entanglement
31. Bremen's river
32. Connery
33. Harriman's nickname
34. Arctic base
35. —— Devi, Indian peak
36. Piece of gossip
37. Schnauzers
39. Mexican shawl
40. Hindu's fast to get justice
41. "—— Lynne"
42. Kyle or Tobin
43. "—— My Sunshine"
45. Play the siren
48. Valuable tree of N.Z.
50. Checks
53. —— Kabaivanska, soprano
54. Rathbone
55. Chilean export
57. Use a straw
58. Useless
59. Cyd Charisse
61. Color in French flag
62. Culbertson
63. Shaman
64. Sniggler
65. Blossom in Brest
66. Prof's stand
68. Wailed
70. Drinks noisily
71. Smuts's philosophy
73. Auction word
74. Korean statesman
75. Iosif V. Dzhugashvili
77. Choir voices
79. Knight fights
83. California's Santa ——
84. Pigtail
85. Cluster
86. Cargo unit
87. Grampuses
88. La ——, Honduran port
89. Fissure
90. "—— move on!"
91. Bowl call
92. Count Basie plays it
93. Cathay
94. Braid of gold or silver
95. Small-time
97. Cary Grant
100. Usher's beat
101. Jeer at
102. Emissary
103. Capitol Hill count
104. Worked on galleys
105. Wroth

DOWN

1. Track official
2. Mackerel-like fish
3. Algerian port
4. Author of "The King Ranch"
5. Ken Murray
6. Nonsense!
7. Agalloch
8. Has an oar-deal
9. Sesame
10. Krypton, for one
11. Miss von Kappelhoff
12. Trout
13. Engage in
14. Drink
15. Leila Koerber
16. "The ravel'd —— of care"
19. Tune
20. Flimflam
21. Name for a ship's carpenter
23. Kringle
27. Congou
30. Anagram for "sheet"
31. Baseball's Big or Little Poison
32. Delusion's partner
34. Royal adornment
35. Natasha Gurdin
36. Midwest airport
38. Meet, as alumni
39. Central theme
40. Indian millet
42. Bed of flowers
44. Horse opera
45. Caliban's opposite
46. Chef's spoon
47. Claudette Colbert
48. Narrative
49. Walked
51. Traffic jam
52. Rail sidetracks
54. George —— (Nathan Birnbaum)
56. "—— Three Lives"
59. City in N.W. Italy
60. Actress Gwyn and others
61. Cornflower
63. Girl in "As You Like It"
65. Hosiery color
67. Turnpike fees
69. Old port of Rome
70. Oyster shell
72. Enriching brine
74. Pope John XXIII
75. Recreation
76. Pacific battle site: 1943
78. Drudged
79. Tia ——
80. Battologize
81. Announcement
82. Grind together
84. Lillie
85. Suborned
88. Adduces
89. Reprove
90. Alexander's epithet
92. Like thick rugs
93. Voucher
94. Former queen of Greece
96. Dan Beard's org.
98. Dernier ——
99. Article in Berlin

101 Off and Running by A. J. Santora

ACROSS

1. Child's ailment
6. Prefix for theater
11. Celebrator's sound
15. Michener book
21. Masochist of a sort
23. Inheritances of a sort
25. Advantage
26. Trifles
27. Spanish ladies
28. Cinema's Sommer
29. Pacific island group
30. Sibilant sound of derision
31. Astronaut John and family
33. One of the Joneses
35. Inspiration
37. Orb
40. Harbor boat
41. Comparative word
43. Siesta
44. Madrid wife: Abbr.
47. Emphatic negative
53. Rep.
54. Scorch
55. TV host
56. Sister Eileen's state
57. From A ___
59. Imitative
61. Indian writer
63. Turtle feature
64. "Rain" girl
66. Spools
67. Helper: Abbr.
70. Love 'em and leave 'em
73. Metrical foot
74. Desire
75. Prongs
76. Horse transport
77. "The Rain ___"
80. Spoil
81. Ice-bucket item
82. Sonoran: Abbr.
83. Add
85. Indian ape
86. Using the rink
88. Peaked
89. Wicked city
90. River areas
91. To be, in Paris
92. Just in time
96. Sky animal
97. Spore sac
98. Long times
99. Augury
100. Correlative
102. ___ one talk
104. Tennis unit
105. Turkish lake
106. Rye or corn
110. Lamented
111. "___ in the stilly night"
113. All-inclusive
118. Pronoun
119. California's Big ___
120. Bridge positions: Abbr.
121. Charged atom
122. Luau instrument
123. Like a rain forest
125. Conger
127. Yellow-green hues
130. Melville title
132. Pineapples
134. Fragrance
136. ___ fours
139. Omaha's achievement
141. Radio men
144. Controlling firmly
145. Final stage
146. Undertakes
147. Paris suburb
148. "Can't teach ___ dog . . ."
149. Prevent, in law

DOWN

1. Greek letter
2. ___ de jambe
3. Approximately
4. Taking advantage
5. Piano part
6. Height: Abbr.
7. Napoleonic battle site
8. Indian verandas
9. Mild cussword
10. Nettled
11. Elite
12. "I ___ dream"
13. Minstrel performer
14. Washington newsman
15. Biddy
16. Reaches a total
17. "___ me!"
18. Bristles
19. Some voters: Abbr.
20. Magazine number: Abbr.
22. Spanish coin
24. Sounding sheepish
32. No, in law
34. Roman emperor
36. Other shoe
37. Compass point
38. Hebrew day
39. And the like: Abbr.
42. Reach
44. Cobbler
45. Cranes' relatives
46. Floodlights
48. Accommodation
49. Assent
50. "A man may see . . . with ___"
51. Mountain passes
52. Certain Hindu
53. Mas d' ___, French town
54. Cut-rate
58. Pindar output
60. Bacon order
62. Sinclair
63. Hard blow
64. Tunisian port
65. Book man
67. Goals
68. Deploys, as police
69. Sinks the cue ball
71. Hybrid tongue, with 112 Down
72. Handicap race, for one
78. Presiding spirit
79. Space agency
81. ___ knot
82. Planet
83. Overshadows
84. Norse god
87. Aligned
88. Attacked
89. Ornamental patterns
90. Pack animal
93. Retreat
94. Deer
95. Vagrant
97. Town in Italy
101. Musical dir.
103. Rake
105. Gaelic
107. French drink
108. Flatboat
109. Ike
112. See 71 Down
114. British explorer
115. Male hawk
116. Trough
117. Establish
119. ___ march on
120. Church councils
123. Classmen
124. ___ Gras
126. Low Hindu caste
127. Prefix for naut
128. Ink: Fr.
129. Heaven's ___!
130. Whether ___
131. Coin of low value
133. Piercing tools
135. Lord in "Winter's Tale"
137. Baltic native
138. Wolf: Prefix
139. Poke, in Scotland
140. Id ___
142. Law degree
143. Engine power: Abbr.

102 Word Assortment by Nancy W. Atkinson

ACROSS

1. Put together
6. What sopranos give dogs
14. Zenana
19. Philosophy of a sort
21. Italian seasoning
22. Bijoux
23. Unspecified time
24. Timetable listing
25. Wacky
26. Enlists
28. Silent star Naldi
29. At no extra ___
31. Pianist Peter
33. Start
35. Zones
37. Ship's hoist
39. Repute
40. Backfield players: Abbr.
42. ___ team
45. Perspectives
50. Large decanters
54. Bold ones
55. Area of Europe
56. Fading politico
58. ___ packing
59. Some fishermen
60. Mindanao natives
61. Gallery sounds
63. Certain believers
65. Mineo and others
66. Color for the Baron
67. Eskimo knives
69. Bristle
70. Capuchin monkey
71. Cheese
73. Threesomes
75. Wrinkle
77. Kind of berry or bug
78. Barbarians
80. Cheerless
82. Bemoans
84. Native of Provo
85. Kind of iron
87. Most stereotyped
88. Flower parts
89. Fastens again
91. Lush
92. Greenland settlement
94. Strips
96. Installs
100. Wins recognition
106. Trophies
108. Use straws in a way
109. Russian range
110. Police weapon
112. Effrontery
114. Creek
115. Break one's word
117. Come to terms
120. Faint clues
121. Quit trying to argue
122. Water animal
123. Heraldic bearing
124. Analyze in a way

DOWN

1. Andes animal
2. Appraiser of Snow White
3. Opposed to
4. Cabinet man: Abbr.
5. Flying jib
6. Developed
7. Inferior one
8. Home: Abbr.
9. Lawyers: Abbr.
10. Like one in a monastery
11. Depend on
12. In any ___
13. U.S. composer
14. Chinese dynasty
15. Flower spike
16. Arm bones
17. Muse
18. Yucatan native
20. When the scholar comes
21. Certain Oscar winners
27. German conjunction
30. Old shields
32. Roman poet
34. Antelope
36. Booted
38. ___ much as
41. Check suddenly
43. First king of Egypt
44. More flamboyant
46. Capitol Hill men: Abbr.
47. Cherish
48. Skyways
49. Most flip
50. Flies off the handle
51. Recent time
52. Cage bird from India
53. Looks high and low
57. Low Indian caste
59. Puts on
62. Fountain order
64. Kind of poker
68. Bondmen
72. Ceylon ape
73. One-fifth of the Union
74. Havens
76. Flats: Abbr.
77. Shook up
79. Strong winds
81. Livid, old style
83. Vientiane's land
85. Name in U.S. journalism
86. Kind of power: Abbr.
90. Babe Ruth or Hank Aaron
93. French spirit
95. Few and far between
97. Overdue debt
98. Contaminates
99. Bundle up
100. An ___ the ground
101. On the job
102. Attacked
103. Relative
104. Sorrowful, in poems
105. Century plant
107. Arabian nomad
111. Japanese measures
113. Eucalyptus wax
116. Eur. language
118. Babylonian god
119. ___ culpa

103 City Landmarks by Marjorie K. Collins

ACROSS

1. Loos
6. Christie and Magnani
11. Malay sailboat
15. ___ Nova
18. Grinding tooth
19. Had in mind
20. Civil War men
21. Voltage term in physics
22. Literary work
23. Philadelphia
26. Burdened man
27. Musical passage
28. Sheep
29. European blackbird
30. Boston
32. New York City
34. Not in vogue
35. Move with care
36. Seamen's quarters
37. Presidential initials
38. Cherish
41. Binge
42. Wound memento
45. "Dear ___"
46. Prepare for action
47. Man's name
49. Cur
51. Rhythmic tunes
52. Make an opinion
56. Style
57. Witch town
58. Steering blade: Abbr.
59. "Zhivago" character
60. Word of afterthought
61. San Francisco
64. City in Oklahoma
65. Egg on
66. Recent: Prefix
67. Insect homes
68. Wild and white
69. Gangsters' disciplinarian
71. Hair jobs
72. Handled
73. Jannings
74. Chemical suffixes
75. Diamond lady
76. Gabor and Little
78. Companion on the range
79. Woolen fabric
84. College degree: Abbr.
87. Bedaubed
89. Valley
90. Scull
91. Washington
94. Miami
97. God of Islam
98. Wire: Abbr.
99. Outer coat
100. 1964 Olympic site
101. Pittsburgh
105. Printers' frames
106. Before, to poets
107. Hymn word
108. Did business
109. Goliath, for one
110. Two: Sp.
111. Beach sight
112. Europeans
113. Kefauver

DOWN

1. Certain sportsman
2. On time
3. Of the lower back
4. Foot bone: Prefix
5. Metric measure
6. French town
7. Heckle
8. Port of Brazil
9. Reply: Abbr.
10. Farm area
11. Does squad-car duty
12. Disposes of again
13. Outmoded: Abbr.
14. ___ in the dark
15. Maligned
16. Take care of the lawn
17. Lithe
22. Peasant's shoe
24. Respond
25. Pronoun
27. Burn
31. Medical prefix
32. Copse
33. After primo, in Italy
36. Baltimore
39. Houston
40. Venue
41. Terrazzo worker
43. Bow shape
44. Detroit
46. River of Southwest
48. Subtle shading
49. Persian, for one
50. Risky
51. Cabinet post
52. U.S. Indians
53. Possessive pronoun
54. Evaporated
55. U.S. inventor
56. Plum variety
57. Pintail duck
61. Seize and hold
62. Exposed
63. Veterinary degrees
68. Downfall
70. Red or Yellow: Abbr.
71. 5-point type
75. Respirator
77. Much in love
78. Main Line town
79. Sky sights
80. Split
81. Have a ___ (give the once-over)
82. Perry Mason and others
83. Guthrie and others
84. Put on
85. Green: Prefix
86. Beauties
88. Forever, in poetry
89. Openwork barrier
92. Ill-bred person
93. ___ of steam
94. Kidney or liver
95. Spirit of a people
96. Crow
102. Seamen's group: Abbr.
103. Do sums
104. Teachers' group: Abbr.
105. Little one: Suffix

104 Phraseology by Bert Beaman

ACROSS

1. Canadian resort
6. Comprehending words
10. Make possible
16. Spanish ladies
21. Edie or John Quincy
22. Process that makes water bubbly
24. Fourflusher
25. Err
27. Fizzle
28. Famous bridge jumper
29. Dead duck
30. Rhythm, in Britain
32. Renovate
33. One kind of man
34. Morning song
36. Man: Prefix
38. Looked happy
40. Equipment for Leinsdorf
41. Math abbreviation
42. Berth
43. ___ grade (succeed)
46. Go off
47. Uses a crystal ball
48. Western alliance
51. Zola
52. Ocean salvaging equipment
55. Develop
57. Yummy
59. Exposed
60. Sped
61. Verb suffix
62. Heraldic term
63. Hersey's town
65. Images
67. Kind of vessel
69. Award: Abbr.
70. Mirthful
71. Accustom
72. Drub
73. 3-R centers
76. Victory celebrations
79. Retreats
80. Bushlands
82. Like some foods
83. N. Y. subway
84. Clasp
85. Chou ___
86. Reserves
87. River to Danube
88. College official
89. Alder or birch
90. Generate
92. Of an old Nile city
94. British Lady of note
96. Zero, to athletes
99. Blackthorns
100. Confronted
101. Make ___ of things
103. Doctor's concern
104. Escorts
106. Lawyer's problem
108. Nonpartisans: Abbr.
109. Inverted V
110. Wear ___
112. Vermont city
113. One kind of relations
114. Stupid one
117. Cape near Lisbon
118. Philippine bananas
120. Prefix for a poison
122. Execrate
124. Turkish carriage
126. Put aside and forget
129. Eastern faith
130. ___ lips (slips out)
131. Capitol features
132. Name for a pitcher
133. Derides
134. Western hill
135. European

DOWN

1. Loquacious
2. Antarctic cape
3. Bags: Sp.
4. Postal abbreviation
5. Judgments
6. Kind of cap
7. Cotton processor
8. Mistaken: Abbr.
9. Black
10. Rapt
11. Slangy retort
12. Kind of pile
13. A Duke of Courland
14. Bewildered
15. Invigorated
16. Student's objective: Abbr.
17. Brian
18. History-making move
19. Vacuum tube part
20. Church council
23. Kind of town
26. British waste land
31. Gardner
35. Touched, as a starting line
37. "___man with seven ..."
39. Girl's name
40. Misrepresent
41. Prefix for a metal
42. Woods dwellers
43. French wines
44. Wild West talk, for one
45. Celebrate
46. Certain New Englanders
47. Food birds
49. Like some college courses
50. Pythoness, for one
53. Mexican timber tree
54. Annoyance
56. Condescend
58. Acclaimed
64. Indian timber trees
66. Fellow
67. Most undeveloped
68. Babylonian god
70. Disturb
71. Land area: Sp.
72. Line a roof
74. College town
75. Standish
77. Money in Uppsala
78. Urgency
81. Cools
84. Gouda's relative
85. Irregular
86. Limits
87. Estuary
89. Kick over ___
91. Side entrances
93. Small planets
95. At any ___
97. German river
98. River to Danube
102. Rotterdam's river
105. Fish in a way
107. ___ Mater
108. Resort off Florida
109. Light craft
110. Thin as ___
111. Eric, for one
112. Bench, in Spain
113. Sierra ___
114. One at ___
115. Did a blacksmith job
116. Common item
119. Bartlett's relative
121. Mouth: Prefix
123. Acknowledge
125. Poet Lowell
127. Manuscript abbreviation
128. Youth org.

In Good Season

by Eva Pollack Taub

ACROSS

1. California mountain
7. Metrical accent
12. Coldest
18. Of rock debris
19. Hangman's symbol
20. Hot-dog topping
22. Eugene Field subject
24. Polish city
25. Pats, in Scotland
26. Property
27. Task
29. Tout's specialty
30. Expert
31. Plant fiber
32. Garish
33. "___ but the brave..."
34. Renovate
36. Grain
37. Film award for animals
38. Less dangerous
39. P. I. rope fiber
41. Freshwater fish
42. Butler's milieu
43. Kind of cheese
46. Profoundness
47. Place for a glider
48. Earth pigments
49. Statistician's concern
50. Postponers
53. Actor John
54. Coax
55. Takes out
56. Comic-strip cry
57. Doctrine
58. Fancy trimmings
60. Relative of st.
61. Perceive
62. Town in Iowa
63. Domestic help
64. Scatter
66. Of an early Greek doctrine
68. Pickles
69. Frenchman's four
70. One of an early rabbi group
71. ___ panky
72. Cowboy
73. Hard
75. Onward
76. Car part
77. River to the Missouri
78. Shallow boats
79. Fireplace problem
80. Russian press agency
84. Lacquer: Sp.
85. Folkways
86. Gossip
87. Navy man: Abbr.
88. Common verb
89. Item in a London parlor
90. Classes
92. Spoken
93. Ziegfeld musical
95. Sherlock Holmes of films
98. More close-fitting
99. Pupil: Fr.
100. Red colors
101. Garden flowers
102. Road curves
103. African insect

DOWN

1. Water channel
2. Kept close to
3. Gardner and others
4. Term of respect
5. Fabric strip
6. Flavoring
7. Confined person
8. Short surplice
9. Lacerated
10. Employ
11. Male seal
12. Give form to: Var.
13. Spicy dish
14. "___ what you mean"
15. Diminutive endings
16. Superior people
17. Athletes' helper
18. Be, in Spain
21. Deception
23. City in N.Y.
28. Quiet
32. Cloister courtyard
33. French city
35. Of a grain
36. Tatters
37. Candies
38. Girls' names
40. Expose
41. "___ porridge..."
42. Pushed a raft
43. Bovine
44. Writer Sean
45. Of an Old World tree
46. Argentine statesman
47. Chinese waxes
49. Suffix for photo
50. Acts
51. Well-known horseman
52. Rod for meat
54. Leg bone
55. In a deadpan manner
58. Old ___
59. Afghan town
62. Organic compound
64. Done for, familiarly
65. Be silent, in music
67. Greek letter
68. Wall game
69. Four: Abbr.
71. Insect
72. Extend
73. Sun rooms
74. Russian ruler
75. Roll up
76. Plant pest
78. Conic lines in geometry
79. Moves in a way
81. Spanning
82. Foster's river
83. Shoe parts
85. Taxi part
86. Initiative
89. Buster Brown's dog
90. Chemical sugars
91. Marie and others: Abbr.
92. News piece
94. Army org.
96. Jolson, etc,
97. Otto I's domain: Abbr.

106 Countdown

by Herbert Ettenson

ACROSS

1. Liquor units
5. Not worth ___ of beans
10. Naval officer: Abbr.
14. Water nymph
19. Old English moneys
20. Daises
21. Certain vaudeville show
22. Hudson town south of Kingston
24. ___ store (place to buy notions)
26. Play about tinhorn bettors
28. Pianist Gabrilowitsch
29. Comedian Danny
30. Nonpaying friend
31. Frost piece
32. Biblical people
34. Korean soldier
36. Town in Sicily
37. Perceive
38. Uncanny
39. The end
41. Love affair
43. Presidential middle name
46. Dogcart
48. Branch of study
52. Make one
53. Title of respect
54. Computer stuff
56. Record keeper
57. Ferber
58. More judicious
59. Outdoor
61. Dwarf: Prefix
62. Shady agreement
63. Exhibitionist
64. Most favorable conditions
65. Alcohol burners
66. Subsidiary
67. Released a claim to
71. Concerning
72. Garnish green
73. Last card of a suit
75. W. W. II town
76. Glacial trough
77. Noted name in West
78. Role for Michael Caine
79. Sew a hawk's eyelids
80. Detachable page
82. Assn.
85. Afro-Asiatic language
86. Filled the bill
88. Shelter
89. Sky: Fr.
90. Girl friend in Paris
91. Ailment
92. Assembly in old Greece
94. Cruising
95. Nut-and-fruit bread
97. Mouth: Prefix
98. In addition
99. Glacial term
100. East Indian shrews
102. People fleeing a land
104. Gems
105. Sauce, in Italy
106. Tin, in Paris
107. Epithet for Clio, Erato, etc.
108. "___ will is the wind's will"
111. Speaker of baseball
114. ___ for one
115. "Had a ___ big as a whale"
118. Sunburns
119. Caps of a kind
121. The fat ___ the fire
123. Literary villain and namesakes
125. Obscenities
127. Necessity à la Thomas Marshall
129. Water animals
130. Cell terminal
131. Spent
132. Fuzz
133. Body: Prefix
134. Gambling game
135. Rimy coatings
136. Silk: Sp.

DOWN

1. Equally
2. Junk
3. Medieval guild
4. Dreggy
5. Soldier's address
6. Game
7. Light bulbs, in the comics
8. Streaked
9. Slugabed
10. Bivouac
11. "___ a Grecian Urn"
12. Windfall
13. Graph of muscular contractions
14. Approaching
15. Residue
16. Relative of a jingo
17. Kitchen wear
18. Italian actress and family
21. Beat it!
23. Dotted, as enamelware
25. Kind of bathing suit
27. Time of the new moon
33. Attempt
35. Fuegian
37. Diamonds, for one
39. Golfer's word
40. Scouring items
42. Bouquet
43. Curfew: Sp.
44. Covered by
45. Rare case
46. Cans
47. Hat
49. Another's meat, so to speak
50. Nursemaids
51. Biblical man
53. Anna's land
55. Grieg character
58. Reporter's question
60. Without distinct form
65. Part of Q.E.D.
67. Control
68. Metric units
69. Ennoble
70. Gloomy
72. Port opposite Gibraltar
74. Method of crop rotation
78. Intend
81. Possessive
83. Singer Della
84. Product of sand
85. Kind of drum
86. Ominous
87. Dinner topper
89. Whip
91. Valley
92. Tax day
93. Singer Campbell
96. Grasslands
99. Spatial
101. Area of Borneo
103. "My ___ Sal"
104. Asian sheep
107. What two fins make
108. When life begins, in a title
109. Northern Europeans
110. Only ___ a customer
112. ___ ear ...
113. Curved metal bar
115. Old Greek temples
116. Farming student
117. ___ so
119. Supreme
120. Taro root
122. Shadow: Prefix
124. Spanish girl: Abbr.
126. Refrain part
128. Football scores: Abbr.

107 Fractured Curios by Frank Nosoff

ACROSS

1. Close watch
6. Perform
9. Certain flights
15. Covering over a throne
21. Old Italian port
22. Favoring
23. Chop's relative
24. Creature lacking color
25. Fruity tree, perhaps
27. Old man at the baccarat table, e.g.
29. Slangy negative
30. Ivy League campus
32. Cups' friends
33. Coarse sound of laughter
34. Girl's name
36. Future tulip
38. Spanish agate
39. Duck of a kind
40. Predecessor of British Airways
41. South Pacific native
43. Yo-Yo or top
44. Frame of mind
45. Living-room item
47. Costs
49. Dreadful
50. Husband of Bathsheba
51. Couple
53. Poems
54. Make a ___ case of
57. Type
58. Rural, in France
60. Wind instrument
61. St. Pierre, e.g.
62. Fraternal man
63. Culmination
65. Obligation
66. Container
67. Image
68. Uncle: Scot.
69. Cubes
70. Fixture of midtown N.Y.
72. Low cabinet
76. Large flowerpot
78. Extraordinary
79. English designer's fruit, perhaps
81. Majority
82. German number
83. Talking bird
84. Fares
85. Colleen's home
86. Childish pouts
88. Kind of dance
91. Hgt.
92. Musical passage
93. Baby carriage
95. Future roses
96. Edge of woven fabric
98. Very: Ger.
99. Bank function
100. Morse and others
101. ___ does it
102. Classman
104. Monochrome
106. Minor slip
108. Gov't. agency
109. Accounting word
111. Winged
112. Work on copy
113. Conjecture
115. Gentlemen
116. Passed over
119. Pronoun
120. Czech composer
122. Sitting
124. Attention
125. Underground artists, maybe
128. Was pertinent
130. City of N. W. Spain
131. Distracted: Fr.
132. Shrill bark
133. Actor Delon
134. Centaur of myth
135. Give more medication
136. Hindu title
137. East ___

DOWN

1. Irish woman patriot
2. Everyday
3. Verging on
4. Slower, in music: Abbr.
5. Train unit
6. Burning
7. State: Abbr.
8. Trunk façades
9. Seafood item
10. Large cask
11. Lawyers: Abbr.
12. Of old Troy
13. Avenges
14. Exterior wall coverings
15. Framework
16. Beverages
17. Knicks' league: Abbr.
18. Rich Texan of 1800s, perhaps
19. Of the lungs: Prefix
20. New ___
26. Veranda
28. Wriggly
31. Abner's partner
35. Wanderer
37. Overdecorated symbols of bad luck?
39. Entice
41. Dakota Indians
42. Insect nest
44. Skin
45. Seed covering
46. Elizabethan song
48. Letter
49. Overcame
50. Luau music maker
52. Star: Fr.
54. Ring weapons
55. Accompanying
56. Eyeglass: It.
59. S. A. Indian
60. Musical notes
63. Minor prophet
64. Teaching
66. Upright: Abbr.
67. Isfahan's land
68. Austen novel
69. Graduation awards: Abbr.
70. Market again
71. U.S. author
72. Spanish beds
73. Reichenbach's hypnotic force
74. Homers by Mickey, perhaps
75. Lyric poem
77. Arena performer
80. Shade of green
85. Set of values
86. Signified
87. Indian buffalo: Var.
88. Old English coach?
89. European river
90. Road curve
92. Instance
93. Japanese coin
94. Quoting France's XVI, perhaps
95. Gaucho weapons
97. Immense
98. Marine art
100. Popular American decor
102. Moira or Norma
103. Put out a new edition
105. Rumanian king
106. Instruction
107. Stick to
108. Stock
110. Seminary title: Abbr.
113. Pearly items
114. Basted
116. Low Greek pillars
117. Dine at home
118. Sluggard
120. Christ, in poetry
121. Incan beaker
123. Box
126. Important workers: Abbr.
127. Relatives of sts.
129. Culbertson

108 Adverbs a la Tom Swift by Edward O'Brien

ACROSS

1. "Cards?" asked Tom ___
10. Mild oaths
17. ___ Swifties
20. Buy stocks in hope of a rise
21. "It will fly," said Wilbur ___
23. Good guys
24. Possibilities in a 3-way armature
25. "___ see"
26. "Times try men's souls," said Tom ___
28. Wept: Scot.
29. Relatives of inches: Abbr.
30. Assert
32. Reclined
33. Man's nickname
35. Patronal feast
37. Agcy. of 40's
40. Adjusts to
45. Singer Perry
48. Mend socks
49. Messy food
50. ___, error: Baseball trio
51. Incite
52. Waste allowance
53. Cow part
55. Girl's name
56. Life: Lat.
58. Once-controversial plane, the F ___
60. Of unbelievers
63. Macaw
64. "Instant coffee," said Tom ___
66. Expect: Lat.
68. "___ thing," said Midas touchingly
70. "Moo," said Elsie ___
71. "I can't," ___ philosophically
73. ___ Grande
74. "Here," said Tom ___
75. Fate
78. Prisoner ___
81. Hilly City
82. Korean city
84. Rel. of a xylophone
87. Men of the cloth: Abbr.
88. "___," sighed Beatrice infernally
91. Red gem
92. Ohio town
93. Wolf: Prefix
94. "Take heart," said ___ coolly
95. Onassis
96. Squirming
98. Self
100. Family man
101. Stein words
102. Droop
105. ___- bitty
109. Words in Xmas hymn
114. Fiji pine
116. Heavyweight name
118. "It adds up," Tom said ___
120. "Be witty," ___ epigrammatically
121. Of voting
122. Cricket sides
123. "Bad music," said Milton ___
124. "I sang and danced," said ___

DOWN

1. "Love," said Don ___
2. Vine-covered
3. Religious units
4. Vibrato: Abbr.
5. ___ challenge (is tested)
6. Indian word
7. Flying time?
8. She-wolf: Lat.
9. City in Michigan
10. "Martini," said Tom ___
11. Mature
12. Pasts
13. Ideas: Abbr.
14. "___ you it's true"
15. Of a decade
16. Toper
17. Russian ruler
18. Spanish jar
19. Agatha Christie work: Abbr.
22. City on Skye
27. Denial
31. Constitutional addition: Abbr.
34. South Bend campus
35. Communist boycott of a parley?
36. Three: Ger.
37. Aged
38. Dais
39. "___ for your thoughts"
41. "John ith," lisped ___
42. "Drop by drop," said ___
43. "Neap," said Tom ___
44. Actor Keach
45. Knight: Abbr.
46. Kimono sash
47. "I ___," said Simon simply
49. "I've no last name," said Hilda ___
54. Postal initials
57. Antoinette
59. Eskimo hut
61. Indisposed
62. Rio ___
65. Norse city
66. Indian lute
67. All: Prefix
68. S. A. mammal
69. "___ mark, get set . . ."
71. Salmon
72. Peaks: Abbr.
76. Took excessive medicine
77. Short skirt
79. Curved line
80. Relative of Army Q.M.
83. Where: Lat.
85. Golf duffers, so to speak
86. Locomotives: Abbr.
89. Digit
90. Glue: Sp.
96. Army woman
97. The date: Sp.
99. ___ mio (dear me)
100. Table mat
102. Bagpipe sound
103. Large halls
104. "The Beggar's Opera," wrote John
105. "___ sorry"
106. Sir, in Asia
107. Pronoun
108. Synagogue instrument
110. Defense offices: Abbr.
111. But, in Paris
112. Israeli airline
113. Donkey: Lat.
115. To the king, in France
117. Romans' 2,100
119. Old farmer's monogram

109 Country Air   by Arnold Moss

ACROSS

1. Rural crossing
6. Italian poet
11. Attach
16. "The ___ Fellow"
21. Ataturk
22. Water animal
23. Register
24. Excessive
25. Kind of sandwich
27. Barrier
29. Verne hero
30. Trifles: Fr.
31. Con ___, in music
32. Mercury
33. Ten percenter
34. Cloth trimmings
35. Turner
36. Manolete et al.
40. Moon stage
41. Animal feet
45. Baffles
46. Hangman's tool
47. Transported in a way
48. Bum ___
49. Andrea ___
50. Snack-tray items
53. Sitar music
54. Signed
55. Hep
56. Buzzing
57. TV personality
58. ___ were
59. Tanker
60. Scaloppine
61. Preparing for an exam
62. Mayday's cousin
63. Antlers of Sherwood Forest deer
66. Army command
67. Native places
69. Unfashionable
70. Cud
71. Fruitcake ingredient
73. Words of bafflement
79. River, in Thailand
82. On ship
83. Clears
84. Revolted
85. Insect nests
86. Recently
87. Broadway offering
88. Arrow poison
90. Venetian bridge
91. Uno, dos, ___
92. Odd couple
94. Waters
95. Suffer
96. Wallops
97. Go for, as a pitched ball
98. Existentialist writer
99. Tennis-court limit
101. Paint filler
102. Like a courtyard
104. ___ da-fé
105. One who grieves
106. Shoe gadgets
107. Medical
110. Vogue
111. Hear of
112. "South Pacific" star
116. Congé
118. Food for Pahlavi
120. Bonne ___
121. Judge's call
122. Dine, in Bonn
123. Spirits
124. Supervises
125. Dull
126. Metric measure
127. Trail

DOWN

1. ___ deep
2. Gallic head
3. Moslem leader
4. French composer
5. Whitney
6. More classy
7. Site of U. of Georgia
8. Stretch, in Scotland
9. Indian weights
10. Pirate gold
11. Shawnee chief
12. "Who . . . believed ___"
13. Sevareid and others
14. ___ avail
15. Norse name
16. Made a chess move
17. Open
18. First mate
19. ___ of thumb
20. Wrigglers
26. Odysseus's dog
28. Wall St. items
31. Debacle
33. Beat ___ horse
34. "Hamlet" role
35. Also-ran
36. In ___ res
37. "Tempest" role
38. Driers
39. Go on ___
40. Models
41. Muskets
42. Eastern times
43. Conestogas
44. Sprinkle
46. U.S. Japanese
47. Playwright Brendan
50. Gulps
51. Durant
52. Jug
53. Hindu title
57. "You've ___" (I give up)
59. Upright
60. Do a civic duty
61. Kind of hydrometer
63. Atlanta university
64. Gulps down
65. Charioteer
68. Some exams
70. Picardy output
71. Harvard man
72. Michener opus
73. Tardy
74. Mets and Yanks
75. Eye swelling: Var.
76. Cerumen
77. Snake
78. Actor Rip
80. Cling to
81. Deceived
85. Explosive, for short
87. Peter Nero's forte
88. Lined, as a roof
89. Complete
90. Pinnipeds
92. Hairpiece
93. Dense tree growth
96. Channels
98. Opera part
100. Won
101. Colanders
102. Pencil part
103. Herb genus
105. Home of many Goyas
106. Succinct
107. "___ first you don't . . ."
108. English composer
109. State: Abbr.
110. Region: Abbr.
111. For fear that
112. Power Source: Abbr.
113. Novelist Grey
114. "___ love with you"
115. News item
117. Cut off
118. Footlike part
119. Explosives: Abbr.

110 Two-Way Middles
by Joan DeRosso

ACROSS

1. Shepherd of Tekoa
5. Something for Garcia
12. Quartz
18. Familiar, old style
20. Arranged; disarranged
21. ___ Thule
22. Extreme
23. One who says "I do"
24. Whirl past
25. Long cloaks
27. D'Annunzio's inamorata
28. Flu symptoms
29. Spanish eights
30. Turn away
32. Incited, as a dog
34. Articulated
36. English county
37. Thailand's neighbor
38. Codlike fish
39. Cautious
40. Softens
41. Genetic initials
44. Golf club
45. Twisted
46. ___ order
47. Mast
48. Cassowary's cousin
49. Subdue; baton stroke
51. Telegram
52. Take off
54. Maple genus
55. Beaches
56. Beak membrane
57. Lighter
59. Bearing
61. Zeus's blood
64. Spring beer
65. Scales
69. Mastwood
70. Impend; aftermath of sorts
74. Stop ___ dime
75. Aria
76. Small change
77. Avifauna
78. Complacent
79. Poets' early days
80. Imparts
81. Places
82. Metric unit
83. German craft
85. Portions
86. Dental problem
87. Forks' tablemates
88. Did a hair job
89. Interrupt
90. Community character
91. English composer
92. Le Mans events
95. Pretty girl, familiarly
97. Arrived, with a bar
100. Reef
101. Illinois city
102. Some British students
103. Island near Zanzibar
104. Most strange
105. Thickly
106. Believe

DOWN

1. ___ of good cheer
2. Breakwater
3. View, and be careful
4. Afflicted
5. Longitude lines: Abbr.
6. W. W. II initials
7. Everything
8. Leggy
9. Encourage
10. Alluvium
11. French verb
12. Menu word
13. Andes animals
14. Troublesome
15. Fool with a bowling target
16. Plant
17. Beams
19. Minces
20. Goddess of hope
26. Offspring
30. Lend ___
31. Zodiac sign
32. Apia's area
33. "___ my heart in ..."
34. Recoils
35. City in Italy
36. "On the Beach" author
37. Cornelia, for one
39. Fad
40. Potato
42. Ointment
43. Greek god
45. Milldam
46. Quondam
47. Proust man
49. Uncle Remus word
50. ___ straight line
53. Image: Prefix
55. Scorch
57. Brest and Boston
58. German exclamations
59. European thrush
60. St. Pierre and others
61. ___ dixit
62. Composed
63. Rob, and support
64. Divers' affliction
65. Premium
66. Enter with a paycheck
67. Accustom: Var.
68. Wise ones
70. "Neptune's ___"
71. Outlets
72. Static
73. Avarice
78. Channeled
80. Undoes
81. Hippie park events
82. Petty ruler
84. Man of odds
85. French revolutionist
86. Nasty one
87. Endured
88. Penned
89. Alley dwellers
90. Roper
91. Word on a brandy bottle
92. Pika
93. Bohemian river
94. Bridge bid
96. Inactive: Abbr.
98. Never: Ger.
99. Relative of qt.

111 Bundle of Nerves by Frances Hansen

ACROSS

1. Wee: Scot.
4. Injures
9. Lincoln Center ladies
14. Dewlapped
20. Between quatre and six
22. Standish's advocate
23. Zola
24. Crown in a way
25. Moving: Lat.
26. Massey
27. Outer reaches
28. Former German republic
29. Honshu city
30. Purport
31. Attach
32. Royal fur
33. Dice maneuver
37. Packs tightly
38. "Be it ___ so . . ."
39. Hearty drink
40. Canines
42. Colette novel
45. Dixieland, for short
48. Jewish eves
51. Grand or Petit
55. After 38 Across
57. Echo of the Third Reich
59. Alas, in old Rome
61. City near Boys Town
62. Early church pulpit
63. Tree
68. Cap
69. Extend over
70. Morris's naked ape
71. Most artless
72. Adorned: Fr.
73. Loy
75. Choir member: Abbr.
76. Sappy trees
77. Played an ice game
79. Greenland base
81. Made a catty sound
82. "Oh dear"
83. Minos, for one
86. Two ___
88. Grate on
90. Make ___ at
94. Brinker
95. Shoo, early style
97. Under
99. Girl's name
100. Lupino
101. Robin Hood's backpack
103. Recess
104. Town S. W. of Saigon
106. Branches: Bot.
107. Forsaken
108. Interweave, as twigs
110. Roots
112. In ___ (befuddled)
115. What is it?
117. Heady stuff
118. Adjective suffixes
120. Island off Sumatra
122. Present
124. Ship post
127. Joe Jacobs's remark (with "I")
135. Buddhist monks
137. Suffix for flirt or visit
138. Terrain: Abbr.
139. Miffed
140. Boil inwardly
141. Date-ripening stage
142. Rouse
143. Quiz
144. Hospital worker
145. Coolers
146. Come up again
147. Senor's assent
148. "And ___ not into . . ."
149. Organ stop: Var.
150. Duel preludes
151. Lepidopterist's aid

DOWN

1. Analyzes verse
2. Biblical prophet
3. Sinuses
4. Proprietor: Fr.
5. Listening intently
6. Surprise wedding response
7. Forget ___
8. Foul-ups
9. Lose hope
10. Encroach on
11. Bit of food
12. Star near Mizar
13. "Eyes have they, but they ___"
14. Brilliant salesman
15. Oddball
16. Trinket
17. Keats poem
18. Antelope
19. Works of a French painter
21. Friends' hats
34. Kind of eye
35. Civil War general
36. Breathers
41. Noun suffix
42. Deep gap
43. Like a camel's back
44. Hinder
46. Topic
47. Virile one
49. Do a job on a lily
50. Slice thinly
52. Special kind of day
53. Midwest terminal
54. Yclept
56. Biblical suffix
58. Saud
60. Compass points
64. George Herman
65. Daunted by
66. Town in north Nebraska
67. Engrave
72. Grammarians' concerns
74. ___ loss
76. Likewise
78. Fringefoot
80. Korean apricot
81. Prado locale
82. Lined up
83. Marx brother
84. Speed-trap item
85. As a friend: Fr.
86. Hindu god
87. Fluid affliction
88. Lewis
89. Incomparable
91. Marriage pledge
92. Soap plant
93. Man in white
96. Cherry brandy
97. Relative: Abbr.
98. Compass point
101. Give up
102. Shake like ___
105. Distraught
109. Atmosphere: Prefix
111. Quonset huts' relatives
113. Pyrenees state
114. Ben-Gurion, for one
116. Unnerved
119. Penetrate fully
121. Spectral types
123. Lawn tools
124. Flavoring leaf
125. Good-night girl
126. Greek letter
128. City on the Mohawk
129. Green colors
130. Symbol of ring defeat
131. Shadowy: Lat.
132. Corner
133. Blot out
134. Resign
136. Road-routing sign

112 Phrasing It Right
by Jack Luzzatto

ACROSS

1. Boil down
7. Fine feather
12. British orderlies
18. Charm
19. Marrying in haste
21. Hard area of a strawberry
22. Device showing the solar system
23. McLuhan word
24. Kind of card
25. Busy
26. Nasty impulse
27. "He knoweth the way that ___"
29. Ideology
30. Monastery man: Abbr.
31. Composer Albeniz
33. Irish lord of yore
35. Reed common in Calif.
36. Hebrew letter
38. Prong
39. Gormandizers
41. Apart from
43. French movie
44. Sun: Prefix
45. Kind of battery
47. "Fidelio" overture
50. Windshield cleaner
53. Formal scolding
55. Old clothes
56. Flowed steadily
59. Choral work: Abbr.
60. Jargon
62. Holy Roman emperor:
63. Make over
64. In error
68. Cap ___
69. Refined guy
70. Swell
71. Pikelike fish
72. Job for the lazy
74. Garroway
75. Junior snowplows
77. Name for Shropshire
78. Old word for sailors
81. Poet
82. Seeker of the flame
84. Stringy
85. Preserves
87. Memory
91. Deadly kind of race
92. Peak
96. Irish island
97. Infallible authority
98. Fight off
100. Put the whammy on
101. Edge
102. City
103. Central parts
105. Unconnected
107. Ocean-study craft
109. Ringed, as a belle
111. Strike back for
112. Open up
113. Western ranges
114. Closet item
115. Steady
116. Cause to think twice
117. In the wake

DOWN

1. East Indian cedar
2. Dress in
3. West Indians
4. Straw in the wind
5. Welsh dog
6. The least one can do
7. Summer flounder
8. Hopeless, as a cause
9. Rendering fruitless
10. Farrow
11. Manipulate events
12. Sponsor unwisely
13. Square area
14. Article
15. McLuhan word
16. Leave on a lonely shore
17. Tennis players
19. Put on a jury list
20. Gain entry
26. Pronounced
28. Author Sholem
32. Meddling
34. Certain cartoons
35. Threefold
37. Stoppage
40. Journalist Abel
42. ___ Arabia
43. Work with
45. Ship taken by Jones
46. Music maker
48. Seize, old style
49. Word in Kansas motto
51. Appears
52. Made a new hand
53. She-wolves: Sp.
54. Like a beaver
57. U.S. missiles
58. Active people
61. Crescent-shaped article: Var.
62. Baby bird
65. Coal barge worker
66. Ambassador
67. Hollow stone
73. Unemotional
74. Amusing
76. Passport entry
79. Spider
80. Diatribes
83. German title
86. Diamond appraisers
87. Ankle
88. Express of fame
89. Condiment
90. Imprisons
91. Unpaid bill
93. Shift
94. Combination
95. Hosp. aide
99. Scoria
102. Faulty pitch
104. Monster
106. Held in
108. Tennis shot
110. Gosh!
111. So!

113 Musically Speaking

by Alfio Micci

ACROSS

1. Fares
6. Provides
11. ___ days
16. Dark color
21. Strad's cousin
22. Relation
23. Indian of Peru
24. Storms
25. Telephone sound
27. Child's game
29. Marie and others: Abbr.
30. At the: It.
31. Representations
33. Claws
34. Wing: Fr.
35. Abusive person
36. ___ de-camp
37. Politely
41. Lebanese port
42. Gaelic
43. Black Sea arm: Var.
47. Blackbirds
48. Untidy one
50. Vacation spot
51. Make joyful
52. Street sights
53. King of Judah
54. Gets
55. ___ wolf
56. Arachnid
57. Agenda
61. Aliped
62. Relative of ltd.
63. River into Lake Chad
65. Constellation
66. Misses a deadline
68. Inquire
69. Postal warning
73. Roman way
74. Pitcher
76. Porgy of Japan
77. Gazelle
78. Hasty
80. Old slave
82. "___ in air"
88. Uncle: Scot.
91. Go over with a brush
93. Corrode
94. Prods
95. Needlefish
96. Countrywide: Abbr.
97. Cavalry men
100. Turkish inn: Var.
101. Girl's name
102. ___ bagatelle
104. Swedish district
105. Bequeaths
106. Cheeses
107. Water worms
108. Took a match to
111. Entreaty, in France
112. Resting places
113. Shipbuilder
114. Like dirt roads
115. Farm man
116. House plant
117. Coins
118. Eur. land
119. Extended
123. Purport
124. Potpourri
125. "Je t'___"
129. Question for a vanishing lady?
131. Musical troublemaker
134. Semblance
135. Bits
136. Of a space
137. Unrefined
138. Discourage
139. "___ are my jewels"
140. Abodes of a kind
141. Three grains

DOWN

1. Locomotive areas
2. Neglect
3. Labyrinth
4. Vous ___
5. Form a lap
6. Over-ornamented
7. Ern
8. Burner
9. Day: Sp.
10. Entreats
11. Pundit
12. Lend ___
13. Myrna and family
14. City official: Abbr.
15. Pedantic
16. Feel for
17. Grate
18. Author James
19. Equal
20. Arctic People: Abbr.
26. Navigates
28. André
32. Zip ___
34. ___ in one's bonnet
35. Composer Erik
36. Peaceful place
37. Fielding title
38. Criminals
39. Musical creator of monster?
40. Der ___
41. Fraction
42. Comfort
43. Exclamation
44. Quinn, Norwegian style?
45. Decorative
46. Rankle
48. Scottish landowner
49. Exclamation of disgust
50. Observed
52. Govt. agent
57. Eastern title
58. Tough cord
59. Military initials
60. Architectural rib
63. Pronoun
64. Conceal
65. Be ___ man for it
67. Fleur de ___
70. On the ___ (fleeing)
71. Biblical mountain
72. In a random way
75. Sopping
79. Legal chiefs: Abbr.
80. Verdi opus
81. Tar
83. Movie initials
84. Kind of harp
85. Degrees
86. Musical syllables
87. Car parts: Abbr.
89. Ravel's "___ l'Oye"
90. Pencil part
92. Highways: Abbr.
98. Course
99. Conclude
100. Pleated skirts
101. Colleen's isle
103. Thorough-fares: Abbr.
105. Petty pier thief
106. Spoiled one
108. ___ over
109. Disease of plants
110. Smoke, in Rome
111. Monastery man
113. Want
115. Cooks in a way
116. Hen
117. Painter of dancers
118. Animal cry
119. Roman poet
120. Woman, in law
121. Campus group
122. Margin
123. Head: Fr.
124. Stove part
125. Emanation
126. River to the Danube
127. Tableland
128. Whilom
130. Indian of Northwest
132. Exist
133. At times: Abbr.

114 Merry Month   by Barbara H. Lewis

ACROSS

1. Life story: Abbr.
5. U.S. eider
9. Catty sound
13. "___ wit's end"
19. Irish exclamation
20. Munich's river
21. Auk genus
22. ___ it out
23. Glove
24. Fork part
25. Fibs: Scot.
26. Cockneys' aides
27. Residue
28. Coarse cloths
29. Cried
30. Thirst, in France
31. Spartan serf
33. Italian city
35. This: Sp.
37. Threshold
40. Tricksy
41. More adroit
43. Two ___
45. Food fish
46. Compass point
48. Addams
49. Old Rumanian coin
50. Plant
51. Without tines
54. Panay native
55. Late actor Robert
57. Evergreen
58. Montague
59. V.I.P.'s in Br. navy
61. Rich men
64. Ramble, old style
66. Eur. capital
68. Grain
70. "'Twas ___ oyster" (Pope)
71. "Let all thy ___" (Quarles)
76. Charity
77. ___ minute
78. Defective: Prefix
79. Seed coat
80. ___ eye dog
82. Hebrew letter
84. Wander aimlessly
86. Certain vote
89. Saturated
91. Pan-cook
92. Yelling
94. Suffix with dull or drunk
96. Yellow bugle
97. Homestead, old style
99. W.W. I initials
100. "A ___ B as..."
101. Mormon word
103. Gas
105. Oz figure and others
107. Stain
108. "Woe ___!"
110. Arabian gulf
111. English composer
112. Own: Scot.
114. Caesar's alas
116. Cabbages
118. Hither's partner
120. Drum
122. Pressure unit
123. Paton
124. Tool
125. Greek letters
126. Dominion
127. Take it easy
128. Neighbor of Thailand
129. Spring time
130. Mine yields
131. Panama: Abbr.
132. Unfledged bird

DOWN

1. Crimson Tide, for short
2. Tales of Old Sod
3. "...fairer than the day ___" (Wither)
4. Channel
5. "I shall love you in December ___" (Joyce)
6. Land mass
7. Ingredient of steel
8. Throng: Fr.
9. Springtime words of Chaucer
10. Robt. ___
11. Realm of Cyrus the Great
12. Rebecca et al.
13. "In March, July, October, May the ___ day"
14. Venus locale
15. Like a snake
16. Spring aphorism
17. Mal de ___
18. Lengths: Abbr.
28. Sea call
32. Mortgage
34. Between tic and toe
36. Related
38. Zodiac sign
39. Wallace
40. Discern
42. Dine in
44. Food fish
47. Lion slain by Hercules
52. Snatch
53. Black stuff
56. Astern
60. Descendant
62. Farm sound
63. Messy place
65. Bone: Lat.
67. Fish delicacy
69. Dress
71. Man's name: Abbr.
72. Corrida cheer
73. Utter
74. Auto man
75. Innkeeper, in Italy
81. Black: Fr.
83. Man ___
85. Order of woody plants
87. Animal parasites
88. Greek contest
90. Arab shrubs
93. Ruler
94. Classified items
95. Old car
98. Tiny one
102. Exalted
104. S.A. monkey: Var.
106. Fr. pronoun
109. Paris subway
113. Jot
115. Gardner
117. Wear
119. Cape
120. Pro ___
121. Honshu town
124. Drink

115 Peering In by Mary M. Murdoch

ACROSS

1. Woolly fabric
7. Poplar
12. Blacksmith's need
17. Hindu deity
21. Vines
22. State
23. Treaty org.
24. ___ du Salut
25. Flower
27. Old railroad showpieces
29. Classmen: Abbr.
30. ___ one goes (stays solvent)
31. Small sum
32. Hawaiian emblem
33. Corbett or Braddock
34. Rulers
36. Caama
37. Beverage
40. Nymph wed to Paris
42. Gun extra
46. Burden
47. Spoil for a fight
51. British parallel of U.S.M.A.
52. Agreement
53. Destitute of water: Abbr.
54. Black
55. Comic-strip captain
56. Ness, for one
57. Revolutionary figure
58. Some temples in Japan
60. Gypsy village
61. Kind of house or boat
62. Sly look
63. Chem. suffix
64. Window part
65. Eye part
66. Graduated series: Abbr.
67. Birds
72. Appoint
73. Hot-dog places
75. "___ but you"
76. Saddle horse
77. "...ate ___ meal"
79. Compiler of certain rules
81. Girl's group: Abbr.
84. "___ midi d'un Faune"
85. Kiss
86. Land measure
87. Mil. groups
88. Sing in a way
89. Indian
90. For ___ being
94. Dash
95. Sacred bull
96. Adversaries
98. Horse
99. Girl's nickname
100. Eye cell
101. Fasten
102. Fish stocks
105. Whale
106. Pro football team
108. Access
109. Dept. store employe
110. Picnic guests
111. Flagmaker
112. Throw off balance
116. Ornamental stone
119. Rows
120. Rail rod
121. Auditor
124. Dance
126. Flowers
129. Will-___-wisp
130. Lake ___
131. French king
132. Gob
133. Dictator
134. Smarted
135. Plus-side item
136. Bristle

DOWN

1. "___ well"
2. Story teller
3. Tablets
4. Some
5. One of the magi
6. Shillong's land
7. Wrong
8. Capuchin monkey
9. Apple parts
10. Direction
11. Saul's uncle
12. Yearns
13. Tidies
14. Farewell: Lat.
15. Give ___ try
16. Poetic Hall
17. Make abundant
18. Soviet range
19. Blackbird
20. Holly
26. Caustic
28. Comforts
31. Counting-out word
33. Cap-and-bells fellow
34. That's ___ (not allowed)
35. Friars
36. Oaks: Scot.
37. Tree resins
38. Very soon: Slang
39. Lace
41. Summary: Abbr.
42. Urbane
43. Some people's hair
44. TV personalities
45. Shout
47. Ballet step
48. Inconvenient
49. Paraphernalia
50. Dizzy and Daffy
56. Blackmore girl
59. Ship-shaped clock
60. French stations
61. Heyward character
64. Famous Quaker
65. Murmuring sound
67. Girl's name
68. Opposites of exts.
69. Current
70. Old-time tubs
71. Implement
72. Jury member
74. Root plants
76. Wool fabric
77. Cartoonist
78. Fiend: Sp.
79. Pursuit
80. Cudgel
82. Golf term
83. Equally close
85. Fox and Rabbit
87. Get back
90. Tipsters
91. Word in an O'Neill title
92. Fr. pronoun
93. Letters
96. Hosiery-counter items
97. Baseball term
98. Type sets
102. Irish tribe
103. Dispenser at a clambake
104. Soubriquet for Clemenceau
107. Angry one
109. College post
111. Large ball: Sp.
113. Strike again
114. Truck union: Abbr.
115. Italian dish
116. Tax
117. Butter units
118. Section of Vedic writing
119. Locale of Diamond Head
120. Containers
121. Headgear
122. Guard: Abbr.
123. Movie dog
125. Angkor ___
126. Nepal native
127. Norway town
128. Numerical prefix

116 Going Places by Bruce R. Shaw

ACROSS

1. Name in U.S. banking
5. Record: Prefix
10. Beer feature
14. Small blister
18. Dies ___
19. Beach product
20. Years: Lat.
21. Fence
22. Skin: Prefix
23. Custom-house: Sp.
24. Folding money
25. Blue: Prefix
26. Trolley center of note
29. Interest moneys
31. Organ stop
33. Counting-out word
34. Tossers, usually of mud
35. Trap
37. Brontë
39. Stand: Lat.
40. Young one
41. Dusting powder
43. Coalition
44. Immoral
48. Hagen
49. Intertwine
52. Weak
54. Egg: Prefix
55. Hair job
57. Bounces off
59. Abstruse
60. Of a Bronze Age culture
61. Chemical prefix
63. Knockout punch
65. Sequin
67. 4,000 chilly miles
72. Japanese wax trees
73. Mountain chain
74. Defendants, in law
75. Skillfully
76. Kiln
78. "Last of the Romans"
80. Choke
84. There: Lat.
85. Rasping sound
87. "___ my right arm for . . ."
89. Arts degree
90. Sky sight
92. Seaweed substance
94. Truly
95. ___ gratia
96. Catch
97. Chides
99. 8-point type
101. Qualifies
105. Fastener
108. Leaflike parts
109. Bearded
110. Train-tune town
112. Melody
113. Game fish
115. Illinois city
116. Over
119. Bell sound
120. During
121. Special
122. Advice, old style
123. Surfeit
124. Vogue
125. Finnish lake
126. North Sea tributary

DOWN

1. Eye part
2. Galena
3. Puffball-like fungus
4. Wail
5. City slicker
6. Take effect
7. Stanza
8. Tooth
9. Out ___ (insecure)
10. Lot
11. Undivided
12. Cancel
13. St. Louis sight
14. Cause
15. Old weapon
16. Duck
17. Joy
19. Nob Hill sight
27. Sound off
28. Byron heroine
30. Caper
31. Prepare
32. $100 bill
34. Old Chinese money
36. Jazz lady
38. Bi-level British bus
42. Medit. tree
45. Let pass
46. Palate part
47. Preferred
50. Pennsylvania wagon place
51. Abrasive, in France
53. Plateau
56. Virile
58. Bull: Ger.
60. Strip of gear
62. Davis domain: abbr.
64. World ___
66. Brew
67. Teach
68. Hasidic leader
69. Improvise
70. Danube tributary
71. ___ bell
77. Goes up
79. African fly
81. Surrenders
82. Precipitation
83. Poker holdings
85. List
86. Cabbage milieu
88. Before febrero
91. Specified amount
93. Backslide
98. Smooth cloth
100. Caprice
101. Old oaths
102. Water wheel
103. Spoil
104. Fluid swelling
106. Roman wear
107. Fruit gadget
110. Morse, for one
111. French resort
114. Fit out
117. Pindaric
118. Each

117 Step On It by Threba Johnson

ACROSS

1. Kind of warrant
7. Bullfighter's cloak
11. Khan
14. Iowa town
18. A kiss ___
20. Junto
21. It. coins: Abbr.
22. Italian philosopher
23. Sculpture site
25. ___ draw
27. Historic island
28. Do a pitching job
29. Small passage
30. Bible book: Abbr.
31. English astronomer
32. Within: Prefix
34. Kind of mother
35. Nichols hero
36. Vital item in the West
41. 1965 movie
44. Rapid view: Fr.
45. Handbag
47. Hairpiece
48. Goose egg
49. Of Apollo's island
50. Slave
51. Bulwark
54. Part of a journey
57. Meager
59. English school
61. "Life ___ dream"
62. ___ cry
63. Impassive
65. Disburse
67. "___ the chief"
69. East Indian tree
72. Fall apple
74. Glacial stage
76. Famous poem
77. Trivial amount
80. Daily grind
82. After-drink drinks
84. Pavlova and others
85. Open a bit
87. Sister of Orestes
89. Ship's rope
90. Place for Italian drama
92. Certify
94. "Five-foot-two, ___ blue . . ."
97. Norse goddess
98. Army man: Abbr.
100. Adjust
102. Heard a court case again
105. Arabic place name
106. More thorny
108. Thin
110. Alert color
112. Hezekiah's mother
114. Nouns: Abbr.
115. Point of dispute
117. Lung part
118. Ordinary
122. Newman movie
125. Major or Minor
126. Part of a Marquand title
127. ___ Khan
129. Take for ___
130. Tumble: Scot.
131. Certain flower
133. Make wide changes
135. Aoudad
139. Control-tower data
141. Beginning of a fast trip
143. " . . . by ___ unresting sea"
144. Got: Abbr.
145. Rockfish
146. "___ Kilimanjaro"
147. Outside: Prefix
148. Chemical prefix
149. Drinks
150. Photo print

DOWN

1. Identical
2. Chemical compound
3. Rub- ___
4. Frog genus
5. Lab man: Abbr.
6. Gilden novel
7. Arrived
8. Upstairs
9. Family people
10. Drink
11. African grass
12. Midwest city
13. "Stay ___ you are"
14. Scottish alder
15. Part of the navy
16. Imitative
17. Small Asian bird
19. Folksy poet
20. Exercises
22. Bashful
24. Plod heavily
26. Blue Nile source
29. Man's nickname
31. Pour gently
33. Beat ___
35. Greek nickname
36. Hula hoop or skate board
37. Copies
38. Order to broker
39. Efforts
40. ___ Dimittis
42. Weight: Abbr.
43. Explosive
46. Fix leftovers
50. Galway's land
52. Assess a fine
53. Cheer
55. Greasy-spoon
56. ___ Pointe
58. Girl's name
60. Fast train
62. Pretensions
64. Rid of vermin
66. Relative
68. P.I. native
69. Thinker, for one
70. Hummeling machines
71. English satirist
73. French writer
75. Rocky debris
78. Course
79. Medit. land
81. Does a tailor's job
83. Harvard club
86. Part of a nursery rhyme
88. Phoenician port
91. Against: Abbr.
93. In a scary way
95. Threatening words
96. ___ mignon
99. Seine
101. Strained
103. Jewish month
104. Having gold
106. Thor's wife
107. Doctrine
109. Transports again
111. Cold ___
113. Scarf
116. Ate noisily
118. Drum sound
119. Of the Finno-Ugric language
120. Kind of dress
121. Adjective suffix
123. Wool: Prefix
124. Ant and Black
128. "When shall we two ___?"
131. Exclamations
132. Skink
134. Gil ___
135. "A one, ___"
136. New Yorker man
137. Space mysteries
138. Undecided
140. Man's name: Abbr.
141. Sky Altar
142. ___ -de-rol

118 Choice Words by Jean Reed

ACROSS

1. Bridge call
5. Make ___
11. Heroes of W.W. I
17. Provides power
20. Make a member
21. Brush holder
22. With "not," firm disavowal
24. Roll
25. Cargo: Abbr.
26. City on the Aare
27. Human group
29. Half a fly
30. Novelist Kingsley
32. Yellow-fever pioneer
33. British plotter
35. Fr. pronoun
36. Riviera resort
38. Poetic word
40. Expense-account item
41. Expert
43. M.I.T. grad: Abbr.
44. Closet catastrophe
46. Car or steak
47. Fairway cry
49. Tills
50. Some peaches
54. Puzzles
58. Enormous
60. China city
61. Indigo
62. Part of Macbeth
64. Social reformer
66. Bosses: Abbr.
67. Escalate
68. Make Greek
70. Musical ending
71. Cleric's degree
72. "Mens ___"
73. W.W. I land
75. European airport
76. Tide's havoc
79. Does edging
81. Ropes for ship ladders
83. Buffet dishes
85. "... ___ your houses"
87. Injury, old style
88. Legal job
89. Candy
92. "___ can never hurt me"
96. Brine
98. Airfoils
99. U.S. dept.
100. "___, dull care!"
101. Sum: Abbr.
102. Standards
104. "... or ___ Hecuba?"
106. Being: Lat.
107. Roy
108. Praying preyer
111. Landmark
113. One: Ger.
114. Medium's specialty
117. Monetary maxim
120. Slow
121. Bone-breakers of 92 Across
122. Sagacious
123. Compounds
124. Evening glory
125. Impart

DOWN

1. Sweet sorrow, to some
2. Latin case: Abbr.
3. Boor
4. Divides
5. British writer
6. Single: Abbr.
7. Cut short
8. Sharpen
9. Fat
10. Enticing trap
11. City for W.W. I doughboys
12. Pirate gold
13. Pronoun
14. Disaster of 1876
15. Depletes
16. "Union Now" author
17. Blot out
18. Thomas
19. "... the ___, the yellow leaf"
23. "... and ___ grow on"
28. Mil. officers
31. Cold sign
34. Eastern port
37. Chem. compound
39. Snow remover
40. Buffet
42. Peso in Spain
44. Kind of marine
45. "All this and ___"
46. French shouts
48. Home: Abbr.
51. Transfer property
52. Sell
53. Tries
54. Delilah, briefly
55. Grieg girl
56. Ultimatum
57. Eyed
59. Adjust sails
63. Map area: Abbr.
65. Moslem dress
69. Cosa ___
70. Invented word
72. Lyons fabric
74. Marie
77. Moon areas
78. Dramatist
80. Rudiments
82. Smooth, in phonetics
84. Dieter's goal
86. Feature of living
90. ___ quo
91. Form foam
93. Ambled
94. Badge
95. "... eyes, but they ___"
96. French writer
97. Cicero words
98. Angelico
100. Of the north
103. Signs
105. Ascot and Windsor
109. "... ___ the pumpkin"
110. Parallel words: Abbr.
112. Neck part
115. Dir.
116. About: Abbr.
118. Between bee and dee
119. Adam's original

119 Literally So by Anthony Morse

ACROSS

1. Moslem prince
6. Rulers
11. Oceanic tunicate
16. ___ as the eye can see
21. Excuse
22. O'Grady
23. Hum
24. Eli word
25. Maid forages in the pantry
28. Aoudads
29. Duck
30. Subtle qualities
31. Chore
32. 18th century English novelist
33. Dancer of a kind
35. Enclosures
36. Like a football shoe
37. Oriental temple
39. Campus queen
40. African tree
41. Rough
42. Youngsters
44. Rolling pins
48. Chemical suffix
51. Reach for
52. Blacksmith
53. Lumps
54. Sly as ___
55. Fumes
56. Guys
57. Interlude
58. Plantagenet country
59. Fictional Georgia site
60. Lace pattern
61. Beneficiary
62. Forbid to fly
63. Sailors in July and August
65. Bird sound
66. Br. fliers
69. Flag
70. Vietnam port
71. The best
72. Time periods: Abbr.
73. Flexible
75. Moynihan at a White House reception
79. Enter in a way
80. Coquette
81. Miss Lisa et al.
82. Galatea's lover
86. Alaskan native
87. In the natural state
88. Ex-dictator of Venezuela
89. Disposed
90. Cheerio
91. Set of bells
92. Brainy ones
93. Shooting affair
94. Kirghiz city
95. Bargain for Peggy Fleming
97. Iron
98. Glossy cover
100. Spanish city
101. Tops
102. High, in music
103. ___ halt (stopped)
105. Papal vestment
107. Yield
109. Blues
110. Stoop to
111. Austrian province
112. Part of a play
115. Polite refusal
116. A-one tutor
119. Type size
120. Babylonian abode of dead
121. ___ a time
122. Sideshow figure
123. Stage settings
124. Trapshooting
125. Low joints
126. Conditions

DOWN

1. Hosses
2. Moslem teacher
3. Telegrapher
4. Better prepared
5. Twice
6. Groups of thespians
7. Went bad
8. "...wagon to ___"
9. Originate
10. Wine quality
11. Nova ___
12. Okie's neighbor
13. Choice cuts
14. Frost
15. Reply: Abbr.
16. Mitigating agents
17. ___ a boil
18. Seven-plus summer days
19. Straighten
20. Tore down: Var.
26. Current author
27. Groom
32. Chunks
34. Chillers
35. River of Rumania
36. Sloping runway
37. Clever
38. Biblical prophet
40. American author
43. Little chief hare
44. Early source of oil
45. Next to nothing
46. Sleuth material
47. Come in last
49. Neighbor of 12 Down
50. Gives out
52. Wedgelike pieces
54. Wild ox
56. Risible
57. Pushed a punt
58. Court decree
60. City on the Po
61. Cow
62. Namesakes of Italian star
63. ___ out (stay to the end)
64. Divide
65. Gem
66. Stiff collar of 1600's
67. Greek war cries
68. Turn toward the orchestra
71. De Mille
74. Jaeger
75. Decline
76. Currents
77. Daughter of Cymbeline
78. Greek musical works
80. Wife of Odin
82. Greek gulf
83. Dairy farmer
84. Totally
85. Ukrainian river
87. Lobster claw
88. Canal Zone town
89. ___ Vecchio
91. Greek island
92. South Seas wear
93. Rhubarb
95. Food dispenser
96. One of the pharaohs
97. Modern composer
99. Excellence: Sp.
101. North wind
103. Thrashed
104. Chem. compound
105. Carnivora
106. Passage
107. Fruit drink
108. Abalone lining
110. Weapon
111. Ethiopian lake
113. Group
114. Bores
116. Notes
117. Go bad
118. Back

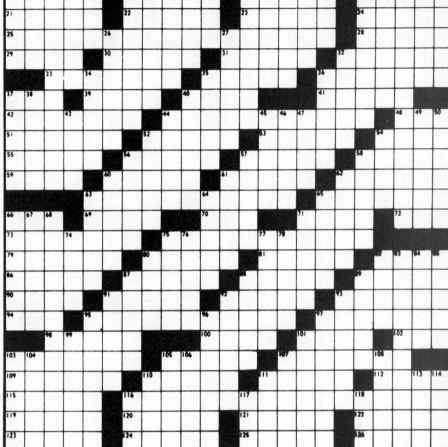

120 Finding a World by Cornelia Warriner

ACROSS

1. Phone book abbr.
4. Wt. units
7. Molasses
14. Marionette-man Tony et al.
19. Involves
21. Burmese port
22. Ghost's need
23. Fish delicacy
24. Indigenous
25. Certain side of life
26. Paving mix
27. Choose
28. Timber spike
30. Math branch
31. No-people
32. Tropical tree
33. Pilot's concern
36. Bakery worker
37. Wood platter
39. Print style: Abbr.
40. River nymph
41. Sea eagle
42. Nautical word
43. Medieval swords
47. Turner
49. Like a hard rain
51. As a friend: Fr.
52. Words describing 1400-1700 A.D.
56. Run in Bea Lillie's hose
57. Guile
58. Certain dives
59. Name in baseball lore
60. Queen of Hearts product
61. Hymenopteron
62. Snack-table item
63. Gloomy Dean
65. Standards of behavior
67. Shattered
72. Bay off White Sea
73. Berry nub
74. Queen Isabella's goal
76. Village in Haiti
77. Memo books
78. Flowing hair
79. Drop in on friends
81. Gas: Prefix
82. Six, in Italy
83. Weskit
87. Earth Day subject: Abbr.
88. Of the stars
90. "To ___ his own"
91. Navigator's route
95. Skill
96. Microwave device
97. Horse color
98. Tree knot
99. Times of day: Abbr.
100. Sly
101. Divert
103. Creatures
106. Easing of tensions
107. Marquis and others
108. "___ d'Arthur"
109. One joining a toast
110. Kind of preview
111. Tenants
112. Gibraltar, for one: Abbr.
113. Noises: Abbr.

DOWN

1. Add varnish
2. Magnify
3. Began
4. Turkish coins
5. Coalition
6. Compass point
7. Cutting tool
8. Declaim
9. Remnant
10. Epoch
11. Long wave
12. French river
13. Applauding for more
14. Draft org.
15. Seneca's prediction in "Medea"
16. Keep on subscribing
17. Columbus's birthplace
18. Block: Var.
20. Title conferred on Columbus
27. ___ sea
29. Moderate
32. Charges
33. Put aside
34. Wobble
35. Scalp parts
37. Care for
38. Athenian demagogue
43. Whatever
44. Aria part
45. Came out
46. Title of respect
48. Astern
49. Weight abbr.
50. Tax agency: Abbr.
52. Play part
53. Magna ___ (Gr. colonies)
54. Mundane
55. Weekday: Abbr.
56. Sass
59. Bacon
61. Tennis score
62. Agnus ___
64. Chemical suffix
66. Untouched
67. Guevara
68. Repair in a way
69. ___ camp
70. Kind of drum
71. Chiefs: Abbr.
72. Everest, for one: Abbr.
73. Elec. unit
74. Geom. lines
75. Jib
77. On the whole
80. Secure
82. Indian weights
84. Curved handrails
85. Like some love letters
86. Reading, etc.
88. Fabrics
89. Egyptian king
91. Kind of widow
92. Cato, for one
93. ___ vie
94. Princess of India
96. Taxi feature
99. Old one: Ger.
100. Fabric
102. Arctic native: Abbr.
104. Sept. and Dec.
105. Land measure
106. Refugees: Abbr.

121 Stepquote by Eugene T. Maleska

ACROSS

1. Start of a 12-word Stepquote ending at 142 Across
7. Infancy
13. "Things ___ what they seem"
19. Poet of Shakespeare's day
20. Permissive
22. Guernsey lilies
24. Greek port
25. Seminole chief
26. Miss Hard, former tennis player
27. Siouan
28. Devours
30. Toned down
32. Preacher's talk: Abbr.
33. Flower holder
35. Pan-fries
37. City in S.E. France
38. Spyri heroine
40. Castle of yesteryear
42. Part of Stepquote
44. Hears rumors about
46. Ali Baba word
48. With 13 Down, source of Stepquote
50. Unventilated
51. "___ 18," Uris novel
53. Best ___
54. Melville novel
55. Diving ducks
58. Legal paper
59. Flower
60. Gives a hand
64. Winnie the Pooh
65. Resumé
67. Dress
69. Extent
71. Follower of Mar.
72. Take off flab
74. Pardon
75. Blandly urbane
76. Visit briefly
78. Bread spread
80. Office gal
81. Companion of Paul
82. Lawyer's homework
83. Of earth: Lat.
85. Native of: Suffix
86. Diner dish
88. In the phone book
90. Judge
91. Liszt's teacher
92. Sonoran Indian
93. Second-hand
95. Port ___
97. Foreordain
99. Cremona creation
101. Hall of Fame name
103. Waste time
104. Spongelike cake
107. Bruised
109. Spread rumors
113. Item that gives confidence
115. Part of Stepquote
117. Scapegrace
118. Concur
119. Head monk
121. All
123. Voluble
124. Shaveling
125. Forceful
127. Atelier items
129. Nabokov heroine
130. City in Calif.
133. Naught
135. Misleads
137. Boxers
138. Magnify
139. Cued up
140. Italian resort
141. Faculties
142. End of Stepquote

DOWN

1. Fourth Sunday in Lent
2. Dictates
3. "Conning Tower" man
4. "___ Kleine Nachtmusik"
5. Greek vowels
6. Part of Stepquote
7. Aaron, Ruth, etc.
8. Held in esteem
9. Olden: Abbr.
10. Was left on base
11. Arrowsmith's wife
12. Photo developer's device
13. See 48 Across
14. Decipher
15. Blunder
16. Nonexistent
17. Way-clearer's words
18. Aegean island
19. Frankish king
21. Sets aside, as a motion
23. Printer's cross-strokes
29. Tree of Pacific
31. Big A action
34. Captivate
36. Surgical instrument: Var.
38. Sign on
39. Form a coalition
41. Give out
43. Part of Stepquote
45. Did dishes
47. Field-hockey team
49. Account book
52. Dry-as-dust
54. Wavered
55. Fencing position
56. Joyful singer
57. Made a slip
59. Undone
61. Man from Teheran
62. Aficionado
63. Folksinger Pete
64. Hines, Tozzi, etc.
66. Mite or tick
68. Skip
70. Town near Padua
72. Appear
73. Troublemaker of myth
77. Hudson River sight
79. Arrives
80. Strong man
84. Offshore hazard
87. City on the Po
89. Thin
91. Dam foundation
94. Author of Stepquote
96. Ending
98. Captured
100. Place for a child's house
101. Islands off New Guinea
102. Presents again
104. Graduated
105. Wild sheep
106. Green
107. Hut: Fr.
108. Place for V.I.P.'s
110. Crusaders' foe
111. Plain
112. Vitiate
114. ___ Saud
116. Part of the Stepquote
120. Tenth part
122. Former queen of Italy
125. White House monograms: 1953-61
126. Oriental Sherlock
128. Bridge bid
131. Baseball V.I.P.
132. Uncle: Scot.
134. Office holders
136. Rubber tree

122 On the Bounding Main by Jogen Rohledge

ACROSS

1. Mil. quarters
4. German hall
8. London network
11. Boom
15. Mineral
16. Entrée
19. Indian shrub
20. Yarn
21. Invincible Armada
25. Melody
26. Launce
27. Shower time
28. U-boat's aid
30. Not so much
31. Go wrong
33. Norse mariner
35. Response: Abbr.
36. Show grief
37. Esoteric knowledge
38. Yellowish brown
43. Kind of sayer
45. Ice: Ger.
46. Forward end
50. Gun attendant
52. Life jacket
54. Tentacle
56. Sea mammal
58. Do a double take
59. Strived
60. British queen
61. Penury
63. Middle East capital
65. Draft agcy.
66. Salty accounts
70. Resin
71. System of plowing
72. Submissive
73. Jurassic division
75. House of
77. ___ River in Poland
79. Chancel seats
81. Mounts
82. Kind of garden
84. Repeated
85. Model's concern
86. Biblical father
87. ___ circle
89. Concise
90. Direct
93. Bikini part
94. Gibbon
97. Never mind!
98. Old warship weapon
99. Moves in circles
103. Navigator's aid
105. Relief org.
107. Offender's concern
110. Musical-work
111. Certain travel fee
114. Get under one's skin
115. Israeli name
116. Group meeting of a kind
117. Tangle
118. Beverages
119. ___ Alte
120. Editor's word
121. Roof finial

DOWN

1. Name for Tweed
2. African village
3. French river
4. Bank items
5. Asian tree
6. Like some bridge hands
7. Shelter
8. Neck wrap
9. Utter joys
10. Lacks ability
11. Navigator's aid
12. Arctic wear
13. Foreigner
14. Old Sp. coins
17. Sea maneuver
18. Drench
19. Relaxes, nautically
22. British body: Abbr.
23. Old salt's words for novices
24. Title of respect
29. Cricket sides
32. Space
34. Censure: Abbr.
38. Code word for A
39. W. Va. town
40. Clingers
41. Defunct auto
42. Caddoan
44. Golf area
46. Born: Fr.
47. Tar
48. Prepares, as a sloop
49. Aphrodite's aide
51. Pays in a way
53. Old habitats
54. More open
55. German number
57. Sierra ___
59. Grove features
62. Triton
64. Daughter of ___
67. Acquired character
68. Eight: Fr.
69. Type style
70. Speak imperfectly
74. French marquis
76. Charge
78. Serai
80. Mil. group
82. River in Bolivia
83. Wax, in prescriptions
86. After Hamlet's "or"
88. Unrestrained
90. Gulf state: Abbr.
91. Like some tuxedoes
92. God of fire
94. "Ad ___ per . . ."
95. Risk
96. Drive out
99. Attack
100. Br. fliers
101. Reproach
102. Purse part
104. ___ the line
106. Privileges: Abbr.
108. Verb suffix
109. Himalaya wonder
112. Mideast initials
113. Sp. article

123 Away From It All by Nancy Schuster

ACROSS

1. My Gal and others
5. Panama city
10. Argyll resort
14. Taiwan city
20. Quality
22. Well's companion
23. Diet
24. Like some beds
25. Manikin: It.
26. Mets, Muses, et al.
27. Flutter
28. Stoppage of fluid
29. Kit-bag advice
33. Purposes
34. Guthrie
35. Guide
36. Beach substitute
38. ___ la
41. Particles
43. Exclamation
45. Goes on the town
48. Galileo's crime
50. Skiing place
53. Silent
55. Harem room
56. Brit. sea unit
57. Handy
58. Proverb
60. Houston initials
62. Honshu town
64. Prepared chestnuts
66. Big deal from the boss
70. Whale
71. "Wish you were ___"
72. Admit
73. Ancestor: Ger.
74. Most important
77. Dickens heroine
79. Hebrew letter
80. Bird output
82. Roman bronze
83. Toll road
85. Kind of seer
87. Gather
89. Golf place
90. Dim
92. Ring
94. Rose of ___

96. Pie à ___
98. Research room
99. Genesis wife
101. Danish weights
102. Ten: Prefix
103. Twain book
106. Igloo dwellers
110. Name in Cuba
111. German title
112. Mug
114. Common contraction
115. "___ dien"
116. Prefix for derm or gram
119. Harness strap
121. Time spans: Abbr.
122. Travel ___
123. Ballet gear
126. Oliver's partner
128. Broadway role
130. The fair ___
131. Kneecap
133. Sea term
136. Youngsters
138. Skipper, familiarly
140. Blasé remark of tourists
146. Straightens
148. Steady
149. Abrogate
150. High nest
151. One of a Biblical tribe
152. Number for a Henry
153. Sierra ___
154. Reaches port
155. Okayed
156. Poet Wilcox
157. To the point
158. Plant part

DOWN

1. Telegram word
2. Vergil word
3. Secular
4. ___ putt
5. Grand place to visit
6. Medley
7. "Peanuts" character
8. Manifest
9. Bird
10. Soldier ___
11. Sumatra wildcat
12. Sons of Ishmael
13. ___ ultra
14. Scuffled
15. Pismire
16. Moslem leaders: Var.
17. Mug shot of a kind
18. Miss Adams
19. Rudolf or Myra
21. Accommodation to avoid
30. Shrewd move
31. Paper measure
32. Inner: Prefix
37. Woman with ___
38. Yonder, out West
39. Repeat
40. Code for callers

42. Instrument
44. Madame de ___
46. Word for parasol users
47. Playing card
49. Downs or salts
51. Printing process, for short
52. Authorities
54. Sandy ridge
58. Nabokov work
59. Folk dance
61. Aft
63. Exclamations
65. Solar event
67. Luggage man
68. Judicious
69. Smokes in a way
74. Childish fare
75. Swell
76. Jet-set delight
77. Scarcity

78. Aegean island
81. Turn right
84. English theater name
86. Compact
88. Tour offering
91. Tropical tree
93. Light beam
95. Judge's word
97. City V.I.P. in France
100. Rodents
102. Retreat
103. P. I. tree
104. Gangplank strip
105. Lady of the waves
107. Kind of store
108. Not repeatedly
109. River of myth
113. Theory
117. Crowded

118. Groundless
120. Place for a chignon
122. Eastern nurse
124. Astringent
125. Garment part
127. Describing some diets
129. Churchill's successor
132. Verdi chorus
134. Jeanmaire
135. Melchior, for one
137. Lab sample
138. Bounders
139. Jai ___
141. Eye: Fr.
142. Hebrew letters
143. River of Italy
144. Venetian resort
145. For fear that
147. After printemps

124 Wise Words by Jennie Lemmo

ACROSS

1. Occupation
6. Lesser Sunda island
11. Ran a spread
18. Ancestor of human race
19. Habituate
20. Smoke-eater's gear
21. Eat crow
22. Snooped
23. Friml's forte
24. Become weedy
26. Man with a ladder
28. Fountain order
29. Take out
31. Saharan hackney
32. Fish
33. Poet's word
34. Lured
35. Hateful person
36. Like some apples
38. Judgment
39. Helsinki native
40. Potato chip's friend
41. Noel Coward's spirit
43. Campaign
45. Predicament
49. ___ Hélène
50. Abundance
51. Approach
52. Made up for
53. Drink flavor
54. Beauty parlor job
55. Narrow margin
56. Ocean route
57. Breed of sheep
59. Loop in anatomy
60. "Roger and ___"
61. Fillet
62. Current
63. 1936 campaigner
65. Suspect
67. Sweetie pie
68. Space a paragraph
69. Least challenging
70. Poem division
71. Furs
72. Writings: Abbr.
73. Bona ___
74. Smoothed a pillow
76. Cash, for one
79. Tuscan city
80. Commemorative coins
81. Goddess: Lat.
84. Tangle
85. Roast slightly
86. End on ___ of sadness
87. Authenticate
88. Variety of non-clam
92. Enact again
94. Well-read
95. Hale character
97. Pitcher
98. Brightly inlaid
99. White sauce
100. Refer, with "to"
101. Not coincidental
102. Tenor role in 49 Down
103. Arctic explorer

DOWN

1. "Key Largo" Oscar winner
2. Shrink
3. Soprano Lucine
4. Mild cussword
5. Confirmed
6. Cowboys' table setting
7. Daughter of Cadmus
8. Went by dog team
9. Mountain: Prefix
10. Tending to diminish
11. Rushed headlong
12. Of a space
13. St. Philip ___
14. Snow goose genus
15. More summery
16. Regard highly
17. At great cost
18. Sometimes purple output
20. One on the other side
25. "___ est laborare"
27. French river
30. Sowing season
34. Italian seven
36. Strategem
37. Munificent
38. Gourmand's big moment
39. Flint
40. Thin coin
41. City in N.Y.
42. Queen of the beasts
44. Frolic
45. Bird
46. Ramble
47. French houses
48. Downright
49. Strauss opera
50. Viewpoint
51. "Of Human Bondage" hero
54. Up for grabs
57. Army
58. Suggestion
61. Smack
63. "Stop the World" hero
64. Ponies up
66. Support
67. Felt in one's bones
70. Kid of the West
71. Mexican grass
73. Solidified
75. Embellished
76. British novelist
77. Like seawater
78. Of any of fifty
79. Called it quits
80. Austrian composer
81. Las Vegas employe
82. Lunchroom
83. Not easily fooled
85. Famous clergyman
87. Pergolesi's "La ___ Padrona"
89. Altar area
90. Harte
91. Moved violently
93. Primitive
96. I love: Lat.

125 Sleight of Hand by Hume R. Craft

ACROSS

1. Remains
6. Ponselle
10. Corn-husk contents
16. Rio de la ___
21. Diagonal line
22. Mich. and 5th
23. Greek places
24. Overhangs
25. People on certain diets
27. Puzzle
29. Cabinet dept.
30. Court jester
31. Great Plains sight
33. ___ brief for
34. Triflers
36. Electrical pioneer
38. Church platform
41. Lazy times in Monte Carlo
42. Early Jewish mystics
44. Navy off.
46. Cat
48. Burma's neighbor
50. Metamere
52. Copper or gold: Abbr.
54. Sailboats
58. Fight ___
60. Callao's land
61. British gun
62. Government program
63. Grassy square
64. City near Des Moines
66. Wisconsin town
68. Mimicking bird
69. Adjusted sails
71. Fortification
72. ___ polloi
73. Exuded
74. Kind of partner
75. One with a trained eye
76. Italian resort
79. Some flutists
83. Ivan et al.
84. Of a bird part
85. No-good one

88. Ariz. Indian
91. Slav rulers
92. Hereditary factors
93. Materialistic
94. Exalted
97. Clothes or saw
98. Main idea
99. Color
100. Paul's family
101. Singer Lily
102. Scratch
104. Butler
106. Alarms
107. Amusement park feature
108. Tasks
110. Cockney abodes
111. Japanese trees
113. Relative of olé
115. Stalk
117. Hindu hero
120. Virginia willows
122. Despicable one
124. ___ Pointe
127. Neglectful one
129. Ties up
131. Br. composer
133. Opposite of ant.
134. Scavenger mollusk
137. Helps a magician
140. Radio name
141. Croquet term
142. Earl of Avon
143. Legerdemain, in France
144. Activists
145. Throws out
146. Word for Ben Jonson
147. Golfer Sam

DOWN

1. ___ as a pig
2. Irish bay
3. His contracts had escape clauses
4. Direction
5. Wool gatherers
6. Assess
7. Tie-breaking periods
8. Sun. discourse
9. Helpers: Abbr.
10. ___ Zee
11. Ailment
12. Particles
13. Biblical lion
14. Wool: Prefix
15. Biblical queen
16. Strip
17. Stairway for leather-footed conjurers
18. Sea call
19. Plating alloy
20. Old Greek vase
26. Orbital point
28. More raucous
32. Robt. ___
35. Let up
37. Arabian ruler
39. Frank
40. Radio's ___ and Abner
43. Drugged
45. Author of nature books
47. Fitzgerald
48. Endures
49. Love
51. Soup bowls
53. Man's nickname
55. Missouri River dam
56. Kind of school
57. Spanish painter
59. Pie à ___
61. Fireworks
62. Aviary sound
65. Botanical part: Suffix
67. Intention
68. Of melody
70. Hypnotist's credo
71. Takes a break
72. Fences
75. Hairnet
76. Shrill cry
77. Hot fragment
78. More sordid
80. "___ moi, le . . ."
81. Ages
82. Spirit's dispatch
86. Mexican grass
87. Certain pups
88. Linen marking
89. Guinness
90. Soviet river
92. Hopeless case
93. Planted
95. Expanse
96. More irritable
97. Scuttle
98. Overseer
101. City of Italy
103. Cuts off
105. Entire: Prefix
107. Be sorry
108. Snow-goose genus
109. Roadside scenery
112. English historian
114. White poplars
116. Some candies
117. Itinerant
118. Starch: Prefix
119. Cotton thread
121. Cachets
123. Fall flower
125. Ex-member of U.A.R.
126. Done
128. Sawbucks
130. Asian area, for short
132. Pierre's friend
135. Portion: Abbr.
136. Born: Fr.
138. Oklahoma city
139. U.S. neighbor

126 Breathing Exercise by Adelyn Lewis

ACROSS

1. Veranda
6. Ignoble
10. Young salmon
15. Three: It.
18. A fond ___
19. Astringent
20. Wartime vessel
21. Small deer
22. Circles: Fr.
23. Source of iodine
24. Large snake
25. Unspoiled site
26. "What glorious sunsets have their birth ___" (Davies)
30. Outstanding
31. Containers
32. Mother of Artemis
33. Moon module
34. Sutherland specialty
35. Feel tired
40. "Fill'd the air with ___" (Milton)
43. Paris parties
45. Oil container
46. English village
47. Oxford tutor
48. Cassowary's relative
49. Some monsters
51. Pale
52. Fr. composer
54. April ecological event
56. Becomes taxing
57. "___ Spring"
58. Salt: Prefix
59. Adjusts
60. Fade away
61. Disprove
64. Marsh bird
65. Name for W. J. Bryan
69. Sour substances
70. Ready: Fr.
71. Preserves
72. Greek letter
73. Labor org.
74. Encourage
75. Church part
76. Laborer
77. R. L. Stevenson line
83. Solid fats
84. Suffix for Cyprus natives
85. Wine: Prefix
86. Nautilus man
87. Silver: Abbr.
88. Ready to perform
92. Hamlet's words for the air around him
98. Space
99. Zodiac sign
100. Some predictions
101. ___ Canarias
102. Stingy
103. Caretakers of a sort
104. German river
105. Uncritical
106. High, in music
107. Word for some cities
108. Summer times
109. Noun suffixes

DOWN

1. Apple-giver of myth
2. Dental prefix
3. ___ doigts: Fr. finger bowl
4. Marks under consonants
5. Shady dealer
6. Cascade peak
7. Drinks
8. Like some pollutants
9. Big store
10. Sets of bells
11. French cleric
12. Fourth of an acre
13. Keeps talking
14. Extended one's vacation
15. Confusion
16. Bad odor
17. Serf
21. Suckfish
27. Metrical foot
28. Spanish articles
29. Musial
34. Proper order
35. Places for statues
36. ___ Park
37. Clothe
38. Disdain
39. Opinion
40. Eye chart, to some
41. Stevenson
42. "Streetcar" sign
43. Relative of a social
44. Doctors' org.
49. Indian ranges
50. Fruitless
51. Inclined
52. Hazes
53. Chorus girl
55. Dull sound
56. Culture centers in Rome
57. Powdered, in heraldry
59. Golf areas
60. Van man
61. Invasions
62. Acclaim
63. Flower: It.
64. English railway town
65. Instances
66. ___ - do-well
67. W.W. II area
68. Norse sea goddess
70. Speech-sound character
71. Geometric solids
74. Yalta people
75. Listened to
76. Plant substance
78. Malaysian town
79. ___ Rabbit
80. "And ___ bed"
81. Hebrides island
82. Of wasps
87. Pantywaist
88. Parts of cricket games
89. Of a royal court
90. Serious
91. Road curves
92. Biblical miracle site
93. City on the Oka
94. Undiluted
95. Japanese race: Var.
96. Hardwood tree
97. Worry

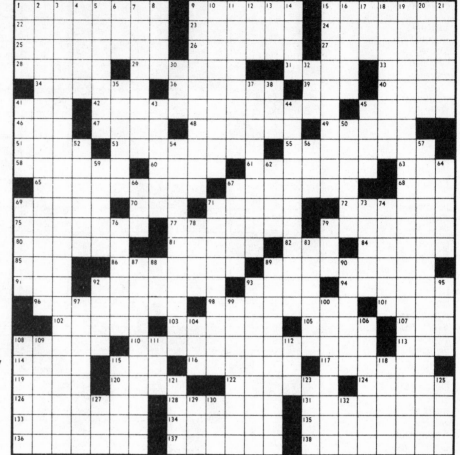

ACROSS

1. Bottom part of a record
9. Jockey Bobby ___
15. Took off in a hurry
22. Cut with the grain
23. Take shorthand
24. "How to Handle a Woman"
25. Blanch
26. Stir: Ger.
27. Whammy
28. Alcohol heaters
29. Ahead: Fr.
31. Graf ___
33. City of Ukraine
34. Injury
36. Biblical father of Obed
39. Spring month: Abbr.
40. Strip, in Scotland
41. Opp. of plaintiff
42. Will-have-been tense
45. Like delicate edging
46. Friend, in France
47. Dixmude's river
48. Dwarfish-ness
49. "___ to the Trees"
51. Artist Joan
53. Jivaran shrunken heads
55. V.I.P.
58. Human soul
60. Votes against
61. Academic protest
63. Monk's title
65. Encounter informally
67. Dickens family
68. Neighbor of Md.
69. Modern name of Emmaus
70. After-thoughts: Abbr.
71. Put a label on
72. Chinese name of Dairen
75. Enzyme
77. Capable of
79. ___ a pig
80. Significant
81. Rather
82. Bee: Prefix
84. Word of surrender
85. Rural postal initials
86. French playwright Jean
89. Slang for a bungler
91. Father of Osiris: Var.
92. Blowhard of sorts
93. ___ bug in one's ear
94. Forget ___
96. Part of a place setting
98. Magic spore, in old lore
101. Contemporary hairdo
102. Pirandello
103. Golf tourney
105. June 6, 1944
107. Parson bird
108. Lacks, for short
110. Where the girls are
113. F.D.R.'s successor
114. City in South Korea
115. Harrogate, Tenn., campus
116. "___ Rag" of jazz fame
117. Alpine hideaway
119. "Who's that knocking ___ door?"
120. Western hero
122. "...and we shall ___ family"
124. ___ far as the end of one's nose
126. Was injured
128. Three, proverbially
131. "___ assumption" (pretty sure)
133. Prohibitive odds
134. Ballet step
135. Laid the groundwork
136. Secret
137. Informal wear
138. Elementary school class

DOWN

1. Part of f.o.b.
2. One afraid of spiders
3. Sentiment on souvenir sachets
4. Animal loin
5. Oyster plant
6. Frigate bird
7. International breathers
8. Apple country
9. Not regretted
10. Segment of Oregon Trail
11. Napoleon's retreat
12. Attention
13. Highway: Abbr.
14. Cravings
15. "Good night; ___"
16. Lid
17. Ancestors: Lat.
18. Poe's heart
19. Victim of Dorothy's landing on Oz
20. Pal of Pooh
21. U.S. poet
30. Thrice: Prefix
32. Moccasin
35. Dismissal
37. Plato's pupil
38. Baseball positions: Abbr.
41. Moist
43. Planet
44. U.S. trade laws of 1800's
45. German river
50. Variations
52. Sea: Sp.
54. Fallacy
56. Pierre's "here"
57. Advice from countess in "All's Well"
59. Attacks
62. Part of Q.E.D.
64. Parsonage
66. Disclose in verse
67. Taxes' partner
69. Stravinsky et al
71. Like Daisy's beau's bicycle
73. In ___ (angry)
74. The girl: Sp.
76. Long John Silver had one
78. Who: Lat.
79. Be indisposed
83. Plato work
87. Of coins
88. Honshu river
89. Nice aspects
90. Printer's line
92. Gad about
93. Defrosted in advance
95. "Honi ___ qui..."
97. Skating leap
99. Concession, in rhetoric
100. Teacher
104. ___ disant
106. Agreed, old style
108. Hero sandwich
109. Bent over
111. Pronoun
112. Elevations: Abbr.
115. Writer Jones
118. East wind: Sp.
121. Concordat
123. Scottish isle
125. Fence: Sp.
127. Calif. Rep.
129. Terrify
130. Regret
132. Depot: Abbr.

128 Roman Holiday

by Philip K. Youritzin

ACROSS

1. Letter-opener for some
6. African gazelle
10. Duel souvenir
14. Rustle
19. Rustic place
20. Time periods
21. White: Prefix
22. Church income
23. Zeal
24. Play an ice game
25. Eldest of the Pleiades
26. Kind of band
27. Apparatus
28. You: Ger.
29. Well-soaped
31. Quibble
32. Locust tree
36. Disengage
38. Stock-market word
41. Asian sea
42. Czech town name
44. Symbol of power
47. In ___ way (tunefully)
49. Alas, to Caesar
50. Western lake
52. Scene of old Roman war games
54. ___ churchmouse
56. Downstairs: Fr.
57. Caesar's way
58. Taken
59. Film actor Arnold
60. Church areas
62. Asians who sealed Marcus Crassus's fate
63. Moscow money
65. Traverse, as through tulips
66. Emperor who started the Colosseum
70. ___ hair (lava froth)
71. Egypt's hub
76. Like a babe
77. Role for Liz
78. Boo-boo
79. Having a wall bracket
80. Father of Latin poetry
84. Graze past
85. Western Indians
86. "Let that be a ___ you"
87. Nevertheless
88. Lacking experience
92. Mexican coin
93. Army V.I.P.
94. Loan shark
95. Beverages
97. Off-center
100. Gin's friend
102. Chinese pagoda
103. Elec. units
107. Shrew
109. Napoleonic battle site
110. Visitor to Siam
112. Ennoble
113. French year
114. Culture medium
115. Garish
116. Andrea ___
117. Max and Buddy
118. Little Helen
119. ___ majesty
120. Go onstage

DOWN

1. Ore refuse
2. Disrupted
3. Saga's relative
4. Athenian center
5. Debussy topic
6. U.S. power agency
7. Mistress of Caligula
8. Singer Callas
9. Wight
10. Uncle and Spade
11. Robert Graves's emperor
12. Remains
13. Cookouts
14. Ways: Abbr.
15. Broom user
16. Willow
17. Persian tiger
18. Hired hands
30. Ox of Tibet
33. Famous Roman reformer
34. Bows
35. Loom part
37. He wanted Carthage destroyed
38. Tempos
39. Lover, in France
40. Cuban dance
42. Recoils
43. Fear: Fr.
44. Maureen or Scarlett
45. German flowers
46. Neckwear
48. Extend over
49. Diminutive suffixes
51. African sheep
53. Up
54. Hair lines
55. Vision: Prefix
58. Cod or Horn
60. In ___ (beset)
61. Land map
62. Flier
64. One who benefits
65. Certain ages
66. City in Sweden
67. Ink: Fr.
68. Tapir's pride
69. Opera's Lily
70. Carried on
72. Pisa's river
73. Metal-drum hook
74. Way
75. Welles
77. Clever
80. Hill of Rome
81. Domitius ___, Roman jurist
82. Gardener's need
83. Sum, ___, fui
89. Zany one
90. Kind of ancient horse
91. Make an error at bridge
94. Shoe part
95. Portage item
96. Britisher
97. Famous whaler
98. Turner
99. French river
101. Psychologist Jung
102. Like some stories
104. Trade center
105. Ballet movement
106. Top banana
108. O.K.
111. Drink
112. Dutch town

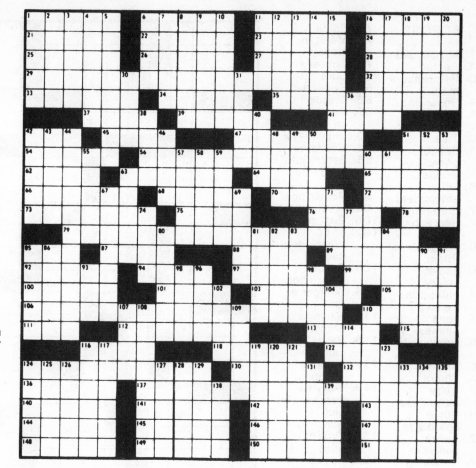

ACROSS

1. Must
6. Aye-aye
11. Biblical titles
16. Mosey along
21. New York city
22. Fatuous
23. Dull
24. Actress Leslie
25. Chaplain
26. Jot
27. Deer: Prefix
28. Stadium features
29. Start of a verse, with 56, 79, 106 and 137 Across
32. Bleak
33. Grievously
34. Metric measure
35. Speak gobble-dygook?
37. Kind of apple
39. Mature, legally
41. Bit of foolishness
42. Bags: Abbr.
45. Fraulein's refusal
47. "When I feel you ___"
51. So!
54. Stocking cap
56. More of 29 Across
62. Border on
63. Not ripped
64. Soil: Prefix
65. Goose eggs
66. Assertions
68. Buddhist saint
70. Marsh bird
72. Egg-boiling aid
73. Certain shipments
75. Body: Suffix
76. Asian priest
78. Not natural: Abbr.
79. More of 56 Across
85. Scenery chewer
87. Present
88. "And ___ is awfully rich . . ."
89. Thingumbobs

92. Vestment
94. Easily bruised things
97. Across: Prefix
99. Town near Sandy Hook
100. Derring-do
101. German valley
103. Verdi opus
105. Relative of "oh, dear"
106. More of 79 Across
110. Curl of the lip
111. Kind of lettuce
112. Foams
113. Facile
115. Unburden
116. Ben Adhem
118. Suffixes for young and old
122. Father
124. Civil War battle site
130. Disney's middle name
132. Soprano's warm-up
136. Welcome to Hilo!
137. End of verse
140. Stares
141. Do-nothing
142. Squelched
143. Old Greek temples
144. Turn inside out
145. Nine: Latin
146. Form of Helen
147. Queen ___ lace
148. Starts an urban renewal job
149. First name in movie lore
150. Nelson and Mary Baker
151. Sprees

DOWN

1. Indians
2. Place to remember
3. Jewish festival
4. Pâtisserie items
5. Solo
6. Bean
7. Geraint's wife, et al.
8. ". . .owed by so ___ so few"
9. World relief group
10. Parasite fish
11. Start of learning song
12. Sheepish remark
13. Body sac
14. Well-known chorus
15. Caramel candy, for instance
16. Misbehaves
17. ___ d'hôtel
18. Stroke of luck
19. Peter of films
20. Send upward
30. Cithara's cousin
31. Within the law
36. Gerald O'Hara's pride

38. After "tres"
40. Wagnerian goddess
42. Sharply, in music: Abbr.
43. Xanadu name
44. Standish, to hippies?
46. Naldi of silents
48. Man from M.I.T.
49. Mrs. Helmer
50. French star
51. Cyclotron
52. Nonsense!
53. ". . .like ___ in spring"
55. Practical
57. Defeat
58. "But when ___ I cannot tell"
59. A friend: Fr.
60. Strapped, financially
61. Thee: Fr.
63. "Give ___ tools . . ."
67. Kipling poem, with "Mine"

69. Unspoken
71. "Green Pastures" role
74. Withered
77. Polynesian
80. Rue
81. Zimbalist
82. Puppeteer Lewis
83. Hair rinse
84. Madison Ave. worker
85. Cry or June
86. Writer Jorge
90. Former Japanese news agency
91. Mortimer
93. Mountain pass
95. Painful sound
96. If it fits, put it on
98. Stated
102. School curriculum, once
104. Compass points
107. Blossom: Sp.
108. Intimidating

109. You, in Madrid
110. Summer theater
114. Thin cover
116. Stick to
117. Burdened ones
119. French President's home
120. Lewd
121. Fried lightly
123. Lily maid
124. $2 item
125. Caste of India
126. Bandleader Vincent
127. Witch's home
128. Puzzle out
129. Weather word
131. Impassive
133. Theater-in-the-round
134. Enticing one
135. Pile up
138. First word of "Aeneid"
139. ___ much as

130 Drawing the Shades by Marjorie K. Collins

ACROSS

1. Mr. Coward
5. Rested
10. Reference mark
14. Regarding
18. Nimbus
19. Hackneyed
20. Title
21. School chore
23. Brains
25. Letter's antecedent
27. Utah range
28. Scoreboard listing
29. Daughter of Priam
30. Lap of luxury
37. Indeed, in Ireland
38. June beetles
39. Geologic time
40. Ship part
44. Where we're weightless
49. Cut to board size
52. Italian genius
54. Knocking sound
55. River to North Sea
56. Tropical fruits
57. Metric measures
59. Balance
60. For a ___ (cheaply)
61. Biblical land
63. German numeral
65. At full speed
67. Exhortation for le roi
71. Manner
72. Shallow
74. French painter
75. Mosque priest
76. Attention-getter
77. Snide
78. Mexican money
79. Chooses
80. Cure
82. Eye part
85. Steady
87. Casts ___ on
90. Chin: Prefix
92. Maintains
95. Betting info
97. Hinder, in law
98. Roman poet
99. Indifferent
100. Boat gear
102. 1956 Wimbledon champ
104. Fast, to slow: Abbr.
105. Sources of junk
113. Having a grudge
116. Dallas campus
117. Yucatan Indians
118. The view from here is nice
120. Sorcery
125. Type of edge
126. Logical
127. Tidal flow
128. Western org.
129. Counsel, old style
130. Models: Abbr.
131. Planes
132. Chinese island

DOWN

1. Plater
2. Possessive
3. Pitcher's concern: Abbr.
4. Store
5. Ladd movie
6. ___ Miles, girl in old tire ad
7. ___ run
8. Acadia's Grand ___
9. Norse god
10. Nature writer
11. Western lake
12. Small cavity
13. Literary initials
14. ___ of woe
15. Dried flower, in a way
16. Distant: Prefix
17. Sign
22. Before automne
24. Wire measure
26. Breakfast treat
30. Brace
31. Container: Sp.
32. Posse's quarry
33. Campus unit
34. More unrestrained
35. Offspring
36. Antiseptic: Prefix
41. Siamese twin
42. Far sound: Sp.
43. Heraldic flower
45. Live it up
46. Law man: Abbr.
47. North, for one
48. Enduring
50. State of India
51. Floor cleaner
53. Johnson
58. Red and others
60. Naps
61. Unusual power
62. ___ Passos
64. Certain kind of stitch
66. Ones: Scot.
68. Paper size
69. Winemaker's need
70. Type measures
73. Brontë's Jane et al.
81. Biblical judge
83. ___ pink
84. Back porch
86. Youth org.
87. Exclamations
88. ___ canals
89. Parts of gals
91. Ocean fish
93. Fix the piano
94. Plane types: Abbr.
96. Convened
101. Go after a fly again
103. Injure
106. Big name in cards
107. Edit
108. Decoys
109. Shell layer
110. Children
111. "Pants" man
112. Yoga posture
113. Fishing term
114. Finished
115. Entwined
119. W.W. II group
120. Poker word
121. Gibbon
122. Pod
123. Japanese statesman
124. Demure

131 All to the Goods by Anne Fox

ACROSS

1. Miss Page
6. Greek letter
9. Cabal
13. U.S. dept.
16. English engineer
19. Part of the Erechtheum
24. Uninvited one
25. Killjoy
26. Radioman's room
27. Spanish relative
28. Way out
30. ___ mater
31. Effrontery
32. Fictional plantation
33. All ___ up
34. Gov't. sleuthing agency
35. Shout
37. Reprove
38. Valley of Europe
40. Spanish port
42. One of the F.F.V.
43. Wool: Sp.
44. Milk ingredient
47. Scull
48. Dean
50. Think
52. What Sam Goldwyn said to "include me in"
56. Chic
60. Viking name
61. ___ B'rith
62. Swiss canton
63. Elec. unit
65. Hep
66. Tonsorial call
67. Car part: Abbr.
68. Indian greeting
69. Inventor Howe
71. English poet
72. Dakota sight
74. City of Peru
76. Aardvark's delicacy
77. Reside
78. Fictional pair
84. "___ a little shadow..."
85. Hunter's limit
86. Sandpiper
87. British ___
88. Service
89. One's word
91. Came in first
92. Make obscure
93. Mexican sandwich
97. Chemical compound
98. ___ pro nobis
99. Honshu peak
101. ___ d'Azur
102. Scrammed
103. Western capital
105. U.S. writer
109. Type of school: Abbr.
111. Coconut fiber
112. Kayoed
113. Crying items
114. Doubles and triples
116. Somewhat: Suffix
118. Newark's county
120. Alley sound
121. Puerto Rican city
122. Portico
124. Exclamations
125. Invite
126. Arabian gulf
130. Gem stone
131. Heat standard: Abbr.
132. Well!, in Spain
134. Abner
135. "...bitten, ___ shy"
136. Congressman from Ill.
139. Firemen's training structures
142. Play by Ibsen
143. Town named for Syrian saint
144. Cooking abbr.
145. Uh-huh
146. Miss West
147. Cut the lawn

DOWN

1. Czech capital
2. Perfume
3. Perry Mason's debut
4. Fictional friar
5. Type of verb: Abbr.
6. Fix
7. Site of Berwick market
8. Réunion, for one
9. Size of type
10. Van, in London
11. Kind of world
12. Drink
13. Constellation
14. Words by Eugene Field
15. Get back
16. Not for: Abbr.
17. Drink
18. Scairt
20. Lined, as a roof
21. Gov't. agency
22. A Fitzgerald
23. First name with 3 Down
29. Eastern U.S. borough
33. Flier
34. Car part, for short
36. Nevada city
37. Queen, for short
39. Kind of line
40. Moslem judge
41. Bantu language
44. Possum's cousin
45. Wheel part
46. Tunisian port
47. ___ even keel
49. Cut of meat
51. Rulers: Abbr.
53. Railroad tool
54. Counsel, in Nice
55. Singer Frankie
57. "The Lady ___"
58. Fusty
59. According to ___
64. French sailors
68. Bad actor
70. Old cry of surprise
73. Chem. suffix
74. Harbor craft
75. Skillful
77. Postal limbo: Abbr.
78. Run-down
79. Snivel
80. Jackson's war secretary
81. Borneo native
82. Bill
83. Took in
89. Peeved
90. ___ importance
92. Pay, as the bill
94. Lily plant
95. Part of a honeycomb
96. Sees red, in a way
100. Narwhal
101. Main feature
104. Of another sort
106. Repeat
107. Farm tools
108. As well
110. Foggy
114. Chinese province
115. Miffed
117. Rugged
119. Food fish
120. Thousand: Prefix
121. Larboard
123. Irish river
125. Bosh
127. Honey: It.
128. Biting
129. State: Suffix
131. Parcel: Abbr.
133. Ansate cross
134. Money in Italy
135. "___ the mornin' to you"
137. Small drink
138. Girl of song
140. Ad ___
141. Male animal

132 Workaday World by Barbara Lewis

ACROSS

1. ___ or nothing
4. "___ Three Lives"
8. Biblical word
11. Elec. unit
14. Biblical name
15. Hawaiian shark
16. Garden tool
17. Two-wheeled vehicles
20. Heating vessel
21. Fundamentals
22. Greek letter
23. Spa
24. Hear a case again
26. Oil, in old Rome
28. Response
30. ___ of Cutch
31. ___ seedling (plant)
32. Dawn goddess
33. Dark
34. Argues in favor of
36. Go back
39. Italian beach
40. "...the giftie ___ us"
41. Some G.I.'s
43. Sensed
44. False god
45. Donkey
46. Doer: Suffix
47. Certain space flights
50. ___ in a poke
52. Pub drink
53. Guarantee
55. Scoff
57. Remove
60. Prepares clams
62. Cause: Prefix
63. Six-day Biblical advice
67. Perfume: Var.
68. ___ God
69. Somewhat: Suffix
70. First-rate
71. Groom
73. Mischievous one
75. By any chance
77. Lacks truth
78. Spanish cape on Medit.
79. Stand-off
80. Maintained
84. Scottish river
85. "Arma virumque ___"
86. Go wrong
87. Concerning
88. Murderous person
92. Labor Day orator, perhaps
95. Roman emperor
96. Housewife
97. Girl's name
98. Mellowed
99. ___ in his life
102. Off the cuff
103. Writer Marsh
105. Star in Draco
106. Lie
108. Jacket
110. Asian country
111. Pours
112. Stir
113. French verb
114. Uncles, etc.: Abbr.
115. Small bird
116. Rocky peak
117. Victory margin
118. Peers: Abbr.

DOWN

1. Sky body
2. Retarding, in music
3. Advice from Longfellow
4. "___ little teapot"
5. Grant's words about toil
6. Inserts
7. A ___ one's own medicine
8. Words by L.B.J.
9. In demand
10. Indeed
11. Zoological suffix
12. Gender: Abbr.
13. A job for heaven
14. Poet's above
18. Huron or Erie
19. Endured
23. The dead may "___" (Bible)
25. Chem. suffix
27. Place of ideal perfection
28. Eggs
29. Direction
32. Sounds of hesitation
34. Roman 151
35. African spirit
37. Move shrubbery
38. Suffix for acids
42. Trick, in Italy
47. Racetracks
48. "Flow-gently" river
49. French river
51. Little, in Paris
54. Korean G.I.
55. ___ Casazza
56. Building beams
58. Start of a jazz piece
59. Dentist's degree: Abbr.
61. Ivy leaguer
63. ___ Vegas
64. Bird of prey
65. Rumanian folk song
66. One: Scot.
72. Winnie
74. All in
76. Part of speech
79. "___ the judge"
81. Made lovable
82. Landed slaves: Var.
83. Three: Prefix
85. Coins: Abbr.
88. Camper's gear
89. King Arthur's father
90. Greek letter
91. Scottish alder
93. "My Sister ___"
94. Fleming
100. Prefix with bus and present
101. Bedim
104. Cricket sides
106. Kind of cat
107. Marriage words
109. Born: Fr.

133 Words on Parade by Ross L. Jamison Jr.

ACROSS

1. Purpose
7. "Gil Blas" author
8. Daisy Mae's creator
17. Fugue composer
21. Small space
22. "Cymbeline" heroine
23. Oriental nurse
24. Gingko
25. Prying
27. Hamlet's forte
29. Rumanian coin
30. Fugue part
31. P. I. natives
33. Developed
34. Nibble
36. Circle, in Germany
37. Truck compartment
38. First name in British letters
39. Aromatic seed
42. Surface measure
43. Growing in pairs
45. Roof ornament
46. Roman scholar
48. Hang fire
49. Mysterious
51. Hindu land grant
54. Hero of Norse myth
55. Consisting of 50 days
60. ___ shirt
61. In the manner of
62. Hungarian Communist
63. Charley's relative
64. City north of Genova
65. As well as
66. Moon: Prefix
68. Move with a rustle
70. Fasten anew
71. Teachers' org.
72. Moslem saint
73. Heed
74. Alley of the comics
76. Reasonable
78. ___ law

81. City on the Rio Grande
85. Lock
86. Cheated
88. Dull finish
89. Pronoun
90. ___disant
91. Samovar
92. Lunisolar difference
95. Designated
97. Mr. ___
101. Remote-control bomb
102. Hitchhiking fish
104. Broth, to a Scot
105. Day times: Abbr.
106. Goose eggs
107. Two: Prefix
108. Astrological aspect
111. Blue, in Spain
112. Egg part
114. Yugoslav river, to Germans
115. Dwarf
116. Water-level measure
118. Bible book: Abbr.
120. Runs
122. Druggist's drops: Abbr.
124. Dealers in certain cakes
125. On ___ (aggressive)
128. Sweep
129. Weighed a container
131. Socialite
132. Off-color
133. Spore sacs
134. Byproduct of divorce
136. Possessive
139. Animal that sponges on another
141. Dropping of legal action
144. Large toad
145. Wild plum
146. Consecrate
147. Perceptible
148. Old English court
149. Sound from the sty
150. Old weapons
151. Sanction

DOWN

1. ___ Eireann
2. Sea bird
3. Consecutive
4. Chit
5. Sparkle
6. Political cartoonist
7. Educators, writers, etc.
8. Ham
9. Military mission
10. Exchange premiums
11. Region: Suffix
12. Interweaving
13. Melon
14. O.T. book
15. Buddy
16. Sorority name
17. Organisms sharing a trait
18. It was auld to Burns
19. Insect sound
20. Called attention
26. Vex
28. Burden
32. Bike
35. Indigo
38. U. S. tree
39. Jumping insects
40. Former gold coin
41. Whisky
43. Gets a hit the hard way
44. Linen fabric
47. Luminary
48. Andean wind
50. Aquarium fish
52. Trojan hero
53. Military fruit salad
56. V.I.P.
57. Senate voting concern
58. Word of respect
59. 2,240-pound units
62. Breeches
67. Grand
68. Musical piece: Abbr.
69. Garden tool
75. Examined
77. Rainbow: Prefix
78. Robust
79. Western gulch
80. Tall and gaunt
81. Water
82. Arabian tea: Var.
83. Eccentric
84. Indian bean
87. Foils
90. Saturday, in Paris
93. Feather trim for hats
94. Administrator: Abbr.
96. Sassy kid
98. African area
99. Cosmetic
100. Razor clam
103. Hollow space in birds
105. Panay native
109. Hill of Rome
110. Endeavors
111. U. S. writer
113. Citrus fruit
117. Molting
119. Hawaiian island
121. Hide and ___
122. French
123. Chemical compound
125. ___ balloon
126. Be contingent
127. Big-money racehorse
129. Claw
130. Buzzing beetle
133. At another time
135. Temporary star
137. Malayan sir
138. Sediment
140. River of Asia
142. ___ shoestring
143. Sigmoid figure

134 Tall Titles
by Eugene T. Maleska

ACROSS

1. Scopes
7. Plea
15. Ablutions
20. Sideshow man
21. ___ boom
22. Kind of committee
23. Sequel to "Dad's Awakening"
25. The ending
26. Spy name
27. Dockers' union: Abbr.
28. Math ratios
29. "Yes, ___" by Sammy Davis
30. Kittiwake
32. Town on the Hudson
34. Main force
35. Most miserly
39. Abbreviation in physics
40. More chichi
42. Ham it up
43. Buzzes
45. Ruler's epithet
46. Resin
49. Masefield heroine
50. Addison's colleague
52. "As You Like It" girl
53. Forum garb
54. Leghorn's largesse
56. Encomium
57. Bills
58. Less perilous
59. Civic center
61. Signify
63. Coat fur
64. Chits
65. Cupola-shaped
67. Oriental nurse
68. Bishop's headdress
70. Inflict
71. Benefit
75. Throbs
76. Ring champ, 1934
77. Dissuade
79. ___ Pea of Popeye strip
80. Shea occupants
81. Sesame
82. Feel by insight
84. Native of: Suffix
85. Blonde shade
86. Rails
87. Subject to
88. Poe's foster father
90. Dines at home
92. Part of U.K.
93. Musical flourishes
95. Shade of brown
97. Astaire
99. Do pruning
100. Greedy
101. Wine and dine
103. Ad ___
104. Bullring cries
108. Under legal age
110. "Portnoy's Complaint"
113. Provide with
114. Pupils, at times
115. Roman goddess
116. Takes it easy
117. Finale on Broadway
118. Tool for boring

DOWN

1. Miracle drug
2. Asian deer
3. ___ Rabbit
4. Discernment
5. Spanish uncle
6. Doddering
7. Fitzgerald
8. We: Lat.
9. Braces
10. Peals again
11. Avenging spirit
12. Lost
13. Post-picnic catsup bottles
14. It is so
15. ___ Dai of Vietnam
16. Esteem
17. Medusa's coiffure
18. Navaho lodge
19. Meager
24. Sentry's call
31. Salt Lake City team
33. German localities
34. Snippet
35. Belief
36. Mature insect
37. Orchestral variation
38. Tale of a so-so adult student
39. Heavy shoe
41. Chinese pagoda
44. Dr. Gesell's co-author
45. Ligurian port
47. Askew
48. Vikki the songstress
51. Bohea and congou
52. Granting
53. Tamerlane's people
55. Siesta sounds
58. About
60. Colors
62. Ice, in Berlin
66. Unfolds
67. Town of Italy
68. Sound from a doll
69. Sherbets
70. Michener title
72. Emotional disorder
73. Bristles
74. Part of a lifetime
78. Goal
81. Cattle genus
83. Anklebones
86. Swinery
87. Expose
89. City in Indiana
91. "Over ___" (sign-off)
92. Writ against a debtor
94. Open
95. Circus performer
96. Of birds: Var.
98. Put up
102. Stratum
103. ___ majesty
105. Pilot's maneuver
106. Sicilian spouter
107. Burmese group
109. In medias ___
110. Refrain syllable
111. Evangeline's Grand ___
112. Remote

135 Both Directions by Keith Blake

ACROSS

1. Kind of pride
6. Struck out
11. ___ homo
15. Proofreaders' marks
20. Eared seal
21. Like Humpty Dumpty
22. Old Irish writing
23. ___ firma
24. First family greeting
26. Threadbare
27. Gibson garnish
28. Wheat: Fr.
29. Theatrical devices
30. Sign in animal shelter
32. Greenbacks
33. "Looking Glass" game
34. "I did, ___?"
35. Month: Abbr.
38. Coasted
39. Carbons
40. "One ___ hope"
43. Bucket passers
45. Artist Edouard
46. Get on toward midnight
47. Plural ending
49. Gil Blas creator
50. Make lace
51. Certain muscle
53. Confess
54. Pupil, in Paris
55. Outdoor area
57. Maple genus
58. ___ de menthe
59. Glut
60. Radar, sis and arara
63. Gazed dreamily
64. "___ for the show"
65. Used up
66. British sand hills
67. Body substance
68. Philo and others
70. Following
71. Warning
72. Humdinger
74. Punjab town
75. Moves in a slinky way
76. Scrap
79. Coaches
80. Challenge to Sir Noel
82. Recognized
83. Astaire partner
84. Person
85. Lock
86. Ex-Dodger star
87. ___ en scène
88. Prudent
91. German article
92. Video set
93. Greek letter
94. It is permitted: Lat.
95. Auto-safety man
97. Exalted
98. Chemical compound
100. Scotsman's tossing-log
101. Sea bird
102. British House: Abbr.
103. Put away, old style
104. Small bell
105. Legislative body
106. Why owls shun the tropics
110. Coin game: Var.
112. "___ Sir Oracle"
115. Town in C.Z.
116. Image: Prefix
117. When a certain man was able
119. Honshu city
120. Slackening bar on a loom
121. Sierra ___
122. Arabian title
123. "Win a few, ___ few"
124. Coaster
125. Southern constellation
126. Battle of the ___

DOWN

1. Search widely
2. Type face: Abbr.
3. ___ mecum
4. George's lyricist
5. Cornice molding
6. Minister: Dialect
7. Baffled
8. Stows
9. Greek letters
10. Party man: Abbr.
11. Barnum's "This way to the ___"
12. Money substitutes
13. Elder or Younger
14. Editor
15. ___ one's rights
16. Bowling target
17. Iroquoian
18. Pony
19. ___ serif
22. Octet: It.
25. Irish princess
30. Blacksmith, at times
31. Forty - ___
33. Swindle
35. Most capable
36. Future attorney's course
37. Advice to a seated M.P.
38. Seasoning
39. Fabric
40. Delicacies
41. Advice for good people
42. Navy-clerical men
44. Conveyed
45. Early prayer
46. Shoe parts
48. Nobel
50. Wayside Inn fare
52. Circus expert
53. Bouquet
55. Writer Walter
56. Random grouping
58. Inner areas
60. Sets the tempo
61. Kind of rocket
62. Kind of play
63. Progressed
65. Between: Fr.
67. Filaments
69. Take ___ in a play
70. Call ___ to (stop)
71. Ritzy quality
72. Impress
73. Dweller in a certain colony
74. Noise abroad
75. Pledge
77. Sow again
78. Sporting wear
80. Distributed
81. Concern of Robert's Rules
82. Indian hemp: Var.
84. Groups
86. Check
88. Loop of lace
89. Type of bed
90. Boston name
92. Third: Lat.
94. Ky. racetrack
96. Retreat
97. Kind of diver
99. "Wherever I hang my hat ___"
100. Lost interest
101. Basketball scores
104. Opted
105. ___ base (be stranded)
106. Comet part
107. Hep
108. Wood sorrels
109. Eastern vine
110. Forest sight
111. "___ the night..."
112. Holly
113. Busy as ___
114. Spoils
117. Tree
118. Scottish uncle

136 Brief Mention

by Elmer Toro

ACROSS

1. Misbehave
6. "___ to be you"
11. East, in Spain
15. Draws a bead on
21. Thicket
22. ___ prayer
23. Relative of etc.
24. Novice
25. Level with
28. Picnic
29. Reveals, to poets
30. "___ a star...?"
31. Besmirch
32. Spade of TV
34. Blade
35. Kennedy
36. Unique
37. Electrical unit
38. Duct
40. Black or green
41. Esthetic doctrine
46. Pshaw!
48. Resolve
51. Endure
52. Seaman
53. Astaire
56. Valley of Europe
57. Abundantly
61. British title: Abbr.
62. Crew member
63. Foreign
65. Commando command
68. Spartan magistrate
69. Famous island
70. Land of the Peacock Throne
71. Shoot dice
72. Cat, in Rome
74. Gums: Prefix
75. Histories
77. Use a curb space
78. Similar
79. Inc., in Britain
82. Yutang
83. Like Pauline's rescuers
86. Poetic word
87. At the age of: Abbr.
88. Negatives of a sort
89. Turkish weights
90. Kind of hosen
91. Pagoda
92. Headwear, in Chaucer's day
94. Lily plant
95. U. S. Indian
96. Land of King Solomon's mines
98. Hebrew letter
100. Hold fast
102. Jerks
103. Moon crater
104. Serf
105. Old coins of Japan
107. Town in China
108. Master, in India
109. Ocean: Abbr.
110. Over, in Paris
112. Colorer
114. Buckeyes' campus
115. Hotrodding
120. ___ Simbel
122. Eastern bay: Abbr.
124. Hymenopter
125. Like, teen-age style
126. Relative of Sandy
129. Dash off
131. Farm sound
133. Virginia
135. Opulent, in Ponce
136. Game
137. Feverel's burden
139. Hoodwink
143. Restless
144. Pulitzer Prize novelist
145. Scottish slopes
146. Useful quality
147. Part of an insect's wing
148. Scepters
149. Sight, for one
150. U. S. Pioneer in mental hygiene

DOWN

1. Churchman
2. Fabric
3. Kind of TV show
4. Stringed instruments
5. Kind of rug: Abbr.
6. ___ March
7. Locarno's canton
8. Mad one
9. "___ Alone"
10. Time periods
11. Most uncanny
12. Delays
13. Color
14. Fraternal men
15. Coffee quality
16. Note
17. Particle
18. "Forget it"
19. Eldest daughter: Fr.
20. Ancient city of Greece
26. Cigarette type
27. Knox and Dix
33. Prevent
36. Suffix for dull or stand
39. Spoil
41. Clothes-drying frame
42. Fred or Steve
43. Ottoman slave
44. In any way
45. Marx
47. Choose
48. Dread Count
49. French saint
50. Invisible symbol
54. Where Regulus is
55. Goof
58. "Your ___ only peacemaker..."
59. Clyde, Forth and others
60. Take out
61. Phil Silvers role
64. Thwart
66. Pursued
67. Operates
72. Leading
73. Highest point
76. Med. subject
77. Actress Molly
78. Tread
80. Mosey
81. Opener of sorts
84. Hale character
85. Armada: Sp.
93. Point in an orbit
94. Eniwetok
95. Wont
97. Trick
98. Skill: Lat.
99. Mauna ___
100. Stiff hair
101. Ping follower
104. Casals
106. ___ David
110. Conclusions
111. Within: Prefix
113. Bartender's need
116. Used a certain utensil
117. Supreme Court justice
118. Roman magistrates
119. Playful
120. Near
121. Carried
123. Actor Williams
126. Big game
127. Tree
128. Legal expenses
130. Lions or Bears
132. Glacial ridges
134. Decays
136. Sit for
138. Enzyme
140. Self
141. Choler
142. Gift of sorts

ACROSS

1. U. S. missile
8. Nile feature
13. Ignominy
18. Combative
19. Ethiopian town
20. Source
22. Elevation
23. Mansion
24. Princeton color
25. Range
26. Tactful one
28. Assail vigorously
29. Campbell
30. Ruin
31. Neighbor of Turkey
33. Modified organism
34. Attention
35. Tobacco mixture
37. Daughter of David
39. Amory, for short
40. Elmo
41. Willamette Univ. site
42. Smoker's gadget
43. Type of playhouse
46. Evening: It.
47. Golfer's wear
48. Inspire
49. Chinese dynasty
50. Discourse: Abbr.
53. Purport
54. Lively
55. Hobby hours
58. ___ acid
59. Sometime city flood source
61. Austerity
62. U. S. system of W. W. II aid
64. Florida cape
65. Spanish corn bread
66. Compass reading
67. Malay gibbon
68. Word of mouth
69. City in Conn.
70. Earthen building material
71. July 4 parade feature
73. Inhabit
76. Kind of lily
77. Lively dances
78. In company with
79. Racetrack fences
80. Gaze
81. Mil. award
84. ___ temperature
85. Nobleman
86. Stadium sounds
87. Strip of wood
88. With extra calories, so to say
90. Encounter
94. Kind of code
95. Carrying on
96. Nymph loved by Minos
97. Rapid-fire joke
99. Immediately
100. Antelope
101. In a stringent way
102. Stage direction
103. Playing marble
104. Foot lever

DOWN

1. Stuffed olive
2. Kukla's friend, formally
3. Cambric or damask
4. Used up
5. Famous fan dancer
6. Occurrence
7. Pick up speed
8. Famous friend
9. Dutch cheese
10. Large moth
11. False friend
12. Swiss river
13. Golf club
14. Injury
15. Strauss opera
16. Threatened
17. Impress deeply
18. Coalesce
21. British marshal of W. W. II
27. Part of a jar
28. Tribunal
32. Crash into
35. Financing
36. English limestone
37. Fancy vests
38. Toward shelter
39. Cozy bistro setting
40. Take a safe dueling role
41. German river
42. Find out
43. Certain pub drinkers
44. Like a frog
45. Choice segment
46. Alan Ladd film
47. Mate of a sort
50. Register
51. Hammed it up
52. Sought office again
54. Cognizant
55. Shoe
56. Aimless drifting
57. Headbands
60. "West Side Story" girl
63. Dude territory
68. Tiresome person
69. Musician Richard ___ Bennet
70. Calif. range
71. Army camp event
72. TV newsman Harry
73. Pacific island
74. Imitate
75. Geometric figure
76. Jalopy
79. Scottish explorer
80. Trifle
81. Weedy grass
82. English essayist
83. Cautious
85. Trimming device
86. Like snakes' eyes
87. Scottish landowner
89. Formerly
91. Spoken
92. Pit
93. Granular snow
96. Shell-game item
98. Grassland

138 Habit-Forming by Alfio Micci

ACROSS

1. French composer
6. "Golden Boy" author
11. Off balance
16. Subway for René
21. Night sound
22. Delicate
23. Wife of Abraham
24. Put one's ___
25. Family garment of sorts
27. Track event
29. Kind
30. Fertile
31. ___ de-lance
32. ___ now
33. Comparative ending
34. Discards
36. Toys
38. Family girls: Abbr.
39. Name in motors
40. Large boats
41. Rabbit's title
42. Stadium area
44. Cuzco people
46. Prince of drama
48. Length of some plays
50. French Alp
53. Mango parts
54. ___ boredom
56. Amount ___ (insurance term)
57. French story
58. Rooted
60. Horse color
61. Changes into particles
63. Sunk without ___
64. Shaped
66. Bauble
67. German pronoun
68. Musical speeds
69. Stone
71. Earth, in Berlin
72. Summer hours: Abbr.
75. Kitchen utensil
77. White stuff, in Scotland
79. Affirming words
81. Dejected
82. German numeral
84. "___ d'arte"
86. Kind of train
88. Tiny: Abbr.
90. Low walls
92. Cooking direction
94. Ships' ropes
97. Full
98. Jewelry part
99. "Will you ___ parlor, said the..."
102. Potato-soup ingredients
103. Rejected, to poets
105. Hamlet
106. Graf ___
107. Road curves
108. Ballet garment
110. Letters
111. Passover rite
112. Relatives of Martians
114. Arden and others
116. Have on
117. Wading bird
119. Gumbo: Var.
120. Feels poorly
121. Enzyme
124. Negation
125. Dumbarton ___
126. Romaine
127. Italian sculptor
129. Typist's abbr.
130. Weds
133. Family garment
135. Fault
136. Lasso
137. Hearth
138. Biting
139. French remainder
140. Cuts, old style
141. Winter wear
142. Misplaces

DOWN

1. Light ___
2. Sam, for one
3. Literary garment
4. Age
5. Upholsters anew
6. Teutonic hero and others
7. Uninteresting
8. Some flowers
9. A ___ two (occasionally)
10. Lawyers: Abbr.
11. Residue
12. Arabian tambourine
13. Kind of verb: Abbr.
14. Homestead and other legislation
15. Unfashionable garments
16. Majority
17. Attention
18. Hiking garments
19. Put through a sieve
20. Topnotchers
26. Morsels
28. Señor's assent
31. Postal term
35. Classroom equipment
37. Still
38. Czech city
39. Former
42. Kashmir alphabet
43. ___ charge account
44. Business abbr.
45. Okinawa city
46. Hair's partner
47. W.W. I group
49. Western Indian
51. List
52. Examined
54. Double-crosser
55. Memo-pad word
59. Foray
62. Waiting for ___ to come in
65. Certain records
66. Full of a grain
68. Hardy heroine
70. Elude
72. Spot
73. Climbs
74. Some bridge hands
76. Urban garments
78. "Exodus" man
80. Sign
83. Harbor sights
85. Composer Jacques and family
87. Helper: Abbr.
89. Hungry-one's cry
91. ___ car (overtake)
93. Genus of frogs
94. Waterers: Abbr.
95. Boxoffice stars
96. Pintail duck
98. ___ notte
100. Long time
101. Slangy pronoun
104. Rind of a kind
109. Sixth-century date
111. Sedative drug
113. Ark builder
115. Texas city
116. Decline
117. Among: Prefix
118. Drink, in Paris
120. Jots
121. Tahoe and Como
122. Miss Thompson
123. Terrapins
125. Wine-bottle, in Italy
126. Shelter
128. Spanish painter
131. Toper
132. Scottish negative
133. Hack
134. Sgt., for one

139 Squarely Figured

by A. J. Santora

ACROSS

1. After-midnight hours
7. Last Commandment
13. Spring date
20. Green crust on metal
21. "Give the devil ___"
22. "Peekaboo, ___"
23. Chem. compounds
24. Italian city
25. "...sleep, perchance ___"
26. Dine
27. Sharp sound
29. Defeats
31. Goddess of infatuation
32. Malay dagger: Var.
34. Hank of yarn
36. Deer
37. Court judgment
39. New York street
42. Japanese coin
44. Makes an offer
46. Not at home
47. Cornbreads
49. In ___
50. Spar on a sail
52. Shouted
54. Eases off
58. What some scouts look for
59. Vaulter's concern
61. Renew old school ties
62. Ex-Senator from Nebraska
63. Male deer
64. Provided that
66. Fairly old auto
67. Gypsy
68. Contended
70. Smother
72. Sesame
73. Jewish month
75. Room in a casa
76. Phila. team
77. Whole
79. Part of a book
81. Hitter
83. Repeats
84. Sam and J.C. of golf
86. Note declining an invitation
87. Pulverize
88. Planet
90. Glistened
91. Strange
92. Caveman of comics
96. Friend in Paris
97. What a duffer does at times
101. Small pair
102. Raffle-ticket marking
104. Ulan ___
107. Anna's land
108. Spigot
109. The ___ be counted
111. In unison
114. Numerical prefix
115. Bulldog, for one
118. Verdi opera
120. Explosive
122. Expires
123. Mews: Fr.
124. Council of 325 A.D.
125. Impost at Aqueduct
126. Annoy
127. Smarts

DOWN

1. Kind of swimsuit
2. Italian spice
3. Ear trouble
4. ___ hand
5. Over again
6. Cattle feed
7. Show gratitude
8. Door piece
9. Spanish coin: Abbr.
10. Famous London address
11. Gum tree
12. Learned
13. Stage fright
14. Service-club units
15. Little Edward
16. Always, to poets
17. Life span of a locust
18. Exactly
19. Heraldic bars
28. Pale
30. Bribe
33. Gapes
35. Mine strike
37. More likely
38. Popular song about a highway
40. Catnap
41. Rat ___
43. Prefixes for recent
45. Lubricate
47. Mine sweeps on ships
48. Underlying layer
50. U. S. Playwright
51. Peacock's pride
52. Student
53. Lao-tse's followers
55. Type of pump
56. Not ventilated
57. Mesta et al.
58. Destructive insects
60. W. W. II group
65. Pullman
69. Fordhamite
70. Douay Bible name
71. Repeat number
74. Pipe-cleaning tool
76. Brass in a musical
78. Arborvitaes
80. Phileas Fogg's travel time
82. Turkish title
85. Hit sign
89. Voiced sounds
91. River of Spain
92. Where 126 is
93. Put on cargo
94. Ida of films
95. Opposite of neg.
98. Young pet
99. Tahiti wrap
100. Fifth of the Indy 500
103. Sign of the flu
105. Aunt in Paris
106. Willow
109. Mouthy
110. Factual
112. Code letters
113. Send out
116. Initials on a crate
117. Elec. particle
119. Lawyer: Abbr.
121. Chemical prefix

140 Coded Phrases
by Edward J. O'Brien

ACROSS

1. Old timer
8. "On ___ of Bibles"
14. Card game
17. Concern of Congress
20. 43,560 square feet
21. By law: Fr.
22. Half a story
24. 19th century advance
27. Main et al.: Abbr.
28. Allay
29. Hospital doctor
30. Canapé spread
31. Christian symbol
33. Skill: Lat.
34. Play the shrinking violet
36. Doorway: Abbr.
38. In ___ (fearing)
40. German road
43. Numerical prefix
45. ___ dinner (entertains)
47. Cartes
48. One ___ million
50. Quiet flower
52. Leading
55. Classman: Abbr.
56. ___ of armor
57. Leaves for, in a casual way
61. Adds juices
63. Highways: Abbr.
64. Get
65. Medical drains
67. Titanic
69. People of Brazil
70. Drink
71. Northwest people
72. Constellation
76. Stellar, sportswise
78. Addicted to cigars
81. Germane
82. Rubbernecked
83. Roman 1501
84. Russian secret police
85. Cookery style
86. Of a poison: Prefix
87. Trojan et al.
91. Elephant
92. French cup
93. One more: Abbr.
94. Habitat: Prefix
95. Summer mos.
97. Vietnamese holidays
98. "... room to ___ cat"
100. Warrior of Japan
102. Neighbor of Den.
103. Pursued
105. Throw an apostle overboard
107. College groups
110. Wool: Prefix
111. Carries on
113. Relative of Able and Baker
114. Charm
116. Sets of boxes
118. Unsophisticated
121. Stop!: Sp.
123. Spectral
124. "___ Macabre"
125. Crimean or Boer
126. Think ___
128. Simpson and Grange: Abbr.
130. One, in Naples
131. Roman 151
133. U.S. sculptor
135. Tittle
137. Hosp. vehicle
140. Lapidarists' concern, with "Will"
145. Reemploy
146. ___ all
147. The measure: It.
148. Footlike part
149. Man's name
150. Book of Apocrypha
151. Beauties

DOWN

1. Old wooden tubs
2. Body of soldiers
3. Debating sides: Abbr.
4. Morse sound
5. Jaundice: Prefix
6. "There must be ___"
7. Peggy and Pinky
8. Suitable
9. "I___ with my own eyes"
10. Ditch outlet, in a way
11. "It's ___ much for me"
12. Gaggles
13. Large vat
14. State V.I.P.
15. Still
16. Pianist Peter
17. Bklyn. campus
18. Girl's name
19. After midnight
23. Roller or fitter
25. Undiluted
26. John Wilkes Booth performance
32. West Coast inst.
33. Mame's corsets
35. Prison breaks
37. Dundee denial
39. Floors with sunset views
40. Youth org.
41. Exclamations
42. Kind of figure
44. Milan opera wear
46. Do lacework
49. Pronoun
51. Calif. campus
53. Touches on
54. Small quantity
58. Whether going ___
59. Uncoerced
60. N. C. Cape
62. Indonesian island
66. Steady customer's bar order
67. Attacks
68. Excessive
69. In style
73. Wall St. house
74. Sublease
75. Yankees: Abbr.
77. Freshens
79. Small bird
80. Moldings: Abbr.
85. Gem wts.
87. Bantu language
88. Hitler aide
89. One ___
90. Italian arrest
96. Embellishes
99. Noun suffix
101. ___ tree
102. Falcons, Eagles et al.
103. Wins big
104. Descriptive of a lone ram
106. Jennet
108. Across: Abbr.
109. Pen
112. F.D.R. agency
115. Mundane
116. Indiana campus
117. Dry-plaster painting
119. Added items of decor
120. Judge Crater's last words
122. Norse Red
125. More discerning
127. Girl's name
129. French chemist
132. Jacob's son
134. Fraternal org.
136. Sooner
137. Aleutian island
138. Blackbird
139. Rels.
141. These: Fr.
142. Lady of Spain
143. G.I. wear
144. Ship-shaped clock

141 Hidden Blemishes by Arthur Bennett

ACROSS

1. Fine violins
7. Type designs
12. Restrictions
18. Endurance
19. Originated
20. Flatbush and others
22. Certain fighters
24. Dessert
25. U.S. inventor
26. Merle
27. Guided and others
29. Harem room
30. Peer Gynt's mother
31. Corrida sounds
32. Israeli port
33. Southwest wind
34. Decades
36. Top banana
37. All: Lat.
38. Have ___
39. Disabled
41. Golf veteran
42. Like an ox
43. Secret doctrines
46. Thing done
47. France: Prefix
48. ___ - skelter
49. Canoes of Malaysia: Var.
50. Acrid-tasting
53. Zodiac sign
54. Milton
55. Devoured
56. Direction
57. Geological stage
58. Singer born in N.Y.
60. Detective of fiction
61. Channel
62. Atropos et al.
63. Neglects
64. Casino money
65. Man against the ___
67. Campus groups
68. Broadway play of 1969-70
69. Tall and lean
70. ___ of humor
71. Exposed to risk
72. Certain animal
74. Salt trees
75. Spanish girls
76. Unkempt
77. Word with case or well
78. Partner of snick
79. Hillock, in England
83. Hurries
84. Hammer parts
85. Suffix for rheo or thermo
86. "___ a drop to drink"
87. East, in Bonn
88. Circulated
89. Shoe
91. Vehicle
92. Easily dominated
94. Babe
97. Ionosphere layer
98. Cancel
99. Meanness
100. Real ___
101. Bother
102. Horses

DOWN

1. Military command
2. Actor Karl
3. Sums: Abbr.
4. Ascot
5. Japanese box
6. Surgeon, to a gangster
7. More comely
8. Old Greek city
9. German botanist
10. Superlative ending
11. Verse forms
12. Ivory palms
13. Ward off
14. Power units
15. Fuegian
16. Way to make a mountain
17. Beer mugs
18. Churchill word
21. Peevish
23. Fished
28. Fetid
32. Big birds
33. Strong as ___
35. Early schoolroom needs
36. Persian name
37. Like a good pitch
38. Part of Poe's name
40. Beverages
41. Staircase, in Rome
42. Delicacies
43. Ballpark cry
44. Antenna
45. Certain insects
46. Molding edge
47. Wooden shoes
49. Marquette et al.
50. Fountain drinks
51. Blackbirds' place
52. Perfumed
54. Balmy
55. Choice group
58. Tropical fruit
59. Collect
60. Messiah
62. Boggy
64. Priest: Sp.
66. "Downstairs" people
67. Cat genus
68. Rozelle
70. Keep one's cards
71. Lays claim to
72. Stranded
73. Kind of time
74. To ___
75. Chaotic
77. Halcyon
78. Fixed
80. New
81. Drives
82. Kind of vote
84. Automatic ___
85. Alone
88. O. T. name
89. Moth
90. Indian peasant
91. Heavenly being: Fr.
93. Life ins. man
95. Scottish one
96. Teens

Turkey Talk
by Frances Hansen

ACROSS

1. Soft shoe
4. Got: Abbr.
8. False gods
13. Dr. Dolittle's pig
19. Winchester
21. Cheerful sound
22. Smiling broadly
23. ___ time
24. Perth of New Jersey
25. Drag strip for chariots
26. Pacific island group
27. It's tutu divine
28. Pyncheon's pride, punny style
32. Deed
33. Reluctant: Var.
34. Ms. men
35. Fr. girl
36. Jabberwocky
40. Recipient
42. "This ___ recording"
45. What it takes to make a wink
46. Runs lukewarm
49. Organic compound
50. Govt. air agency
51. Armada: Abbr.
52. Wall hanging
56. Number one
58. "Waitin' on ___"
60. Map features
61. Gaelic
62. Without exception
63. Police-deploying tactic
67. Sticky stuff
68. Arctic explorer
70. "___ About the Boy"
72. Old card game
73. TV late show
75. Holmes's words for a tea party
81. Wedge-shaped: Prefix
82. Nootka
83. Steam bath
84. Portion: Abbr.
85. Panay people
86. Hat named for a painter
90. Kind of ring
92. Eager
96. No room "in ___"
98. Sidewalk test in July?
100. Comical
101. Ibsen matron, punny style
105. Framing-shop abbr.
107. Blue-black: Dialect
108. Islets
109. Samuel F. B., formally
110. Wander a little
112. Teachers' org.
113. Idaho capital
114. "...produced a ___"
118. Impose on: Scot.
119. Church group: Abbr.
122. Dinner course
123. Siouan
124. Warning in a Riley poem
131. Garden shrub
132. Kind of yell
133. Small case
134. Surprised exclamations
135. Consign to perdition
136. Sound of a knight's approach
137. Yo-ho-ho drinks
138. Old musical symbol
139. Kind of prunes
140. Nincompoops
141. Small baracuda
142. Carriers: Abbr.

DOWN

1. Copy: Prefix
2. "To tell children ___ and goblins"
3. Near
4. "___ I had the wings..."
5. Had it out
6. Eat high off ___
7. Risk
8. Ignoble
9. Century plant
10. Kind of forces
11. Daniel's arena
12. Catch
13. Ate dessert, in a way
14. Helpless
15. Starr of the West
16. Burst of laughter
17. Shoshoneans
18. Blink the eyes
19. Bowl sound
20. Order to a platoon
29. "___ me, pretty maiden..."
30. Before 'nuff
31. ___ vincit amor
36. Faux pas
37. Walk ___
38. Likewise, I'm sure
39. Ukraine city
41. Choose
42. Entire: Prefix
43. Classify
44. Girl's name
47. Coaster
48. Row
49. Letter
52. Having buds
53. "___ of God, I come!"
54. Hut of Guiana
55. Dinner course
57. Suit material
59. ___ Ashbury
62. Wire: Abbr.
64. "Words have ___ life than deeds"
65. Japanese game
66. S. F. hill
69. "...go to the Warres in ___"
71. Metric units: Abbr.
74. Moth
75. Tyrone or Arlo
76. Town in Spain
77. Gobble
78. Artist's need
79. Lead
80. W. W. II craft
81. Lion trainer
87. "And more ___ more"
88. Get an ___ effort
89. City: Lat.
91. Urge
93. "Don't ___ dinner!"
94. Kukla's friend
95. Language: Prefix
97. Monogram for Jesus
99. "___ your pardon"
100. Loss of rank
102. Letter-shaped bar
103. Morning hrs.
104. Third Reich name
106. Gog's partner
110. Preen again
111. "I hate to be ___"
113. Puccini's "La ___"
115. Columbus campus
116. Antisocial ones
117. Fracas
118. Kind of boss
120. Rhyme schemes
121. Fully: Lat.
124. In ___ (vexed)
125. Pheasant group
126. Killer whale
127. B.P.O.E.
128. Itemize
129. Elec. units
130. Employ
131. Science degrees

Office Doings

by Gladys V. Miller

ACROSS

1. Open house
7. Battery terminal
12. Singer Clark
18. Alcohol
19. Defiant one
20. Desk items
22. Leroy Anderson work
24. Clerical cap
25. Ear part
26. Plasters over
27. Sky body
29. Kind of space
30. "___ Old Spanish Garden"
31. Awkward
32. Exams
34. Liven, with "up"
35. Instance: Fr.
36. John and Mark: Abbr.
37. Falling-out
39. Miserly
41. Union Pacific et al.
42. Parents' need, at times
44. Vitality
46. Pry
48. Tennis placements
50. Roof décor
52. Arena V.I.P.
55. Tammany man
59. Light color
60. "Blossom in purple ___"
61. Vapor
62. African village
63. River features
65. "How stupid ___!"
66. Letterhead abbr.
67. Suffix for acids
69. Vivid display
70. Lamb, old style
71. Standard
73. Gillette and Louise
75. Appraisals: Abbr.
77. Galatea's lover
78. Takes a rifle position
80. Depression initials
81. Galápagos sight
83. Bouts
84. Lose one's bankroll
86. Carry on
87. Flower
89. New star
90. Truman and Myerson
94. Kind of stool
96. Action
98. Verne hero
100. Air group: Abbr.
101. Jungfrau
102. Writer Seton
104. Removes dross
106. Church man
108. ___ breve
109. Zodiac sign
111. Where: Lat.
112. Entrance
113. Out of bed
114. Swizzle stick
116. Third Reich et al.
119. Muster
120. Nursemaids
121. "It makes ___ to me"
122. Voters
123. Chair piece
124. Foot in the door

DOWN

1. Acropolis city, to Greeks
2. Omega
3. Throw one's ___ the ring
4. Cameo stone
5. Mass of hair
6. Chooses
7. Unstable
8. Cosmetic implement
9. Fragments
10. Aberdeen's river
11. Baseball statistic
12. Small stones
13. Silkworm
14. Edible root
15. Finish
16. Pat
17. Highway
18. Principles
21. Shirts, in Scotland
23. Chinese dynasty
28. L.A. player
31. Broadcasts
32. Policeman
33. Anna and Clara
36. Faction
38. Inspired
40. Between A.M. and P.M.
43. Certain master
45. First
47. Church calendar
49. Attack
50. Builder's afterthought
51. Covered with clay
53. Forward
54. Danish port
55. Name in 1950 robbery
56. Greek nymph
57. African raptor
58. London borough
64. Flower oil
68. Copies
72. Baseball team
73. Resources
74. "___ qui peut"
76. ___ Mater
77. Greek god
79. Movie studios
82. Eye part
85. Eggar
88. Freshens up a perm
91. Cracker
92. Certain shape
93. Meager
94. Life raft
95. Grieg dancer
97. Alehouse
99. Russian province
100. Zero
103. Pianist Claudio
105. Tycoon
107. What to do with your boots
108. Tribe of Israel
110. Chemical group
112. Adjective suffix
113. Aide: Abbr.
115. Consume
117. Opposite of exp.
118. Swoboda or Nessen

144 Keeping House

by Christine Valence

ACROSS

1. Beach sight
7. British ___
12. Little terror
16. Heretofore, old style
20. Did a July 4 chore
21. Sharp-pointed
22. Greek letter
23. Slangy denial
24. Seeing eye of a sort
26. Access for Hans Brinker
28. Ox of Tibet
29. Streamlet
30. Russian city
32. So-long!
33. Weekday: Abbr.
34. Fleer
36. Certain eggs
37. River to the Elbe
39. Partner of groans
41. Somerset spa
43. Track officials
45. Certain athletes
46. Mural artist
47. Expect
49. Now: Lat.
50. Curtain material
51. Divide
54. Poured
56. Warm up
58. Certain transoms
60. Unpredictable
62. Jumble
64. O'Casey
65. Diminutive suffixes
66. ___ Moines
67. Laugh
69. Thus: Lat.
70. Drop in for ___
72. Printer's mark
73. ___ of Cremona
75. Planned
77. Yokels
78. Kind of farm
80. Slides for some children
82. Organ stops
83. Decorative plants
84. Small room
85. Amen
87. Basics
88. Certain bags
89. Louis or Philip
91. Young animal
92. Reign, in India
95. Field sound
96. Marquis de ___
97. Godhead
100. Copious
102. Third degree, in a way
105. Because
107. Forge apparatus
108. Bases of bone tissue: Var.
109. "___ your pardon"
111. Sale condition
113. Relative of groovy
114. Spot
115. Closely-knit group
116. Poplars
118. Sisters
119. Indisputable things
121. Dartmoor, for example
122. Line, as a roof
123. English city
125. High in pitch
126. Certain shape
128. Ascend
130. Holm oak
131. Boxing units: Abbr.
134. Embryo house
137. House area
140. Forsaken
141. Mixture
142. Huntress and namesakes
143. Small cavity
144. Views
145. Cried
146. Appetizing
147. Grew more interested

DOWN

1. Imitate
2. Opera excerpt
3. Type of intrigue
4. Lawyer: Abbr.
5. Sinew: Prefix
6. Without aim
7. Here: Fr.
8. Many-windowed places
9. Luck and others
10. Jackets
11. Makes clothes
12. One club or one spade
13. Ways
14. Perfume
15. Social grace
16. Pass-catcher
17. Attic, so to speak
18. Golf club
19. Sea swallows
21. Hole puncher
25. Impish
27. Piper's milieu
31. Composer Jerome
35. Tableware
36. Extend
38. Make a boo-boo
40. Not imit.
41. Laid open
42. In the know
44. River of central Europe
45. Sneaky ___
46. Chair part
48. Ties up
50. It's out for welcome guests
51. Golfing name
52. Voices
53. Sibilant sounds
55. Personal book
57. Bring out
59. ___ rose
61. Tea
63. Singular
68. Dispute settler
71. Middles: Abbr.
72. Somewhat, with "of"
73. Spirits
74. Great ___
76. Dined in a café
77. Money deliverers
78. Prohibits
79. Building style
81. Love ___
82. Courage
83. North Dakota city
84. Fogies
86. Jazz form
88. Tannish
90. Resident
92. Place to play
93. Colorado resort
94. Mocks
96. Errs
98. Nothing: Fr.
99. Picture holder
101. Recovered
103. Word of caution
104. Eur. measure
106. Sesame
110. Fragrance
112. ___ bill of goods
115. Mint variety
116. Wanderer of fiction
117. Alternate
119. Tall story
120. Brass or steel
121. Trickery
122. Roman ___
124. Newspaper edition
127. Bird known for straight flying
129. Letter-signing servant: Abbr.
130. Possibilities
132. Pass out
133. Timetable, for short
135. Being, in abstract
136. Add up
138. Arthurian knight
139. Father of Abner

145 Fitting Phrases by Bert Beaman

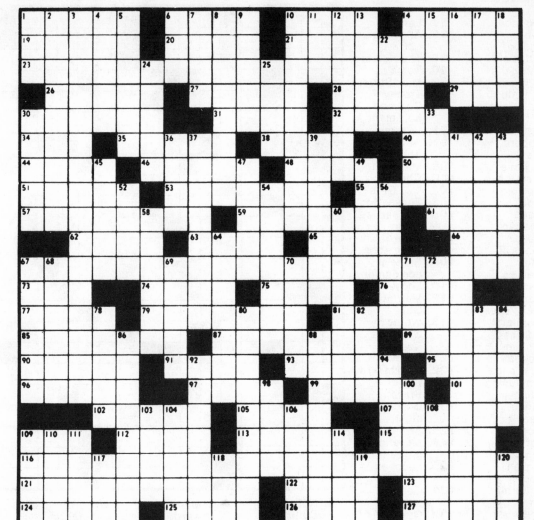

ACROSS

1. Peachy
6. ___ California
10. Wine barrel
14. Kind of comedy
19. Malaga raisin
20. Norse name
21. On the blink
23. Prepare to shave
26. Insurance problems
27. Pass off
28. Author's concern
29. Relative of Mme.
30. Opposed to
31. Calpurnia, for one
32. Paris areas
34. Publisher's abbr.
35. Some racers
38. Brood of young birds
40. Attacked
44. Beery
46. Himalayan denizens
48. Electrical units
50. Before febrero
51. Great Horde division
53. Depreciate
55. Bills
57. Glasses
59. French pince-nez
61. Drills
62. Ineffectual
63. Branches
65. Come-on
66. Wheel spoke: Fr.
67. Designate in a way
73. Suffix for drunk or cow
74. Table extender
75. Kind of case
76. Roman emperor
77. Strains: Scot.
79. Intertwines
81. Eradicated
85. Accord
87. Trouble
89. ___ administravit
90. Road to Alaska
91. Cake ingredient
93. Show rudeness
95. Snorri Sturluson creation
96. Some looks
97. Old recompense
99. Wives, informally
101. Roll of hair
102. Elapsed
105. Eggs, in Bonn
107. Cape Vert natives
109. African charm
112. Mine: Fr.
113. ___ in the right direction
115. Stone pillar
116. Done with
121. Guiding principle
122. Pinza
123. Composition
124. Riding schools: Abbr.
125. River to North Sea
126. Music sign
127. More protected

DOWN

1. Ship departure: Abbr.
2. Got rid of
3. Egg on the chin
4. Public figures
5. Large hurdy-gurdy
6. Cattle genus
7. Hebrew letter
8. Kind of window
9. Fasten
10. Scheming one
11. Same: Prefix
12. Reliable pitcher
13. Down-under attraction
14. Certain samples
15. Heavy-duty wire: Abbr.
16. Stadium sounds
17. Party equipment
18. Soup ingredient
22. Sherry mold
24. School assignment
25. "The frost ___ the . . ."
30. Hawks
33. ___ Rosa
36. Phone part: Abbr.
37. Light
39. Swings
41. Gardener's faith in his carrots
42. Debtor's situation
43. ___ the towel
45. Biblical enemy of Jews
47. Ragout of game
49. Seed: Prefix
52. Gibe
54. Significant
56. ___ the road
58. Horn
60. Mother, for one
64. Cordial
67. French mathematician
68. A.L. player
69. Boys'-book writer
70. Deeds
71. Kind of light
72. Guitar opening
78. Boa
80. Party-going dandy
82. Breath: Prefix
83. Patience
84. College officials
86. Subjugates
88. Release, as hoarded funds
92. Kind of bill
94. ___- Japanese War
98. Region: Abbr.
100. Arrangements
103. Indication
104. Stew
106. Clear sky
108. Networks
109. Silly
110. Farm ___
111. Spanish pot
114. Greek letters
117. ___ man out
118. Caucho tree
119. In demand
120. Neighbor of Den.

146 Christmas Thoughts
by Anne Fox

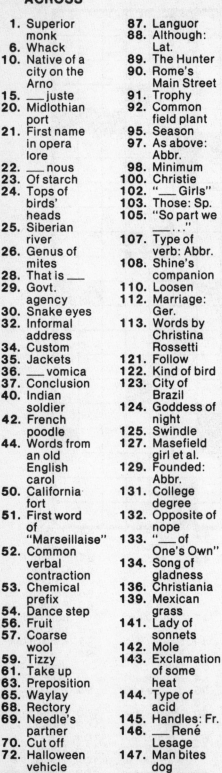

ACROSS

1. Superior monk
6. Whack
10. Native of a city on the Arno
15. ___ juste
20. Midlothian port
21. First name in opera lore
22. ___ nous
23. Of starch
24. Tops of birds' heads
25. Siberian river
26. Genus of mites
28. That is ___
29. Govt. agency
30. Snake eyes
32. Informal address
34. Custom
35. Jackets
36. ___ vomica
37. Conclusion
40. Indian soldier
42. French poodle
44. Words from an old English carol
50. California fort
51. First word of "Marseillaise"
52. Common verbal contraction
53. Chemical prefix
54. Dance step
56. Fruit
57. Coarse wool
59. Tizzy
61. Take up
63. Preposition
65. Waylay
68. Rectory
69. Needle's partner
70. Cut off
72. Halloween vehicle
73. Biblical brother
75. August occurrence
77. Henchman
78. ___ rasae
82. Words from St. Matthew
85. Beach grass
86. With a crest.
87. Languor
88. Although: Lat.
89. The Hunter
90. Rome's Main Street
91. Trophy
92. Common field plant
95. Season
97. As above: Abbr.
98. Minimum
100. Christie
102. "___ Girls"
103. Those: Sp.
105. "So part we ___ ..."
107. Type of verb: Abbr.
108. Shine's companion
110. Loosen
112. Marriage: Ger.
113. Words by Christina Rossetti
121. Follow
122. Kind of bird
123. City of Brazil
124. Goddess of night
125. Swindle
127. Masefield girl et al.
129. Founded: Abbr.
131. College degree
132. Opposite of nope
133. "___ of One's Own"
134. Song of gladness
136. Christiania
139. Mexican grass
141. Lady of sonnets
142. Mole
143. Exclamation of some heat
144. Type of acid
145. Handles: Fr.
146. ___ René Lesage
147. Man bites dog
148. Demand

DOWN

1. Italian mountain soldier
2. Lebanon's capital
3. Mississippi city
4. Native: Suffix
5. Words by Frederic W. Farrar
6. Have place
7. Resemble: Suffix
8. Flipper
9. Spume
10. Words by Thackeray
11. Business abbr.
12. ___ Bethlehem
13. Ravine
14. Gender: Abbr.
15. Words by Charles Wesley
16. Put on an act
17. Nursery-rhyme character
18. Buck heroine
19. Certain gifts
27. Religious groups
31. March word
33. Berkshire village
38. O.T. book
39. Convinced of
41. Times: Abbr.
43. Four inches
45. ___ brown
46. French pastry
47. Kids
48. Stolid ones
49. Olden time
54. Musical work
55. Novel of 1895
57. "Welcome ___"
58. Leather-stocking name: Var.
60. Estate in India
61. Genus of plant pest
62. Chemical compound
64. The hunted
66. Upholstery fabric
67. N.C. cape
71. Where the Acheron flows
72. Arctic bay
74. Thailand money
76. Warning
77. Mouse: Fr.
79. City of Peru
80. Black ___
81. Pharaohs' land
83. Type of cheese
84. Postal limbos: Abbr.
90. Conn. village
92. Spanker
93. ___ —Finnic
94. Causing wonder
96. Court word
97. Fuel
99. Hgt.
101. Japanese native
104. Weaver's reeds
106. Mosquito genus
109. Opera part
110. Middle East org.
111. Christmas ___
114. Again
115. Type of library
116. New Hampshire city
117. Jostles
118. African antelope
119. Purely intellectual
120. Look for
125. Offenses against law
126. Monitor lizard
128. B'way group
130. Go to ___
135. Finial
137. Pronoun
138. Wallace
140. Strain

147 Dress Circle
by Thomas Sheenan

ACROSS

1. NKVD's predecessor
4. Affix
9. Wrap
14. Invasion craft
18. Victorian mouthwash
19. Cigarettes, at times
20. Impulses
21. Okla. Indian
22. Coffee containers
23. Reverses in a way
25. Asta's mistress
26. Underskirt
28. Blood: Prefix
29. Showing an emotion
31. America's Cup entry
32. Apiece
33. Brazilian plant
34. Pastry order
36. Screen fare
43. Zoological suffix
44. Bugaboo
45. Like some sheep
46. Actor Dullea
47. Song of joy
48. Chilean seaport
50. P. M.'s address
51. "___ Magic"
52. Gridiron seizure
55. Scene for bit players
56. NBC and CBS
58. Riverfront Stadium team
59. Snake charmer
61. Placed: Lat.
62. Chemical compound
64. Gushed
68. Kind of jet
69. Scottish slope
70. N. Y. street
72. Singing voice: Abbr.
75. Bar offerings
79. First-down yardage
80. Shipshape
82. Playwright Jones
83. Name in evangelism
84. Coin
85. Ethan or Fred
87. Words to a sentry
89. Bedouin
90. Cowards
92. Charles ___ Stengel
94. Rumanian coins
95. Pioneered
96. Opposite of a busy signal?
97. "___ Go Gentle into . . ."
98. S.A. monkey
100. Slows down
104. Kind of dancer
105. Capt. Corcoran's command
108. Melville romance
109. Arrow poison
110. Degrade
111. Spoken for
112. House plant
113. Look a ___
114. Roman spirits
115. Occur
116. Religious title

DOWN

1. Tennessee's Albert
2. Milquetoasts
3. Resident of Buffalo, e.g.
4. Lithographer's liquid
5. ___ water (hard put)
6. Literary pseudonym
7. Gust, in Scotland
8. Baseball great
9. Deceitfully agreeable
10. Gum or rubber
11. Irish writing
12. Celtic Neptune
13. Output of 6 Down
14. Silver
15. Holder of many records
16. Conservative one
17. Great amount
18. Higher: Abbr.
24. Luster
27. Here: Fr.
30. Slangy denials
32. Full: Prefix
34. Atoll
35. Late-show time on TV
36. Ventures upon
37. French political unit
38. Bitter words
39. Norse hero and others
40. Kings, queens, etc.
41. Small combo
42. Uppity one
44. Kind of football field
47. Examination
49. Herring
52. Dorsal
53. Indians
54. Chance's partner
57. Barrister's accessory
60. Old times
62. "Will and intellect ___ and the same . . ."
63. Certain bonds
65. Grandma Moses, for one
66. Nevertheless
67. Make a ___ (impress)
69. Justice White
70. Math term
71. Dickens's Uriah
72. Take up quarters
73. Heraldic bearing
74. Glorified foxholes
76. Joins a union
77. Bundled
78. Whale-oil cask
81. Scarlett's in-law and others
84. Enumerates
86. Taboo, new style
88. Coil of yarn
91. Nevertheless
92. Adequate
93. Class
96. Leverets
97. Kierkegaard
98. Godunov
99. ___ dixit
100. Tunisian port
101. Norse god
102. ___ song (cheaply)
103. Dahomey native
104. Cratchit
106. Executive's degree
107. Used up

148 Button Up by Herbert Ettenson

ACROSS

1. Part of a refrain
5. Tobacco kiln
9. Part of a Taiwan name
13. Roadhouse of sorts
20. Salad ingredient
23. Broiled-meat order
24. Gossip
25. Lincoln's Ann
26. Eastern state: Abbr.
27. Revoke, as a legacy
28. Offers bait
30. Asian ox
31. Iroquoian
32. Underlings: Abbr.
33. Rises to prominence
34. Wide of the mark
35. Camillo, for one
36. Superlative suffix-
37. Macaw
38. Muhammad et al.
39. Nidologist's concern
41. Town near Rome
44. Boating hazard
47. He wrote "Devotions"
49. Oldtime movie actor
52. English historian
54. What Polonius hid behind
57. Hyalite and harlequin
58. "___ through the coming day!"
60. Uses thread
61. Nasty look
62. Feature
63. Civil War battle scene
65. Sandwiched
67. Colt or filly
68. In the direction of movement
69. Home-buyer's burden: Abbr.
72. Asian partridge
73. Relative of 1 Across
74. Be loyal
76. Gumshoe
77. Feudal vassal
80. Certain paintings
81. Facial annoyances
84. "Like-it-is" talk
87. Speleologist's concern
88. Imparted
89. Man ___
91. Survive
92. Eateries
93. Old Roman receptacles
94. Vehicle of a sort
96. Suspension of activity
99. Partner of snicks
100. "When I was ___"
102. Superb
103. Digs
106. First word of Xmas poem
107. Belief
109. Roman spirit
110. Hagen
112. Linden
113. "...no ___ birth and death"
116. "...bit of ___ the best of us"
119. Perfume: Var.
120. Sea bird
121. Dogcart
122. ___ boredom
123. Other: Fr.
124. Well-thought of
126. Poet
129. Sharp-tongued critics
130. President
131. Maple and Walnut
132. Fleuret
133. Affectations
134. Oregon bay

DOWN

1. Had a speech problem
2. River of Woe
3. Of jungle royalty
4. Between a rag and a hank
5. Scrap
6. Dismayed
7. Cutter and pung
8. Jewish month
9. Ancestral line
10. Cry's partner
11. Skin condition
12. Professional mourners
13. Respite
14. Observances
15. "___ well"
16. Adjectival ending
17. Certain fan
18. He wrote "Red Star Over China"
19. Olid
21. Japanese outcast
22. Word with chic or bien
23. Young, lively one
29. Enraptured
32. Holly of southern U.S.
33. Of a time
34. King in "The Tempest"
36. Suffixes for numbers
37. Bothers
38. Fruit drink
40. Gives the willies to
41. Wine pitchers
42. Beau
43. Joust
45. Brightest star
46. Nasser
48. Navy officer: Abbr.
50. Body of knowledge
51. Toasts
53. Checks for errors
54. Canting
55. Adoree of the silents
56. Du Maurier heroine
59. She: It.
62. Entice by music
63. Like anthracite
64. River bottoms
66. Snitch
67. Quaker
70. River in England
71. Exploits
73. "The Bridges at ___-Ri"
75. ___-than-thou
78. City on the Mohawk
79. Claude ___ famous highwayman
81. Cloth of India
82. Public
83. ___ majesty
85. Harrowing experience
86. Gave a new appraisal
87. May or Horn
89. Gives approval to
90. Maxwell Anderson play
92. Sure thing, to a Britisher
93. Autocrat
95. Edition: Abbr.
97. River to the Elbe
98. Israeli name
101. French kind of tour
104. "Theirs ___ and die"
105. "The ___ down to rise upon ..."
108. Nix
109. ___ death
111. Mountain ridges
112. Youngsters
113. Long-tailed sky body
114. Customers
115. Energy units
116. Cheap cigarette of India
117. Sicilian mount
118. Pipe-organ stops
119. Like gold
121. Printing term
122. ___ Dag, Turkish mountain
123. Union group: Abbr.
125. Dutch commune
127. Wheat: Fr.
128. Aurora

149 Calling All Men
by Betty Leary

ACROSS

1. Le Mans sight
6. Traveled in a way
12. Norwegian saint
16. Convict's goal
17. Appropriated
19. Adriatic wind
20. Summer boon to parents
21. Fond of music
23. Kick ___
24. Card game
26. Late afternoon, usually
27. Jewish month: Var.
29. Umps' companions
30. False gods
32. Team members: Abbr.
33. Ranger's status
34. Letter
35. Whipper-snapper
39. Silver
41. Joins
43. Part of Q.E.D.
44. Sea call
45. Teeth
47. Strong emotion
49. Chinese guild
50. Old car
51. Exudes
52. Recondite
57. Eight: Ger.
58. Words of annoyance
61. Upward: Prefix
62. Silk from France
63. Other: Prefix
64. Egyptian heaven: Var.
65. Recipe abbr.
66. Cosmic cycle
67. Pink
71. News item
72. Outpourings
74. "There was ___ woman..."
75. One of an evil seven
76. Ms. people
77. Pointed instrument
79. Alarm clock for some
81. Add up
84. A thou
85. Emotion
86. Censures
88. Conform
90. Gardner
93. Pressure units: Abbr.
94. ___ Claire
96. Vehicles
97. Sibs: Abbr.
98. Nonsense!
99. Dog
103. Roman money
104. Soil
105. Imitate a jumping jack
108. Mosaic piece
110. Wife of Cuchullainn
111. Tardy
112. Fur
113. Letters for a hostess
114. Does a framer's job
115. Staggers

DOWN

1. Words for Pollyanna
2. Son of Zeus
3. Fuel
4. Tree
5. Succeeds
6. House part
7. Item for a tray
8. Night, in Paris
9. Heraldic fillet
10. Hebrew measure
11. At ___ door
12. Music maker
13. Chaney
14. Home of the Hopi
15. Garment parts
16. Leaves
18. Fragment
20. Challenge
22. Science degree
25. Trees
28. Parts of yards
30. Subside
31. Familiar symptom
33. "C'est ___"
35. Bad luck
36. Court decree
37. Do a class chore
38. W.W.II area
40. Terre ___
42. Blank: Ger.
45. Ends
46. ___ of ice cream
47. Go ___ (become seedy)
48. Iterated
49. Bunk
51. More ___
53. Part of a casa
54. Crowded quarters
55. Gunther title word
56. Eggbeater
58. Grovels
59. Cassini
60. Milton of the silents
65. Body part
67. Edge furtively
68. Duke of Hollywood
69. Entrance
70. Irish lakes
73. Lasts
75. Entrée order
78. Word with little and late
79. Old car style
80. Lord Boyd and family
81. Nicholas
82. Ale time
83. Drums
85. Widgeon
87. Percolate
88. English artist
89. Antelopes
91. Your: Fr.
92. Somali people
95. Urchin
97. Red Square name
99. Paint thinner: Abbr.
100. Move slowly
101. Cheese
102. Hurdy-gurdy
104. Girl's name
106. Girl's nickname
107. Soak
109. Before

150 Choose Your Weapons by H.L. Risteer

ACROSS

1. Total: Abbr.
4. Remonstrances
7. Camelot notable
14. Well-known street and others
21. Beach sight
23. Clam's big brother
24. Dixie river
25. Behave stubbornly
27. Mideast land
28. Legal copy
29. Stage monarch
30. Italian philosopher
32. Normal: Abbr.
33. Water bird
34. ___ tables
36. Praying figure
37. Fare for Miss Muffet
38. Malaccan measures
41. Wallet items
42. Street urchins
44. Subjunctive and indicative
45. U.S. balloon pioneer
46. Calendar source
47. Bridled
48. Binge
49. Man's nickname
50. Wall St. purchase
51. Shetland natives
52. Demand
55. Rocks
57. Ship officer
58. Table wine
59. Odorless gas
60. Rare animals
61. Impudent
62. Bloodhound feature
63. McKuen
64. Darnay's friend
65. Like some excuses
66. Ferrer
67. Charges
69. Satire of 1894
72. Haberdashery items
73. Salutation
74. Yawn
75. Kind of biscuit
76. Fed. agency
77. Western team
79. Armadillo
80. Dour
81. Finally
84. Enlightens
86. Authors' concerns
87. Merchant of drama
88. Business deals
89. Did a job in Denver
90. Italian locale
91. Educ. group
92. Malay weapon
93. Villella, e.g.
94. Olympian
95. Periods
96. Marksmen's sport
98. Eel
99. Bloom
100. Scottish stipend
101. Excavations
102. Noted Italian
103. Vestment
104. Common abbr.
105. Brew
106. North Sea feeder
107. Book of N.T.
109. Eating place
114. Alaskan peak
116. Stabbed in a way
119. "The ___ Worker"
120. Recorded
121. Beginning
122. Musical groups
123. Beverage experts
124. Campus V.I.P.'s
125. Roman 151

DOWN

1. Church section
2. Channels
3. Pluck
4. Petitioners
5. Valhalla man
6. Las Vegas opening
7. Started, in poems
8. Poplars
9. Light beam
10. Sea growth
11. Net time of a football game
12. Mass. cape
13. Discovers
14. Arty gatherings
15. Decide upon
16. "Quién ___?"
17. Jidda garb
18. His living depends on net income
19. Was theatrical
20. Scotchmen
22. Foaming
26. Manifesto city
31. Sally or Ayn
35. Printery supply
36. Old card game
37. Bulky cloth
38. Winged
39. Heavy shoe
40. Fast-draw trio
41. Light shades
42. Wartime plenty
43. Zodiac sign
44. Shed feathers
46. Tiresome one
47. Ring of policemen
48. Make tight
50. Give way a little
51. ___ del Este
52. Railway employee
53. Beginning
54. Movie units
56. N.M. art colony
57. Sentence-analyser
58. Salty one
60. South American plains
61. Russian whips
64. Fabrics
67. Traveler
68. Escape
69. Marbles
70. Atomic expert
71. Summoned
72. Marsh: Prefix
76. "___ boy!"
78. Startles
80. Because
81. Loop in anatomy
82. Tuscany city
83. Banquet feature
85. Came to rest
86. Slight amount
87. Delicate
89. Short cape
90. Money in Madrid
93. Juan and Quixote
94. Dance
95. Performer's bonus
96. Bursts of activity
97. Highlander
98. Lost ___
99. Be reflective
100. European capital
102. Distributed
103. Dear: Fr.
104. Ardent
106. Meek ones
107. Tiny quantities
108. African weight
110. Flier's word for bombs
111. Wash. tribunal: Abbr.
112. Jib
113. Although: Lat.
115. Riga coin
117. Put ___ pedestal
118. Dental degree

151 Inflation by Mel Rosen

ACROSS

1. Medieval fabric
7. Earth pigment
12. Recede
15. Air-gun pellets
18. Chemical compounds
19. Papal cape
20. Gershwin
21. Exotic island
22. New name for old whip
24. Needlefish
26. Western capital
27. Apparitions
29. Convictions
30. Location
32. Words of denial
33. Jaunty
34. Make over
38. Snooped, with "about"
41. Comedian Mort
42. Curve
43. Love in Turin
45. Door sign
47. __ nibs
49. DiMaggio
52. Low-price place, updated
59. Caught, as a fish
60. Suckfish
61. Doolittle and others
62. Huntley
64. Not public: Abbr.
65. Boring tools
66. Low person
69. Social Security abbr.
70. High note
71. She, in Paris
73. French marshal
74. Ingrained
76. Festive
78. In a __ (put out)
79. Shore bird
80. Use hard-sell tactics
82. Hebrew month
87. Plays an oversize piano
91. Drink
92. River of Scotland
93. City of Yemen
94. Flash
95. Overdraft abbr.
98. Dormouse
101. Sonata movement
104. Swiss painter
105. Alaskan town
107. Volcano
108. Village, in Africa
110. Goose genus
111. San Clemente citizen
115. Dross
119. Diner's reading matter
121. Next step for fanciers of the occult
124. Sea-speed unit
125. Tree
126. Growing out
127. Equiangular figure
128. Eastern weight
129. Swindle
130. Kind of geometry
131. Abandon

DOWN

1. Neighbor of It.
2. Oriental nurse
3. Small sum
4. Matinee __
5. Heads, in Reims
6. Russian poet
7. Away, to a Scotsman
8. Crop
9. Broadway show
10. Fitzgerald
11. Pine products
12. Bliss, modern style
13. Dye pigment: Var.
14. Profession
15. Twelve, nowadays
16. Cheerless
17. Milksop
21. Waits
23. Defense pact
25. "__ down!"
28. Done __ turn
31. German donkey
34. Headland
35. Man's name
36. Part of an Eastern hymn
37. Medit. port
39. Put into action
40. Crummy joint
44. Pass-catcher
46. Metal molds
48. Furtive
50. "__ Ben Jonson!'
51. In disorder
53. Poured
54. Old letters
55. "Thin Man" wife
56. Dernier __
57. Pivot
58. Poke: Scot.
63. Slam bid, maybe
66. Rope
67. Chorus topic
68. __ your thoughts, new style
69. Soviet city
70. Otherwise
72. Tilt
75. Suffix for hill or bull
77. Sound of disgust
78. Musical sign
81. Fibber
83. Chang's companion
84. Defraud
85. Indigo
86. Filament: Suffix
88. With gravity
89. Kind of bag
90. Marie, e.g.
96. Target game
97. Minor league club
99. Hostelry
100. Bridge calls
102. Old verb
103. Flower
105. Pillages
106. Empty
109. Chaser of a sort
112. Strange: Prefix
113. Shape
114. Pacific grass
116. Old cars
117. Author of "Bus Stop"
118. Ancient lyre
120. Brain-wave record: Abbr.
122. Nickname
123. Door: Abbr.

152 Words In Place
by William Lutwiniak

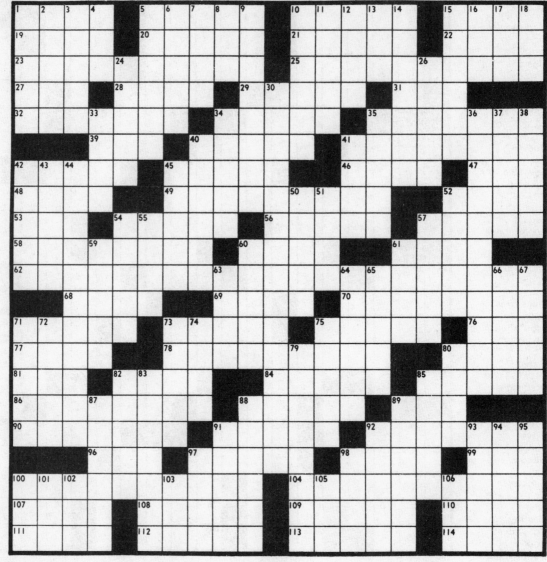

ACROSS

1. Eastern big wheel
5. Shut-eye
10. Boo-boo
15. Haul
19. Komsomolsk's river
20. Eccentric
21. "I want __ ..."
22. Mountain: Prefix
23. Clipper feature
25. Chaotic
27. Cockney idol
28. Person
29. Chemical compound
31. __ Andreas
32. Means
34. Friend of Trajan and Tacitus
35. Bars
39. Accomplished
40. Footpaths, old style
41. Turnips and cabbages
42. Equity member
45. Cuckoopint, for one
46. Occult character
47. Army off.
48. Famed comedian
49. Go-between
52. Rough cloth
53. Native: Suffix
54. Pulpits
56. Ukase's cousin
57. Relative of Mauna Loa
58. Indurated
60. Today's youth
61. Study hard
62. Not a sideshow
68. Featureless
69. River areas
70. Keep
71. "__ Is Born"
73. Rustle
75. Thread
76. Neighbor of Ger.
77. Semiaquatic creature
78. Hockey area
80. __ and now
81. Panay native
82. Oyster
84. Takes heed of
85. "Waiting for __"
86. Companies
88. Greek city-state
89. The works
90. Employs
91. Property
92. Macule
96. Direction
97. "... __ horse to ..."
98. Hall: Ger.
99. Letter
100. Like the green traffic light
104. Unfathomable
107. Mil. acronym
108. Brilliant glass
109. Nonprofessionals
110. Fodder
111. Pond
112. Playing cards
113. Colorado park
114. Blackthorn

DOWN

1. Merited
2. Con __
3. Knight's shirt
4. Neighbor of Uru.
5. Went it alone
6. Oners
7. Common Latin abbr.
8. Sea bird
9. Like a flower part
10. Some Americans
11. Suffering
12. Speak, with "up"
13. Elders: Abbr.
14. Blissful
15. Peerage members
16. Timetable word: Abbr.
17. Race an engine
18. Nursery item
24. Out of bed
26. Cup: Fr.
30. Place for Sunday drivers
33. Reputation
34. Exerts pressure
35. Main impact
36. Virtuous
37. Great expanse
38. African cattle
40. Electron tube
41. Bric-a- __
42. Leaning
43. Net
44. Political group
45. Sphere of action
50. Norse epics
51. Weather word
52. Alliance
54. Erect
55. Blanc, for one
57. __ Triomphe
59. Fanfare
60. Not quite wet
61. Poker move
63. Ballgame delayer
64. Dense areas
65. Flowers
66. Colorado county
67. Vocal group
71. Within __ of
72. Writer Ernest Thompson __
73. Thumbs through
74. Dampens
75. Within the law
79. Trustworthy
80. Evergreen oak
82. Musical sign
83. Appropriate
85. Flicker
87. Saddle part
88. Yaks
89. Bronze and pewter
91. Cantankerous
92. Mesa's cousin
93. Consummate
94. Sixth: It.
95. German state
97. Mislay
98. Have __ (begin)
100. Loud sound
101. Use credit
102. High rock
103. Seagoing: Abbr.
105. Western org.
106. Spanish article

153 Solving Material · by Martha Dewitt

ACROSS

1. Traffic light
6. Lieu
11. Competitor
16. By-product
21. Sight from Apollo craft
22. Do the honors at dinner
23. Hovel or house
24. Rope
25. Things within a stone's throw
27. Lucky girls
29. City on Danube
30. Piquant
31. Motors
33. Dip again
34. Junkyard, for one
36. Part of Troy's trouble
37. Kind of party
39. __ van Delft
40. Hand holder
41. Wise men
42. Hash
44. Thicket
47. Entertainments
49. Surgical instrument
53. Asian nurse
54. Yields
55. Ends' associate
56. Gossip
57. Glove-compartment item
58. Spices
59. Run
60. Swiss river
61. Bull or Olsen
62. Class of mollusks
64. Nonconformists
66. Way to cook tough meat
67. More composed
68. Euterpe
69. Home of some Alaskans
70. Asian goats
71. Rend
73. Type of TV tube
75. Julia of cookery
77. West Asian
78. Minnelli
79. Card game
82. Harridans
83. Thousand-legger
85. Transitory
86. Mike's look-alike
87. Auctioneer's last word
88. Macadamias
89. Small bays
90. Furrow
91. On the brink
93. Air outlet
94. Rock blend
95. Busy city
96. Ascetic
97. Ignored
99. Musical pieces
100. Lacking sunlight
102. Cleaves
103. Medieval tale
104. Collard's family
107. Measure
108. Parisian parents
109. Vestige
113. One with endurance
115. Fishing boot
116. Metropolitan thrush
117. Anaconda
118. Hardwear
121. Vulnerable ones
124. Old town in Asia Minor
125. Peers
126. Indian's castle
127. Force out
128. Appears
129. Schedule
130. Ship area
131. Late Chicago mayor

DOWN

1. Debate
2. Girl's nickname
3. Censure
4. Loop sights
5. Give back
6. Twenty
7. Kind of ship
8. Hesitant sounds
9. Means
10. One who wants
11. Red, white and black
12. Nile creature
13. German prefix
14. Say more
15. Regard, in a way
16. Soviet city
17. Light-bulb part
18. __ -ral
19. "__ told by an idiot"
20. Beam
26. Injure
28. Career military men
32. Movie fade-out
35. Window part
36. Surfaces
37. Pride, envy, etc.
38. April 15 items: Abbr.
41. Was partial
42. Update
43. Have it made
44. Vacation places
45. Peruvian volcano
46. Opposites of wolves in sheeps' clothing
47. Working on interiors
48. French brainstorm
50. Hallway fixture
51. Fisherman
52. Tartan trousers
54. Cavort
56. Hides
58. Unit
59. Firmly fixed
60. High point
63. Cable spools
64. Hazy condition
65. Scottish island
66. E. I. heartwood
68. Crumbly earth
70. Shades
72. Whine
73. Joshes
74. Desert animal
75. Onion's relative
76. Cods' relatives
78. Well-educated
80. Ridicule
81. Singers
83. Banker
84. Calembours
85. Broods
87. Lollobrigida
89. Spelunkers' milieu
92. Something to be done
93. Amphora
94. Spread
95. Rack's companion
97. Variety of peeve
98. Oversees
99. Marred
101. Bifocals, e.g.
103. Son of Jacob
104. N. Z. birds
105. Got up
106. Lax
108. Old hat
109. Age
110. Seething
111. Time-being
112. Savory
114. Navy facility
115. Shoe part
116. Textile worker
119. Holbrook
120. Mouths
122. Tarzan's foster parent
123. Zsa Zsa's sister

154 Valentines

by Dan Girardi

ACROSS

1. Bible book: Abbr.
4. Swedish island
8. Coxa
11. Angel or short
15. Whatever
16. "Lohengrin" bird
17. Sleeve card
18. Suppose
20. Memphis deity
21. Almost: Prefix
22. Corded cloth
23. Little Jack
24. Turn back
26. Miscued
28. "__ straws"
30. Bandleader Jones
31. Like some steak
32. Coal size
33. Table d'__
34. Cheat
36. Wages
39. Comedian Sahl
40. Roman money
41. Nibbles
43. Berber tribesman
44. Sailor's gear
45. Hamelin denizen
46. B.&O. et al.
47. Novelist Moravia
50. German river
52. Terminal: Abbr.
53. Picadors, in a way
55. Nap
57. Pewter coin
60. Work-heat units
62. River to Moselle
63. Feb. 14 symbols
67. Mortgage
68. Elegance
69. Earth: Prefix
70. Handle: Fr.
71. Ma Bell's concern
73. Ape
75. River crossing
77. Nice and Lido
78. Chem. suffix
79. Postage item: Abbr.
80. Army men: Abbr.
84. Building beam
85. Prefix with present
86. On __ level
87. Borders: Lat.
88. Learning time
92. Its emblem was an eagle
95. Maddened
96. Rodrigo Díaz
97. Angler's flies
98. Purse items
99. Freeloader
102. Fried, in Toledo
103. Eastern Christian
104. Hatbox toters
105. Impair
107. Pout
109. He, in Italy
110. Soft-__
111. Pirate gold
112. Doorways: Abbr.
113. Asian holiday
114. Robert Burns word
115. Glen Canyon, e.g.
116. Noted "racketeer"
117. Call on

DOWN

1. TV fare
2. Word repetition
3. Cole Porter sentiment
4. Serpent
5. Sub-rosa deals
6. Cook a certain way
7. Homer, with none on
8. "__ Savannah"
9. Kind of cap
10. Willie of ring fame
11. Eccentric one
12. Months: Abbr.
13. Film of 1950
14. Spanish months
19. Clio's sister
20. Optical devices
23. Miss., Ala., Ga., etc.
25. Zonal clocking: Abbr.
27. Moths
28. Yarn measure
29. Cyst
32. Portions: Abbr.
35. Relief org.
37. Do a transplant job
38. "Henry VI" character
42. Defunct rulers
47. Set right
48. Niobe's output
49. Declaim
51. Morning moisture
54. Campus people: Abbr.
55. Monastic officer
56. Dancing Castle
58. Holds sway
59. Nepal peak
61. Stifle
63. Completely
64. Kind of football pass
65. Religion
66. Head feature
72. Timber wolf
74. Actor Carl or Rob
76. Poker term
79. Rich cheeses
81. I.O.U. recipient
82. Tear into
83. Takes care of
85. Ref. book
88. Sample
89. Charley horse
90. Exalted ones
91. "... the giftie __ us"
93. Where the 600 rode
94. Southwest campus
100. O'Casey
101. That, to Ovid
105. Up-to-date
106. Macaw
108. Compass point

155 Central Activity by Gladys V. Miller

ACROSS

1. Anna or Maria
6. Finally
12. Island near Corsica
16. Knob
20. Binges
21. Certain clock
22. Cadence
23. Israeli name
24. French singer and Chinese V.I.P.
26. Bradley
27. Dog's name
28. Metric measure
29. Slovenly woman
30. Oahu neckpiece
31. Moon goddess
32. French seasons
33. Ancient Briton
35. Louisiana feature
37. British gun
39. Naval officer: Abbr.
41. Steel city
43. Wartime concern
45. Explosive device
49. Lincoln Center tenant
51. Forms a mosaic
55. McPherson of evangelism
56. Bulwark
60. Leander's milieu and high priest
62. Expend
63. Peep shows
67. Liner of tragedy
68. Arrow poison
69. Clear of
70. Muse and wall writing
72. Remedied: Abbr.
73. U.S. President
76. Capital of Honan
77. Teasdale
79. Hayward or Stanford
81. Improvise in jazz
82. Track concern
86. Ambrosia's companion
90. Blue-green hue
92. Chorus
95. __ a tune
96. Shangri-La V.I.P.
99. Arty district and actress
104. Tropical tree
105. Upper: Ger.
106. Emote
107. Swarmed
109. Adjective suffix
110. Winter Olympics site of 1956 and movie star
113. Commissions
115. Stock-market listings
116. Of a 19th-cent. essayist
120. Make edging
121. Detective
123. Expresses again
125. Drives and putts
129. Highway
131. Immovable
132. Soviet chain
134. Masculine
135. Site
138. Money boxes
140. Hindu title
141. English town
143. Words in ode titles
144. Coagulates
145. Malay boat
146. Thieves' nemesis and French cake
150. Foolhardy
151. Stravinsky
152. Abuse
153. Winter hazards
154. Away from weather
155. Hawaiian goose
156. Like a lawn
157. Observes

DOWN

1. Extra tires
2. Soviet cooperatives
3. Educ. group
4. Carnegie or Cal.
5. Mohammed's associates
6. Needle: Prefix
7. Certain Ranger
8. Scorecard data
9. Tree of India
10. Expanse
11. Numerical prefix
12. Conceal, old style

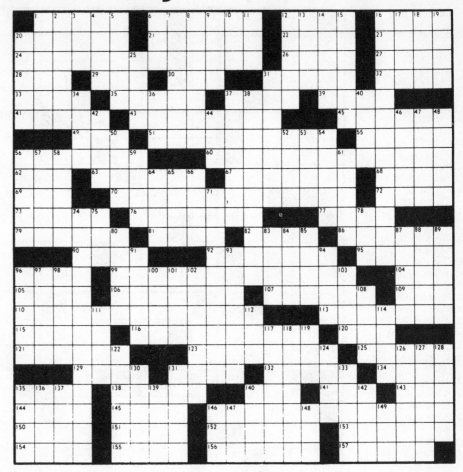

13. Bean
14. Famous Mont
15. "The Lady Is __"
16. Egyptian queen and S. A. lake
17. News item
18. Florida county
19. Son of Seth
20. __ capsule
25. Irish script
31. Name for Adenauer
34. Weather-ear abbr.
36. Nickname of ex-Giant QB
37. Add chips to the pot
38. Scolding
40. Martin
42. Imminent
44. Soviet city
46. Kind of acid
47. What asterisks do
48. Postpone
50. Mine car
52. Cardinals or Orioles
53. Early menial
54. Prolongs, with "out"
56. Bucolic
57. Stage remark
58. Hero's reward
59. Migrate
61. Blue area on map
64. Greek org. of W. W. II
65. Homeric
66. Living-room piece
71. Does a math job, in Britain
74. U.S. general and tennis ace
75. Ship's plank curve
78. Cook's guide: Abbr.
80. Apply lightly
83. Mild oath
84. "I __ you!"
85. Beget
87. Metroliner, for one
88. Hungarian hero
89. Old Scottish coins
91. Flaring stars
93. Goes to a restaurant
94. Alaskan port
96. Ness and neighbors
97. Seething
98. Unite
100. Pilot's place
101. Leading man, in Italy
102. French political writer
103. "Bird thou never __"
108. Haul
111. Math ratio words
112. Insect study: Abbr.
114. Particle
117. Family of pianist José
118. Football passes
119. Depression agency
122. Old feminine weapon
124. English river
126. Shaped with a machine
127. Mocks
128. Joinings
130. Funeral song
131. Signal light
133. Abridge
135. Taj Mahal site
136. Sincere
137. Other
139. Diving bird
140. Hindu deity
142. Kind of log
146. S. A. country
147. Irish god
148. Turkish title
149. Female ruff

156 Stepquotes by Eugene T. Maleska

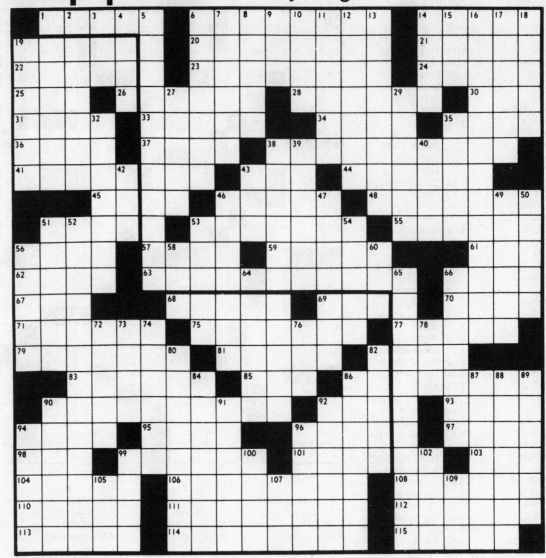

ACROSS

1. Start of a six-word Stepquote ending at 115 Across
6. Recorder of events
14. Estate
19. Gone up
20. _ roof
21. Perkins purple
22. Yacht's home
23. Author of Stepquote
24. Pyromaniac's crime
25. Items of interest
26. London artery
28. Even: Brit.
30. Ring decision
31. Notch
33. Jots
34. Sailors' saint
35. _ Rabbit
36. Artist from Spain
37. Augury
38. Source of cameline oil
41. Buttercups' kin
43. Marsh
44. Shows disdain
45. Gallimaufry
46. Ten, for Cicero
48. Lingers
51. Beaches
53. Calms a patient
55. Prepares to drive
56. TV camera screen
57. School subject
59. Road stopover
61. Refrain syllable
62. Teases
63. Part of Stepquote
66. Loser to Braddock
67. Hockey star
68. Name for Rayburn
69. "_ a man with . . ."
70. Writing fluids
71. Garden tool
75. "On _" (Source of Stepquote)
77. Seed covering
79. More rigorous
81. Feudal domestics
82. Ruler in Teheran

83. Harmoniously
85. Native: Suffix
86. Places to eat
90. Chews
92. South of Ky.
93. Indonesian boat
94. Snack spread
95. Gnawed: It.
96. City in Pripet Marshes
97. Yemen capital
98. Caliph's name
99. Clobber
101. Priscilla's in-laws
103. Hebrew letter
104. Small papal coin
106. Gregarious
108. Kind of rock
110. Successor to H. H. H.
111. Tiptoer's opposite
112. Sausage
113. Stands the gaff
114. Kennedy and Baker
115. End of Stepquote

DOWN

1. Man from Tabriz
2. Wondrous event
3. "_ was saying . . ."
4. Clan
5. Part of Stepquote
6. Invents
7. Island off China
8. Cocktail garnishes
9. Wild Bill Donovan's org.
10. Trawler equipment

11. Noted, as a detail
12. Escutcheons
13. Inner-city sight
14. Oriental nurse
15. Edsel
16. Like certain paints
17. Called forth
18. Madrileño
19. "Private Lives" heroine
27. Man's slipper
29. Tried to claw
32. Dressing gowns
35. _ l'Etang (French port)
38. Bivouac break-ups
39. "Had _ many"
40. Withered
42. Glory or maid
43. Nourished
46. Gape

47. Part of prosody
49. Calif. motto
50. Bowsprits
51. Evening party
52. Inc., co., etc.
53. Suffixes with mob and gang
54. "_ as a seal . . ."
56. Develops
58. Inlet
60. New Guinea port
64. Henry James heroine
65. Part of Stepquote
66. Chess pieces
72. Stupid
73. Whilom
74. Join the pensioners
76. Born: Fr.
78. Concha

80. Glides downhill again
82. Import
84. Former R. I. Senator
86. Proffers
87. Ciceronian activity
88. Marine mammal
89. More polished
90. White wine
91. Fruit-eating bird
92. Steering device
94. Of Paul or Pius
96. Picasso
99. Yields
100. Cotton
102. Silk: Fr.
105. Court call
107. Suitable
109. Conducted

Fragments by Frances Hansen

ACROSS

1. Wheresoever: Lat.
7. Burdens
12. Arab name for Acre
16. Book jacket info
21. Discompose
22. Coypu's cousin
23. Biblical kingdom
24. Demolished: Var.
25. Finally!
26. Before Unis
27. Ives
28. Lab solutions: Abbr.
29. Bellow
30. Beauty spots
31. Ascent
32. Part of a magic word
33. Lone Ranger's friend
35. Jabberwocky word
36. Kind of jacket
38. Between iota and lambda
40. Fur
41. Belay's partner
43. Dutch painter
44. Haunt the mind
45. Thought for Omar's "Sorry Scheme"
48. Balsam
49. Rosé
50. Menu entry
51. Porter
52. Rubbing
57. Needle: Prefix
58. Charon's crossing
60. Church part
64. Stamp on
65. June 14 sights
67. __ on parle français
68. Met patron Otto et al.
70. People in a Sheridan play
71. Yale
72. Major of comics

74. Character-actor Eric
75. Violin
76. House wrecker's big brother
78. Kind of leather
79. Ait
80. Show up
81. The: Sp.
82. Greeting for the Mets
83. Beauts
84. Snooze
85. Wickiup's cousin
87. More lecherous
88. Pueblo Indian
89. Chemical prefix
91. Bern's river
92. Literary backing, of a kind
93. Casa dweller
95. Club men
97. Nettle
98. Between epsilon and theta
102. Bookbindery equipment
110. Girl's name
111. "__ fan tutte"
112. Curaçao's neighbor
113. Hook, in biology
114. Active ones
115. 1956 wedding locale
117. Sign
118. Hebrew months
119. Eyelash: Prefix
120. Nurse of India
121. Not so zany
123. "Let __ as it may . . ."
124. Wan
125. Roast: Fr.
126. Leftward, at sea
127. Effect
129. Make up for
130. Wild guess
131. Rebel against Moses
132. Exactly
133. Czech leader
134. Dame Myra
135. Writer St. Johns

136. Spuds

DOWN

1. Page sizes
2. Defang
3. Peachtree St. locale
4. "Rigoletto" feature
5. Us, in Essen
6. Of age: Abbr.
7. "__ finger writes . . ."
8. Eatery
9. Least newsworthy
10. Bird
11. Right pert
12. Walks about
13. Pairs
14. Boat loads
15. Waving in the breeze
16. Tennyson's advice to sea
17. Tear into
18. Throne seizer
19. Backslide
20. Wall St. purchases: Abbr.
34. Morsel
35. Word with aqua or sub
37. Jannings
39. Ibsen role
42. Puccini girl
44. Export of 112 Across
46. Deplorable deeds
47. "When the __ the cradle . . ."
48. Not so easily duped
51. Rings
52. Blaze __
53. Wells to the surface
54. Montana county
55. Part of A.A.U.
56. Breaks up, in a way
57. Shade of blue
59. Proceed warily
61. Artist's colors
62. __ the arm (boosters)
63. Fit to be tied
65. Like a basset's ears
66. Small amount
69. Segovia and friends
71. Texas city
73. Famed physician
76. Kind of split
77. Krazy __
82. __ gift horse in . . .
86. Kemal
87. Central Texas city
90. Ladies in India
92. Krupp product
94. Native: Suffix
96. Nonclerical
98. British letter
99. Declaim
100. Ski part
101. Kennedy tenant
102. Beethoven's forte
103. Pittsburgh intake
104. Digit
105. Tea
106. Natural __
107. Ape
108. Having more fibers
109. Secreters of Dead Sea Scrolls
111. Prairie wolf
115. Fen
116. City of 1970 fair
122. Like peas in __
124. Movie monster's birthplace
127. Mel
128. Stole

158 Fanciful Tour — Edward J. O'Brien

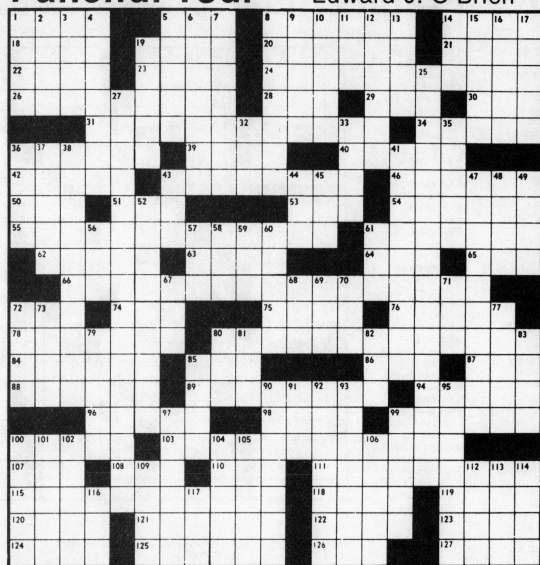

ACROSS

1. Kennedy wear
5. Prepaid: Abbr.
8. Alphonse's pal
14. Silent sister
18. Fraud
19. Hawaiian island
20. Arbiter
21. Preposition
22. B'way hero
23. Liberal or fine
24. Part of Rushmore
26. Southern facade
28. Whole
29. Scottish alder
30. Rolling or bowling
31. Mass. rhythm
34. Goals: Abbr.
36. Hunt cries
39. Tom, Dick and Harry
40. Principle
42. Possess: Fr.
43. Transit to Fisherman's Wharf
46. Inferior imitator
50. And not: Lat.
51. Cousins of 4 F's
53. B. & O., etc.
54. __ one side (swerve)
55. Houston's Astrodome, in a way
61. French opinions
62. Misty
63. Year Richard I died
64. Difficult, to a cockney
65. Ibsen figure
66. D. C. summers, to some
72. Sgt.
74. Annex
75. Alley
76. Organic compounds
78. Tea varieties
80. Conquers the Grand Canyon
84. Invest with
85. Haut or low
86. Shoshonean
87. Melanesian
88. Formidable one
89. Excavation in Chicago
94. Yesterdays: Fr.
96. Result
98. Sole
99. Animal awards
100. Got wind of
103. Autumns in part of N.Y.
107. Harvest goddess
108. Lyric poem
110. Mr. Fawkes
111. Relative of iron duke
115. Dusky divestiture
118. Number of nights
119. Sight of St. Louis gateway
120. Cupid
121. No place __
122. Explosive inventor
123. Handicap or stake
124. Tartan pattern
125. Keep __ mind
126. Diminutive suffixes
127. Honduran port

DOWN

1. Wear for Ann or May
2. New Hebrides island
3. Match
4. Part of e.g.
5. Glance off
6. "__ penny for tribute"
7. Roil
8. Dick
9. Affaire de coeur
10. Foam up: Lat.
11. Can
12. Give __ a few
13. Closely akin
14. Card game
15. Bumbling
16. Discolor
17. Brasses
19. Martin and Tyler Moore
25. Phila. divorce court
27. Miami touch
32. Sesame
33. Hubs: Abbr.
35. Unkempt abodes
36. __ fire (pend)
37. Conjugate __
38. Painted Desert quality
41. "We may __ again"
43. Davis's union: Abbr.
44. __ Magnon
45. Branch
47. Arthur and Veronica, to admirers
48. Natives: Suffix
49. Plane part
52. Workers on a digest
56. Educ. group
57. Initials of "Little Women" author
58. Type of train: Abbr.
59. Kind of tide
60. Eyes: Lat.
61. Cry of disdain
67. Aims of a Q B
68. Pile
69. Units of length: Abbr.
70. Bridge loss
71. Eur. land
72. Night: Prefix
73. African tree
77. Timid
79. Water animal
80. Court
81. Swine: Prefix
82. Outcry
83. Collide gently
85. Lead: Ger.
90. Nursery item
91. Prone: Abbr.
92. Showing favoritism
93. Omitted
95. Has __ (fits in)
97. Harmony
99. __ air (daylight)
100. Tubes
101. Tracing pattern
102. Like __ (probably)
104. Get __ on yourself
105. Cicerone
106. Long times
109. "__ boy!"
112. Dies __
113. Clerical: Abbr.
114. Zeus's mother
116. Concorde, for one
117. Even if, for short

Shaping Up — by Arnold Moss

ACROSS

1. Marsh plant
6. Word of disgust
11. Comes in third
13. Ways
21. Written: Fr.
22. In harmony
23. Realty sign
24. Moral code
25. Pirates' milieu
28. "Hi, __!"
29. Passable
30. Italian river
31. Kind of thief
32. Dig further
33. Flower parts
35. Certain maid
36. Section of Alps
37. Telly network
39. Certain shop
40. Lollapalooza
41. On __ diet
42. Stirring up
44. Khufu's milieu
48. Conway or Holt
51. Disquiet
52. Footnote's place
53. Belgrade people
54. Loosen
55. Quechuas
56. "All __, all dead"
57. Stuffed roast
58. Idiom
59. Norse name
60. To one side
61. Yucatan people
62. Baltimore player
63. Where jacks hang out
65. Utter delight
67. Limits
68. Izmir money
69. Honshu town
70. Et __
71. Verdi opus
75. Classify
76. "__ the Sea"
83. What "sumer is"
85. Gray
86. Like a sumo wrestler
87. Same: Prefix
88. Tent parts
89. Rope fiber
90. Nerve-cell part
91. Row
92. Hula hoops et al.
93. __ Rapids
94. City of Spain
95. Xmas in Pisa
96. Bering or Messina: Abbr.
97. Poor man's Riviera
99. Pre-school artist
100. Stomach woes
102. Sale-tag words
103. Musical lines
104. Road curve
105. "Much Ado" role
107. Lithium, for one
109. "...thou, __, art far more fair..."
111. Moths
112. Legacy law
113. City near Cleveland
114. __ Eireann
117. __ once
118. Crystal ball, to some
121. Pee Wee
122. Irene's concern
123. One of the media
124. Musical "ssh!"
125. Peace Nobelist, 1911
126. Saracen quarters
127. Willow
128. Watchful

DOWN

1. Wanes
2. Nymph of fable
3. Skirt hoop, in a way
4. Leg of mutton
5. W. W. II area
6. Amateur Santa's need
7. Mugs
8. Chesapeake Bay arm
9. Pony up
10. Who, in Bonn
11. Kind of comedian
12. Before moon and dew
13. Prince Igor's wife et al.
14. "One-and-a-two" man
15. Anne, for one: Abbr.
16. Faded slowly, with "out"
17. Olympian
18. Large brass container
19. Takes on
20. Vista
26. Complaint
27. "That which __ today..."
32. Food shops
34. Equal to a mile
35. Where Manila is
36. Disney film
37. Men from U.C.L.A.
38. Auto hood in Leeds
40. Adam's mythical first wife
43. Let
44. Equipment
45. Violinist
46. Showed an old movie
47. Certain lights
49. Arthurian lover
50. Boundaries
52. Like a man-about-town
54. U.S. Indian
56. Kind of whale
57. Party gift
58. Shaw
60. Outsider
61. Dixon's friend
62. Chemical compound
64. Ballet movements
66. Painter's gear
67. Girl's name
70. Field of activity
71. Berbers
72. Brilliance
73. Student milieus
74. Sports men
75. Analyze ore
76. Puppeteer Lewis
77. Poisons
79. Page facing a verso
80. Conformist's fun
81. Light fabrics
82. Raincoats
84. __-mémoire
86. Forward
89. Horse quality
90. Purpose
91. Sauce for pasta
93. Students
94. Strasbourg's region
95. Standard
97. Flight of a kind
98. Juvenal works
99. Tend
101. Wrinkle
103. "Yowzah" band-leader of yore
105. Brazilian state
106. Eyes
107. Writer on seapower
108. Choose
109. Children's book
110. Perfect
112. German count
113. College degrees
115. Cake decorator
116. Man from Riga
118. Ostend or Brest: Abbr.
119. Peruvian gold
120. Lizard

A La Mode by Jay Spry

ACROSS

1. Sourdough's concern
6. Place
11. "... for man or __"
16. Calif. Indians
18. Actress Wendy
20. Zodiac sign
21. So-so
23. Covered gallery
24. Sphere
25. Run off
26. Risky ventures
28. Prosecutors, for short
29. Harem rooms
31. Affront
32. __ were
33. Goes out, in a card game
34. Partake of
36. Ski turn
38. Take place
39. Nudge
40. Endings for major and cigar
41. Workhorses
43. Short-order initials
45. Hindu dance dramas
46. P.G.A. veteran
47. No. 49
50. Deadly snake
54. Faucet
55. Chinese dynasty
56. Bother
58. Epiphany figures
61. Troubles
63. Purpose
67. As to
68. Flock of mallards
69. Paris area
70. Tower
71. Artistic feat
75. Arctic command
76. Org.
77. Conway of TV
78. Ring arbiter
79. Genève, for one
81. Watery abysses
83. Airport areas
85. Pentateuch
87. Iron: Prefix
91. Favorable times
92. Indelibly impressed
94. Garson
95. Hot pants, etc.
98. Con man
100. Allgood
102. Mud volcano
103. French friend
104. Relative of etc.
105. Czarist state council
107. A-one
108. Encyc. unit
109. Tangles
111. Colorado resort
112. Small island
113. Soothsayer
115. TV bleep material
119. Sines and cosines
120. Shoot up
121. Navy specialists
122. Glaze
123. Cheeses
124. African villages

DOWN

1. Vertebrates
2. Pounds
3. Military weapon: Abbr.
4. Native of: Suffix
5. Clubs
6. Mall visitors
7. Occasion
8. Tree
9. Hebrew letter
10. Manifested
11. Prisoners' see-throughs
12. Business-letter abbr.
13. Longfellow locale
14. Some cars
15. French bit of hair
16. Iceboat
17. Horizontal timbers
19. Lexia, for one
20. Blank check
22. Raccoon's cousin
27. Ice: Ger.
30. More like some summers
33. Understands
35. She: It.
37. Blanc or Tremblant
38. Brazilian area
42. Tight
44. Catch
47. "My kingdom for __"
48. Small hawks
49. Tapestry
51. Stage settings
52. Bets big with a small pair
53. Kind of horn
57. U. S. composer
58. Glove
59. Idiocy
60. Crosspatch
62. Homily: Abbr.
64. Lunchtime hr.
65. Arabian king
66. Conjugation words after eram
72. Bead
73. Veil
74. Merit
80. Heels
82. German coins
84. Trick
85. English novelist
86. Phone operators' gear
88. Prepared to refire
89. Breathes
90. Brother of Electra
92. Gets on the plane
93. Peach or plum
95. Prefers
96. Without ethical precepts
97. Widen
99. GATT treaty: Abbr.
101. Last words
106. Certain entrance fees
109. Deer track
110. Unsounded consonant
111. Dyeing agent
114. French co.
116. Wrap
117. Ingest
118. Knicks' league

161 Along the Grain by H. Hastings Reddall

ACROSS

1. Peak
4. Dr. Rhine's field
7. Jeff Davis, for one
14. Home for some
17. Mat. time
20. Sayings
21. W. W. II area
22. Wilmot, for one
23. Chem. suffix
24. Golfer's problem
25. John Adams's party
27. Lovers of cruelty
28. Certain pitches
30. Work hard
31. Tang
33. Order to a broker
34. Actual being
36. School course
37. Quartet for a world traveler
42. Scheduled
43. Exposes
44. Reactor part
45. One of a Poe pair
46. Grimaces
49. Sweetsop
50. Worried about
51. Birthplace of Mohammed
55. Bible book
56. Persian tiger
57. Boot, in Paris
58. "Money is ___ of . . ."
60. Eur. country
61. Evian and Vichy
62. Entices
63. Gunsight
64. Reine's spouse
65. Attire, in old Rome
67. September times
68. Capricorn
69. Digits: Abbr.
70. Steering brace
71. Stop
72. Uneven
73. Chew of tobacco
74. Ship's complement
75. Handy shopping spot
77. Places
78. Blockhead
79. Embers
80. Greek letters
81. Casabas
83. Insect study: Abbr.
84. Parts of innings
85. Dress up
86. Like Buster Keaton
87. One of a Latin trio
88. Pitcher parts
89. Hoof sounds
90. Exploit
91. Japanese statesman
92. Feelings of malice
94. Disorder
95. Fishing maneuver
96. Max or Buddy
97. Scoff
98. Edge
99. Arrange
100. Antiquated
101. Smidgen
103. Relative
104. Point of land
105. Corrode
106. Land's End, Falmouth, etc.
113. Garment seen at U.N.
114. S. A. monkey
115. Stratum
116. Scandinavian country
117. Flying prefix
119. Deceived
121. Drop ___ (write briefly)
124. Sextant scale
126. Salutation
127. Western state: Abbr.
128. Soup ingredients
129. French season
130. Channel
131. Babylonian god
132. Draft initials
133. People with hunches
134. Naval craft: Abbr.
135. Relatives of mins.

DOWN

1. White House name
2. ___ a kind
3. Transistor
4. Poetic word
5. Posture
6. Salk's conquest
7. Navy guards: Abbr.
8. Stenos' needs
9. Black Chamber workers
10. Three monkey's taboos
11. Inconveniences
12. Superlative suffix
13. Grafted flower unit
14. Chaser of a sort
15. Not alert
16. ___ gratia
17. Put on guard
18. Forth or Clyde
19. Storm Country girl
26. Dodges
29. Snakebird
32. Babbles
35. Outbuilding
38. European land: Abbr.
39. U.S. physicist
40. Defense positions
41. Pointed
46. Bundle of sticks
47. Certain citizen
48. Basic element
49. Exclamations
50. Town in Newfoundland
52. Endless supplies
53. Harmonizes
54. Panay people
56. Tater
57. Case for church cloth
58. Comb, in a way
59. Emotion
61. Put away
62. Bank deals
63. Yokels
66. Greek god
67. Blackbirds
68. Despairing sound
71. Covers
72. Diminutive suffixes
73. Faucet reading
75. Bridge ploys
76. Permeates
77. Tire fault
79. Rope fiber
81. Soften
82. Certain noise
83. Hearing devices
85. Tara, for instance
86. Columbia, for one: Abbr.
88. Navigation aid
89. Tough cloth
90. Fur animal
93. Hardwicke of stage
94. European carp
95. Hairdo
96. P. I. peninsula
98. Thai money
99. Show-off
100. Friend
102. Some dogs
104. English essayist
105. Wading birds
106. Do the honors at dinner
107. Bay window
108. Record parts
109. Rinses out, in Scotland
110. Unusual
111. Stable sound
112. Doleful, to poets
113. Attempt
118. Scraps
120. Ring outcomes
122. Affection, in Scotland
123. W. W. II org.
125. On Social Security: Abbr.

162 Spring Is Sprung by Cornelia Warriner

ACROSS

1. Dog-paddled
5. Abie's Rose
10. Basic fact
13. Confer upon
19. Pueblo Indian
20. Jason's wife
21. Devout, in Spain
22. Unimpaired
23. Strays
24. Heraldic stripe: Var.
25. Greek letter
26. Cossack chief
27. React to spring stimuli
31. Nantes's river
32. "Please step to the __"
33. Wither
37. Dredge
39. Goes on the cuff
42. "... in corpore __"
43. Culture: Prefix
44. Nicene and others
45. Crumb: Fr.
46. Green or split
47. Greek letter
48. Water or musk
50. Live bait
53. Chapters of auto union
55. Seasonal yen
59. Saarinen and others
60. Villains at times
62. Precious ones
63. Glove units: Abbr.
64. Brats
65. Islamic spirit
66. Biblical coins
70. Certain words: Abbr.
71. David's daughter
72. He-man's strong point
73. In a quandary
76. Walton tools
78. Pakistani town
79. Goofs off
81. Nymph
83. Lower-Niger people
84. Capek play
85. Wee, in Scotland
86. Go for flies
89. Queen's spread
91. Cupid
93. Shower curtain, of a sort
95. Fund-drive V.I.P.'s
96. Lost
98. Fling
99. Early fiddle
100. Nature lovers
105. Someday
108. Carpenter __
109. English shrub
110. Standoffs
112. Neckwear
113. Perry Mason's concern
114. Poet who mused on April
115. Avon, for one
116. Tatler man
117. Odin's son
118. Lorna
119. Gambol

DOWN

1. Pronoun
2. Production
3. Spring do for a fiancée
4. Mint improperly
5. Meaning
6. Tear apart
7. Kind of thoughts
8. Sibyl
9. Hall item
10. Has attraction
11. Night spot
12. Coconut fiber
13. Seaside crowd
14. Word on a door
15. State of inertia
16. Cratchit heir
17. Old English money
18. Cyst
28. Metric meas.
29. Note
30. As cheap __
34. Fog
35. January in Peru
36. Soils
37. Scrape off metal
38. Flammable gas
39. Caesar's forehead
40. Split
41. Collect
44. Woodwinds: Abbr.
49. Pitchers
50. French river
51. Start of a toast
52. Lady's vest
54. Put the tennis ball in play
56. Swelling
57. French historian
58. Scottish landowner
61. Steal: Sp.
63. Branches of animal kingdom
65. Table-hops
66. October wear
67. Seasonal storm
68. Move clumsily
69. Former Indian soldiers
71. Portuguese city
72. Yearly: Abbr.
73. Pertinent: Lat.
74. Bull: Prefix
75. Cyclades island
76. Euphrates town
77. French menu item
80. Spend the summer
82. Low Hindu
86. Stroll
87. River of Bavaria
88. Asserted
90. Dance
92. Silk filament
94. Sham
95. Take out
97. Record, old style
99. Cleric's gown
101. George of films
102. Refuse: Lat.
103. Recital group
104. Antitoxins
105. Sens. and Reps.
106. Carney
107. Scot's denial
111. Devious

163 Roundup by William Lutwiniak

ACROSS

1. Then: Fr.
6. Tallow ingredients
11. Smash, in show biz
16. Small armadillo
20. Scuba user
21. "__ Gloaming . . ."
22. Arabian demon
23. Residents of Aarhus
24. Intercepting, Western style
28. Girl-watch
29. Stew ingredient
30. __ to high heaven
31. Card game
32. These, in Paris
33. Bird cries
34. Clerical headgear
35. Most leisurely
36. I.O.U.'s
37. Young kangaroos
38. Timetable, for short
39. Area of Asia Minor
41. Beg: Scot.
42. Fork feature
43. Diminutive ending
46. Answer to a Matt Dillon query
53. Greek city
54. Literary device
55. Hangs laxly
56. __ Alto
57. Seamstress's angle
58. Ducks
59. Favorite song
60. Continues
62. The works
63. Patisserie item
64. Lyrical creation
65. Bern's river
66. Familiar ultimatum
75. Shutter's companion
76. Well-known Camino
77. Common Latin verb
78. Ace
79. Scram, to Hamlet
82. Rubbish
83. Reputations
85. Uncluttered
86. Height: Prefix
87. Be eminent
88. Short-haired dog
89. Merchant guild
90. Champion survivor of frontier days
95. Indian greeting
96. ". . . __ won fair lady"
97. Palm leaves: Var.
98. Cognizant
99. Small bit
100. Nursery kind of ache
102. Hebrew leader
104. Cold wind of France
108. Adorn
109. Ghastly
110. Brace
113. Dormant
114. Suspect's defense
115. Undergo chemical change
116. Popular garnish
117. Relative of "Came the dawn"
121. "Aux __!"
122. Thermoplastic
123. C'est __
124. Point of view
125. Snug place
126. Championship
127. Ulan __
128. Vestibule

DOWN

1. Kind of committee
2. City of Belgium
3. Roundish shapes
4. Counsel, of yore
5. Hindu title
6. Document seal
7. Frees
8. Mores
9. "__ there were none"
10. Educational inst.
11. Football score
12. Bids
13. Marsh bird
14. Carson et al.
15. Cooperstown name
16. Custard apple
17. Lake of Finland
18. Outplays
19. Resource
23. Cryptography man
25. Not at all
26. Prized pearl
27. Last Chance Gulch, today
33. Defrosts
34. Eel
35. Removes cream
36. Mexican avocados
37. __ Hopkins
38. Fashion
39. Cause quivers
40. Wine and dine
41. Put away
43. Addams
44. French composer
45. N. C. college
46. Cigares et cigarettes
47. Rain cloud
48. Pick up the tab
49. Concede
50. Name-giver of a weekday
51. Out on __
52. Expedite
58. French river
59. City on the Odra
60. Unit of magnetism
61. Caen's river
63. Kind of gun
65. Allege
67. Withdrawn
68. European iris
69. Stratagem
70. Not live
71. Red Sea country
72. Kitchen must
73. Warm-sea fish
74. __ home (out)
79. City of England
80. Little Sir __
81. Flourished
82. Heat unit
83. "There's __" (impossible)
84. W. W. II coalition
85. V.I.P. of India
87. Baseball ploy
88. Daft
89. Conformed, with "to"
91. Merry ones
92. Angel
93. Of modern Greece
94. Native salt
100. Of an allied group
101. Polished
102. Spanish numeral
103. Toxophilite
104. French family member
105. River of France
106. Door sounds
107. Doctrine
108. Ready
109. Part of what stet means
110. Drab
111. Sam or Tom
112. Additional
114. Turkish regiment
115. Russian council
116. Hand, in Rome
118. Adherent
119. Hebrew measure: Var.
120. Queen's pilots

164 Words In a Row — Jordan S. Lasher

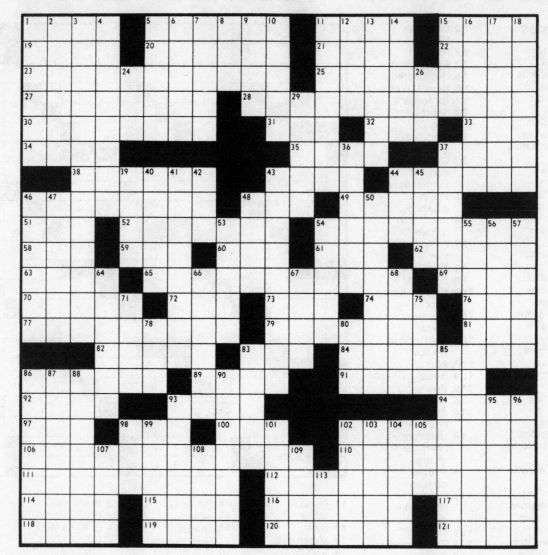

ACROSS

1. "Hell __ no fury . . ."
5. Ivanhoe's beloved
11. Red: Sp.
15. Oh, dear
19. Jamaica's __ Rios
20. Atlantic islands, to Portuguese
21. Hebrew letter
22. Soliloquy words
23. Vehicle for a gardener
25. Rosemary
27. Ploys of a sort
28. Road sign
30. Balloon or blimp
31. Recent: Prefix
32. Certain vote
33. Dejected
34. Tied
35. Event of 1944
37. Image: Prefix
38. Infatuate
43. Japanese salmon
44. Chinese soup
46. Day brightener
48. Certain review
49. All smiles
51. Spanish queen
52. Poor rating
54. Copenhagen, in song
58. Spring mo.
59. Certain reply
60. Audience
61. Ararat visitor
62. Girl's name
63. People of Brazil
65. Predatory bird
69. Door sign
70. Uneven
72. Timetable abbr.
73. Court
74. Portal: Abbr.
76. Marseilles season
77. Time, Times, etc.
79. Toaster
81. __ Locks
82. Jane and namesakes
83. After Harry
84. Get rid of a hangover
86. Game stick
89. Tim
91. __ to (ignores)
92. Wine prefixes
93. Insincere talk
94. Argo or Titanic
97. Map abbr.
98. Durocher
100. German name part
102. Do séance work
106. TV personality
110. Astronomer's field
111. Maine county
112. Tip of Alaska
114. "__ horse!"
115. Action: Suffix
116. Victim of a political shake-up
117. Alaskan port
118. Paradise
119. Mango parts
120. Chemical compounds
121. __ Pea, Popeye's friend

DOWN

1. Words of commiseration
2. More pained
3. Comic-book cousin of Superman
4. Square dances
5. Moroccan port
6. Florida city
7. Defeat
8. Be human, in a way
9. Broadway gas
10. Nile dam
11. Firearm devices
12. Hodgepodge
13. St. Lawrence, e.g.
14. Go __ oneself
15. Italian town
16. __ over (domineers)
17. Lawyer of Madrid
18. Attached, in a way
24. "__ Sylphides"
26. Common verb
29. Fortified work
36. Borealis's predecessor
37. Menu item
39. Bridge call
40. Gets ore
41. Bridge call
42. In medias __
43. Spoonerism
44. Bankroll
45. "A __ lama is a priest . . ."
46. Gobs
47. Tainted
48. Carson's predecessor
50. Old school-desk items
53. Firma or cotta
54. Game fish
55. Yerby novel, with "The"
56. __ length (inch or meter)
57. Most recently from
64. Evaluate
66. Awn
67. Roused
68. Struck, in a way
71. Tortoise genus
75. Shoe holder
78. Poetic word
80. "__ was saying . . ."
83. Being hauled
85. Horses' foot parts
86. Ropes
87. Weighed a container again
88. Citizen's right
90. Conjures
93. Celestial halo
95. Give __ thought
96. Ex-Dodger Reese
98. Football positions: Abbr.
99. Devoured
101. Section of a cone
102. Thrust
103. Join
104. Jazz instrument, for short
105. Herb genus
107. Of the dawn
108. Move back and forth
109. Pronouns
113. N.Y. subway

First Reader

by Nancy W. Atkinson

ACROSS

1. Advance sampling
8. In proximity
14. Certain readers
21. Swiss lake
22. Did a tailoring job
23. Count
24. Miracles
25. Popular English novelist
27. Hemingway novel
29. Cassette
30. Scottish now
31. Faction
32. Beneficiary in a suit
33. Scottish weather
34. Relative
35. __ war
38. Present times
40. Verne captain and others
42. Unhappy states
43. Designed
45. Minor college sport
48. Good friends
50. Small duck
52. Frankie
53. Braised meat dish
56. Arabic letters
59. Uppity one
61. Pacific porgy
62. Author of "Wall Street Jungle"
66. Scottish resort
68. Gardner and others
70. Patrol vehicle
72. Compiègne's river
73. Valley of fame
75. Number ending
76. Blew up photos
78. Youth org.
79. Popular nonfiction book of a decade ago
83. Hitler aide and writer of memoirs
85. Missive: Abbr.
86. Starlike
88. Dutch commune
89. Preserves
90. Paris seasons
92. Ready to go onstage
94. "Uneasy __ the head that . . ."
96. Steady fare
97. Fragrant herbs
99. __ capita
101. Explosives
103. Honshu town
104. Voice source
105. Dreams: Fr.
107. Heart and __
109. Orchid tubers
111. Small fish
114. Word in Miller title
118. Norms: Abbr.
119. Fun's partner
121. Bristle
123. __ reason at all
124. Reception
125. Prattle
126. P. I. native
129. Room, in Madrid
131. Gabor
132. "Do you __ car?"
134. Writers Leon, Charles and Antonia
139. Writers Shirley and Irwin
141. Impetuous lovers
142. Introduction
143. Oddballs
144. "It makes __ to me"
145. Picket-line member
146. Out-and-out
147. Fly's nemesis

DOWN

1. Laments
2. Terminates
3. Popular science
4. Musical subject
5. Joyce's land
6. Prunes, in Scotland
7. Swiss canton
8. Gift for a man
9. Root or Yale
10. Appraises, with up
11. To some extent
12. Creditors
13. River to the Fulda
14. Allen and Frome
15. Belief
16. Japanese statesman
17. Strained
18. Unredeemed man
19. Backings on floors
20. Races
22. Subscriber's encore
26. Uganda people
28. Admired one
36. Danube tributary
37. Charges
39. Out!
41. Archy's friend
42. "__ you really know?"
44. Andrews
46. Inlets
47. In reserve
48. Red wine
49. Pronoun
51. Erich Segal's tear-jerker
54. Authorize
55. Rawhides
56. Author of 79 Across
57. On the verge of
58. "No Exit" author et al.
60. Uses to the utmost
62. Trundle, as ore
63. Home of Lagos
64. Early mystics
65. Add __ one's life
67. Annamese measure
69. Mini-test
71. __ cruise
74. Epoch
77. Award
80. Steep slope
81. Edible herb
82. Kipling hero
84. Vessel of a kind
87. Orator Chauncey
91. Betrays, with out
93. Wife of Siva
95. Bounce, in Scotland
98. Miss West
100. Accelerates
102. Beach sight
105. One making a new try for grass
106. Vacillates
108. Card game
109. Writer Donald Ogden __
110. As graceful as __
112. Pupil
113. Musial
115. Offer
116. Direct opposite
117. Less fine
118. Noisy dances
119. James or John Nance
120. Nichols hero
122. Early New Englanders
125. Safari V.I.P.
127. Danube tributary
128. Geologic stage
130. Running
133. "__ want for Xmas is . . ."
135. Forsyte, for one
136. Writer Moss
137. Ponselle
138. In __ (peeved)
140. Diving bird

166 For a May Queen
by Alfio Micci

ACROSS

1. Mountain ash
6. Medicine unit
10. London policeman
16. Taxpayer's hope
17. "__ is Paris!"
19. "...maids __ row"
20. Ancient Urfa
21. Economy
22. __ pin
24. Present for Mother
27. Geometrical solids
28. Mad one
29. Partitions
30. Prepared to propose
31. To be: Lat.
34. __ left field
36. Andes animals
38. Kind of whale
40. Dernier __
41. Follow
42. Warplane crewman: Abbr.
45. "__ of All Flesh"
47. Posse's critters
50. Wisconsin city
52. Seeks to attain
54. Spad
55. Arabian cloak
57. Oodles
58. Kind of dive
59. Heathen
61. Remoras
62. Madrid attraction
65. Honor card
67. Galena
68. Grating
69. Burr
70. Gluttonous
74. Collar
76. Chowder
77. Donkey
78. Noun suffix
79. Fill the plates
83. Saves
85. Like some night skies
87. Garçon's name
88. Direction
89. Convene anew
92. Wonder
93. Partner of trick
94. Loos and others
96. Pacific island group
99. Porter

100. Acquired characters
104. __ hand
106. Kind of cord
108. Singers
109. Present for Mother
114. Outdoor area
116. Aloft, in France
117. Shut again
118. More like Snow White
119. Finishes furniture
120. Builds
121. Does garden work
122. Army man: Abbr.
123. Feminine suffixes

DOWN

1. Italian naturalist
2. Brain matter
3. Present for Mother
4. Confused
5. Draw __ (approach)
6. Present for Mother
7. Other: Sp.
8. Turkomen
9. Big name in towers
10. Certain boxers
11. Bull
12. Russia's Riviera
13. Gnawed
14. Silly
15. Stand
16. Kind of book: Abbr.
17. Time in the jug
18. Flour and sugar
23. One connected with: Suffix
25. Heating abbr.
26. Williams hero
31. This: Sp.
32. Globes: Abbr.
33. Ooze
35. Jewish month
37. Atmosphere
39. Get rid of, in a way
42. Life stories, for short
43. Ready
44. Untidy
46. Assent
48. Thor's wife
49. Whitney
51. Present for Mother
53. Adam's son and others
55. Gas: Prefix
56. Suffer
60. Present for Mother
61. Toast
62. Old-hat
63. Has it made
64. Sharp ridge
66. Aurora
71. Understand
72. __ fog
73. Discard
75. Pourboire
77. Have __ for (desire)
80. Mountain: Prefix
81. U.S.S.R. range
82. French head
84. Arm badge
85. Positions
86. Some dogs
90. Pirate John and others
91. Willow
95. Arrests
97. Express
98. In bondage
100. Corrode
101. Bass and treble
102. Set __ for (ambush)
103. Andrea __
105. Large rooms
107. Warn
110. Additional: Scot.
111. Fairy-tale word
112. Charlie Brown expletive
113. Navy police: Abbr.
115. Letter

ACROSS

1. Bank features
6. Fills
11. Deceived
16. Sometime money
21. Follow
22. Pick up the tab
23. Hole __
24. Stage
25. Pastoral district
27. Inlet
29. Western pact
30. Viewpoint
31. Hari et al.
32. Farm machine
33. Fretful
34. Relatives of oaters
35. Chicago landmark
36. Dominate
40. Conserve, in a way
41. Dispossessed
45. Hebrew god
46. False
47. Mosquito genus
48. Scottish name
49. Band instruments
50. Strenuously
53. Bondman
54. Musical group
55. Whales
56. Comparative endings
57. Relied: Var.
58. Glaciation stage
59. Gatsby, for one
60. Catkin
62. Bit
63. Numerical suffix
64. Sieve
66. Divination
67. West Indian sorcery
69. "__ the land of . . ."
70. Emotion
71. Visible
73. Give the once-over
79. Fail
82. Expunge
83. O. T. book
84. Family member
85. Seventh-century date
86. "__ a Man"
87. Indian of Sonora
88. Miss Toklas
89. Irish writer
90. Printing direction
91. Spare, plus
94. Actor Walter and family
95. Sabbath talk: Abbr.
96. Cowboys' wear
97. Shield bands
98. "Chanson __"
99. Magazines
101. Outdoorsy cloth
102. Overlappings in music
104. Central or Estes
105. Church part
106. River to the Amazon
107. Hans's shoes
110. Strips of rock
111. Crazed
112. Snappish person
116. Like an English king
118. Jams
120. Part of a certain even trade
121. French beast
122. Of hearing
123. Restrict
124. Beginnings
125. Stair part
126. Controls
127. Guitar parts

DOWN

1. Laurel of comedy
2. Old Irish oath
3. Matter-of- __
4. Vestige
5. But, to Cicero
6. Impassive
7. Mysterious
8. __ -bopper
9. Direction
10. French church abbr.
11. Pipe-organ stop
12. Green
13. Fleshy fruits
14. Son of Seth

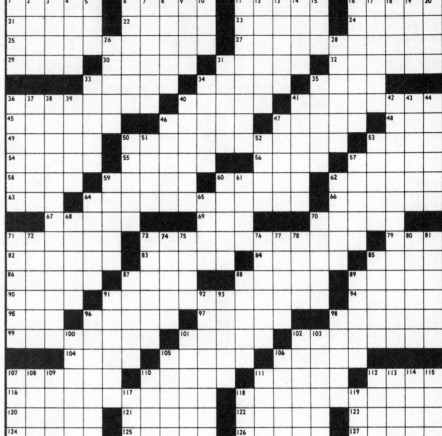

15. Court case figure: Abbr.
16. Milieus
17. Two-times
18. Grate upon
19. Response to "Get it?"
20. Bosc
26. Soviet river
28. Kind of agent
31. Band man
33. Kind of wrestling
34. Thomas and others
35. Noontimes in Provence
36. "Two Years __ the Mast"
37. Evoke
38. Highway hazards
39. Old pronouns
40. Take turns
41. Scarcity
42. Place for doubloons

43. Worker
44. With skill
46. After-theater snag
47. Concerning
50. Pentateuch
51. Gideon's victim
52. "Mon __!"
53. Twilled fabric
57. Dubliner's lake
59. Brightness
60. Protozoan: Var.
61. Sahl
62. Squalid
64. Rhythms
65. Variety of apple
68. Meadow sound
70. N. Z. trees
71. "Potemkin" locale

72. Axis
73. Pronoun
74. Rhino features
75. Wash. agency
76. Like the moon at times
77. Greek tourist sights
78. Story start
80. Broadway district
81. Laundry cycles
85. Bookkeeper's entry
87. Lie in hiding
88. More qualified
89. Strips
91. Scant
92. Reply to the expected
93. German numbers

96. Scythe handles
98. Hiatus in war
100. Name giver
101. Steal
102. Summer covering
103. Singing gymnastics
105. Sky Whale
106. Writer Angelo
107. Scoria
108. Elder: Fr.
109. Smuts, for one
110. True, in Tours
111. Grimace
112. Dam
113. Height
114. Burlesque number
115. Whispering sounds
117. Continent: Abbr.
118. Candy shape
119. Vietnam-war initials

168 Pecking Order by Jack Rosenthal

ACROSS

1. Masked man's No. 2
6. Made neat
12. Where No. 2 is No. 1
18. Noisy
19. Stassen
20. Tied to
21. Terra __
22. Jacqueline's No. 2
23. Photographer and family
24. Hairy, as a leaf
26. Tyler's No. 1
28. Pea of India
29. Acquaint
30. Photo-developing abbr.
31. Cowpoke's mount
35. "My __" (embarrassed)
40. Casual throw
42. Touch
43. Boston fixture
44. "Jane __"
45. Bundle again
47. Italian painter
48. Slanting: Abbr.
50. Vapor: Prefix
54. Trimmed
55. Vents frustration
58. Between holier and thou
59. TV logo
60. Take __ garbage
61. Infinite: Abbr.
62. No. 2 in 1968
71. Cuckoo
72. Eclipse sight
73. Old Dutch measure
74. Fibber
76. Readies a fishing line
80. Chemical sugar
83. Bone: Prefix
84. Service initials
85. Ontario river
86. Adjusts
87. Between ifs and buts
90. Does cobbling
92. Initials of a No. 1 and others
93. Endure, in Scotland
94. Pirates
96. Salinger character
97. Willie Winkie
99. Finally
101. Adjust
103. Corps member, to Nixon's No. 2
105. Kind of nabobs, to Nixon's No. 2
111. Most valorous
112. Homely one
115. Pass the buck
116. Fogs
117. Declared
118. Mediterranean union
119. Small fish
120. St. Lawrence, for one
121. Stealthily

DOWN

1. G.O.P. No. 2 in 1952
2. Spanish town
3. Standard
4. Vapid
5. Praying figure
6. Key Biscayne products
7. Dies __
8. No. 2 in Madrid
9. French pronoun
10. Letter addressees
11. Covet
12. The Spirit of __-six
13. Political collegian
14. Spanish nothing
15. Repents
16. Dovetail part
17. Ford
19. Shout
20. Grape residue
25. Like a bird with a crest
27. Circumference formula
31. Dwell on
32. Higher, in Bonn
33. Split-level places
34. Posture
36. Coupon: Abbr.
37. Sword
38. N. Y. college
39. Nixon's No. 2
41. County hub
44. Root or Yale
46. No. 1 in Shakespeare drama
48. "__ be in England . . ."
49. English spa
51. Strom's family
52. Long hair
53. Just
56. __ generis
57. Radiation unit
62. Moon sight
63. Etats __
64. Southwest campus
65. Wagner of baseball
66. Scraps
67. Horse
68. Rutledge
69. Revere
70. Chemical compound
75. "Step to the __"
77. Chinese poet
78. Relative of etc.
79. Switchblade
80. Ortega y __
81. Appear
82. Being, in Rome
88. Most groovy
89. Abhors
90. Slum hazard
91. Took five
93. Slander
94. Pedro or Fernando
95. Town on Hudson
97. Fabian Society pioneers
98. Zimbalist
100. W. W. II craft
102. Political tenures
104. Pernicious
105. City in Japan
106. Deucey's No. 1
107. Sincere
108. Problematical
109. Armstrong
110. Neutral
113. Greek letter
114. Handful

ACROSS

1. Flowers of Whitman poem
7. Goldish
11. Papal name
15. Indian's word with big
19. Obsession for repeating certain words
22. Relative of abracadabra
24. High-level argot
25. Baby talk spoken by adults
26. Dollar bills
27. Hayworth or Gam
28. Radio or TV remote
30. Tahoe or Louise
31. Moon vehicle
32. Pig genus
33. British blackjack
34. Goriot
35. Tent fixtures
36. Plant stem
37. Hector
38. Cobwebby things
40. Decrees
41. Wavy, as a leaf edge
44. Business title abbr.
45. Store event
46. Yellow ocher
47. Like neon
48. Fervor
49. Pick out
50. Sweet wines
54. "Complected," for one
56. African antelope
57. Bob Feller specialty
58. Hesitant sounds
59. Predilections
60. Putting on guard
62. Certain bones
63. Like Irish eyes of song
65. Barbara __ Geddes
66. Eccentricity
67. Nonprofessionals
68. "Do not __, spindle or . . ."
69. Voters
72. Equanimous
73. Antwerp man, to French
75. Festive
76. Nineties, for one
77. Throb
80. Hawaiian thrush
81. Florid language
83. South Pacific sight
85. Pagoda
86. Headache
88. Cordon __
89. Mispronunciation of "r"
91. Patagonian trees
92. Addition word
93. Laundry item
94. Ruffle, as hair
95. Gourmand
96. Spanish aunts
97. ". . . are __ forgotten"
98. Snaky sounds
99. Town __
102. Vitamin source
104. Chimney output
105. Rockfish
106. Engendered
107. Latin verb
108. Social science: Abbr.
109. Young doe
112. German cry
113. Hebrew letter
114. Jerk's cousin
115. Western state: Abbr.
116. Toots
117. Relative of gibberish
120. "All well stop send money stop"
123. Chelly tree, for example
124. Speech that runs like sixty
125. French seasons
126. New York's way
127. River to North Sea
128. Sitting, as a statue

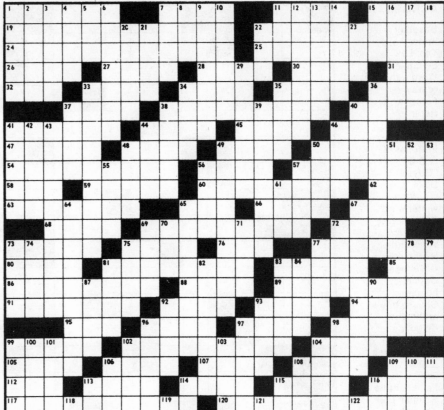

DOWN

1. Reason, in philosophy
2. Turkish statesman
3. Places for earrings
4. Envoys: Abbr.
5. Coolidge
6. Kind of hormone
7. Cuckoo
8. Daughter of Cadmus
9. Elsa, for one
10. Certain bettors
11. Volcanic hill of France
12. Entreat
13. Prowlers of W. W. II
14. Hose
15. Ben __
16. Wife of Iago
17. Away
18. French apples
20. Horace, for one
21. Story of gods
22. Unit of conductance
23. Fellow
29. Size up
33. Melodious
34. Swimming or car
35. Hoosegow unit
36. Letters such as b and m
37. Snide remark
38. Metric weights
39. Relative of soft soap
40. Dossier
41. Currant genus
42. Equip for war, old style
43. Frivolous talk
44. Actress Edna
46. Marionette man
48. Enthusiasm
49. Speaks to privately
50. Fur
51. Meaningless talk
52. Came down
53. Murder
55. Rip
56. Chinese weight
57. Skin-diving gear
61. Rifle range: Fr.
64. Nonstop talkativeness
65. Hokum
67. Relative of 123 Across
69. Bundle
70. Every
71. Interdiction
72. Secret group
73. Village barrier in Africa
74. Ludwig
75. Cotton and sloe
77. Ship deck
78. Armor plate
79. Soprano Emma
81. Victory: Ger.
82. Talk noisily
83. "__ with a view"
84. ". . . thicker __ water"
87. Acidity
90. __ à dire
92. Like some pipers
93. Quality
96. What the brave deserve
97. Shore plants
98. Water-cooled pipes of East
99. Hold protectively
100. Paint over
101. Deposit in the earth
102. Miserable one
103. Nitty- __
104. Steep slope
106. Baa
108. High-strung
109. "One of __ days"
110. Red dye
111. Super
113. City official: Abbr.
114. Metric length: Abbr.
115. Very: Ger.
116. Fish delicacy
118. Air-rifle fodder
119. Baton Rouge campus
121. Spear: Abbr.
122. Before: Prefix

170 Extra Values by Keith Blake

ACROSS

1. Baseball throw
4. Ten: Lat.
9. Egyptian god
12. Word with air or way
15. Forebear, in Berlin
16. Fault
18. Singing voice
20. Princess of G. & S.
21. "Guys and Dolls" guy
23. "__, thou winter wind"
25. Collection
26. Miss Page
27. Work unit
29. Hit the hay
30. Cover again
32. Optical beams
35. Checks one's arithmetic
36. Spigots
37. Off balance
39. Mother's plea
41. __ Dai
42. Dry
43. Faulkner title
47. Scottish port
49. Kahn et al.
50. English school
51. Deal in hot tips
52. Inscribed
53. Dress up
54. Kind of talk
57. Hepburn role
60. Jezebel's king
61. Service initials
62. Kelp, for one
63. Frost line
68. Heavy cart
69. Direction
70. Mountain snow
71. Spanish zither
72. Skelton or Holzman
73. Evangeline's Grand __
74. Upstate N.Y. county
76. Word of disgust
77. "Umble" person
78. __ avis
79. Sines, e.g.
81. Round words
84. Way: Abbr.
86. Men's org.
87. King Cole
88. Half a Jules Verne number
89. Plain in Spain
91. Ones with low IQ's
94. Large, in Italy
96. "But there's __ in your eyes"
98. __ régime
99. Brynner
100. Like raisins
103. Someone, in Seville
104. Son of J.F.K.
107. Reproof for the angry
110. Wolframite
111. Extinct bird
112. Calm expanses
113. Essence
114. Cape
115. Greek letter
116. Fourth-down maneuvers
117. Political victors

DOWN

1. Barnum
2. Bivouacked
3. Before whiz
4. Depression
5. Give out
6. Roman saint
7. Before
8. See 63 Across
9. "__ Ballads"
10. Wing
11. German theologian
12. Water barrier
13. Broadway show
14. Grows light
15. What Bismarck called politics
16. Indonesian
17. Wheel part, in London
19. "__ is me!"
22. Discs: Abbr.
24. Tattle about
28. Kind of monkey
31. Vermont mountain
33. Like a Mid-east alliance
34. Day of worship: Abbr.
37. Aid's partner
38. Mao __-tung
40. Fly
43. Commandment breaker
44. Type mold
45. Lack of accent
46. Record
48. Certain votes
52. Reporter's question
54. Entreaty
55. "Rome of Hungary"
56. Hemingway
57. Naval off.
58. Rent
59. "When I was __"
60. Mellow
61. Samovar
62. Brass instruments
64. Admission fee to child's show
65. Operatic barber et al.
66. Mouths
67. Mexican's assent
73. Through
74. "... succeed __ again"
75. "__ a Camera"
76. __ Alto
77. Narcotic
79. Cruise port
80. Remain mounted
81. Jo, Meg et al.
82. Hang back
83. Map-making device
85. Textile devices
86. Mexican state
90. Be __ loser
91. Serious
92. Province of Saudi Arabia
93. Pry
95. Inning units
96. Conjunctions
97. Dutch town
101. Tenant's concern
102. Annoys
105. Chiefs: Abbr.
106. We, in Italy
108. Burmese people
109. Roman 1,101

Type Casting by Fay L. Gieschi

ACROSS

1. Motionless
7. Racing site
12. Word of regret
16. Penults, sportswise
21. Mexican fare
22. One who snoops
23. Frank's wrap
24. Some writing
25. Popular line for printers
27. Kind of press
29. Tennis term
30. Of the ear
31. Baby talk
33. Severn tributary
34. Poetic word
35. Solo
37. Do a farm chore
39. Movie dog
40. Railing support
42. Log
45. Drudgery
47. Vegetable
48. Soothe
51. Zodiac sign
53. French titles
55. Wheys
59. Worship
60. Where to learn the score
63. Suez peninsula
64. Filch, old style
65. Tipplers
67. Begins, poetically
68. Davis or Ryder
71. Come upon
72. Blanc, etc.
74. Slicker
77. Roman dictator
79. Even up
80. November sky sight
82. Kilns
83. Do galley labor
85. Term of respect
86. Golfer's goal
87. Common verb
88. Got ready to drive
89. Kind of "we"
92. Triple Crown horse
95. Vast plains
98. River of France
99. Approximates
100. Trifling
102. Light carriage
103. Stub —
105. Intersperse
106. "— deal"
107. — avis
109. Le Gallienne
110. Earth, to Plautus
112. Peanuts' showcase
116. Kind of beam
118. Synthetic
120. Photog's solution
121. Sandy's to
122. Decline, in Arles
123. Wearing brogans
125. Time periods
127. Surprise
130. Won back
134. Oafs
136. Old wheat measure
137. India, China, etc.
141. Red Baron, e.g.
142. Building beam
143. Ardor
144. Applications
146. Direction
147. Help Wanted, for one
150. Vehicles for debs
154. Gold unit: Var.
155. Distant: Prefix
156. Dewy
157. Aerie tenant
158. Eye swellings
159. Port of Algeria
160. Seed: Prefix
161. Inhibits

DOWN

1. Inscribed pillar
2. Yam's relative
3. Violin maker
4. Oriental morality
5. Pelvis: Prefix
6. Middle
7. Sidewalk sight
8. Lawn waterer: Abbr.
9. Spanish hero
10. Maryland town
11. Obvious fact
12. Fish of Brazil
13. Spanish article
14. Preakness winner in 1942
15. Eastern European
16. Thistle parts
17. Period
18. Choral piece
19. French river
20. Passover feast
26. Southern fish
28. Soft drinks
32. Certain dancers
36. Discordant
38. — Alto
41. Letter stroke
43. Cheers
44. Irish sea god
46. Relay-race unit
48. Twice-told
49. Roman official
50. Typesetters
52. Indians
54. Established
56. International precedent
57. Violent desire
58. Word with lop or one
60. Terminals: Abbr.
61. Greek letter
62. Tiff
66. Sent for
69. Gums: Prefix
70. Guy Fawkes, for one
73. In a — (excited)
75. Short fibers
76. Peaked
77. Flower arrangement
78. For — (not free)
81. Mashie, e.g.
84. Accounting: Abbr.
86. Virgil of cartoons
87. Cry of triumph
89. Gladden
90. Fond grandparent
91. Samoan bird
92. Like auto-seller's extras
93. Varied: Abbr.
94. "With — of thousands" (movie ad)
95. Cookie
96. Overhangs
97. Kind of tire
101. Swiss canton
104. Remove
106. Used unduly
108. Shepard
111. Nonbelievers
113. Grandchild, in Dundee
114. Pagoda
115. Take it easy
117. Batman
119. Snake deity
122. Showing surprise
124. Unheeding
126. Fits of energy
128. Faithful
129. Dismiss
130. Draws off wine
131. Applause
132. Relative of darling
133. Laundry unit
135. Nose
138. Phase
139. Scoff
140. Dry runs
145. Prophesy: Scot.
148. Auto group: Abbr.
149. High note
151. Labor initials
152. Mideast land: Abbr.
153. Govt. sleuth

172 Man's World Thomas W. Schier

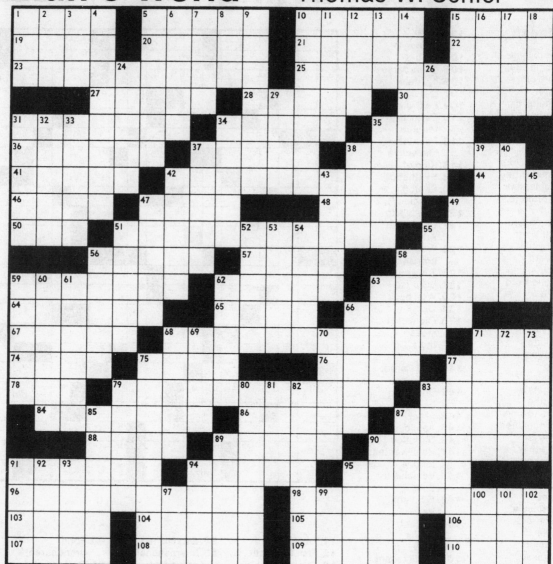

ACROSS

1. Beats it
5. Footnote words
10. Old newsreel name
15. One spade, etc.
19. Sleep like __
20. Under, to poets
21. Kind of den
22. Alaskan island
23. Tropical sight
25. Childish shooting
27. Relatives of cols.
28. Gelatine devices
30. Emissary
31. Jersey resort
34. Aides to Santa
35. Goalie's specialty
36. Chemical compound
37. Shankar's instrument
38. Came to pass
41. Approach perfection
42. Former Italian domain
44. __ Cruces
46. Eve's eldest
47. Twist
48. Nail part
49. Confined
50. N. E. cape
51. Offerings of some museums
55. Transition in music
56. Thorn, in old Rome
57. __ even keel
58. Newsman
59. Child's swing, at times
62. Fabric finish
63. Place for a pea
64. San __
65. Behold, à la Cassius
66. Oak's beginning
67. Roman official
68. Chesterton creation
71. Dance step
74. Fund-raiser's word
75. Tarry
76. Old French coins
77. Rumor personified
78. "Fables in Slang" writer
79. Prayer
83. Mehta's need
84. Chronic loser
86. Sweetened the pot
87. Bull Run, for one
88. Jungle denizens
89. Oklahoma Indians
90. Dismiss summarily
91. Forearm bone
94. Blazing
95. York or Devon
96. Russian physiologist
98. Promote, in a way
103. Sahl
104. Queen for Louis
105. Be stationary, as a ship
106. Cut of meat
107. Beards of grass
108. Well-worn pants areas
109. Berry tree
110. Exercise cult

DOWN

1. Circuit
2. __ loss
3. Janitor's need
4. Moon walkers
5. Equal in value
6. Kind of cash
7. Sedans
8. Native: Suffix
9. Topics
10. Trees
11. Footless creatures
12. Hot info
13. Squeeze
14. Rivaled
15. Slammed
16. Light-bulb lighter
17. Game item
18. Terrier
24. Mandarin's quarters
26. Leeward island
29. Cacholong
31. Approximately
32. Kind of flu
33. Enter informally
34. Did a job in Hamelin
35. Attack
37. Health-resort feature
38. Ex-champ
39. Legal writ
40. Blue river
42. Kind of geometry
43. Title for Macbeth
45. Bullock
47. Coiled: Prefix
49. Juan or Eva
51. Think
52. Dog
53. Reserved
54. Chef's implement
55. Disdain
56. Steps
58. Evinces
59. Ending
60. Pretentious
61. Twaddle
62. Poet's concern
63. Work on pans
66. Formed a bow
68. __ a fiddle
69. Arabian gulf
70. Animals, in France
71. Page
72. Soap plant
73. Less wacky
75. Warrior in Norse lore
77. Kind of advice
79. Infield fly
80. Hometowners
81. __ about
82. Village sight
83. Mideast port
85. N.O. players
87. Legal deliverer
89. "A Majority __"
90. Paratrooper's need
91. Fissure
92. Declare
93. Embroider
94. "I cannot tell __"
95. Raced
97. Worthy of honor: Abbr.
99. Unctuous speech
100. Ripe old age
101. Sharp movement
102. Spanish queen

173 Sea Fare by Frances Hansen

ACROSS

1. Half an operatic name
6. Court of equity: Abbr.
11. Where Luang Prabang is
15. Beanie wearer
20. Believer: Suffix
21. Hoople, for one
22. Titan
24. Where Ephesus was
25. Boojum
26. In embryo: Lat.
27. Lobster claw
28. Fish
29. Folk-opera names, fishy style
32. Unscrupulous ones
34. Latin infinitive
35. Office-seeker: Abbr.
36. Take the hook
38. Lost-mail dept.
39. Attractive paella
48. "The __ the Pussycat"
52. Words of inquiry
53. Rolled a log
54. __ time (pronto)
55. Flower: It.
56. Between a and f
58. Fuel again
59. Celestial spectral type
60. Proceed clumsily
63. Us, in Berlin
64. Yugoslavian town
65. Kind
66. Dravidian
67. Derisive sound
68. Pou __ (base)
69. Fig-bird
70. Stadium
72. Desensitized
74. Kaffir village
76. Weapon: Fr.
77. Ski-trail pattern
80. Exclamation, menu style
85. Kind of code
86. Comic-strip girl
88. "__ the morning to you"
89. Stamped on
90. Fish dish
93. Writer Josephine
94. W. W. II craft
96. African river
98. French pronoun
99. Of __ to (inclined)
100. Hurok
101. Warning to the undecided
104. Sorrowing figure
105. Medicine-cabinet item
107. Bridge hand
108. Where Wiesbaden is
109. European capital
110. Popular salad
111. Army unit: Abbr.
112. Group of five
113. What Pistol said to Falstaff
118. Purchase
119. Moore work
120. Noun suffix
121. Delays
125. Treat for 29 Across, maybe
131. Relative of yipes
135. Mature
136. Letter
138. Turnpike features
139. Ruth's mother-in-law
140. Earl Carroll specialty
141. Like an old sweater
142. Spry
143. Steel city
144. Dominion
145. Lear's Pobble hasn't any
146. Stendhal character
147. Shellfish

DOWN

1. Canadian peninsula
2. Peter et al.
3. Some fishermen
4. At __ (on the lam)
5. Like a squid's weapon
6. Musical key
7. Treat
8. Do __ on (trick)
9. Resurging star
10. Bob and Bing
11. Wax ingredient
12. Muscular
13. Kitchen staple
14. Senora's room
15. ". . . __ the sea" (Genesis)
16. City on the Tevere
17. Corker
18. Worm product
19. Sailors
23. Launces
30. Endorsed: Abbr.
31. Dr. Ota __, Czech reformer
33. Slipped, old style
37. Jewish month
39. Concerning
40. African people: Var.
41. By __ (incidentally)
42. Baby steelhead
43. Grassy plain
44. Most dubious
45. Musical vamp
46. French delicacy
47. Vast number
48. Distant in manner
49. "How __ marry . . . ?"
50. Pretty gal
51. Islands off New Guinea
56. Source of 90 Across
57. Prepare, as fish
58. German river
59. "One __ master . . ."
61. Bill collector
62. Like a certain bucket
68. My gal
69. Furniture decoration
71. "There's __ in the sky"
73. Filleted
75. Deep gulf
76. Appearance
78. Decree
79. Certain vote
81. Bar orders
82. First __
83. Alcott
84. Revised
87. Jewel piece
90. Boat: Fr.
91. Mennonite
92. __ d'orchestre
93. Trifled
95. On __ (active)
97. Upper space
100. Terrier
101. Madden: Lat.
102. Like a grain
103. Big or Gentle
106. Mexican state
110. French vineyards
111. Shark suckers
112. Orchestra part: Abbr.
114. __ dictum
115. O. T. book
116. Like Simon
117. Prickly herb
121. Restrain
122. Came up
123. Paired
124. Walk like Theda Bara
125. Fish
126. To that point: Lat.
127. Between s and x
128. Chimney part
129. Vivid display
130. German king
132. Como or Nemi
133. Norse giant
134. Experienced
137. Rickover et al., to friends

174 Literary License by Eugene T. Maleska

ACROSS

1. Sells or tells
8. Vacillated
15. They need good memories
20. Armpits
21. Restlessly, in music
22. Cove
23. Tale of a colicky cherub
25. Brazilian dance
26. Con __ (vigorously)
27. Five-star headline name of 1934
28. Granada girl: Abbr.
30. Formed a lap
31. Fruit punch
32. Complete defeat
33. Teachers' org.
34. Allied org.
35. Main point
37. Early Mexican
39. No bid
40. Topnotcher
41. Like some butterflies
43. Coin for Plato
45. Class
47. Mots of a sort
48. Emulates Petruchio
50. Inviting word
52. Revivalist's advice
55. Least ruffled
57. Vashti's successor
59. Tilled land in Texas
60. Swedish port
61. Viscount's superior
63. Antitoxins
64. Calendar abbr.
65. Monstrous hot-dog with beer
69. Hebrew letter
70. Pielet
72. Seed for a plot
73. Homes, in Ponce
74. Where a belle might dwell
76. Packed
78. Pittsburgh pro
80. Triplets
81. Yemen's neighbor
82. Used a whetstone
83. Control
84. Business-letter abbr.
86. Price
87. Discusses at length
91. Savoir-faire
93. Bald __ eagle
95. Accent
98. Third Reich salute
99. Nobel chemist
100. Waikiki wreath
101. Where to find an M.D.
102. Sky Altar
103. Hodges or Blas
104. Line of cliffs
106. Beldams
108. Mardi __
109. Quink or brant
111. Tale of a scale
114. Big Bertha's birthplace
115. Saint-Exupéry
116. Oeufs à __ (menu item)
117. Loved too fondly
118. Man with a yen
119. Insecticide, sort of

DOWN

1. Collections of trivia
2. Introductions
3. Most neat
4. Further
5. Inauspicious
6. "The best __ schemes..."
7. Bars used in shipbuilding
8. Graceful tree
9. Italian broker
10. Roman streets
11. Catch-all abbr.
12. Bowl calls
13. Ceaseless
14. Fishing boats
15. "David and __"
16. __ rut
17. Sequel to "The Beggar's Opera"
18. Discount
19. Machine part
24. County in Montana
29. Assignment
34. Music works
36. Did a stenog's job
37. Add color
38. Treatise on economy
39. Mad or had
42. __ the mill
44. Nectar expert
46. French pronoun
48. Filibuster
49. City in Michigan
51. Part of H.S.H.
52. Catamarans
53. Printing mistakes
54. Tale of missing cubes
55. Malaccas
56. Tamerlane
57. Wallach
58. Kind of gin fizz
60. Frantic
62. In medias __
66. Disencumber
67. Valley
68. Of the nostrils
71. Score
75. Shore
77. U.S.N.A. grad
79. Aurora
80. Hardy girl
83. Orthographizes again
85. Aftershave item
86. One of Sadat's people
87. U.S.S.R. river
88. Next
89. Organ-pedal coupler
90. Swordsman, at times
91. Pulled hard
92. Melodious
94. St. Lawrence
96. Sovereignty
97. His work is on the house
104. Mail
105. Fiber plant
106. Chew the fat
107. Side dish
108. Surfeit
110. Grasp
112. Cockney's oath
113. Lippo Lippi

175 Independence Day by Sylvia Baumgarten

ACROSS

1. Five, for Cicero
8. En __
13. Shade of green
20. Rare-earth metals
21. Of a mouth part
23. Withstood
24. Toothed, as a leaf
25. Enliven
26. The Magi, e.g.
27. Methods: Abbr.
28. Overall fabric
29. Serve tea
30. Crucial signal choice from North Church
37. Rate of interest: Abbr.
40. Foreign
41. Opposite of a magnum
42. Scottish county
43. Jumping
45. Common French verb
46. Juilliard degree
49. Porridge choice
50. Kadiddlehopper
51. Batters anew
53. Yr. Obdt. __
55. __ Mater
57. Casino game
58. Seven: Prefix
59. Sounds of inquiry
61. Mrs. Priest and others
62. Blitzen's buddy
63. Word for Rome
66. Shorten sail
68. French season
69. Ties
70. Element in uranium series
71. Mascara recipient
73. Prefix for derm or plasm
74. Grow rapidly
75. Capable of an answer
76. Hymn tune
80. Hardy girl
81. More out of practice
82. Woman's accessory
83. "__ Again"
86. Writer Anais
87. Isaac's son
88. Go Marcel Marceau one better
89. Worn away
90. "The Razor's __"
92. Religious degree
93. Impatient
94. Shensi city
95. British country wear
97. Gumshoe
99. Igneous rock
100. Brace
101. Quiet!
102. Disastrous defeat
104. Scottish hillside
106. Missile platform
107. Style
108. Prop for a stage extra
110. Matured, as fruit
112. Wool: Prefix
113. Date of a famous warning
119. Certain word
120. Part of a phono record
121. ". . . upon so __ subject as myself"
125. Leeward island
128. Damaging, as a fender
129. Color of embarrassment
131. __ (Beetle) Smith
132. Pastoral scene, to French
133. Angels' home
134. Type of pass
135. Combatants in a certain battle
136. Mortarboard adornments

DOWN

1. Math abbreviations
2. Nobel chemist
3. Saud and others
4. Capone lieutenant
5. Apparently
6. Draft program: Abbr.
7. Mariner's direction
8. Windfalls
9. Adjusted
10. Organizer of 57 Down
11. __ Zagora, Bulgaria
12. Consumed
13. Helmsman
14. Make an __ (finish)
15. Without __ (certainly)
16. Like some winter coats
17. Wash. neighbor
18. Atmosphere: Prefix
19. Kildare and Welby
21. Follower of 30 Across
22. Yorkshire city
28. Textile workers
31. Enemies
32. Honorary mil. commission
33. Having twin A.C. circuits
34. Spanish greeting
35. Small hole
36. Weapons suppliers
37. Doers of a grammar chore
38. Spotted cat
39. Sub's weapon
44. April 19 in New England
47. Latin adverb
48. Emulates the grasshopper
50. Battle town
52. Troops at 50 Down
54. Junior Pliny
56. Embattled farmers' place
57. Significant party of 1773
60. Blinds, as a falcon
62. Nazi camp near Munich
64. Entertained
65. Circuits
67. Groove in a pillar
72. Chasm: Var.
73. Imitate
77. Mrs. John Adams
78. Thin layer
79. Family name of dukes of Bridgewater
83. "Seven __ Baldpate"
84. Cromwell's son-in-law
85. Having sound
86. Wifely pick-me-up
91. Nigerian
95. Behind __ (in trouble)
96. Colonial grievance
98. Cleveland Clinic founder
99. Snake charmer's clarinet
101. Mollusk genus
103. Up on deck
105. Bee: Prefix
108. Poet Alan or singer Pete
109. Girl's name
111. Lopez et al.
114. Historic Danish family
115. Cricket term
116. Hot-goods handler
117. Pirates' domain
118. Twice 100ths
122. "Born __"
123. Linden tree
124. Nimitz and Halsey: Abbr.
125. Shoemaker's tool
126. Basketball org.
127. Asian holiday
129. Vampire
130. Spanish queen

176 Reversals by Paul R. Barnes

ACROSS

1. Backward spring month
6. Simpleton
10. Trick
14. Anser or brant
15. Occupy
16. Wheys
17. Sherman or Reynolds
18. Cartoonist Hype __
19. First man
20. Aides of drs.
21. Writer Carson
23. Lucrezia
24. Occult doctrine
26. Asian sea and town
27. "I __ to a suggestion"
29. Island off Naples
32. Heavy blow
33. Piles
34. Of age: Abbr.
37. Imagine
40. Mold anew
42. Part of E.S.T.: Abbr.
43. Person
45. Fish sauce
46. Begin a meal
47. Buckingham, for one
49. Towaway __
52. Dutch city
54. Pepper's partner
55. Houston eleven
57. Peer Gynt's mother
60. Head: Fr.
61. Tiny thing
62. More accurate
64. Got off
65. Within: Prefix
66. Big artery: Fr.
67. Deteriorates
68. Bonded laborer
69. Hebrew prophet

DOWN

1. Sew a falcon's eyes
2. Unless, in old Rome
3. Bright room
4. Cut off
5. Kind of grape
6. In __ of a mess
7. Small flute
8. Exchange premium
9. Berber
10. Decisive point
11. Macaw
12. Riding contest
13. Disconcert
22. Burrows or Lincoln
25. Implement
26. Exclamations
27. Mild oath: Var.
28. Deodar or baobab
30. Listen
31. Ginger
33. Little devils
34. Most heartless
35. Sheltered
36. Rubber
38. Metal
39. Happy: Fr.
41. Every
44. Bien __ (of course)
46. Turns informer
47. Freshwater fish
48. Brave
49. Printing marks
50. Name
51. Upstate N.Y. city
53. Norman Vincent __
55. French names
56. Repute
58. Endings with sen and jun
59. Hari
63. Consumed

177 After You Alphonse by Frances Hansen

ACROSS

1. Milquetoast
7. Teen-age party wear
14. Goose variety
20. Grounded
21. In fashion
22. Small simian
23. Impassive
24. Separate
25. Cesar of films
26. Certain employee
28. Prisoner's remark to judge
30. Ridge
31. Indians
32. Big birds
33. Cheese
35. Autocrat
39. Daunt
42. Legal claim
45. Motto of Oxford unit
51. Parser's concern
53. Refrigerator bin
54. Gay
55. __ out (evade)
56. Western org.
57. Seine areas
59. Among: Prefix
60. File
62. Falcon's source
63. Antimacassar
64. Apology to Clementine
70. Catface
74. Daub
75. Intensifies
80. Defeat
82. S.A. Monkey
83. Boxer's move
86. Potter's tool
87. Superior
88. East or West
90. "It takes __ livin' . . ."
91. Cleveland Amory people
95. Handle: Lat.
96. Browne
97. Lafayette College town
98. Lawyers: Abbr.
100. Gallup item
102. Fashion name
105. Mosquito genus
109. "Oops, sorry"
113. Bump in a road
116. __ mind
117. Singer
119. Right away
120. Not seemly
121. Illusion
122. Handgun
123. Cowboys
124. Regrets
125. Navigator's aid

DOWN

1. Roman conspirator
2. About
3. Thrust
4. Social asset
5. Coated, as a seed
6. Magenta, etc.
7. Churchman
8. Vibrant
9. Breeds of fowl
10. Sun god
11. Sahl
12. Military asst.
13. Ooze
14. To Bugs Bunny's taste
15. Footless class
16. Remote TV broadcasts
17. Danish measure
18. Skin: Prefix
19. Stub __
27. Girl's name
29. Running wild
34. Writer Eric
35. M.D.'s
36. Discovery
37. Sniffs
38. "Mind and Society" author
39. Violin
40. Declined
41. Ledger item
42. "Green Pastures" role
43. Prefix for logy
44. Girls' names
46. Sgt., e.g.
47. Initials of the 30's
48. Ice: Ger.
49. Color or corn
50. Cue
52. Whitelaw or Ogden
58. Chalcedony
61. Take five
62. Wall: Fr.
65. José's friends
66. Loathe
67. __ middling
68. High tea
69. Uh-huh
70. Horse of 1955
71. Lethal snake
72. "__ With a View"
73. Invitation initials
76. Satisfy fully
77. Esprit
78. Fiber knots
79. Portico
81. Golf word
83. Peerce
84. Cuckoo
85. __ nose
89. After "hoot"
92. Lets up
93. Tea and sympathy
94. Not any
99. Bovine
100. Baby food
101. Willow
102. 1912 Nobel physicist
103. Unmoving
104. Vegetables
106. Tapir
107. Early colonist
108. Young fish
109. Ivory: Lat.
110. A kind of phobia
111. David, for one
112. O. T. book
113. Spruce
114. Unique place
115. Sweetheart, British style
118. So!

178 The Gang's All Here by Nancy Schuster

ACROSS

1. Voracious S.A. fish
7. Gave support
12. A Davis
17. Having wings
18. Disregards
20. City of the Prater
22. __ one's own
23. Historic do
25. Curl
26. Miss Merrill
27. Purloin
28. Remorseful one
29. Pronoun
30. Pain reliever
33. Preceding month: Abbr.
34. __ facias
35. Flimsy pretense
37. News edition
39. Group having a common culture
40. Mark of disgrace
42. Sky item?
43. Fail, familiarly
44. Stendhal
45. Name coined in 1880
51. Scold
53. Form of Greek language
54. Flour base
55. Ne'er-do-well
56. Swiss canton
57. Arranged
59. Fashion name
60. O'Hara home
61. Play about
63. Islands off Galway
64. Christ: Poetic
65. River to North Sea
66. S. A. capital
67. Female swans
68. Part of the street scene
71. Decimal base
72. Maple genus
73. Swedish river
74. Dostoevski heroine
75. Eats greedily
77. Game some people play
80. Sick's partner
81. Lamb
82. __ de mer
83. Fortune-telling cards
85. Sugar or salt
88. Brown pigment
90. Pond sight
93. Flynn
94. Common verb
95. Tag again
97. Ginger or pepper
99. Italian lake
100. Like neon
102. Father
103. Words on a valentine
105. Fundamental of democracy
108. With "all," a smarty
109. Tranquil
110. Discourses
111. Move back
112. Old instruments
113. Campus V.I.P.'s
114. Stage remarks

DOWN

1. Snag
2. Sacker of Rome
3. Dashing
4. News article
5. Aid and abet
6. Sullivan and Begley
7. Pain
8. Mad
9. Morse signal
10. Olympian
11. Fitted with teeth
12. Race track
13. Use a straw
14. Emergency group
15. Moldering
16. Intestine: Prefix
18. Footnote word
19. Engraved pillar
21. Actor Lew
24. Mother's plea
26. Sidestep
31. Pinner
32. Spread out
34. End
36. Cruising
38. Spike
39. Churchman
41. Marketplaces
43. Baseball term
44. A full glass
46. Nothing, in Paris
47. Indian state
48. Cooked
49. Serving dish
50. Aches for
51. Coarse cloth
52. Beethoven's Third
53. Central part
58. Devil: Var.
59. Stop
62. Killjoy
64. Crossroads: Abbr.
67. Cocoon dwellers
68. Janitor's concern
69. Bird
70. Busybodies' delights
74. Thrust
76. Evening, on a prescription
78. Whoop
79. Absorbed in
80. Seneca, e.g.
84. Some clocks
85. Factions
86. Implement
87. The art of heraldry
88. Noted chemist and family
89. __ one's laurels
91. Declared
92. Conquer's partner
94. Amazon or soldier
96. Legal claims
98. Distributes
100. Angers
101. Ancient port
104. Places
106. Chemical suffix
107. Scottish wee
108. Ape of India

179 Stir Crazy by Edward J. O'Brien

ACROSS

1. Postal items: Abbr.
5. Decline
8. Filipinos
15. Balcony: Abbr.
18. Shout for attention
19. Teachers' org.
20. Glossy paints
21. Santa's sounds
22. 63481, 71120, 52893, etc.
24. Plucky penologists
26. Possess
27. Bound
28. Steal: Slang
29. More pleasant
31. "Life __ an empty dream!"
33. Tuscaloosa inmate's song
38. Wrong
39. Roman god
40. Jannings
41. Whales
42. Ventilate anew
43. Ziegfeld
44. Sarcastic telegram
47. Riboflavin: Abbr.
48. Western state: Abbr.
49. Dine
50. In itself: Lat.
51. Wing
53. __-cat
54. Rice-field vehicle
57. Golf's Palmer
59. Mil. medal
61. "I'm doing well, __?"
62. Red gurnards
64. "Master, __?" (Judas's question)
66. Lemon color: Abbr.
67. Independence monogram
69. "... as lovely as __"
70. __ fit (clothier's offer)
72. Ancient flint
74. Pronoun
75. Stare, in England
76. Inmate's side of the story?
79. Recipe units: Abbr.
83. Spanish uncle
84. "... could __ horse!"
86. Conclude
87. Eur. nation
88. Gas: Prefix
89. Black Maria?
92. Grid scores
93. Las Vegas area
94. Corded fabric: Var.
95. Chem. compound
96. Wander
97. Allen and Lawrence
98. Convicted bigamist
102. Pretenses
103. __-missabib (Jer. 20:3)
104. Day: Abbr.
105. Growl
107. Printing devices: Abbr.
109. Value of yeast
113. Stack of mod records
115. Master: Var.
116. Gush back
117. Miss Arden
118. Closing word
119. Tokyo coins: Abbr.
120. Lies atop
121. Attention
122. Old rulers

DOWN

1. Toadfish
2. "__ heart shall be called prudent"
3. Keystone prison conditions
4. Opp. of antonym
5. Antagonism
6. Lager
7. 24 hours in a Paris jail
8. Mendicant
9. As a whole
10. Where Pago Pago is
11. "I am __ of the rabble"
12. Evergreen
13. Carte or mode
14. Eurasian union
15. "__ Nights"
16. They power cells?
17. "His glassy __ an angry ape"
23. Dilute: Sp.
25. Book of lives: Abbr.
30. Boxing units: Abbr.
32. Incarcerate Bambi?
34. Peking name
35. I go round: Lat.
36. Mine: Fr.
37. Harvests: Abbr.
38. Afternoon, in Australia
43. Angelico
44. Cattle fold
45. "__ off" (sale ad)
46. Affluence
48. Thesis abbr.
49. Optometrist's cherished alma mater?
52. The, in Nice
55. Deplete: Dialect
56. Piths
58. Spins again
60. Last night: Scot.
63. Front yards
64. In a small-minded way
65. Birdman of Alcatraz
68. Ph. D., for some
70. Deputy: Abbr.
71. Hydrocarbon
73. Eye part
77. "... an __ a sail"
78. Suffix with joy
80. Moment for a tennis player
81. Brit. writer
82. Bribes
85. Arabian gulf
90. Climbs skyward
91. Eclipse
92. Hebrew letter
93. Wading bird
94. Phono-record abbr.
96. N. Y. village
97. Typewriter bar
99. A Wright, for short
100. Brit. ridges
101. Release
106. Flaring star
108. Wash. men
110. Misjudge
111. Born: Fr.
112. Plane parts: Abbr.
114. Bed, to some

180 After-Hours by Mary Ann Code

ACROSS

1. Jewish feast
6. Kind of tow or boot
9. Uses a scythe
14. "__ steals my purse..."
17. Nerve conductor
18. Charged atom
19. Transfer permit
20. Sumptuous
22. Cain's home
24. Call up
25. "Be Prepared," for one
26. Museum offering
27. Activate a cradle
28. Linden tree
29. Sweetened the kitty
31. Roman 650
32. Chuck-a-luck unit
33. Old anthology
35. Biblical coin
37. Warning
38. Other
39. Succinct
41. Kind of storm
42. Gloomy man
44. Serling
47. Diminutive ending
49. __ publica
51. What lilies don't do
53. Asserts
55. Moslem mascaras
57. Sound of despair
60. Glowing
62. Rumanian composer
64. Saunter
66. Disengaged
67. Society gal
68. Condensed: Abbr.
70. Relating to eight
71. March or Holbrook
72. Decrepit boat
75. Spooky
77. __ the track
79. Membrane
81. Like Sherlock's methods
84. Used an ax
86. French city
87. French tree
88. Musical ending
90. Oriental principle
91. Greetings for Orphan Annie
92. Antelope
93. After upsilon
94. Scottish river
97. Server
100. Ball
103. Trade combine
105. Gypsy
108. Comment of Henry Ford
111. Gain
112. West
113. Take in
114. Relatives
115. Computer fare
116. Certain records
117. Emulated Mata Hari
118. Halt abruptly
120. Toasts to Morpheus
122. Bridge reverses
123. Lena
124. Drink
125. Pyle
126. Lease
127. Filled
128. Thor or Zeus
129. Teams

DOWN

1. Vegetable dishes
2. Eastern church title
3. Retiring child's wisecrack
4. Pass-catcher
5. Stock up
6. Because
7. Nutty one
8. Neither Dem. nor Rep.
9. Some TV fare
10. Salon events
11. Group of Greek dialects
12. Man of pipes
13. U.S. violinist
14. Maligns
15. Song of 1942
16. Singing group
21. Scuttles
23. Rapiers
25. Jouster's wear
28. Hole: Fr.
30. Chemical suffixes
33. Famous last words
34. Sea god
36. Boat parts
40. Work unit
43. Jesse of Calif.
45. Admit
46. Time abbr.
47. Squeezed out
48. Kind of poem
50. Speech pauses
52. Rock Hudson movie
53. Confounds
54. Henry or Edward
56. Hard to get
58. Old chest
59. Mountain gap
61. Duck genus
63. News piece
65. Geneva, for one
69. German state
73. Fliers' org.
74. Prohibits
76. Continent: Abbr.
78. Educ. group
80. Kingdom
81. Hammarskjold
82. Sea eagle
83. Behold: Fr.
85. U. S. money: Abbr.
89. Flying
93. Paris area
95. Flew with a flourish
96. Camera part
98. Math branch
99. Is charitable
101. Relaxing
102. Burden
104. Classify
106. Serving dish: Var.
107. Certain replies
108. Famed W. W. II internee
109. Urge
110. Slangy affirmatives
111. Carried on
115. Queen of Carthage
119. Neckpiece
120. Plater
121. Dernier __

181 Wild Flowers by Mary M. Murdoch

ACROSS

1. High and reverse, e.g.
6. You love: Lat.
10. Bureau: Abbr.
14. Levels
19. Rent again
20. Parcel of land
21. Seaweed
23. Sherry
24. Flower's parting words
26. Elite of flowerdom
28. Flowery proposal in old song
30. Broadway signs
31. Paris airport
32. Some cats and dogs
33. Shoe parts
36. Run __ in the paper
37. Italian pot
38. Waldorf, for one
41. Ocean: Abbr.
43. Estimate
47. Word with way and sea
48. Danish measures
49. __ -Magnon
50. Remnant
51. Flowery put-off
54. Aspen gear
55. Cloth strainer
56. Kind of alcohol
57. Boxing outcomes: Abbr.
58. Scabbard part
59. Alike: Fr.
60. Gem weight
61. Weekday: Abbr.
62. Gay ones
63. Kind of room, for short
64. Very wealthy flower
67. Arbor
68. Frog sound
70. Up to __
71. Opera voices
72. Make even
74. Flowery animal groups
80. Rested
83. Four-baggers
84. Long time
85. Dances
86. Pianist Hess
87. Fuses
88. Buses and trains: Abbr.
89. Guardian of sailors
91. Aspect
92. Rehan et al.
93. Transgress in a flowery way
95. Lasso
96. Peleg's son
97. Girl, in Paris
98. Old big-game guns
99. Shout
100. Spread hay
101. Scolded
102. Bits
103. Fraternal org.
105. Fortification
107. Pub offerings
108. Perry's creator
109. Italian island
113. "Aster no questions __"
119. Halt, in a flowery way
122. Stein words
123. Of birds
124. Swift descent
125. Open
126. Paint worker
127. Furious
128. Early slave
129. TV's Parker
130. Methods: Abbr.

DOWN

1. Luggage pieces
2. Fisherman
3. __ the good
4. Puzzle
5. British gun
6. Benedict or Hap
7. Virile
8. Sharp
9. Bachelors' dinner, e.g.
10. Fliers
11. Cooper et al.
12. Baby's bed
13. Gypsum
14. Surpasses
15. Green, in Paris
16. Time period
17. Seine
18. Draft system: Abbr.
20. Headpiece
22. Cardboard box: Abbr.
25. Utopias
27. Available
29. Close again
34. Listless, gardenwise
35. Kind of bass
36. Snakes
37. Wife of Ahasuerus
38. One who pillages
39. Slack, old style
40. Camera part
42. __ bet (wagers badly)
43. Flower
44. Actors' milieu
45. Shrubby kind of degree
46. Ludwig
47. Deadly
51. Scoundrel: Scot.
52. Artificial fly
53. Small case
54. Put-ons
58. Brooch
60. Dice game
61. Edible root
62. Scottish hillsides
64. City on the Loire
65. Preposition
66. Eastman
69. Orchestra section
71. On earth
72. Frustrate
73. European buck
74. Convict's goal
75. Cured
76. Kind of wolf
77. Emancipators
78. Vends
79. Blood: Prefix
81. Mountain ridge
82. Soviet republic
86. Certain delivery
88. Pinball flash
89. Put up
90. __ Russia (title of Ivan IV)
91. Cleaving tool
93. Food
94. Author of "Phineas Finn"
97. Kukla, __ Ollie
99. E. Indies weights
103. Prickly plants
104. Braid
106. __ Lama
107. Illinois city
108. It's nobody __ business
109. Ex-pitcher Face
110. Civic club
111. Assail
112. Son of Jacob et al.
114. Wall and State: Abbr.
115. U. S. inventor
116. Some poetry
117. Moved, as a ship
118. Cereal
119. Smoking __
120. Gardner
121. Women's __

182 Observations

by Henry V. Straka

ACROSS

1. Syrian city, to French
5. Vehicle
9. Pair up
14. Fighter planes of W. W. I
19. Greek dais
20. Roofing piece
21. Zola
22. Paine product
23. Indians
24. Indian plum
25. Mass. port
26. Nest
27. Playboy's version of a right
31. Harem
32. Force: Lat.
33. Newspaper section: Abbr.
34. Radical
35. Roman writer
38. Restrain
42. "I wasn't there"
46. Flaunted
47. Bright bird
48. Tabula __
49. Laws: Abbr.
51. W. W. II vessel
53. Blue glass
54. Coal dust
55. Ankles
56. Troupers
59. Reno leavers
60. Horse
62. Yokel
64. Formality
66. Possible query of a zoo ape
72. Sir Robert
73. Indian of West
74. The Met forbids these
76. __ cry
80. Depletes
82. Salinger girl
84. Louvre name
85. Pacific island group
87. Guinness, e.g.
88. Kind of breath
89. Coins in Riga
90. Three in one
92. Plane-engine housing
95. Units of force
96. Reparation
97. Nail décor
98. Keresan Indian
100. Kind of bunt
102. Saratoga, for one
103. City near L. A.
108. Millionaire's pad
114. Cottontails
115. Lag behind
116. __ over lightly
117. Binge
118. Small ones: Suffix
119. French year
120. River to Elbe
121. Instrument
122. Germs
123. Rises high
124. Time periods in Wild West
125. Goes down

DOWN

1. Borders on
2. River of Hades
3. Eastern prince
4. Kemal __
5. Basic item
6. Serene
7. Tucson suburb
8. College figure
9. Scylla's strait
10. Gathered
11. Spanish linden
12. Musical symbol
13. Rope fibers
14. Track officials
15. H-hour at a newspaper
16. Egyptian abode of dead
17. Roman 602
18. Word on a proof
28. Fields: Lat.
29. Baseball great
30. Capable of
35. Swift output
36. Ancient Briton
37. Gather on a surface
39. Deception
40. She, in Paris
41. Soaks flax
42. Alms box
43. Girl's name
44. Moslem faith
45. Well-known deer
46. Buddy
49. Restrained
50. Oilers
52. Old galley
56. Eggs on
57. Game fish
58. Removed pits
61. Mischief-maker
63. "Once __ a . . ."
65. Common abbr.
67. Lily maid
68. What crystal gazers do
69. Xmas plant
70. Of a lake area
71. Trace: Fr.
75. Lip
76. Movie dog
77. MacDonald's asset
78. French friend
79. Early English Puritan
81. Mideast land
83. Marie, for one
86. "Days of Wine __"
88. Pasture sound
91. Genesis name
93. Drum out of office
94. Pierces: Var.
95. Lulu
98. Pele's game
99. Annoying ones
101. Spectral type
103. Old Asian coin
104. Sedans
105. Weeper of myth
106. Hoof: Scot.
107. Diminutive suffixes
108. "Now hear __!"
109. Sound
110. Gardner
111. Sea bird
112. Blue Nile source
113. O'Hara Pal

183 Urban Renewal   A. J. Santora

ACROSS

1. Becomes clogged
6. Beyond
10. Steeple
15. L.A. time
18. Stroller
19. Lover
20. Breadwinner
21. "__ Gang"
22. Earhart
23. ". . . fetch __ of water"
24. Box-office bargain
25. Sky object
26. Theatrical lament
29. Provisory
30. Hawaiian tree
31. Old come-on in book ads
33. Blood prefix
35. Strong point
36. Medley
37. Doing a bar job
41. Nuclear pact
43. Hockey star
45. Gust of wind
47. War vessel
48. Natives of Cagliari
50. Wine: Prefix
52. Come __ halt
54. Asian antelope
55. Splash
58. Metal sheets
62. S. A. city
64. Average
65. __ debt to society
66. Air-booking problem
67. Place for the moon
70. Nasal bones
73. Weird
74. Portland product: Abbr.
75. Snake
76. With dispatch
82. Three, in Naples
83. Noun suffix
84. Units of fluidity
85. Missile charge
87. Unique birds
90. On the canvas
92. That: Lat.
93. Snare
94. Wire: Abbr.
95. Remainder
97. Storm
99. Partner of older
101. Auto of yore
103. Writer Levin
104. Boron's table listing: Abbr.
106. Barnstorming
108. Drain
110. Flying group: Abbr.
113. Put __ (halt)
117. O. Henry output
119. A-one
121. Moon goddess
123. Norwegian name
124. Where a heart is
127. State: Abbr.
128. Arizona city
131. Legal eagle
135. Metric unit
136. Spinets
137. Sierra __
138. Former U.N. name
139. Athens letter
140. Directionals
141. Type of beam
142. Works in concert
143. Diego or Remo
144. Resources
145. Printing word
146. St. __, Leeward island

DOWN

1. Person
2. Morning-after items
3. French composer
4. Svelte
5. Attempt
6. __ the picture
7. In __ of speaking
8. French river
9. "Holy" city
10. Looked into
11. City in Utah
12. Overrun
13. Stage direction
14. Make a bevue
15. Backless couch
16. Word addition: Abbr.
17. Kind of weight
18. Gape
19. Speed-trap item
20. Of a people
27. Savings item
28. Presidential name
29. Racing classic
32. Fuegians
34. Phrase for baseball busts
35. Diet
38. Dialect
39. Vamp of silents
40. Suffix for ana or epi
42. Dance, in Paris
44. Answer in kind
46. Slang for money
49. Traffic sign
51. Magazine
53. Tune
55. Medic
56. Truant
57. River of Bolivia
59. In __ (so to speak)
60. Put to __
61. Salmon
63. Triple Crown winner
66. Biblical name
68. Left-hand pages
69. "This __ treat"
71. Present
72. Spy
77. __-Bains, French spa
78. Scarlett et al.
79. Kind of interest: Abbr.
80. Lopez theme
81. Salvador
86. Eastern state: Abbr.
87. News or fine
88. Must
89. Doer: Suffix
91. Airline-board abbr.
93. Deuces
96. Footballer's protection
97. Handle: Lat.
98. Drinker
100. Mar
102. Streams
105. Samoan bowl
107. Breathe
109. Swamp
111. Fatty
112. Angler's need
114. Make believe
115. Gifts
116. Bachelor __
118. Wasteland
120. Fishing leaders
122. Gray drab
125. Curtain fabric
126. Part of a golf shoe
128. Chatters
129. Sky bear
130. "Meet __ St. Louis"
132. Breaks
133. To you: Fr.
134. Querying word
136. Miss Mason

184 Surnames by Elaine D. Schorr

ACROSS

1. Porridge
5. Covenant
9. Abbr. on a map
13. Kind of shoe or suit
17. Operatic prince
18. Covering: Ger.
19. Mitigates
21. Foot: Prefix
22. Slum-clearance problem
24. Lookout for some
26. Fictional hero's larder
28. Deprives, in a way
31. Slant
32. Author Victor
33. Stradivari's teacher
34. Italian poet
35. Honest name
37. Grafted, in heraldry
40. Appoints
41. Cooper
42. Lord's demesne
44. Neighbor of Neth.
45. Ratite birds
46. Leaf division
47. Russian saint and others
48. Schurz
49. Compass point
50. "Blithe Spirit" author
52. Roulette choice
53. Delibes opera
54. Singer Frankie
56. Result
58. Kind of girl
59. Lobby décor
61. Epic poem
62. Words of apology
63. Tenant
64. Valentino locale
65. Balances
66. Latin abbrs.
67. Nontalker
68. Harrow
71. Graduate degree
74. Air: Prefix
75. Cowpoke's need
76. Macaws
77. French coins
78. Family member
79. Inscribe
80. Perdition
81. Georges of opera
82. Poets' words
84. __ through
85. General at Gettysburg
87. Gland: Prefix
88. Bridge seat
90. Back talk
91. Property conveyer
93. Certain actress's tonic
99. Where not to go from
100. Helplessly
104. Latin that
105. Uses a mop
106. Adams and others
107. Precious
108. Campus figure
109. Young oyster
110. Loss of value: Abbr.
111. Rodin subject

DOWN

1. Echo's title
2. Bronze or Iron
3. Tiny mass: Abbr.
4. Divides in balance
5. Certain golf strokes
6. Came to rest
7. Shoemaker, in London
8. Rarefied condition
9. Game for a playwright
10. Wash
11. Hebrew lyre
12. Land areas: Abbr.
13. Kind of cake or rubber
14. Wilson aide's largesse
15. Stettin's river
16. Lean and strong
18. Blood: Prefix
20. Does ship carpentry
23. Columbus, to friends
25. Greek letter
27. Use a shuttle
28. Some are great
29. Moslem leaders
30. Boston patriot's plant
34. Ali
35. Miss Dickinson
36. Wild beast
38. One serving a sentence
39. A Queen
41. A Champion
43. Vocally
46. An isolate
48. Leslie of films
50. Commends
51. English writer's hideaway
53. Certain beam
55. __-Saxon
57. Penpoint
58. British chaps
59. Polite word
60. Girl's nickname
61. Choleric
62. City on the Meuse
64. Winged
67. Movie, in Europe
69. Revered event of 1775
70. Seed cover
72. Former tennis star Maria
73. Mary or John
75. Cooks further
77. Ally
80. Stitched anew
81. Scottish child
83. Used a cellar
86. Angkor __
89. Road sign
91. More qualified
92. Ballads
93. Commerce group: Abbr.
94. Aureole
95. Cries of pain
96. Swaddle
97. Log hut in Minsk
98. Blunder
101. Fr. pronoun
102. Mil. officers
103. "Of course"

185 Promissory Notes by John Willig

ACROSS

1. Kind of child
6. Baht spender
10. "... gang aft __"
15. City of Greece
21. River of France
22. "It __!"
23. "__ evil"
24. Imbibed freely
25. Dentist's promise
28. Style, in Madrid
29. Greek letters
30. River to North Sea
31. Start of a June promise
33. Fishy road sign
36. Parrot of N. Z.
38. Deserves
41. Laborious
42. Manpower program: Abbr.
43. Parting promise
46. U.S. journalist
47. Find
49. Ring verdict
50. Effect
52. Portico
56. Loudly vulgar
57. Promise to a hounded postman
60. Operetta man
61. Crate
63. Krone part
64. "__ Sylphides"
65. Turn away
66. Clod
67. What Florida promises
72. Verdon
73. Town in China
75. Light shade
76. __-disant
77. Safari help
80. P. R., for one
81. Most intimate
85. Picture on a fiver
88. Crosses out
89. Refrigerants
91. Sky Altar
93. Hawks of Hawaii
94. Get rid of
96. Toothy look
97. Politician's promise

101. W. W. II org.
102. Crow over
104. "The __ Seed"
105. Haul
106. __-the-board
109. Petulant
110. Police chief's promise
115. Deft
117. Spear-carrier
118. Starlike object
119. Last month: Abbr.
120. Relative of itsy-bitsy
121. Confident
122. Boss's promise to son
126. Plan
127. Cutting weapon
131. Unanimous
132. __ de mer
133. Proof mark
134. What money doesn't promise
136. Pot or bag
139. Mystery-title word
141. Famed express-no-more
142. Tout's promise
149. Forward: It.
150. __ space
151. Stimulus
152. Tin: Fr.
153. Loser to F.D.R.
154. Primp
155. Sound unit
156. Partners

DOWN

1. N.Y.C. subway
2. Encouraging cry
3. Onassis
4. Map feature
5. Salamander
6. Glitter
7. Pres. initials
8. Pallid
9. Paper promises
10. Off base
11. Perfect thing
12. Rumanian coin
13. Pens: Abbr.
14. Attention-getter
15. __ off (get over a jag)
16. Gets on a crowded bus
17. J. J. or Vincent
18. Zoo favorite
19. Ultimate end
20. Be fond of
26. Annie et al.
27. Fishing gear
32. Alto and tenor
33. Corm
34. Con __
35. Broker's stock promise
37. Hormone initials
39. Unruly one, in Scotland
40. Unfeeling
43. Lindsay's remark about N.Y.C.
44. N. Z. tree
45. Running out of
46. Holds esteem
48. Songwriters' org.

51. Rug feature
52. Cut apart
53. Freeloader's promise
54. Thames sight
55. Skill
58. Relating to: Suffix
59. Headland
60. Politician's promise
62. These: Sp.
68. Mideast org.
69. Compass point
70. Bengal native
71. Clock reading
72. Harden
73. Cover
74. Mideast land: Abbr.
77. __ nova
78. Play period: Abbr.
79. Quiet!
82. Poetic word
83. Tool
84. Three, in Asti
86. "No soap!"
87. Iowa college
90. Angered

92. Affected
95. "And __ a big red rose"
97. Wools: Lat.
98. 5-2, for one
99. Besides
100. "The __ Truth"
102. Some drs.
103. Costello
104. Butter at Maxim's
107. Of a Spanish area
108. Hemp fiber
111. Remunerates
112. Irish cry
113. Interior cover: Abbr.
114. Mouth: Prefix
116. Kind
118. A Roosevelt
121. Ancestral religion
123. Not yet existing
124. Grin in a way
125. Semblance
127. Boating hazard
128. Grub
129. Of bees

130. __ time
131. Assyrian god
133. Greek letter
135. "__ on red"
137. Cobras
138. Wolfe
140. Hold back
143. Paris season
144. Before haw
145. Hoodwink
146. Word with cake or meal
147. She, in Bonn
148. U. S. N. A. grad

186 Mixed Pairs by Gladys V. Miller

ACROSS

1. Devastation
6. "As — you can"
12. Past events: Abbr.
16. Fellini's milieu
17. Chestnut clam
19. Bread spread
20. Movie-set area
21. Smasher
23. Stained
24. Guevara
26. Sinful man
27. Female ruff
29. French or Dutch
30. Scorches
32. Ineffective
33. Skin: Prefix
34. Poetic word
35. High-hat
39. Praise
40. De Carlo of films
42. Mystical poem
43. Broadcast
44. Hasty, for one
46. Twilight
48. Scowl
52. Met highlights
53. Walk daintily
54. Wine jug
56. Piquant
57. Jumble
59. Antiquity, to poets
60. Fraternal men
61. Major- —
62. Slant
63. Control
64. Uncle: Sp.
65. Tied
69. Voice
70. Stiff fabric
73. Miss Evert
74. Endorsements
75. Familiar name in tennis
76. Earthy: It.
78. Slander
80. Polite word
81. Twig
82. Ate less
83. Grand, for one
86. Gobbledygook
88. Plant part
91. Armadillo
92. Cretan sight
94. Better's partner
95. Nobel physicist
96. Photo, for short
97. Over — (helpless)
101. Slangy denial
102. Lock part
103. Willy-nilly, to Caesar
106. Ship's nemesis
108. Arab prince
109. Greek: Prefix
110. Carriage
111. "... in corpore —"
112. Reduce
113. Gives a party

DOWN

1. Nursery-rhyme start
2. English river
3. African landscape
4. Shoulder: Prefix
5. Contagious
6. Deception
7. "— was saying"
8. French town
9. Incredible
10. "Pluck — rose"
11. Thatched
12. Holly tree
13. State: Abbr.
14. Lose one's cool
15. Bullring man
16. Boat
18. Sturluson work
20. Tarry
22. Fleming
25. Be unwilling
28. Letters
30. State: Abbr.
31. Stretched out
33. Hog breed
35. Hawaiian yams
36. Asian leopard
37. Indivisible: Abbr.
38. Curling target
39. Metric measure
41. May 8 and Aug. 15, 1945
43. De Mille or Moorehead
44. Pebbly surfaced
45. Of a Russian range
46. Phoenician city
47. West Indian birds
49. Influence peddlers
50. Primitive implements
51. Rudolph feature
53. Consequence
55. Actor Richard
57. Madagascar native
58. Evident: Sp.
61. Check
63. Turkish liquor
66. Stage curtain
67. Vibrate
68. Previously, old style
71. Weeper, in adage
72. Deep blue
74. Vision: Prefix
77. French coin
78. Aspires
79. Direction: Abbr.
82. — mater
83. Gen. Arnold
84. Believes
85. Western port
86. Wonder
87. "O rare" poet
89. Terminate a mission
90. Circus unit
92. Saud
93. Track event
95. Moroccan port
97. Flying prefix
98. Function
99. Wings
100. Radziwill, etc.
102. Whodunit V.I.P.'s
104. Rubbing fluid: Abbr.
105. Compass point
107. Cote sound

187 Time Piece — by Guido N. Scarato

ACROSS

1. Catfish
6. Sample TV film
11. Latch again
16. Like some eyes
21. Spanish month
22. "__ Mio"
23. Remove
24. Proportion
25. Steel, in Paris
26. Clear
27. Squalls
28. Old Times Sq. hotel
29. St. Peter's and Farnese, e.g.
33. Drop __ (suggest)
34. Waste allowance
35. Height: Abbr.
36. Does math work
40. Furnish
42. "__ deal!"
44. Kind of relief
45. Roll-call note: Abbr.
48. Closet items
50. Here, to Caesar
52. Café additive
54. Salad
55. Antique-buyer's choice
62. Chemical prefixes
63. Chemical compound
64. Sea bird
65. Sierra __
66. Colony near Hong Kong
67. Beaks
68. Explorer
69. "I can't __!"
71. Chisholm, for one
73. Italian family
75. Like a grain
77. Miss Claire
78. Sphinxes, etc.
85. Recent: Prefix
86. Mediocre
87. City officials: Abbr.
88. Eastern title
89. More daft
92. Word with shoppe
94. One opposed
96. Latin nine
100. Maple and box elder
101. Rose lover
102. Toxic protein
104. Certain tapestries
109. Shortly
110. Bakery worker
111. U. S. storyteller
112. Sea off Greece
113. Biblical name
114. Decree
115. Cleaner's concern
118. Salutation
122. Actual being
123. After pi
124. Lively: Abbr.
126. Struck
128. Space station, maybe
139. Color over
140. Grind, as teeth
141. Room, in Paris
142. P. I. island
143. Judge's call
144. "My cup __"
145. Shade of gray
146. Works on copy
147. Like some moss
148. Performs, old style
149. Former L. A. mayor
150. Bristles

DOWN

1. Costly
2. Fairy-tale word
3. Guide
4. Kind of code
5. Genoese admiral
6. Visits casually
7. Safety zone
8. Make a __ (finance)
9. Acid suffix
10. Dogma
11. Compunction
12. Ejects
13. Wild party
14. Italian city
15. Take five
16. Plant parts
17. Bridge seat
18. Pacific island
19. Fashion name
20. Poetic time
30. "__ jewel" (words for a new maid)
31. Chilean port
32. Puff up
36. Nautical word
37. Shaw product
38. Column style
39. Italian army men
41. Caprice
43. Fine lace
45. Lamp rubber
46. Blocking
47. As __ sugar
49. Indian state
51. Diamonds
53. Reverence
54. Cygnus
56. Civil War ship
57. Banishes
58. Tease
59. Sea nymph
60. Sawlike: Prefix
61. Woolwich initials
68. Attempt: Scot.
69. Miler's need
70. Sidon's neighbor
72. Handle: Fr.
74. Gardener
76. Liquid ester
78. Islands in Bay of Bengal
79. Geologic era
80. Area of France
81. Peanuts
82. As red __
83. Jury panel
84. Early period
90. Triplet
91. Noun suffix
93. Brooklyn campus
95. Agency of 1930's
97. Lobby pieces
98. Vergil hero: Var.
99. Middle, in law
101. Drink
102. Army address: Abbr.
105. French capital in W. W. II
106. Inevitable accident
107. Of sight
108. Shabby
114. Through street
116. Goes by
117. "I wouldn't bet __!"
119. Early stable man
120. Talisman
121. Extremely
125. Disordered
127. Slackens
128. Too much: Fr.
129. "As you __"
130. Norse myth
131. Russian vote
132. Lowdown
133. Have it made
134. Western alliance
135. Commanded
136. Leave out
137. Statistics
138. Gaelic

188 Inner Meanings
by Anthony Morse

ACROSS

1. Traffic maneuver
6. Swizzle stick
11. Heat milk, in a way
16. Black entry
21. Cold
22. Doddery
23. P. I. island
24. Author of children's books
25. Dostoevsky subject
26. Like a parade
29. English capital: Abbr.
30. Bowl
32. Got the word
33. African banana
34. High notes
36. Stretch out
37. Like S. F. or Rome
38. Pathetic
39. Cushion
40. Constellation
42. Punishment, in law
44. Elec. unit
45. Ooze
46. Capital of Eritrea
47. Object of playing postoffice
50. Quebec, etc.: Abbr.
51. Middle, in law
52. Guides
53. Moss Hart book
54. Jargon
57. Metal
58. Stream
59. Zodiac sign
60. Christian symbol
63. Part of a scarecrow
67. Documents
68. Cover
69. Troubles
70. Korean family
71. Mountaineer's parent
73. Draw a bead on
74. Fat: Prefix
75. Bring up
76. Hammer parts
77. Make out
78. Spenser lady
79. Bow
80. Wing
81. Takes on fuel
82. Channing
83. Sawbuck
84. Linen braid
86. Garibaldis take to the alleys
88. Agreeable word
89. Pine product
90. Russian range
91. Weather prediction
92. Hesse or Ohio
93. Trait of bigotry
94. Timid
96. Italian fare
101. Man's nickname
102. Fibbing before snoozing
104. Pool addict
105. Star in Cygnus
107. College degrees
108. Route to north
109. Land measure
110. Jujube
111. Glove shade
112. Swiss city
114. Jet housing
115. Abbot's counterpart
116. Daughter of Cyrus
118. Canadian peninsula
119. Lighthouses
122. Realm: Suffix
123. University
126. Air: Prefix
128. Witch's home
129. Clown
130. Talk: Fr.
131. Group of ten tones
132. Stingers
133. French river
134. Do a sheep job
135. Joint

DOWN

1. Friend of John Bull
2. Alpine natives
3. Where a baby often is
4. Engine rate: Abbr.
5. U. N. word
6. N. Z. people
7. __ simple
8. Aztec god of sowing
9. Dash
10. Home: Abbr.
11. Sideshow man
12. Place for locks
13. Boiling
14. Put down
15. Power: Prefix
16. Modify
17. Titles
18. Miss America at night
19. Stud with gems
20. __-pont (bridgehead)
27. Stands out
28. Rams or Cubs
31. Bone
35. Pair of horses
37. Sound for attention
38. Valentino role
41. "... __ I saw Elba"
42. Rice dishes
43. Lyric poem
44. Musical group
45. Dressler
47. More willing, old style
48. Changes
49. Bakery workers
50. Taylor or Erskine
52. Denoting more than one
55. One invested in ministry
56. Dutch explorer and family
58. Sinkiang town
60. Damages
61. It rules the waves
62. Puritan penal equipment
63. Sorted out
64. Asian weight
65. Phobias
66. Ledge
71. Takeoff
72. In line
76. Allergy source
77. Fictitious
81. Raccoonlike animal
82. Picked
85. Measure
86. __ "Elegy"
87. Form of diving
90. Prussian lancer
94. Cereal grass
95. This is usually enough
96. Footwear
97. Tropical tree
98. Imitation diamond
99. End
100. Part of a phone number
103. Fuel line
104. George Eliot character
105. Gull
106. Town in Westphalia
107. False god
109. One of the Jacks
111. Tyrants
112. Sew
113. Macaulay's chieftain
114. Italian town
117. Traffic sign
118. African antelopes
119. God of Egypt
120. Take on
121. Bar item
124. Here, in France
125. Downs' partner
127. Buddhist sect

Word Expertise by Diana Sessions

ACROSS

1. Good and plenty
7. Egyptian symbol
13. Shade of red
19. Emote
21. Mosaic gold
22. Ormandy
23. Oscar winner of 1953
24. Force
25. Fits
26. Calendar abbr.
27. Writing flourish
29. Sauterne
31. Undergoes
32. Setter or potato
34. Army officer: Abbr.
35. Various
36. Van __
37. Writer Ernie
38. Light-bulb units
39. __ horse
40. Mrs. Ponti's maiden name
41. Indifference
43. Darkness
44. Tarboosh
45. Whistlelike instruments
48. Small boats
49. Diamond surfaces
52. Be a coward, with "out"
53. Sheepskin
55. Zodiac beast
57. Church taxes
58. Baby bird
59. Prefix for tasse
60. Arab prince
61. Jewelry item
62. Living-room items
63. Girl's nickname
64. Corral helper
65. Gewgaw
66. Title in India
67. Toward Polaris
68. Sociable one
69. Wood-burning kiln
71. Threadbare
72. Place for certain birds
73. Kind of stare
74. Study carefully
75. Disregard
76. Peculiarity
79. Waggish one
80. "__ d'Arthur"
81. Energy units
85. Impel
86. Listen
87. Ornamental tree
88. Go slowly
89. Bear: Sp.
90. Ali __
91. Seeking to get even
93. Letter
94. Serving vessel
96. City on the Moldau
98. Turn to good account
100. Went to Gretna Green
101. "__ said than done"
102. Spoke candidly
103. Lustrous
104. Score
105. Disconnects

DOWN

1. Chat
2. Birdhouse
3. Kind of soup
4. Old Danish money
5. Notched bar
6. Tan color
7. Mrs. Astor's realm
8. Spring harbinger
9. Creature of Egyptian myth
10. Cordage item
11. Beverage
12. Protection
13. Skullcap: Var.
14. Barbarous
15. Turkish title
16. Gentle breeze
17. Part of a jet engine
18. Shrink
20. Costume material
28. Currier & Ives prints: Abbr.
30. Squid's output
33. Examines
35. Swamp
36. Nap
38. Diminishes
39. Hay shelter in England
40. Discourse: Abbr.
42. Cheap operator
43. Alice's tea companion
44. Snake equipment
45. Singing groups
46. Monster of myth
47. Eastern Church litany
48. Sloganlike expression
49. Ward off
50. Quake
51. Piece of needlework
53. Hodgepodge
54. Intellect
56. Distress
58. Do a spooky job, in dialect
59. Relative
61. Guarded
62. Old weapon
64. Calhoun
65. Carousal
67. Isthmus
68. Gay
70. Engage
72. Air __
74. Bridge barrier
75. Art bargain, at times
76. States a price
77. Miss Andress
78. Luzon native
79. Truck area
80. Mozart piece
82. Rail at
83. Odd chap
84. Makes haste
86. Convenient
87. Initiate
88. British pioneer in India
90. Has- __
91. China-shop item
92. All-purpose trucks
95. Roof piece
97. Chilly
99. Coin in Bulgaria

190 Wet Strength by Virginia W. Schneider

ACROSS

1. Fourth or real
7. Day of prayer
12. Badger
16. Source of some cigars
21. Tool
22. Watered silk
23. Blame
24. Of Mars
25. Fabled fritterers
27. "South Pacific" role
29. Wash. title
30. Best __
31. Beings: Fr.
33. Kenya's neighbor
34. July-August people
35. "Some like __"
36. Prune, in Scotland
37. Stir
40. City on the Hudson
41. "All we can do __"
42. Some lenses
46. Troop actions
48. Lizard
49. Guilty, for one
50. Map abbr.
51. Went up and away
52. "__ Me?"
55. Suet: Prefix
56. O'Neill heroine et al.
57. Words of disgust
58. Seagoing initials
59. Play for time
60. Safecracker
61. Smell __
62. Gloves and hose: Abbr.
63. Red
64. Direction
65. Like bustles
70. Plane's route
71. __ fire (hot shot)
73. U. S. writer and editor
74. Vedic god
76. Refer to
78. Tools
81. Thine: Fr.
84. Mickey or Annie
85. Young one
86. Mr. Martini
87. Interlock
88. Peace Nobelist, 1911
89. Beat-up auto
91. Certain room
93. Creator of Ah Sin
94. Good Queen __
95. People who produce corn
98. Water sportsman
99. World aid org.
100. Overdo the toast
101. "Two hearts that beat __"
102. Ghost story
103. __ milk (bland)
105. Commoners
106. Police problem
107. Lowell
108. Dashes about
109. Centers of activity
110. Layer
111. Fixed standard
114. Rejuvenate
115. Scout and eye
117. Espouse
120. "Old __ Sky"
122. Stolen sweet
125. __ -propre
126. Auk genus
127. Expect
128. Heavily favored
129. Boxes
130. Trudge
131. Lab jobs
132. Singer Bobby and family

DOWN

1. Nog ingredients
2. Father
3. Fed
4. Kaline and Capp
5. Hardy heroine
6. The Unready
7. Occupy
8. Sulks
9. German drink
10. Blunder
11. Find a new home
12. Highland brigand
13. Cove
14. Small combos
15. That: Sp.
16. Star in Pleiades
17. Spanish export of 1588
18. Ignoble
19. Sidekick
20. Writer Seton
26. Spreads
28. Persistent creditor
32. Pigs or R's
35. "The good men do __ interred . . ."
36. Music pieces
37. Analyzes
38. Lorna and family
39. Florida's flower
40. Gets even
41. Dope
42. Some tax men
43. Gulf Coast city
44. __ motion (set aside)
45. Pompous
47. Certain drama: Abbr.
48. Arterial trunk
52. Banters
53. English painter
54. In __ (actual)
55. Open-eyed
57. Church list
59. Partly-closed eyes
61. Playing marble
62. Thoreau milieu
63. H. Q. for Sadat
65. Senior
66. Subway supports
67. Dug
68. Labor org.
69. Balfour and Harum
72. Old French measures
75. Gainsay
76. Largest peninsula
77. Certain bridge cards
79. Highland unit
80. Take effect
82. Respect
83. Port's counterpart
87. Crumbly earth
89. Israeli dances
90. Kalpas
91. Insufferable ones
92. Sawbucks
93. Après sept
95. Wet-track runner
96. Bisect
97. "__ you mean"
98. Type of food fish
100. Sports jackets
102. Taxco's sky
104. Therefore: Lat.
105. Edged with scallops
106. Bill of __
109. Telephone call
110. Agreement, of a kind
111. Coarse fabrics
112. __ pump
113. Portico
114. Moon valley
115. Greek letters
116. Drink additive
117. "Able __ ere . . ."
118. Jacket
119. Retreats
121. Mug
123. Have creditors
124. Guide: Abbr.

191 Arithmetricks — by Alfio Micci

ACROSS

1. Cay
6. Moral nature
11. Play parts: Abbr.
14. Alaskan port
18. Ascribe
19. Tai people
20. Emoter
21. Decorator of a kind
22. Mermaid
23. Rings: Abbr.
24. Train mail abbr.
25. Tiber tributary
26. 4
28. Sanction
29. Yale men
30. Weasels
31. 12
33. Aleutian island
37. Tokay, for one
38. Japanese port
39. Preminger
40. Dessert
42. Serpents
43. Ordinal suffix
44. African region
45. Meddles
47. Appears
51. 14
55. Conrail units: Abbr.
56. "To __ His Own"
57. Engage in a sport
60. Goldilocks words
61. Village in Norway
62. Mesta
63. "__ my word!"
64. Locomotive
65. Pontius __
67. Protuberance
68. Car of a kind
70. Partner of haw
71. Aquatic bird
72. Marie, for one
73. Jai __
74. Kind of book: Abbr.
75. 0
78. Enmeshed
80. Cat of Africa
81. Manifest
85. Fedora
86. French pronoun
87. Certain Manhattanite
91. Makes lace
93. Blue colors
94. Plenty, poetically
95. Arnaz
96. ½
98. Not traversed
100. Ericson
101. Dies __
102. 52
107. Eur. capital
108. Raleigh, for one
109. Recognition
110. __ quality (shoddy)
111. Dravidian Indian
112. Fastener
113. Silly
114. Snores and snorts
115. Box
116. Direction
117. Brawl
118. Fisherman

DOWN

1. Hungary's Nagy
2. Slacker: Brit.
3. Stringed instrument
4. Jackets
5. 8
6. Delight
7. 14
8. Leporids
9. __ -over-lightly
10. Titles for Thant and Lie: Abbr.
11. Whodunit sounds
12. Tapioca root
13. Struck
14. 12
15. Leopardlike cat
16. Sheep
17. Blot out
18. "__ all in the game"
27. French roof
28. Dithers
31. Elizabeth's friend
32. Distinction
33. Speed-up: Abbr.
34. While, for short
35. Color
36. Yen
38. Insurance abbr.
41. Dawdle
43. German spa
46. Bone: Prefix
47. Synthetic
48. Paris stations
49. Brilliance
50. __ khan (tiger)
52. Railway car, for short
53. Took more than one's share
54. Larcenist
55. Take it easy
57. No-fat man
58. Bear of Down Under
59. Quechua
61. 19
62. Five-spots in card games
65. Do road work
66. Draw
69. 2
74. Inactive: Abbr.
75. French lass
76. U. S. composer
77. Roman poet
79. Endure
80. Critic Barnes
82. Dutch town
83. Home: Abbr.
84. Numerical prefix
86. Dilate
88. S. A. woody perennial
89. Black earth
90. 1
91. Binds
92. Armpit
93. Nests
96. Openings
97. Bits of hay
98. Mayan month
99. Crusoe creator
102. Unit of loudness
103. P. I. tree
104. Japanese town
105. Garden worker
106. Corp. officials
109. Pronoun

ACROSS

1. U.S. suffragist
5. In short supply
10. Took a break
16. Old plaster source
21. Suffix for cell or pop
22. Less vivid
23. Symbol of rank
24. Nest
25. Bright ones
27. Weapon
29. Certain husbands
30. Uber __
32. Kind of cluster for a medal
33. Biblical twelve: Abbr.
34. Norse god
35. __ fixe
36. Riled
39. Misfortunes
40. Part of F.O.B.
42. Sleeve card
44. Slugger Roger
46. Gay-nineties novelties
51. __ -a-Dale
56. Car groups
57. Indonesian island
58. Ottoman title
59. Area around hockey goal
60. Irish expletive
61. Commercials
62. Reactor areas
65. Togetherness symbol
67. Symington
68. Miss the __
69. Baseball thrill
70. Feel for
71. Rodin work: Abbr.
72. Hero-Leander locale
74. Greek city-state
75. Painter Rockwell
76. Holy one: Abbr.
77. Radiation detectors
82. Raggedy doll
83. Gallery
84. Golf club
85. Merited
87. Mat. days
89. Colonizers
90. Menu items
91. Deface
92. Whimsical
93. Carnival men
95. Sheriff's men
96. Drinking man
97. Zoo exhibit
98. Fitted out
99. Abner or Diamond
100. Musketeers, e.g.
102. Revive a court case
103. Objects of perception
104. Pole vault
109. Day
111. Saul's uncle
112. Items in the black
113. Event in Madrid
117. Pommel accessory
119. Select
121. Exclamation
122. City trains
125. Flappers' hats
127. Songbird
129. Detailed
131. Go for
134. Cartoon family
136. Wild sheep
137. Makes happy
138. Complete: Prefix
139. Advantage
140. Menials
141. Relics found in North Africa
142. Clairvoyants
143. Look in a way

DOWN

1. Brazilian rhythm-maker
2. Finished
3. Powders
4. Caroline group
5. Blabbed
6. Items once eaten as toasts
7. "Woe is me"
8. Tennis gear
9. Common chord
10. Mirror
11. Perry's creator
12. Fruit drink
13. Comedian Conway
14. Direction
15. Runarounds, of a sort
16. Garage sign
17. __ fruit: African berry
18. Spur part
19. Word for Miss America
20. Feudal slaves
26. Laments
28. Nile, as a god
31. Mr. Sprat's fare
35. Peruvian
37. TV award
38. Kind of dance
40. Famous dog
41. Condition: Suffix
43. One of the Plinys
45. Chalcedony
46. Bridge call
47. Spanish directions
48. Flash of wit
49. Warm-water fish
50. Copper money
52. Fishing spear
53. Deep-sea denizen
54. On the briny
55. Fit together
59. Far or battle
61. Neighbor of Hung.
63. Leave undone
64. Weathers
65. Trojan Horse figure
66. Northern island
68. Eur. capital
69. Green features
70. River to Rio Grande
73. Decorations
74. Carries on
75. Biblical verb
76. Celebrity
78. Road for Cato
79. Poet's relative of 'gins
80. Straight
81. Take to the door
86. Units of force
87. Fast planes
88. Edgar __
89. Oyster's home
90. Lawgiver
91. T-man's concern
94. Start a hand
95. Bowler's target
96. Gentlemen
97. Props
99. Inferior
101. Kind of number
102. English streams
104. Strips sugarcane
105. Linen marking
106. Go back abroad
107. Kind of blue
108. Sheds
110. Arena sounds
113. Behave badly
114. Mrs. Luce
115. Japanese city: Var.
116. One of five
118. Hobby
120. Barn features
122. Literary work
123. Fencing move
124. Villain's trademark
126. Dutch painter
128. News piece
129. Partner of forget
130. Ladder rung
132. __ de France
133. Form of Anna
135. Author Harper

193 Choice Words by Jordan S. Lasher

ACROSS

1. Utter
6. To the sunrise
15. Fasteners
20. Mr. America et al.
21. Mr. Wickfield's clerk
22. Barely ahead
23. Cordial flavor
24. Something for good measure
25. City on the Mohawk
26. Skater Sonja
27. Earth pigment
28. Macaw
29. Detecting device
30. Red signals
32. Antipathy
34. Hides
35. Israeli group
36. Do a takeoff
40. Dorado browns
41. Speakers' platforms
46. "Rose __ ..."
47. Conversations
48. In bloom
49. Twists, in Scotland
50. Lobster claw
51. Morally offensive, old style
52. Stem's counterpart
53. Part of the biota
54. Reply to "Are too!"
55. Pacific neckwear
56. Hockeypuck's destination
57. Anthology
59. Batters' concerns: Abbr.
60. Arab cloak
61. System of manual training
62. Of a fertilizer chemical
63. Track-shoe adjunct
64. Mouth-watering
66. Simper
67. Inundates
68. Franklin's wife
69. Gary Cooper's negatives
70. Apprentice
71. Giver of lip
72. Spore cluster
73. Hive
74. Defeatist
76. Listens
77. Certain survey
81. Some cigars
86. Triple Crown winner
87. Period
88. Argentine measure
89. Young hooter
90. Famous empire
91. Secured an anchor
93. New York county
94. "You __ right!"
95. Period of great prosperity
96. Former buddy
97. Auto style
98. Of course!
99. Plant-stem part

DOWN

1. Eastern rulers
2. Principle
3. Kind of acid
4. Taste again
5. Prepares to be dubbed
6. Extol
7. Girl turned into a spider
8. Vacation objectives
9. Sound qualities, in Scotland
10. Buzzing sound
11. Exclamation
12. Road workers
13. Cheapen
14. Props for extras
15. Realty sign
16. Chekhov
17. Paris divider
18. Goblins: Var.
19. Coast Guard girls
31. "__ your hand ..."
32. Loos
33. Feudal slavery
35. Malaysian capital
36. Oak-tree afflictions
37. City on Lake Erie
38. Krypton, xenon, etc.
39. Pray: Lat.
40. Darling, in Nice
42. Part of S.P.C.A.: Abbr.
43. Lunch-hour time span
44. Turncoats
45. Today's painters, mod style
47. Line in a circle
48. Void
50. Satiates
51. Eskimo craft
53. Baking staple
54. Ripeners
57. Work from the ground __
58. U. S. Indians
59. Lily plant extract
61. Absolute necessity
63. Exam-cramming material
65. Instance, in Paris
66. French historian
67. "__ Jacques"
69. __ than (time-limit words)
70. Place for oolong
72. Safekeeping
73. Singer Mimi
75. Medicinal plant
76. Kind of collision
77. African reed instruments
78. Love, in Venice
79. Crippled
80. Forbidden City
81. Ear projections
82. In the middle
83. Run off
84. Kingly
85. Passé
88. Derision: Sp.
92. Spicy

194 Fare Game
by Joseph LaFauci

ACROSS

1. Prepare clams
6. Firefighting needs
11. Wash. agent
15. Roman field
19. Yearn for
20. States or Nations
22. Movie western
24. Old instrument
25. Deserved
26. Nullify
27. Prince Valiant's wife
28. Rawboned
29. Worship
30. "It is to laugh,"etc.
32. Magician's word
34. Kind of house
35. Arizona city
36. Apollo's mother
37. Top bananas
38. Nigerian city
39. Grand old name of song
40. Morning sound
42. Bullet
43. Arabic letter
46. Gems
48. ___ cry
49. Raiment
51. Color
52. Iris expert
54. Feminine suffix
55. "___ on you!"
56. London flophouse
57. Coupled
58. Peep show
60. Cubic meter
61. Thrash
62. Celebes beast
63. Strictness
64. Open-eyed
65. Villella, e.g.
66. Ship-shaped clock
67. Encrust
68. Well-known streetcar
70. Englishman
71. Panted
73. Annoying
74. Not permanent
75. Henry Cabot, etc.
76. Inflame
77. Fish
78. Peruvian city

81. Took a break
82. Spoke at length
83. Brazilian city
85. Handle
86. Stratagems
87. Hunks
88. Took out
89. Splendid
90. Russian city
91. Fido's friend
92. S. A. rubber
93. In an expert way
95. Veneto, for one
96. Guest and Hers
97. Jewish month
98. Great, teen-age style
99. Word in poems
100. Encourage
101. Kind of servitude
103. Bede or Smith
104. Dit's partner
107. Old-hat
109. Wax, in prescriptions
110. Cut
111. Call to mind
112. Facing stone
114. La Scala fare
117. Maria or Cruz
118. Machination
119. Eurasian sandpiper
121. Biblical landfall
122. Eye pencil
123. A bit
124. Playing marble
125. Where R.F.K. served
126. "___ You Glad You're You?"
127. Pitcher
128. European river
129. Taxi feature
130. Verbose

DOWN

1. Bow's partner
2. Shopped
3. Sponge
4. Ward off
5. Iranian's ancestor
6. Certain protests
7. ___ Street (well off)
8. Ancient monograms
9. Common abbr.
10. Egyptian king
11. George Jessel sobriquet
12. Swedish port
13. Early film stutterer
14. Tennis gear
15. German river
16. Poser for Spencer Tracy
17. State: Fr.
18. Italian river
21. Promulgate
23. Ecstasy
31. Comparative suffix
33. Frenetic state
35. De mer and de tête
37. Viscous mud
39. Domestic

40. Chaser, of a sort
41. Kind of news
42. Sudden reaction
44. "Emma" novelist
45. German river
47. Trial action
48. Prefix for naut
50. "I told you so!"
52. Arabian land
53. Chaplin prop
56. "Inferno" man
59. Like fine cheese
60. Broken-arm décor
61. Enticements
63. Went wild over
64. Irani or Yemeni
65. Laughable
67. Hockey goals
69. Boo-boo
70. Certain diet
72. Ford

74. Rose of baseball
75. Annie of song
76. Atelier item
79. Anthracite
80. With competence
81. Verify
82. Buttonhead, for one
84. Winglike
85. Maintained
87. Did lawn work
88. Art style
89. Countersink
91. Kern musical
92. Bread-crumb sauces
94. Campus figure
96. "So long!"
102. Suffix for north or east
103. Make effervescent
105. Take charge
106. Comrade, sea style
108. Do over

109. Minotaur's home
110. Afghan city
111. Illinois city
112. Church part
113. Like some racehorses
114. Alumnus
115. Utah town
116. Bread, to Miss Loren
117. Cabbage dish
120. Swellhead's hang-up

Halloween Thought *by Threba Johnson*

ACROSS

1. English dramatist
6. New-shoe tragedy
11. Drift
16. High style
17. Every 60 minutes
18. Drink for a cold day
20. Start of a quote from "Hamlet"
24. Quantity: Abbr.
25. Dress again
26. Speeds
27. Egg _ yong
28. About: Abbr.
30. Sp. Amer. plain
32. Kinds
33. Use Rotten Row
34. Harden
36. _-Saud
37. Goblin
39. "Now you _ . . ."
40. More of quote
44. Inner: Prefix
45. Part of Mao's name
46. Inc., in Britain
47. Urge
48. Breathe
52. Certain records
54. Cargo
58. High note
59. Artless
62. Bother
64. Pentateuch
65. Eyelashes: Prefix
67. More of quote
70. River
71. Throat-clearings
73. Psyche parts
74. Feature of boxer shorts
76. Wallach
77. October décor
79. Jackie's spouse
80. Mocking one
82. U. S. fliers of W. W. II
83. Month: Abbr.
85. Barn area
88. Inflation concern: Abbr.
89. More of quote
98. Strayed
99. U. S. fur trader
100. "_ the ghost of . . ."
101. Consume
102. Son of Hera
103. Blackbirds
104. Short poem
107. Term of address
108. Go down swinging
109. Breathless
110. Relatives of prelims
112. Reagan, for short
113. End of quote
118. Continent
119. Writer Ramée
120. Approached
121. Candle
122. Prepare to play marbles
123. Inhibit

DOWN

1. Quack dosage
2. Mass. cape
3. Warehouse charge: Abbr.
4. Julia and Elias
5. Use Amtrak
6. The whole works, and more
7. Group of witches: Scot.
8. Process: Suffix
9. _ and wide
10. Routing for a broomstick rider
11. What the plot may do
12. Routines
13. Catch-all abbrs.
14. Kind of degree
15. One who exalts
16. Bahama resort
19. Of a battery pole
20. Implied
21. Tolkien creation
22. Like Troy
23. "Pride _ before . . ."
29. Crawl
31. Concerning: Abbr.
33. Event for old grads
35. Red dye
38. Spooky birds
39. Oct. 31 wear
41. Raid
42. Alas, in Paris
43. France's Saint-_
48. Summarize
49. Root or Yale
50. Witch city
51. Shade of blue
53. One who keeps busy
54. Kind of shoe
55. Charlie Brown's good word
56. Market: Fr.
57. ". . . lost _ mittens"
60. Bean of India
61. Three-min. units
62. Fish of Hawaii
63. Outs' partner
66. Pierces
68. Out on _
69. _ wahr?
72. Bard of old Scandinavia
75. S. A. tongue
78. "_ Were King"
79. Guthrie
81. Insects
83. Italian town
84. Favorite ghost
86. Fine rug
87. Riches
89. Current
90. Roman poet
91. Adjust
92. Colorful bird
93. Partner of to
94. New World native
95. Bar gadget
96. "Let's toast _ comrades"
97. Turn over
103. Brotherly love
105. Vacuum tube
106. "We're off _ the wizard . . ."
109. Resting on
111. Do in a fly
114. Org. of the 30's
115. Sister
116. Connection
117. Mine yield

196 In Good Form by Bruce R. Shaw

ACROSS

1. Queen's baked goods
6. Wastes
11. Shatter
16. Indonesian island
21. Love, in Italy
22. "... upon _ of violets"
23. Hoist
24. Tie score
25. Memento
26. Auto mechanic's ward
29. Street game
31. Relieve
32. Logarithm word
33. Pismires
34. Waiter's worry
36. _ souci
38. Prison camp
40. Author Erica
43. Hebrew measure
45. View
47. Paradise
48. Outdo
51. Flightless bird
52. Gymnast's props
55. Ethiopian lake
57. _ Ste. Marie
59. Tease
60. Lets
61. Big or Little
62. Implied
64. French writer
66. Society-page word
67. Indian chiefs
68. Mountains
70. River of Italy
72. Carries on
74. Author Wiesel
75. Fundamental
77. Orbit
79. Paulo or Luiz
80. Songs
81. Round landmark of N.Y.C.
85. In harmony
87. Traffic warning
88. Word for the rich
89. Gal Friday
90. Booted
91. Items for Astor
93. Inventor of diving bell
95. Manned
99. Vessels
101. Headache compound
103. Aspect of personality
105. "_ nacht ..."
106. Old catapult
107. Fatty acid: Prefix
109. Shamrock land
111. As a friend: Fr.
112. Berlin area
113. Soda jerk's offering
116. Angelico et al.
117. Compass point
118. Wool: Prefix
120. Drunkards
121. Tech grad: Abbr.
122. Spring period
123. French mathematician
125. Near or Ole
127. Wien's river
129. Italian town
132. Voices
134. Trim
136. Gear
140. Incoming pilot's concern
144. Charged atom
145. Town officer
146. Anglo-Saxon coin
147. Spasm
148. Disdain
149. Soprano Emma
150. Deserves
151. Sources
152. French heads

DOWN

1. Pacific root
2. Theban deity
3. Function
4. First-aid gear
5. Plaster painting
6. Hurt: Sp.
7. Sash
8. _-Coburg
9. Reserve item, in France
10. Ship rigging
11. Bahamas, etc.: Abbr.
12. Scottish pool
13. Lake Titicaca's range
14. Royal symbols
15. Screw parts
16. Heir
17. Free from censorship
18. Chow or lo
19. Baseball strategy
20. Copies
27. Pawnbroker
28. Gardner
30. On
35. Risk
37. Moon: Prefix
39. Prank
40. Alou of baseball
41. Arabian
42. N. C. river
44. Gaseous element
46. Doubleday
48. Northern sea fish
49. Lack of vigor
50. Breaks down a sentence
53. Pauses
54. Resting
56. Politician's concern
58. Harangue
61. German article
63. Hindu slave
65. Baghdad native
67. Ermines
69. Talks back
71. Chopin piece
73. Annoys
76. Take it easy
78. Papa Bear of Chicago
80. Grown together
81. Anchoring
82. Record
83. Turn in coupons
84. Soaks
85. Ties
86. Macbeth and others
91. _ annum
92. Glasses, for short
94. Golfing flaw
96. Blaze
97. Violinist Mischa
98. Certain believer
100. "Most Happy" guy
102. Cue-ball shot
104. Fern leaf
107. Hip pain
108. Eye part
110. Gluts
113. _ quarters (crowded)
114. Approvals
115. Sea bird
119. Quickly: Abbr.
123. Annoy
124. Aloof one
126. Hebrew letter
128. Sea call
129. Raison d'_
130. Met home
131. Vibrating, in music: Abbr.
133. Laurel
135. Item of inflation
137. Disorder
138. Distressing
139. Austrian river
141. Recipients: Suffix
142. Officers: Abbr.
143. Biblical land

197 Reverse English by Thomas Sheehan

ACROSS

1. Defensive barricade
7. Doghouse dweller
11. Hayseeds
16. Hercules, e.g.
18. Santa's standbys
19. Pale
20. Edward Bellamy title, taken literally
24. Dance
25. Ms. people
26. Bar items
27. Arrived
29. Time period out West
30. Carol
32. __ anchor (be moored)
33. Nitwit
34. Earthy clay
35. Retaliate
38. Certain movie scenes
40. Mask
41. Irritate
42. Sports: Abbr.
43. Weapon for Aaron
46. Badminton need
47. Malay sailboat
48. Angora fabrics
52. Briefly
54. Be found wanting
56. Screening
57. Theodore and family
58. Answers a phone memo
59. Well-known Benedict
60. Canasta term
61. Retraces one's steps
62. Hindu gentleman
63. Luxuriate
64. Flinches
65. Middleman's specialty
67. __ glance
68. Reverts to
69. Char's millinery
70. Vagrancy
72. Support
73. "__ Mable"
74. Mode of Biblical reading
75. Berne's river
76. Dearth
77. Corday's victim et al.
79. Ready for a duel
83. Holder of the last straw
87. Places of refuge
88. Young __
89. Kind of snake
90. "__ in the Money"
91. Rival of NBC
92. Arctic sight
93. On the __ of (chummy)
96. Dakota Indian
97. N. H. city
99. Emulate John Osborne?
102. Charlie Chan portrayer
103. Exchange places
104. "... toil and __"
105. Weird Sisters
106. Musicians' stints
107. Words for a certain friend

DOWN

1. In-laws of the Mullenses
2. Brigitte of films
3. One who degrades
4. Haul
5. Annoys
6. Faction
7. Wishful winker
8. Albanian coins
9. Nigerian people
10. Self-centered
11. Attention
12. Baton Rouge campus
13. Epitaph for Atlas
14. Land
15. Barber's headaches
17. Racing fan
18. Kind of preview
21. Kellogg-__ Pact
22. Dancer José
23. Beats it
28. Speedometer initials
31. Operculum
33. Returns on the q.t.
34. Miss Hari
36. German sprite
37. Eastern rulers
38. Hits a ball out of play
39. Thai money
41. Reduces, as prices
43. Lobster-eater's wear
44. Lively, in music
45. Emulates a shrinking violet
47. Gets sassy
48. Sham
49. Grampus: Var.
50. Gas-pump word
51. Wall, etc.: Abbr
53. Bandleader
54. Joins the also-rans
55. Bad writer
58. Cleat's relative
59. Area of the wise men
61. Bavarian river
62. Hems in
63. Scrooge word
64. __ de Calais
65. Part of R.F.D.
66. Roof ornament
68. Trumpeter A
69. Abandoned ship
71. Dumbarton, for one
73. Napery fabric
76. Liberal giving
77. After lundi
78. Direction at sea: Abbr.
79. Supporting
80. Old Assyrian city
81. Suffix of origin
82. Tillstrom
83. __ age
84. Organism needing oxygen
85. Cookery style
86. Tipped over
89. Covers
92. River areas
93. Insect
94. Grain sorghum: Var.
95. Dark
98. Compass point
100. Whillikins' partner
101. Hungary's Bela

198 Observations by Bert Beaman

ACROSS

1. Whittier's boy
9. "I saw __ asailing..."
14. Trouble spots of 1960's
22. Show who's boss
23. Puppeteer Lewis
24. Be equivalent
25. Humbles
26. Athapascan abode
27. Memorable lion
28. Astrologer's sign
29. Kind of mine
31. Mary __, fictional ship
33. Dill
34. "Waiting for Lefty" author
37. Sham
38. Blanch: Fr.
39. Navy officers: Abbr.
40. Color: Abbr.
42. Kind of scholar
44. Indian otter
46. Surrenders
48. Burma or open
50. Ancient Asian kingdom
51. Vex
53. Hot pants, for one
56. He, in Rome
57. Horse-breeder's purchase
58. Story opener
59. Vipers
60. Salutation
61. Arising within one
63. Rings
65. Observation
67. Give it a go
68. Chair part
70. Of the kind of: Suffix
72. Guthrie
73. German river
75. Eagle: Prefix
76. Salmon
77. "Try __ for size"
78. Will Rogers words, with 117 Across and 11 Down
84. Greek commune
85. Greeting
86. Cockney steed
87. Biblical son
88. __ instant
89. River to Danube
90. Honey drinks
92. Went through papers
96. __ ear (listened)
98. Hidden
101. Part of Greece
103. Common Market: Abbr.
104. Opposed: Abbr.
106. Bindle stiff
107. Indian maid
108. Threshold
109. Indian title
110. See 35 Down
112. Swing around
113. Silkworm
114. Rice dish
116. City of Rumania
117. See 78 Across
119. Hamilton's bill
120. Mayan god
122. Effect of past experience
124. Long ago
126. To be, in Spain
128. Heart, in Egyptian religion
129. Church sections
130. Emulates Greeley
132. River to the Missouri
135. Suggestive of
137. S. A. shelter
139. Thrusts out
142. "There's no __ an old..."
143. Waters
144. Logical
145. Bridge plays
146. Before febrero
147. Biased

DOWN

1. Madrid marriage
2. Affirm
3. How some tourneys are run
4. Misjudged
5. Canadian river
6. Like: Suffix
7. Pindar output
8. Hardy girl
9. Houston players
10. Valentino role
11. See 78 Across
12. Choler
13. Storied exterminator
14. Intrigue
15. __ Cup
16. See 35 Down
17. __ off (defer)
18. Loosen
19. Has a chance
20. Clear sky
21. Out of __
30. Motif
32. Noble
35. Shaw quote, with 110 Across and 141 and 16 Down
36. Kind of plexus
40. French port
41. Radio O.K.
43. Repairs, in a way
45. Spore sacs
47. Ledge, in Britain
49. Dissimilar
51. Italian astronomer
52. Lafayette College's home
54. Legendary island
55. U. S. arctic explorer
62. Substance
63. Gray poem
64. Extremely
66. Straw mattress
69. Film producer Berman
71. Ehrenburg
74. Greek letters
76. Lazy __
78. Roman officials
79. Coating
80. Lincoln's cause
81. "__ girl just like..."
82. Clear
83. Visits
91. Needles
93. Like some store items
94. Girl's nickname
95. Singer Bob
97. U. S. culture group: Abbr.
99. "Ay, __ rub"
100. Kind of cracker
102. Terre __
105. Alternate non-toll road
107. Charm, for one
111. Lansbury role
115. Winter sight
117. Melodic passage
118. Supplies
120. Grain husks
121. Vietnam capital
123. Verb suffixes
125. More curious
127. Dialect of India
131. Brazilian heron
133. Sarazen of golf
134. Founded: Abbr.
136. Viscous liquids: Abbr.
138. Oven, in Britain
140. Tunisian cape
141. See 35 Down

Seasonal Tidings   by Anne Fox

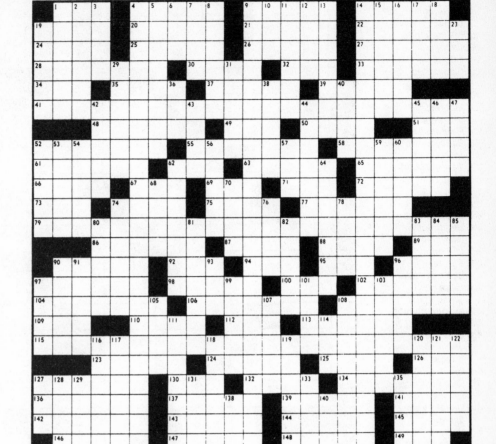

ACROSS

1. Letter
4. Disdain
9. Jabbed
14. Poet Chartier
19. Evidence
20. Minced, in cookery
21. __ Gay (W.W. II plane)
22. Cape Cod Indian
24. Handle
25. To be, in Spain
26. Tiny thing
27. City on the Liffey
28. Selected passage
30. Pig, in Paris
32. Girl's nickname
33. A.W.O.L.
34. Kind of pocket
35. Jezebel's husband
37. "Hasta __!"
39. Not the same
41. Words from an 18th cent. carol
48. Italian glass
49. Part of a certain mountain
50. Bye-bye
51. Gypsy horse
52. Where roses bloomed in song
55. Highway man
58. Magnify
61. Floors: Fr.
62. Extinct bird
63. Eastern U. S. capital
65. __ chance
66. Vegetable
67. Neighbor of Mont.
69. Dick Tracy's trademark
71. Card
72. Be
73. Priest of Shiloh
74. "Mon __ ami"
75. Zestful
77. Lincoln's V. P.
79. Words from a 17th cent. carol
86. Vietnam town
87. Disney character
88. Shakespearean dog
89. Resin
90. Junk
92. Irish rebels: Abbr.
94. Star
95. Egg: Prefix
96. Tom Sawyer's Polly
97. Chinese province
98. Snap
100. Defile
102. Twelve: Prefix
104. Binge lover
106. Termagants
108. Instructed
109. Deplore
110. Gibe
112. Spanish wave
113. Large watch
115. Words from a 13th cent. plainsong
123. Patrician
124. Up __ (cornered)
125. N. M. resort
126. State: Abbr.
127. Moola
130. __ ton
132. Tackles' neighbors
134. Printing process
136. Certain spirits
137. Japanese in U. S.
139. Slangy affirmative
141. __ homo
142. Separate
143. On the way
144. Orleans' river
145. Downfall
146. Badger
147. Substantive
148. Revoke, as a legacy
149. Choose

DOWN

1. Heady drink
2. Supports
3. Entertain
4. Words from a Cornish carol
5. Alexander Selkirk, for one
6. Before Nov.
7. Liszt specialty: Abbr.
8. Orange oil
9. Words by Frederic W. Farrar
10. Can. province
11. African antelope
12. Sailor's saint
13. Florida beach
14. "__ : Fear not ..."
15. Symbol of victory
16. Brown hair color
17. __ de Pinos
18. German denial
19. Tawdry
23. Explosive
29. Obliteration
31. Approach on the double
36. Jonson
38. Logging operator
40. Lug
42. Semblance
43. Explorer De
44. Netherlands city
45. Monsters
46. Rye fungus
47. Willing, old style
52. Dogs, for short
53. Balbo
54. State: Abbr.
56. Indian prince
57. Little __
59. Looseness
60. "La Sonnambula"
62. Dull
64. Man of property
68. Tibetan creature
70. "__ plaisir"
74. Yacht-race category
76. God: Fr.
78. Griffin of TV
80. "... the use of him is more __ can see"
81. Flourishes
82. Lone Ranger's friend
83. More forlorn
84. Weapon
85. Outward: Anat.
90. Monotonous sound
91. "__ angelorum"
93. Blackbird
96. Take up
97. "And they were __ afraid"
99. Slav
101. Concerning
103. Futile
105. Chinese weight
107. Greek physician
108. Think much of
111. Commonplace: Var.
114. Mil. service initials
116. Emptiness
117. Wanderers
118. Cab
119. Spanish permit
120. Barfly's sound
121. Cause
122. Glasgow
127. Pop
128. "Step __!"
129. Sever
131. European capital
133. Booted
135. Son of Agrippina
138. Compass point
140. Speed

200 Breaking With Habit by Eugene T. Malesk

ACROSS

1. Cager's target
5. Intimidated
10. Banter
14. Sticker
19. Code word for A
20. Macaw
21. Ubangi tributary
22. Residence
23. Everywhere
25. Marooned
27. Saw-toothed
28. Refusal
30. Hairy
31. Loom bar
32. Biblical verb
34. Legendary Irish beauty
35. Old hand
37. Former comedy team
41. Have hard going
42. Marine plant
43. Quiet and __
45. Suffix with unit and budget
46. Ibis's relative
48. Coop sounds
51. Coffee type
52. Harper Valley group
53. Pang
54. Scottish port
55. College in Iowa
56. Eraser users
58. Splendid
61. "Vissi __" (Tosca aria)
62. Ref. book
63. Utter confusion
64. Transaction policy
68. Singer in a group
70. Tolstoy
71. __ and Addison
72. Toy with
73. Scene of Tell legend
75. Swift's "The Tale of __"
77. British film maker
78. Good soil
79. Bask
80. Mister of cartoons
82. Dept. store area
85. Cabdriver
86. Symbols of drudgery
89. __ and sticks
91. Mal de __
92. Flash
93. "How __ you!"
94. Ubiquitous G.I.
96. Ten tens: Abbr.
97. Cross-country team
100. Bar order
103. Academic wear
105. Upright
106. German article
107. Buoyantly
108. Alas
109. A sight __
110. Caroler's word
111. Compact
112. Eddie of baseball

DOWN

1. __ and hems
2. Off-Broadway award
3. Taylor, Zachary
4. Burke's subject
5. Lope
6. __ and law
7. U.A.R. political group
8. Time division
9. Weedy grasses
10. Kind of puppet show
11. "__ the land of the free . . ."
12. Like Reynard
13. Stacked
14. Serve the soup
15. Loathed
16. Parisians' park
17. Sharpen
18. Kashmir town
24. Soprano Loeveberg
26. Halo
29. Pulitzer novelist: 1958
32. Mystical poet
33. Last part
35. Exchange
36. Estonian port
37. Planes, for short
38. Indigent
39. Mythical pair
40. Child
42. Resort near Naples
44. Inventor of a sign language
46. Account
47. Cowper poem
49. Better than 58 Across
50. Men from Brazil
54. __ macabre
57. __ es Salaam
58. What con artists do
59. Pub game
60. Faith: Fr.
64. Littleneck
65. P. I. natives
66. Beef casing
67. Debt assignor
68. Dagger and __
69. Cease-fire
72. Dapple
74. Signs a contract
76. Oversboe cord
81. Glutted
83. Start a roulette game
84. Aeolus
85. Time for a good time
87. Boy's collar
88. Rembrandt's birthplace
89. "What is __ as . . . ?"
90. __ and toss
93. Sky animal
94. One of the Fijis
95. Caesar's fatal day
97. Money in Seoul
98. Fordham team
99. Small barracuda
100. Put into type
101. S. A. port
102. Chemical suffix
104. All and __

1

```
AD  RAIL  PHUT  UVAS
LEC ERDA  RASH  NICE
ARUSHKAS KIKNE HERA
ERBIES  SINE  TROWEL
   ETA    EST  SHOO
EDBUTTONS  STICKBUG
TE PEEL  GLENS  IRE
ASP DELF REEK  ALGA
HIRE  MARIEDRESSLER
  DODO   EKE   ROPY
TEVELAWRENCE  NERVE
ERO DREE SAVE  NOIL
RI ASSES  REMO  SOU
RODUCED  CURRERBELL
   HERS   PER   RBI
NGORA  ARNAZ  GIDEON
IRT TIZIANOVECELLI
LAI CLUE  ULAN  SKIN
ESS HERD  SALT   ODE
```

2

```
ELBOW  TREMOR  ADESTE
LEASE  REPAVE  MILERS
MAKESNOBONESABOUTIT
EVE TALES  NILES  OPA
REDS ILL ORDER  CULT
   AILS  OBOES  SUTEE
SHELLS ERIAS  GAT
TONES KNOTS  TAVERNS
ALAS TIE  STRIPE HAI
RIB PETRO SIDED  OTT
EEL ONTOUR  TED  EDIT
DRESSES  TOWED  SIEVE
   LET CODAS  FUSSER
ARSON  CAFES  CREE
MATE  BANJO ERA  NAPA
UNE PATIO STENS  SAC
SKELETONINTHECLOSET
ELDEST ENNEAD  IRENE
RESETS STERNS  DATED
```

3

```
HASTA  ARAB  COOLIT
AMIES  RAGE  ARCANE
SIDEPOCKET  STAVER
AGED CHEETAH   ISM
NAG SHED ERIE  SSE
  LOPER   BERTHED
REAMER  REMORSE
ARNIE  TENOR  EAST
PACT ELATE  TIEA
  TETE METED  RIDER
   ERUPTED  FOMENT
PENDANT  EASES
ALA SLED INCA  TUB
LIP ARRANGE  ARNE
EXOTIC INSIDEJOBS
SILAGE EDEN  TAKAO
TRIPOD DATE  EXERT
```

4

```
COBS ALGA GLEN  FACT
OPEN BEAN RANA  ALLA
META SAFE IGOR  BLOC
ACHIPOFFTHEOLDBLOCK
  LER   IFS   RECK
JAY ABRADE  SEESAWS
ACED  ALA FEAST TIE
WASAFLYBYNIGHT CEST
STORIES  ORAL LOSES
  INT ALLEN  SUN
TRINE PLOT  FALAISE
RANG WASWELLROUNDED
EIS MINOS  ESE  TERN
KNOWING  FETTLE MEA
 CLAD  SAL   OAT
THERIGHTFOOTFORWARD
REND ROOT POOP  ISEE
ECCE ISLE TORE  SHEA
EKED NEAR SLED  TELL
```

5

```
GHATS  NICHE  SPLAT
RATIO PINHEAD HAIKU
ARTOFTHEFUGUE  ARGIL
PPI THY ORI  RHYTHMS
HELI  EST CREME  ITSA
ORATORIO HAY  RET
   ALE LEO  EARLAP
GELD  UNFELT  MILLA
ANCIENT ASSETS NIAS
JOHANNSEBASTIANBACH
AMON WALLIE  CHIMNEY
REICH DUENNA  PITS
  COOPED TER  SUN
  NOA EAT  COMPOSER
WAAC WIDTH AMI  RURU
INFERNO TOT ELI  SIN
LITRE WEIMARGERMANY
LOOTS AGRAPHA  MANGO
ANNOT  GESSO  ARSON
```

6

```
PASO  IRE  ACES  SHAG
SNAP  NATS  LARA  CAFE
HOMEONTHERANGE  AURA
ALI  SAI  AIRY  ABNER
WIGWAMOFNOKOMIS  TSS
     IRENIC   NINEVEH
INGE    TEAK  STAID
CORNER   SCANTS  APSE
ESE  SAVE  ANAI  SLATS
ATE  THELOVENEST  LIT
GENES  NOTE  ARIA  ALE
ERMA  TENORS   TRACER
   ASSET  ENES    TESS
  ANTONIO    REDUCE
ARS   HEARTBREAKHOUSE
CAIRO   AIDA  MAI  RET
OBOE   UNCLETOMSCABIN
RINS  BOLT  EPEE  DANA
NAST  IDES  ADS  ONES
```

7

```
GOLF  OMER  APED  LAZ
AMOR  NINA  DOLE  EBE
FAREWELLTOALMS  HEE
FRESH  SIRUPY  SOIL
     NOS  VAST  BEAGLE
OSLO  PIECE  NORTHER
LEE  KENNELWORTH  FO
GLIBNESS  OSES  ROD
AFFLICT  MOVER  CORE
   WASH  GODEY  SUSA
AMISH  AUDEN  FIREDU
VOTE  IDLE  LATINAT
ETH  ADOLLSSOUSE  NA
REFINERY  INONU  JOH
STANTON  FRAP  PEA
   TWIG  ALEPHS  TROU
HAHA  ROBINSONCARUSO
ODER  ADEN  ALIE  ESA
WORD  MALT  TETE  DEF
```

8

```
FERMI  EVADE  PULLMAN
UMIAK  LAPEL  RIVIERA
LENTO  ANILE  INSERTS
TUG  NOTES  GENT   GET
OTOE  LES  MANTA  PELS
NESTLED  FONTS  WAN
   TIS  MINCE  SEPTA
COWED  SANTE  SPAHEE
AME   OREG  EASTWARD
PES   BURROUGHS  LAG
ENTIRELY  LIGA   ETE
STINTS   AFROS  YPRES
 ANDES  APIAN  PEU
  GUS  PORED  RATTRAP
PAHS  SANER  PEN  TECA
AGO   TRES  ROVES  SMS
NAUSEAS  MEUSE  EROIC
ENSUITE  ORDER  AORTA
LAENNEC  INERT  NOBEL
```

9

```
UBER  BASIC  JOB  TINA
TAXE  CRASH  ROME  SIMON
HAPPYDAYSAREHEREAGAIN
ABELE  LAUGHINGALLEGRA
NARES   ERIN  ANSA  EEL
TATT  GOESIN    GAD
  ECLAT  NOTIME  OCEAN
UME  HORAS  UNARM  OSLO
PALAEO  LAW  ROC  IRAQIS
SANREMO  LOEB  ABNER
 MERRYWIVESOFWINDSOR
  EIGHT  IOTA  SENEGAL
POITOU  ASS  SIR  HORRID
INRE  SALEM  MIDAS  ELS
TEARS  GONEAR  TEHEE
   EAN   LOVESA  NCAR
SAB  ERUA  CASO  SCHMO
CRYONESHEARTOUT  ALIEN
ITSAMADMADMADMADWORLD
REEFY  EERY  NOBLE  SOIE
ELAS  IDS  DOOLY  ENAS
```

10

```
  CABOT  SEWAN  STRO
MIRAGE  CHEERED  QUAS
CIRCLESTHEGLOBE  URIA
OCC  LETHAL  TOUCHANDG
ARULE  ARILS  FLOOR  SE
TOLET  IRAQI  ADLET
  ASST  FECUND  EDDIED
CRI  RETD  AVES   ANTI
REMODELS  CRONE  NEES
ONENAME  THEINE  SCARE
UTA  VICIOUSCIRCLE  NU
NESSIE  RUCHES  AIRBAS
DRUMS  ELKOS  TINSELE
SERIC  SOLO  TANG  STS
DETURS  NETTER  STIR
  EPOCH  DERAT  IDIO
SOL  TARES  RITES  LEAV
PROCEDURES  ORSELL  NA
ANTRA  BERMUDATRIANGL
TOTEM  SIBONEY  ENGELS
STOWS  NOGAS  STEVE
```

1

```
IMP   BTU   SAGA  SLATE
SIA  GAIN  SOLAR  KAREN
ONGJOHNS  ICEBREAKERS
NDEAR  PONCE    STEAM
  ODE  FENCE    STER
IONINWINTER  HAH    SHO
NNES  ART   CONE  ENOL
NT  HIDE  ESAU  THRONE
AH  LES  AMENS  EARWIG
TES  ERI  SPITE  SLOE
ESTE  DOITNOW    ERDA
LITS  ERNIE  ASH  SUNS
MORAL  CITED  REO  NIP
APITA  HOOD  MATS  DSO
IEN  PLAN   DEL  CHEER
DS  DOT  SKIERSCOURSE
  SPAT  LURES   ERN
FLIES  HAREM   ACTSUP
ROMTHECOLD  SLUSHFUND
ANOI  TOROS  SORE  OLDS
NENT  CLAM   OWN   RUE
```

12

```
DRAM  CRESC  OGDEN  ESPS
IOTA  LEACH  PREEN  SCOW
VOICEOFTHEPEOPLE  CREE
EMPHASES  ERNST   THEME
    EVER  CROSS  FAREAST
GRATER  PHONE  SALAAM
ROPES   RANGABELL  TIPI
OUR  CHAR   RAS     NOR
AGES  HAMMERHOME  EAGLE
NEGATORS  NEONS  LAMMED
  NURMI  STARK  CARPE
BEATUP  FOOLS  CHILLERS
RANEE  DRUMMEDOUT  EMEU
IST   AES    EDGY   IDE
MESS  FIREDAWAY   GREET
  IMPOSE  EMIRS  DRESSY
DELANEY  GRANS   SEEM
EVERS   FRITO  APPEALED
LENT  ENDEDONASOURNOTE
ONCE  RARAE  ALERT  DAUB
STER  RESTS  SPATE  SNIT
```

13

```
INGHAM  ALES    DOE   SLOT
FINALE  SAREE  DIRTY  PYRO
FLAMINGSWORD  ONTHEMARGE
YEW  ETHANS  ISLES  LORES
    HAYS    FAIR  ALIT
PRO  ROTS   KILN  OVERACTS
SAFROLS  CHICAGOFIRE  HAW
ADLAIS  ALONE  LAOS  CARE
LIARS  FLANK  CAIRN  HARTE
MOKE  NITS   TOPOT  LARIAT
SSE   FORESTFIRES  FACTOR
  LEANER  HORNS  DOCKET
PENROD  PUTOUTFIRES  OSA
SABERS  PALOS  ENDS  EFTS
CRAMS  SINES  HOMES  CAFES
AIRY  MANI   SINUS  DESIRE
NAG  FIRECRACKER  CASTROS
SHEBANGS  ALOE  VANS  ELS
  ARUS  ODOR    BALS
  SPRAT  AMATI  DENIED  BAR
INATHEATER  FIERYFURNACE
AONE  SMOGS  YALTA  SUITED
OWER   IMA    NESS  EMBERS
```

4

```
ASH  BASIS  SPEWS  PALS
TOE  AVERT  PLEAT  AMOK
THALLOWEENIALWAYSBUY
ANDOLIN  PINNY  BESIDE
  LOAD  RUPEE   RILE
EMAND  LOPPY  ROLL  COU
RAM   SAUTE  ROLEO  HUN
ENPOUNDSORSOOFSWEETS
CO  FLEET   ACME   RARE
STRUTTER  HANKY  PORTER
  KERR  BAWDY  HALO
ABANA  CARNY  GETALONG
AMES   PORT  WOMEN  CAR
UTEVERYYEARIFINDITSI
ASS  EXILE  MELON  NEAP
EY  NUDE  COVER  RATTLE
  FILE  CAREY  POME
ASPECT  BANAL  SATURDAY
WHOSEATENALLTHETREATS
ROUT  NITER  EVADE  SLOE
ORE  TEARY  RAYON  TIER
```

15

```
HORSE  REAP  TARE    PIN
ACUTE  INTO  EROS  SEINE
STEER  DOESBENNETTCERF
  NILES  TAPES  RIOTOF
AMICES   OLE    ATLAS
GODISDEADNIETZSCHE
ATILT  GRI    RATTY  LAP
TIOS  REATA  ETA   ISA
EFT  NIETZSCHEISPEACHY
  MONTE  ARID  ARNIE
ABORTS   DOR   GRANTS
BEAME   MESA  GEESE
BUTSARTRESMARTRE  SEC
EST   WAN   ASTIR  AERO
TEE  PRIZE  RPI  ENTRE
  NIETZSCHEISDEADGOD
  BAITS   REA   CROONS
CANNOT  STARR  ASTAR
ISJONATHANSWIFT  CROUP
NEONS  IOLE  IRAE  HARTE
ELU   AWES  GARS  ENTER
```

16

```
S R A S   M A S C   S T A T E   M A A M
P O L O S   E N T O   W I G H T   A D D A
A M I N E   D O R R   O A T E S   R I D S
S E E I N T O   E N D O R S E   C R E E K
M O N A O F C R E M O N A   V E L O U R S
    O R R   A T E N S   B E L O W
R O O F   N I S A N   L O A S   L A B
E N H A N C E S   L E N A O F H E L E N A
S T O N E A G E   I N N   T U N I S
    S O R E   C O A X E D   L O L I T A
A H S O   E V A O F G E N E V A   U N A L
B O N N E T   I N F E S T   E B R O
O N A I R   R A T   S N I F F L E S
N O R A O F S O N O R A   P O O L H A L L
E R E   S I T U   E P S O M   O N L Y
    F I L E T   H I P P O   U S N
B E D R O L L   O O N A O F A L T O O N A
R E R A N   L A N T E R N   S M A L L E R
I R O N   P A R S E   E D I T   F U D G E
L I N K   S T E E L   N E R O   F L A R E
L E E S   T E S T S   T E A R   U S E D
```

17

```
A D E P T   A S P I C   R A N U P   C A B A
U R I A H   T A L C O   I N U S E   O L L I
F U R L E D A G A I N   P O L O R E G I O N
  B E L L E   S T E T   I L L   C R E A T E
    S A R A   E R R A N D   S E A N S
O R D   M A R I A   A N T   T W I S T   R C
W H A T B I G G U Y S Y O U H A V E   B E R
N O M E   L O U   I T A   S A D E   H O V E
E D S E L   T A L E S   P E N D   A R L E N
R E I N E S   N I L   M O R E L   L E G R E
S S T   N A V A L D R I P   S E A L   E E L
  E L A T E   S I N U S   Y E A R N
R U B E   R E F S   D I P T H O N G S   C H
A G E N D A   L U B E S   R O C   E S T E E
C A T S U P   E N E S   P Á G E S   T A B L
I N T E R   R E D A   S R I   A M S   L O I
A D E S   B E C A U S E I T S N O T A L O U
L A R   T E H E E   P E N   E S T E R   K M
    S O R A S   C A N C A N   E B R O
E D I T O R S   T A R   I T S A   E A S T S
L I V E L Y H O O D S   P O U L T R Y S U M
A N E L E   E N U R E   L L A M A   A I M E
N O S E D   D E T E R   E L L E N   L E P E
```

18

```
G L A R E   D A D A   C I T E   F A S T
L O N E R   D E D O S   O N E S   I L I E
A C T E D   E P O C H   S D A K   N E N E
C H I S A N B O P S Y S T E M   A G R A
E S S E   E A S T   T A X   P R E T T Y
    S T A T E   S P A R   C A R R A R A
M A T   E T E S   P A N   F A N   P R A M
E L O P E   G O L D F I N G E R
S T R U N G   M A U   A N T   T I L T
T E N T   A L O N S O   R I O   O N E R
A R A T   F I N G E R B O A R D   T O O L
E D H S   N E W   O R E L S E   I N T O
D O E R   A Y A   A S S   O R N A T E
    F I N G E R W A V E   O G R E S
A L A I   O E D   O R E   E D D A   D R S
C O R N E T S   E V E R   N E E D S
H A G G L E   P R E   S I A M   A R C A
F U E L   C O U N T I N G F I N G E R S
B E E R   C H I P   S L I M E   A G N E S
A R R O   P A N T   A L D A N   S E T E E
A S S N   A R T S   R Y E S   A D E P T
```

19

```
  B O D   L A S T   R I L E   C O A T
F I F E   A F T R A   E L E M I   A N G E
R O T C   C L A I R D E L O O N   N E E D
A G H A S T   B A S I L   S T O R A G E S
  E N T O M   D I V O T   E N E R O
T A L I E S I N   S E P A L   U N S O R E
I R A   M E N A T   R E L I C   D I D O S
F I R S   A R A G   S O D A S   E T T A
F A K E D   H A M E S   N O R T E   E A U
  R U S T   I L E S   D E S E R T S
S W A R T H   L I L A C   I N T O N E
A P R I O R I   D A T A   N O E L
T R E   C I R C S   H E R M A   S I R E S
T I N S   A D R E M   D E A L   C E D E
A T O N E   S E T T E   W I S P S   A G A
R E V O L T   S T A R S   M I R A C L E S
  A R B O R   O R A T E   N O V E M
H A T T E R A S   A T O L L   P E T A R D
O B O E   S P A R R O W D I M E   A C I D
L I R R   O I D E A   S E R A L   N A S T
M E S S   D E B T   R E D S   E W E
```

20

```
P R A D O   G N A T   J A M B   P A C
L O C A L   R O N A   O M A R   G O L L
A N T R E   A R G S   L A N A   U N L A
I D O N O T S M O K E I D O N O T D O P
T O R I   O P A L   N E O N   S T E W S
    T A P   A D O   A L A R
R I A   P I C K   A L A M O D E   O S S
I A M A S C L E A N A S I V O R Y S O A
O G I V E   O N C E   K L A N   M A R G
T O N E   B U T T   Z E A L   M I S T E
    W I T   T A D   C I R
T R O W E L   A P E X   M A R X   L I Q
R O D I N   A L O P   S I L O   P A P U
I S E L D O M L I E I F R O W N O N S I
M E R L   T E S S E R A   E N Y O   O P
    I B A N   A X E   M R S
S T A R R   S L O T   R A S P   T A L
N O W M A Y I H A V E A N O T H E R G I
A L I S T   V O T E   M E R E   P A I N
M I N O S   A V E R   A S T I   O I L E
E D E N   N E X T   S T A N   S T E N
```

21

```
HEF  CHIN   GRIN    BUD
URAL AIDE CAESAR    UNI
HEWINGSOFTHEDOVE    CSA
   NONES    HALS  TAKEN
SWINE    STEPS  STOMATA
PINS MACAWS    DAIREN
ING  SAFARI  BRUNT  DPT
RG WHITTEN   LOCK  TWEE
EB HONES GRAPES    HINT
   ABATER TSARS   FENCE
SCALE   CRONE     BORGE
NKLE   CLEFT     MOORED
AFE MOLEST PAGET    ALE
ROS  AVOW HOOTERS   NOT
ER SLEDS EMOTES    SCIO
  MOLARS SWALES   STERN
LATERS SHINS      TERRE
OTTE    BOON      BOONE
NI  TAKEUNDERONESWING
EO  SPARSE FONT    EERIE
RN    TYNE   TODO  DALE
```

22

```
ALTAR  PROM  ALCAN  APICAL
TAURI  ROSA  SOLDI  BIGAMY
ISAAC  EAST  PROVO  ACADIA
CANTHISMARRIAGEBESAVED
      MSS    OUT    REVERE
TAMTAM BENS ASS  ORO   BOM
INART  LIL HENPECK    BANE
ONRYE  AGO  EDNA  HEP ASAD
GUAM  SCOP ROADTEST   LIDO
ALTA  OUTER    EWE  GALLIC
   TERN  MOOED  OSI  MAIMS
MARRIAGEOFCONVENIENCE
SALII  EON  TORII    SEND
CRIMEA OTB   SCOUR   CROW
AMMO  DOGSLIFE  TARS HUGO
LION  OSO  ORAN  ITE SABRA
PONY   SOLOMON  MED OILED
SNY EEE  ODA  USSR INNESS
   ONVIEW  AIM   CHI
WEDDINGBELLSARERINGING
HANDEL ARCED RAVE  LOCAL
OSTEAL DOTHE TREE  ABARE
WHERRY SWORN YELP  WILDE
```

23

```
EKG  EASED  APOD  GOATS
REE ANNEAU  RENO  ORBIT
AET STANDPATTER  TEIMA
SPORTIF OLSEN  SCALDED
ESNE PUT ISLAM  ASSERT
  TYRO  KAKI  MARINE
REH CLEOMES ENERO  CPA
ALERTED ATIC GLOW  HAM
HEHE  ISTH LAY  JAINA
MOA PLO UFOS  POODLES
GETSTHEWINDUPANDBOLTS
UNLOADS EDAD DEE  NYE
STINK  ERE THOU  IDLE
TAN ERGS RUHE MESCALS
OLE BEATS PEERAGE YAP
  BYBLOW  TIDE  GIGI
ATEASE PALOS DAO  ANTS
PRATTLE LANSE FRESHET
PARTO COLDOUTSIDE ELA
LITER ALOE ENURED LEG
ENORM DAWN   APERS LOY
```

24

```
APORT  IDOL   CASH    TAMA
LADIES NOTES ASTI   MOTOR
BRONXNEWYORK BRIDGEPORT
ARR TAMALE ILLER  ARMIES
    PERE  SPEED   FLEA
TRK STED APAS DIE   SWIM
SENATOR RULES SIGN  THRU
EBOLA SHAKERHEIGHTS  EAR
TEXANS EVAS  RESTON  EDE
SAVE RASES  AIN   SOCLES
ERI LITTLEROCKARK  ROIS
  LIESTO  OAT  EASTON
ALDA ANCHORAGEALAS  GSA
CLEANS  AAS  OASES  AWOL
HOT ELAINE  ORTO  SILENT
AGE DODGECITYKANS  MESNE
RING POOR BREIT  CHASTER
MANN ERR PAIR MAIM   VTS
  ASSE  GIRTS  CORN
APERCU SENSE ROTATE  LOO
GALLUPNMEX SOUTHBENDIND
OILED LISI TASTE  DIETED
GLAD  STET  FEAR  DEARS
```

25

```
ADATE  ORTEA  DORAT   TRES
MOTET  NEEDS  INANE  BRAWL
BYHEAVENSIHAVENTANYIDEA
ELON  ERASE  BITTE  OLEARY
RES  DROME  PISO   STARRY
   IGUESSIDONTKNOW
SHELVES  ONER  REINS  PET
TONIER BALED READE   BRAE
ORMER  RULED DANTE  PROSE
UNES  WORLD CATTS  BLAMED
TES  AROSE SORE    DLII
 THISISANOTHERBEYONDME
 LIST   LEAR  LANNY   ALE
LARIAT PADEN MATED  CRAM
ARIAN  FARED MUSES  HAITI
REND  DORAN GALEN  DARNER
DAD  GORED HURT   MENDERS
  ONCEAGAINIMLOST
PEEDEE  ARNE  AEDES   STS
WILSON SALVE INNER   OTOE
ONETWOTHREEANDFORTYDOWN
RUMEN  VEINS  ABORN  EELED
EPIS   SADAT  PERES  ARARS
```

26

```
BLADES  AVOID   IMPART
ERINITE CARNE   MISSIES
PONTCHARTRAIN   PLIABLE
OTERO  GOONS  TAELS  AEN
CHAUTAUQUA  CIRRI   ELSE
HELM  SLUT  ARNA  NORDIC
SRS  ATLE  ORIEL  ODESSA
      ILES  FARMS  SCAB
CRATER  TAHOE  LAKH   APR
OILER  SINEW  TARE   ALAE
HOPATCONG    WHITEFISH
ATES  ORES  BOERS  LISTE
NSS  FEES  MOSES  BANTAM
      SLUR  SEDAN  SATE
TATTER  SHEER  TIRE   HOR
ELIDED  TATS  SIDI   NONE
XATS  ACIDS  OKEECHOBEE
ONA  CLARO  FLEUR  ODONS
MINARET  WINNIPESAUKEE
ANILINE  EMDEN  AIRLESS
EASTER  RORYS  LADENS
```

27

```
ABASH  ASEMS   BELAS
CANOE  MAMIE   ANELE
THEOPHILUSTHISTLE
EST  CENA   THORNTOM
      AROMA     ENA
SWEETBRIARS   SRTAS
DOLT       RILE   EIRE
ROSTER  OOLONG   NEW
    ADAMSNEEDLE
LET  OHBABY  SINGLY
ALIA  SAGU     IOTA
DICTA  SERVINGFORK
      AID   RARER
SOFTSOAP  NAVE  PRE
NETTLESANDDAISIES
ASHOE  ANNEE  GHENT
PESOS  SEERS  EERIE
```

28

```
SHRIFT  OCTO  HAHA  ARTS
PIANOS  KHAN  ONAN  CHAP
ADROOP  RISE  PICT  TINA
TEEST  MALTAMILK  SONGS
    LHO  LENA  ELBAROOM
WIGGUAM    DUO  ELM  SSS
ABLAZE  SHEARER  LOA
CAIRO  STUTTERER  AURAL
ORSON  AERATE  MEMBRANE
    FARAD  UNP  PALANCE
ARUBABALL   RHODESTER
LEBANON  ESE  OASES
OVERCOAT  AVENGE  SCABS
PERRY  COMBATTED  ERNIE
    AFR  TABLEON  EDITOR
UBE  ROK  RAE   POTBALI
LEYTEBUG  TUAN  ANO
STERE  WIGHTLIES  GONGS
TILE  RAJA  IANS  SICILY
EDIE  RIOT  AMEN  AVALON
REDS  STES  NOSE  RESEWS
```

29

```
EDDAS  POLAR  ESTES
PRIORY  ABASE  SHASTA
CONSUMMATIONS  CAPSIZE
OTE  ROBLE  SEEPAGE  NAV
MESS  ROLLO  REAPS  OGLE
ANTED  LOLLS  DIE  PREEN
STONES  TAINTED  MADRAS
    OCTA  VERD  SOLE
THOROUGHFARE  SHAMROCK
HARAR  NEO  DEPARTS  HOI
RIIS  CAROM  SEMIS  BARN
UFO  MATELOT  NOM  MIRED
MANDATES  LOUDSPEAKERS
    ONES  FAWN  SARI
MISTER  TURNIPS  RANDOM
OPTED  BAR  STATS  TIERE
TEES  TARNS  ELAND  SCAN
OCA  CONTACT  AGORA  RTE
RAMPART  COUNTERACTION
CERISE  ERNIE  TINIER
DONOR  SNAPS  SNEAD
```

30

```
ARIOSO  ADDUCE   TURBO
RESTOP  REUBEN  OUTSER
MATTHEWARNOLD  CLEANE
ATL  ORIG  NATURALS  EG
DAES  AMULET  RILE  SDA
ASSAM  PASS  PAPA  MAIN
    BELOIT  CONE  MARCO
SSE  MELA  BOSC  SATIT
TEAROSE  SENSELESS  AP
ENROSE  DOLCE  INCURRE
ETNA  SUGGESTED  UNA
PROMPTER  EISEN  PAROL
SYL  ARNOLDVON  POPULA
    DRIES  EDER  CROP  DR
REBELS  MAES  THERES
EVELS  CADS  RIAS  LEUC
PANS  SHIP  LEERED  SNO
ASN  SPELLOUT  ANIM  AS
SIESTAS  ARNOLDTOYNBE
TOTTERS  NETTIE  DRILL
ENTERS  TOSSES  EASEL
```

31

```
MORON  MOATS  BORED   USMA
EXILE  ANGIE  ENURE   ALCAN
TELEVISIONNEWSBROADCAST
EYES   GOONS  RAILS   SMELTS
RED  BUNNY  SNIDE  SPIRES
   CLASS  STALE  SKITS
BRAIN  DEAN   WHIR   SET
TRANSATLANTICPHONECALLS
RATES  HORDE  ARIAS  OCALA
ENID  PERKS  TROLL  PRIMER
ACT   PAIR   REDO   SYN
THECURRENTNEWSMAGAZINES
ARK   ARAT   GALA   ASP
SOLVES  REAMS  SALEM  YUCA
AVAIL  DEVIE  TOPOL  VISOR
DAILYORSUNDAYNEWSPAPERS
ELD   NITS   PROS   ONEAT
   ABELE  SPOOF  POLES
CHROMY  WELLS  PARIS  GET
AREOLA  SEPAL  EILAT  FUSE
COMMUNICATIONSSATELLITE
ENEAS  RAVEN  APACE  AUDEN
DENS   STEMS  GYNES  BEERY
```

32

```
TOTED  ICHOR  SWINGER
ATONE  DOUSE  PAROLEE
WOODYHERMAN  ELATERS
   SEAN   DUELS   NIT
AREA  FLEET  ACE  ONES
BALLOT  RAH   RHYTHM
SELAH  ESSE   ERMINE
MANX   TBONE   SILAS
IGOROT  IDOLS  CLIP
EMU  ARRANGEMENT  ELY
PAYS  NABOB  COWERS
IGLOO  SCRAP  TWIN
COOLED  NETS  COATI
MOROSE  DOR  HELPER
RIBS  SAX  SNIPE  SEEK
ORA  DAWES  MARK
YARDAGE  TOMMYDORSEY
ANDOVER  ALIEN  HOUSE
LIONESS  READE  LINTS
```

33

```
ADRIFT  RADAR  SHAHS  ASSE
NOSNOW  OSOLE  PARIS  PHEN
SEVERE  BAWLS  HITTHEROAD
ASP  PEAL  NEO  LIP  MATTE
WETBEHINDTHEEARS  GER
HIGHTEA  ANDSEE  SYE  MURS
ALLIED  ANTE  HID  DISON
SLIPS  WISH  TRIESITON
HEMP  RAM  EYRA  BARESKIN
EDOS  DOING  STR  ESIS
ATTRACT  LUGS  ELI  STYLET
CREST  EDEMA  ATONE  ABACK
CATNAP  RAP  IMAN  PERUSES
AMRA  ATE  SYBIL  OLES
PAPERHAT  OENO  ADD  ILSE
PETERSOUT  ACRE  SNEAK
BELOW  PAR  ADAM  SHEAVE
BOAR  NEF  FEODOR  SLOSHES
ABI  HEARTSANDFLOWERS
BELIE  TEY  TUT  ABET  SLA
BRONXCHEER  ICHOS  POWWOW
LOUD  PETRO  MEANT  ENTIRE
ENTO  AROSE  ESTAS  RESTED
```

34

```
HOTEL   DAGGLE  MIAMIS
AERATE  PIGIRON  ALBINO
BROKENSHOELACE  SIESTA
ADZE  ISAR  DSC  ADLER
SEC  ANTSATAPICNIC  ARE
DOST  SEMI  THAN  KIND
WTS   ADES   STRAND
TRAIT  ASHE  RENEGE
DOUBLEFAULTING  DALLAS
URN  AMISS  ARDOR  LAGO
MED  SATED  TRIER  SLY
PROS  TOTES  UNCAS  SEA
YOWLED  PARKINGTICKETS
SNARES  XMAS  DROSS
BILLOW  ATLE  SAB
BRAN  TRIP  IGOR  PEAT
RAT  RAINATAPARADE  LEO
INTRO  IRR  LAZO  BLAT
AGEOLD  UNINVITEDGUEST
NERVES  ALINEATE  GANGES
DRYEST  ENISLE  EDGES
```

35

```
STEELS  RAYA  PACT  ABED
TOSTEP  ETON  SURE  MALI
ARCHAEOLOGY  TRIP  ARES
TIRE  CRANIAL  OSE  ICE
ENOL  TAXES  AERIE  ATTU
NOW  BALED  AMBASSADORS
FATED  TRIAL  CANOE
ACCUSER  SOLAN  BARRENS
BEARS  SLUES  CANE
ASTRONOMERS  DARESTOBE
STEE  ADADS  AARON  AREA
HARDINESS  ADVENTURERS
RATH  BRAID  LIANE
SAPLESS  MARIS  SLANDER
TRAIN  DEBAR  PHONS
IMPRESARIOS  PEENS  GAL
POPE  AMINO  METRE  BARE
PRO  NIB  NAILERS  ABLE
LEOI  TELA  STORYTELLER
ERSE  ENES  TETE  ARSENE
SSES  ESTA  ORAD  READER
```

36

```
KOPEK  CUBAN  COBRA  KICKS
OSAKA  UKASE  AKRON  INERT
LAGER  KENTUCKIANS  RELAY
AGE  ETES  ORLE  DESK  LIL
SETTLES  KRAS  CLERK  ROTE
     AIR  TEIL  POOL  ILE
 TEXARKANA  DAMASK  ANKLE
NISI  IAGO  KORAN  EMPORIA
ELK  KEYS  HUNKS  TRIS  ERG
EDITORS  SILKS  CRETE  MAL
DEMONS  ANTAE  CAUSE  ELSE
   ORG  BACKYARDS  CII
SKIN  LAUGH  HOARS  KARNAK
KEG  MARTS  HORSE  PALETTE
ILL  COOS  WAITS  PINK  ROE
ELOIGNS  KANSA  BUCK  SIMP
SAONE  ENLIST  COCKATOOS
   KEW  EASE  KOOK  KEA
PONY  AVANT  DIRK  LEAKOUT
AME  ERAT  DINO  AIEL  APO
CAPON  NECKANDNECK  ESKER
KHAKI  ESSEN  LEVEE  AMENT
SALAD  STARK  ETERN  FUNDS
```

37

```
RAM    GAT  STAGES  TON
AMIS  CASH  ARNOLD  ILE
NONET  THYME  CADRES  CLU
GINGERBREADS  NEIN  STAT
   URIA  TREM  CANASTA
CASINOROYALE  ENG  PACKE
ACU  TSF  LLB  SPORTIV
SECCHI  IVE  TRKS  AREOLA
 CHESSTER  SONEAR  DEN
RIALTO  RES  NUANCE
CENTI  LIV  TACT  AHA  GE
ANC  CHINESECHECKERS  RA
WIT  ITE  TATI  HSE  APER
 CARTEL  AAR  SIMIAN
CBE  ITALIC  DOMINOES
SMOLDER  JENA  AMA  CARIN
LAYAWAYS  GSA  RPI  NE
PISCIS  IMA  BRIDGETHEGA
 KNEADED  AINU  REAR
OUIJA  RETE  HARDSCRABBL
BELA  RECALL  DOILY  RILE
ALEC  ITALIA  NASO  LUN
DESK  TERSER  EDH  ET
```

38

```
GOAD  TUANS  TOTEM  SCAD
ROLE  ISLIP  ORONO  ELLA
ANUMBRELLA  COMINGTOMY
SAMARAS  ERDA  AMERICA
  NIDUS  EARN  TANKS
HOWDEEPISTHEOCEAN
ERIE  NAHS  NIX  THORN
RAND  REATA  SUTES  OLEO
ACC  LEVI  THEPICCOLINO
THEPOPE  ATLE  RUDDER
 HEARTATTHESTAGE
OHHOWI  EIRE  EPHRATA
EASTERPARADE  STET  RUR
TRIO  SEPTS  LATER  SAMA
AMANA  DOR  HESA  ADIB
 PLAYASIMPLEMELODY
BLARE  POSE  EXALT
REVISES  ISNT  ITALIAN
DEVILSBALL  THATIMARRY
EVEN  ERNIE  ARLEN  KEEN
WERE  NOSED  LOADS  EDDY
```

39

```
PESA  RABAT  GEMS  SMIT
ERAT  ITALO  TABOO  PATE
LOCH  SOREPHALANX  RTES
FOREGONE  SOLENT  LAHRS
 ENATE  COVEN  ABANG
ELDEST  DRIES  INDIGENT
LAI  SOCIALLEOPARD  NOR
AGLEY  ARMS  PENS  SUSA
NEIN  TNT  TECS  FISHY
DRAGOUT  SENORA  SOB
 CONFOUNDFRACTURES
   RUT  LILLES  RETRACT
DREGS  OLDS  BUD  ILLO
ROPE  PRAE  SAID  BAMIA
AMI  FRAGRANTCRIME  OMN
MADELINE  FIEND  OLDNED
 EYING  ARNEE  SUGAR
ARRET  EASIER  ANNOTATE
RIMS  MASHTRANSIT  ECON
IDIO  IDEES  GROPE  READ
ASSN  LEAN  EARED  SSTS
```

40

```
PEWS  SPET  ORIBI  TROV
ECRU  CALEB  FANON  HALC
THEBLACKCLIFFSOFDOVE
EON  ALEE  ACETO  EOLIAN
  APED  AMIN  IRNE
SABLE  OVENS  ANNA  MEN
THEBLUEBADGEOFCOURAG
LENA  NAIL  CRUS  ERGS
OME  ARTS  PATER  ALIA
 TREE  ARLES  DATING
THEWEARINGOFTHEORANG
RELOAD  MISSA  LEAS
OREB  CASTE  REST  LAI
LOCI  BARE  DEMI  SOLO
LITTLEBEIGERIDINGHOO
SCS  ALIT  EPHOD  LUNGE
 GRIN  NAYS  SPAN
ASTAGE  EJECT  ETUI  HOT
THELOVEFORTHREEGREENS
OENO  EBOLI  MARNE  DATE
RASP  DORIC  HOOT  ODO
```

41

```
MARGE  SWAMI  TRAMPS  UPGO
AXIAL  UHLAN  HOBBIT  TARA
GODZILLAVSTHESEAMONSTER
INGE  ULNAS  USED  ANE  TEE
CEY  STEG  ASIT  EXPEND
JOHNSONVSGOLDWATER
ASHORE  BEGAN  OREG  ASOP
PHASER  BLEAR  SCIRE  ONO
LATHS  LEANS  SHALE  MONDE
ELF  NYASA  PLATY  PURVIS
ALII  YOUTHVSAGE  HONESTY
ETHANS  IAN  AERIAL
TOLTECS  GRANTVSLEE  DISC
UNDOCK  MRAND  ITOLD  SUE
BESOT  BEARD  CZARS  TOTED
ENV  LANZA  VAILS  TRIODE
DDSS  AIDE  AIMEE  RUNNER
MONITORVSMERRIMACK
COCOON  ITAL  RAGE  QED
OTC  ROI  ISAN  AMATI  SUVA
BROWNVSBOARDOFEDUCATION
RAYE  ELANET  FAMER  RILKE
ASST  REMADE  AROSE  ARLES
```

42

```
HOE  CONT  TOLL  HUE  ARNE
PORTFOLIO  EPHA  ALLGREEK
INITALICS  HEATHENCHINEE
POSER  VESPERS  OMAHA  ODD
IRS  OTIS  OREADS  ETC
TEAL  RATATAT  YEWS  SAFES
USA  BANTUS  RIO  SRTA
NBCS  KINGSENGLISH  TEND
BURKE  EPEE  BEET  MOLNAR
EROO  STIR  USINE  TECS
ASOF  ION  ENATIC  AMISH
NEKTONS  INDUTCH  RECITER
LHOKE  SCENES  MIL  NOLO
OYEZ  LORAN  COST  SASS
ANNIES  TEMP  HONE  APSIS
BEER  RUSSIANBYRON  LATE
ETSI  IDA  ANURAN  ELI
LOESS  ERAS  NIDUSES  NUMB
HOD  STACTE  ALEE  POI
JAM  FISHY  FITSOUT  CARON
ARABICNUMERAL  SCOTCHING
PIGLATIN  COTE  TENNESSEE
EDIT  APT  USES  ERST  OER
```

43

```
CRAPE  CAPER  SSTS  WEB
LEGIT  OCALA  ICOSA  AXE
ALEXANDERSBELLOWS  TEC
RENI  OATS  INLET  SPECK
ATTEST  AES  AIR  SUER
SHIRLEYSBLACKMAGIC
CAR  ACE  ROLY  HEELAND
AVENGED  SIDE  OLDSTER
PILAR  PTA  MIT  EDS
ELISE  MAINE  FACET
KATHERINESPORTERHOUSE
NESTS  INITS  ELLIN
EHE  MSS  SEE  OGEED
TALIPOT  NATS  STRANGE
RESNARE  IONA  PHE  TED
EMILYSPOSTAGESTAMP
NOSE  RAY  ENA  TSETSE
KYOTO  TABES  AVAS  RAPS
LAR  FAWCETTSMAJORSUIT
EME  FRILL  OMEGA  BONNE
ESS  ANES  BALER  INTER
```

44

```
SIMAR  STABLE  LAIC
SESAME  AIRIER  APRON
CONTRACTBRIDGE  REEVES
ARAL  LURED  AMEER  ERE
RETE  LINED  STIRS  BROW
DSO  SINES  THETA  FEELS
STRICTER  PRASE  SOLDI
NOHS  SLUM  CARIB
REBATE  THESE  ALGERIA
EARNS  AREAS  SPREE  ILL
BRIE  SWEETBRIERS  CDII
ELD  BEAST  RATTY  SAGOS
CYGNETS  PILES  PARENT
EARTH  ADES  RECT
LOTTO  FANGS  NEAREAST
FIFES  HEDGE  TETRA  BLE
LASS  CODAS  HAMAL  ARIA
UNI  CAROM  FILER  SANS
EAGRES  RAILROADBRIDGE
SHARE  ANDEAN  ERODES
SHOD  STEAMS  DANES
```

45

```
WASP  STA  CRATE  DADDY
ILLUSIONS  RUBIN  ASRED
COOLASACUCUMBER  TSIAS
KNOLL  DOLLS  ANIMATED
SEP  TRINKETS  SCI  RLS
SMEE  SWIPE  HADATIT
CHAINS  NEDS  MASHED
AROUND  TAMECATS  NEAR
NOTRE  ERMAS  RAPIDAN
TOTE  SQUATS  ROTI  SAL
INELOQUENT  ALLTHESAME
SSR  VIAL  FRUITS  AHET
TRENTON  RILLY  AVANT
CHAR  EVERYDAY  SNORTS
CRAVED  EBOE  SEDRAS
LINEDUP  SCRAM  WAFS
ETH  RAT  ABROGATE  FLA
TAMBOURS  UNIES  AGAIN
CEDAR  SALTYASAHERRING
IRENE  ELIDE  TREASURES
ESSEN  SATYR  SST  BEST
```

46

```
AGAMA DANS STEAM DARE
RIMER EVAN THAWS AXED
ANISO PERU RATAL VINE
BARNUMANDBAILEY BISON
    ESTRUS APER TAD
BSA ESTE ARES DURANCE
RILLS EGO SERENELY
IAGO MUTTANDJEFF DAUR
ELEV USHER AINT AGREE
FOREGONE OWL GROSS
  ARN ASSENTS AIL
EDNAS PAR ASSAILED
ENIDS SLAG NEWTS AIDE
NORM AMOSANDANDY TREF
CLEAROUT YAM SHAME
EARRING SILK ANTE SAR
  ROE NERO SNARES
DEBIT DAMONANDPYTHIAS
AREA CUTIN PERA HORSE
RING ORATE REEL ENATE
TETE POLED ARAM DENIM
```

47

```
RAPT ALAS MUST SEAM
ALIA TALE ANTI AXLE
YACKAHULAHICKEYDULA
ENTERED MENU ADDON
   SIN FIRER SLEETY
ABDULABULBULAMIR
DEEP ERE RUE TAW
ERR PRAY PAPA FALA
SNAILED CIRIBIRIBIN
ANTON CONGE RILLE
DIGADIGADOO COMMENT
ESEL OMEN LONE LAW
BED TAR AIM PETE
OHBYJINGOOHBYGEE
INSURE ICIAN UAR
NOTTO BENT EMBARGO
THEABADABAHONEYMOON
RING SARA ALAR IDOL
OTOE SMOG SEMI DENY
```

48

```
INSTEP FARGO JADE TOTHE
DENIAL ADEAL ADEN APHID
ONECRACKMIND MOUTHPEACE
LEE SYRIAN HEMPS ORNIS
   BIRN TOLET FROE
CAM AAMS SHRED PANORAMA
AMIABLE SPASM ROGET CON
SIGNAL THEWEIGHOUT SCOT
INHOT TEENS NIPS PAINE
NOTA MEDOC ALANS PADDED
DRY BRIDLESUITE MESHED
  WARBLY ELM AACHEN
HOMEIS SERAPHICJAM TAM
BERING NOVAE ACTON ACRO
EARNS SAFE PRIOR TIRED
ATIS STRINGFEVER HEDONE
TEE HAIDA LITER ZENANAS
ARRAIGNS COVEY SOLD EST
   SPET LEVER LORD
DWELL BONES BALBOA BAA
BRAVEYARDS PROSEANDCONS
EAVES GOGO OUSEL TOORIE
DYERS EWER TEARY OGLALA
```

49

```
SACCO SOLD IPSO SITON
OMAHA EPEE MOLD TAWNY
LOPES VIAL PRAE ONONE
FOURTEENNINETYTWO OOT
ANTI UNI AIR STOLEN
  SARTOS VIA EMINENT
EIGHTEENTWELVE BETTOR
TRI EKE RANSOMS SAWTO
HALO ANCON NENE LOAD
AQABA OPTE RUTS
NINETHOUSANDEIGHTYTWO
  TARN SENT EMIRS
EFTS YETI IDIOT ALII
GOWER MODESTO PHI EST
ARENAS FIFTYFOURFORTY
DENOTED OFA ABLEST
  TRICOT ETA LEA HEMI
BEY FOURSCOREANDSEVEN
ALTAI BOAT BETT ELITE
BOWIE TUBE OREL ALTER
ANOLD STUD ROSY TOAST
```

50

```
LAPPS SOUP SPARE PARMA
AMARA ULNAR ILLER AVIAN
REPEL MICRO GOLDA LANCE
ANUXORIOUSMANWASSOLIGHT
STAYME STEED SHEEN LOOS
   ELA ODA AREA
ABOW INDIA EVEL ENSTAR
HEWASCARRIEDAWAYBYAKITE
HELIO NEARS SEVERE IMPS
ONEFLAG EFLAT ILA ATBAT
WAT DREG LOX ASP ASTORS
HEFLEWOVERTHECITY
CHOIRS MAW LOT DADO LAS
HURTS BID ASPEN SERPENT
ETAH ANILL ENEAS IONIA
SCREECHINGLORDWHATAPITY
SHERPA GEER STATE ENAS
   IRAQ ZIG TMP
ZASU AGUAS BEATA PELOTA
IWONTSEEMYMISSUSTONIGHT
PALLI SNARE SARTO SALEM
PREEN ICTUS ONIQN ENERO
YENTE SHIPS ANNE EASES
```

51

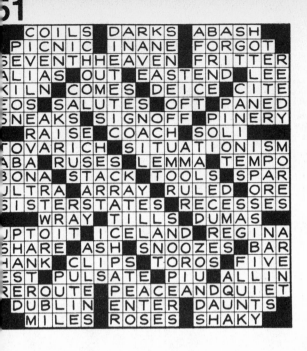

```
COILS DARKS ABASH
PICNIC INANE FORGOT
SEVENTHHEAVEN FRITTER
ALIAS OUT EASTEND LEE
KILN COMES DEICE CITE
EOS SALUTES OFT PANED
SNEAKS SIGNOFF PINERY
RAISE COACH SOLI
TOVARICH SITUATIONISM
ABA RUSES LEMMA TEMPO
BONA STACK TOOLS SPAR
ULTRA ARRAY RULED ORE
SISTERSTATES RECESSES
WRAY TILLS DUMAS
UPTOIT ICELAND REGINA
SHARE ASH SNOOZES BAR
HANK CLIPS TOROS FIVE
EST PULSATE PIU ALLIN
REROUTE PEACEANDQUIET
DUBLIN ENTER DAUNTS
MILES ROSES SHAKY
```

52

```
NOTHIN BUSHER BARDS
TARRING SALTINE PARTIES
ORIENTS CLAUDIA ATACAMA
PRO CHORAL BEGGARED GAR
HALT ENOLA SMALL ALONG
ATEUP EEDSRE ANTA ANTE
TESTED SETOFF SAY TWAIN
ONES DETOUR REAR LCT
TURNUPS DARTED DIET
MARS TACT SMITES MARAUD
AGA HAHA ILONA EDIRNE
NONE UNREGENERATED MIDI
ORISON PRONG TREE SIS
FEASTS SONTAG YELL SENT
ATES DIESES NEOCENE
ICE EWES CRONES DOUR
TAMAR GPS STRAIT TROPES
ALEM MEAD HERPEO BURNT
LENIS EAGER CHIPS SEGO
IND TINKERER HOLLOS CIA
ADAMANT NINETEN ELEMENT
NATIVES EVADERS STRIPES
RENEE SENSES HABITS
```

53

```
BOGS COLOR WRAP ASST
EXAM ARISE HALO ATETE
AUTUMNALEQUINOX STEED
USE ONLY UNTIE STUMPS
NOES MECHS CAEN
KAFIRS BASLE ALFRESCO
ADAMS WINTERGREEN ULM
BULB LAGO AGAS SMEE
OWL OUTOFSEASON TOMAN
BASSINET LAMPS FAMERS
BONER WAGES BOXER
CHALKS TOKEN DANISHES
RACES SOMERSAULTS ONA
INKS SAXE BEES BUTS
MOO SPRINGFIELD RISES
PINDARIC RENTS CELERY
ALAS SALAS SOCK
BOUNTY SETON AQUA FAN
OUNCE SPRINGASURPRISE
ACTED TURF EXEAT AXIS
THOS ADAY READS JEST
```

54

```
METAL COSTA DELAY STAEL
OZONE OPTED EROSE PORTE
BRONXCHEERS CROSSBOWMAN
YALE LENIN PLANT LIESTO
BARON MEANY SALA
FASTENER LEAST ANDERSON
AMIENS LIARS ACIER ENA
MALAE WHISTLESTOPS ACES
IDEST OASTS ERRS TROIS
NINE TOILE PATEN BRENDA
EST FALLENARCHES LANDAU
BLIP LEE IDAS
EQUINE RUBBERBRIDGE TAA
SUTTER ASIAN LURCH MONT
POLES AGAS FOCAL SARTO
ITER STAGECOACHES COIRS
EER MESNE ALIKE PAREUS
DESPISED STIRS CHARISMA
ASTA TAHOE DROSS
MALICE CHIOS LOATH XRAY
INANUTSHELL DUMBWAITERS
LAVIE AIMEE ARUBA BRICE
EMEND GRADS WESER NADIR
```

55

```
SPARED ALMOST PASTAS
CAREER NEEDLER UNIATE
ORGANA ARMOIRE RODMEN
ROAM MANN REGALIA MAS
ELL EASIER RIVET DUSE
DEIGN KAREL VENALIZES
ACMES CERE SNUG
SOLOED CATER ICINGS
REPAID SOPHISTICATION
ADA LOCUM ANARK NACRE
VALE COOPERATION LOGE
ATILT AMANG IONIC BOZ
GENERALISSIMOS CABANE
EREMIC SUZAN TENORS
EMUS BEET PAROL
REINSTATE STERN NOTCH
AUNT ETHAN EVOKES RAE
IRA SNEERED AWAY LIMA
NORATE MIRACLE RIOTER
EPURES ENVIOUS INSERT
DETERS GESTES ESTRAY
```

56

```
EDWARDS ACED FEAR ARTS
LEERIER HOMEPLACE TEHEE
IWEEPFORADONAISHEISDEAD
CASAS ABET STEEDS ARMS
ILL PAYSRENT IMINE
TIETIES REAMOUT STILE
EARTHINESS ANTECESSOR
SAKES EMIT THREADS APE
ARIL APOGEE AGAG
LET SUES ERRANTS AGARS
TOCSINS CATS GOAT BEREA
ELONGATIONS REPRIMANDED
RAWIN OLIO DORE PORTEND
SERGE PANNIER REBS NAL
ISTO CAYUGA RICE
AWN SHIPPED KEPI LUNTS
PATRICIDES SWEETTOOTH
TRIES GALATEA ESTHETE
MATCH RASSLERS RAT
PIRL ATEASE TEER ASFIT
FLOWERINTHECRANNIEDWALL
CLUES DOMINEERS TREACLE
ESTE ELON ELSE SANTEES
```

57

```
ABJURE JANIS SATI NEB
LEASTS EVERT FACILE ONO
EMCEES JACKINTHEBOX PGS
COKE HUSK LOCATE TELIC
TAB POINT BLT ROT OLAN
ONEHORSE SAMARA ALLYE
NIMB PICARESQUE AMES
SIPPED ERINYS UPDO ARA
LAMP DADOES UPAS BAKED
ARBOR LINN BALED ISLED
IAL AAMS STILTS HOCKS
CHEAPJACK ULT OFONESJIB
JAPAN NOBLES ORAN ADE
CAROM BONES HERS ENCLS
PACER TAXI HISSES OKES
ARK TOIT OSIERS DALLAS
ROBE JOHNNYCAKE DUAD
LEVIS OSLERS QUIDNUNC
IQED SES VLS MURES LAR
INUSE PATRIA MEAN ALTA
MII EVERYMANJACK GAMBIT
PAC STALLS DUNCE REMOVE
INK SKYE STEAD STAYED
```

58

```
EBOLI CODED AGES DESK
LENIN AWARE DAMP RITE
LETME TARASBULBA KRON
ACHE CORKSCREW SCIENT
HERTZ LESE AAMILNE
GISARMES GUYS ODI
SORCERIES SUN PANACHE
TREK SPA CHEMIST ROED
IDEST IDOLATER MAENAD
RON ONE CUM SABOT SLY
MUNSTERCHEESE
UME BRICA OPE ATS MBL
NERVES AVOCADOS TIARA
USIA ENRANKS CTO NYET
MANMADE RES THEMAJORS
APL SPYS DESPOTIC
SCIOLTO HEEL REGLE
STEREO POORCLARE TINT
IOOI ULSTERETTE DINAH
OPUS GOUT INHOT AMICI
NASH HYPO STEMS SECTS
```

59

```
MERGE ACT AZOV GBSHA
GAMARI RAH NAME NOTAT
EXODERM GREENCORMORANT
TITAN EAU ACI ODDMANOU
EMERALDFEATHER ASET
MSS DIET NEO EAN DEBAS
VITA MER CENTS SONI
LOINS PUN ADDIOS WIL
CYCLE DESTAEL SQUEALSO
ICAL PORT BALLOU AVIES
DELAMARES DROP ELLEN
SEAGATE PILUS AIRGAP
EYING LCIS TURNSGRA
GORGON RAFAEL OLEG RIP
OVERRATES TRYOUTS LEAP
OUSE SEETHE MRS POESY
PLIED SNEAD PAS LUNN
SENNET GRD MUN BERG PR
LIMA JACKINTHEGREE
CREDITORS BCE OSA RILL
PEREGRINEPICKLE REENTE
APACHE EMIT AIL REGEN
SPLATS TINE STS SNORT
```

60

```
AMPLE  SILK  HEEPS  RIPSAW
KORAN  PLAN  ONTAP  EMOTER
HOOTCHIECOOTCHIE  MALADE
  HEAD  ETAT  DEROGATES
RAHS  SEA  HEPTA  EVEREST
ENE  HURLYBURLY  SPAS
DELLAS  POR  APPEAL  CHEM
SATIRE  HOITYTOITY  HOERS
REDUST  NEE  NAS  UVEAS
ROM  HODGEPODGE  GREB
BOSNS  OWE  SRO  VERTIGO
OAK  COUNTER  BELLAMY  EON
TREPANS  ROT  IAN  SOJAS
LURE  HANKYPANKY  CUE
MATSU  TOR  PIR  ABUSES
BEAM  HOCUSPOCUS  EREBUS
TERN  LETSGO  HRH  ARLINE
HEMS  HOWDYDOODY  EUR
OCARINA  ASTHE  ELI  ASPS
CAROLINAS  IMET  ENOL
ADESTE  HIGGLEDYPIGGLEDY
LESSON  ADORE  IRAN  RINSE
ATTENT  HEROD  TOWS  ENACT
```

61

```
POSTOFFICE  ALB  INAPOT
HEARNOEVIL  HOLESINONE
LAUNDERMATS  TOUCHANDGO
DELFT  ADONAIS  TEL  GASES
EMA  ALT  ROTGUT  SETA
FONDAS  DAVINCIS  CORDOBA
INGENUES  OOHED  TRAILER
CAIRA  ACTON  ARABIA  ODRA
IDUN  MUSES  SNAKECHARMER
TEM  FIX  LLOYDC  RISE  ATA
LON  OFOURSKINS  ODIST
YANGTZE  TIU  SAMPLED
TWEED  CARSONCITY  AUG
OAS  LAHR  AFGHAN  SYS  MAW
PHIBETAKAPPA  LOCHS  FAVI
PICA  BISTRO  ISTOO  AUDEN
ONANOAK  TICKS  TOWNSEND
SENSATO  UNKNOWNS  OTSEGO
RSVP  SEISHU  UGH  YEW
SHAMS  SHE  TSCALES  OMERS
KISSMEKATE  HELLISHNESS
YESTERYEAR  ELEEMOSYNA
ERNANI  OLE  SENDINGSET
```

62

```
MASS  PALM  CAPH  RALSTON
ANIL  EQUI  SAMOA  ELEMENT
EDDO  RUNSACROSS  FINITES
DEVILANDDANIELWEBSTER
TOWATER  IMRE  EERIE
AWAKE  INDIA  OUTRE  SHAWL
RNS  SPUR  TBARS  ENC  AREA
ASHE  SMOLT  FANS  COSTING
LET  LOOKIT  OVERHEATS
OPALS  FLU  ENE  RIFTED
CALYPSO  BEE  DEERE  SOI
UPINYOURFUNKANDWAGNALLS
LAT  ORION  EWA  MEANIES
OUTLAY  STE  COE  PUDGY
CLAMSHELL  ATESTS  GAR
EVERET  EARL  CRIME  ADDA
AMEN  STU  FRESH  EELS  IAN
ASSU  ENCRE  NEARS  OPART
PORTA  CARL  STOOGES
CROSSWORDPUZZLEMAKERS
GUANACO  HORIZONTAL  SANS
ANNULAR  OTARY  ECTO  IMOU
MANSARD  POMS  WHEN  ESTE
```

63

```
ANISE  PASHA  KILN  WASP
MEGILP  TINEAR  USIA  IXIA
MONDAYMORNING  KIBITZERS
STRAINS  DUELS  NEA
MAW  EARLS  ASAMA  STRATA
INES  MAS  SLOBS  BLOODRED
STEPOUT  GHOUL  AROON  MED
HIKERS  QUARTERBACK  ACTE
AGENT  TUANS  OINK  OTHER
PUNT  SHIRT  BATED  SPEARS
SAD  ITOLDYOUSO  THETIS
WISENTS  TRI  STAINER
SAVING  CRITICISMS  GAS
MERINO  COHAN  DRESS  REVE
IRREG  MANU  SLANE  MANET
RAID  POSTMORTEMS  REVERT
APO  MOLTO  BEARS  SEVERAL
GERBILLE  RESTS  SOV  SAGE
ESSENE  BELIE  SABER  LED
AIM  CUPID  MARINER
HINDSIGHT  SECONDGUESSES
ORAL  COAT  KNIVES  ELVERS
SKYE  SAPS  STEER  SPARS
```

64

```
PEST  SCAMP   TBAR    SPUD
ASHE  CANOE   EERY    OHARE
SPONSORS MESSAGE      SANDE
TYE   TREE   LASSO   OILSUP
      ERNS   BINET   CURT
APPLES  KONER   ARTISTRY
CRAMP  PROGRAMMERS    RAE
RIMS  SOIE      OISE   DANA
AMP   NEWSREPORTS     LINER
BEHOOVES   RUNNY    RINSES
      LATER   CONES   SEMEL
SEEKER   NOSIR   SCANDALS
KATES   TELECASTERS    TOP
ATEN  IODO     PONS    LOCI
TEE   INPANTOMIME    CORAL
ERRORHAS   ONETO   TUSSLE
      BRER   STEMS   SURE
LABOUR  TOTUP   AMBI   SOU
EQUIP  TELEPHONEBOOTHS
WURST  ITER   ISTLE   NINE
DIRT   MESS   SCALD   TROD
```

65

```
THEMAN    SADSACK   ALSACE
THEVIEW   AREOLAE  DENIALS
REMATCH   LAPLATA  JOURNAL
ICAN  IOWE  TOLA  GONG  DIA
PAT  RACIST   UNTRUE   PINT
OVINE  ANMAKE   DIOR  TIDES
DECAMP   SARAHS   CONSOLES
       VEEP  NOTATE  METRO
SOLITARY   CAREEN   DISTAL
APIE  RIOTS  DELOS  NOESIS
LETS  LOGE  STREWING   DAMP
TNT    RUNSTHERISK    WEA
USED  FIRSTAID  STOA  MEAD
SERENE  TEAIN  REELS  OLDE
ASSESS   SINGLE   RECALLED
       PETES  RESOLE  SUSA
TRIDENTS   DEBATE  SCRIMP
CHESS  TIER  ASYIST  OSCAR
REVE  BILLET  SOTHAT   ORA
ILE  MIME  ARAB  LEES  SMIT
MALTESE   SMETANA  EPICENE
EMERSON   LEVERET  DILATED
BRYAN    ORIENTE   UCATOR
```

66

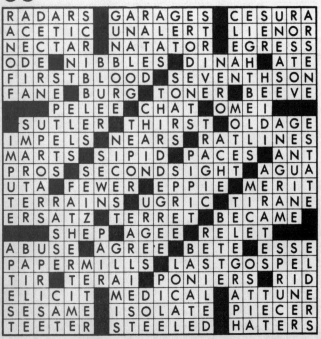

```
RADARS   GARAGES   CESURA
ACETIC   UNALERT   LIENOR
NECTAR   NATATOR   EGRESS
ODE  NIBBLES   DINAH   ATE
FIRSTBLOOD   SEVENTHSON
FANE  BURG  TONER   BEEVE
      PELEE  CHAT   OMEI
SUTLER   THIRST   OLDAGE
IMPELS   NEARS   RATLINES
MARTS  SIPID   PACES   ANT
PROS  SECONDSIGHT   AGUA
UTA  FEWER  EPPIE   MERIT
TERRAINS   UGRIC   TIRANE
ERSATZ   TERRET   BECAME
      SHEP   AGEE   RELET
ABUSE  AGREE   BETE   ESSE
PAPERMILLS   LASTGOSPEL
TIR  TERAI  PONIERS    RID
ELICIT   MEDICAL   ATTUNE
SESAME   ISOLATE   PIECER
TEETER   STEELED   HATERS
```

67

```
ABOMA  CUTUP  RSTAR  POONA
IONIC  ALOMA  AERIE  ALLOT
DUTCHUNCLES   FRENCHLEAVE
ATOE  NOEL  TAFFY  TELAMON
       TIER  TOPIS  BORS
PLANETS  PARIS  HARD  HAHA
HERESY   CUBANHEELS  ARRET
RAGES  CANAL   ILL   PEARL
AGED  ONIC  PORPOISE   BOA
SUN  ASCOT  SUM  OVERLIES
YET  SPANISHBAYONET  EAST
ITER   VIR   NEF    OBAN
SANE  ABIES  IRISHROSE  NOG
CREATION   KAS  EARED   IRE
ROB  INSTATES  CANT   AGIN
ILEDE  ERA  ERRIS   ICHOR
PLEAD  BRAZILNUTS  DOTTLE
TAFT  TRIM  NUDES  TRUSSES
       PRAM  ISNOT  REIS
SEABEES  BLUER  POPE  ALEE
ENGLISHPEER   SIAMESECATS
CORIN  LIANE  EMCEE  GROUT
SWIPE  YOKED  SPEOS  GENIE
```

68

69

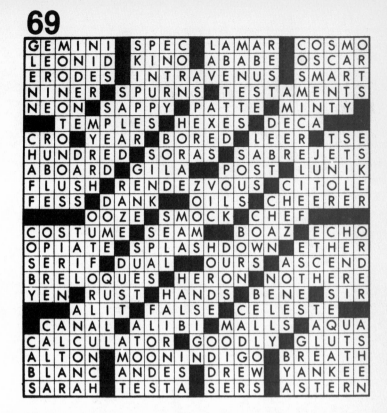

70

71

72

```
SNUB  PIER  CATO   CHIMES
ATHENE  ANNOTATOR  LENORE
BROTHERCANYOUSPAREADIME
BARTERS  EARL  SCOOP  LIP
ADELE  MEDALS  SALON  BENE
EDH  MUDS  CHIEF  PARED
ETCS  ADITS  HEIL  SCAR
THO  GLORY  CARES  ARAMIS
ARI  REIS  ARLES  HANK  ARA
TENSEST  CLEFS  AORTA  KID
SETAE  MATED  ALONG  LESE
PENNYWISEPOUNDFOOLISH
PESO  AIRER  LINES  ADDLE
ANT  LURES  ULNAR  BONSOIR
ICE  APES  FRATS  HOVE  UNA
DERIVE  CLARA  SOLES  GET
DARK  AILS  RUMOR  OHNO
STIES  OGLES  DELE  TEN
ERNS  BRIAR  SUTURE  SABAL
RID  PEART  PERI  RISSOLE
AFOOLANDHISMONEYARESOON
PLOVER  LENTICULA  ANITRA
HERATS  EADS  SEAM  NESS
```

73

```
ICEAGE  TRAIT  PADUA
THEBES  TOESTHE  TURNSA
METROS  ARCHAEOLOGISTS
ORIAL  ERST  LOSES  LORS
STO  ONATOOT  PIT  PLUIE
SNUGASA  RISEN  ROALDS
VIXENS  NAR  OUST
PESOS  PICKANDSHOVEL
MARATS  SERAI  EDS  OILA
ULO  SIMPLON  DREE  TRAP
SARG  OREN  NOES  HUTS
IBAR  OLIO  CANITBE  SEE
NOTA  LIT  GAZED  EXCESS
GRAVELDEPOSIT  ATHOS
EVAS  HAT  SILTUP
DOONES  SATUP  FOEMANS
ORRIS  PAS  PENNERA  OTT
REAM  MELEE  LIES  TERRA
EXCAVATIONSITE  MINOAN
NILGAI  CUSTARD  LOCATE
SEELS  TENSE  ANYDAY
```

74

```
CREPT  DECAP  DAMPS  WHATA
ROBER  ORIBI  ASNAP  HADUP
AGORA  WIDEN  MAORI  OPINE
SUNKMONK  CHOPPERHOPPER
HEYS  STS  TUAN  QUEASY
UPTO  EARLET  ADIPOSE
SIMPLEWIMPLE  ARA  ASANOX
INE  MONTI  STABAT  PERI
DESIGN  ELF  ICESIN  APODS
IZAR  EVER  FARCRY  BYBIT
AGILE  YBARRA  TIA  ONE
PERKYTURKEY  PALLIDSALAD
OLE  RES  ORGEAT  OMAHA
TASSE  IMABUM  ERLE  AMAH
STOPS  VOLUME  ROI  CESARE
HILL  BELAYS  STOOD  LIL
ONEIDA  ESE  VENIALMENIAL
TESTERS  ROOMIE  DELA
STEEPS  STEP  AMU  PROB
KIPPERSHIPPER  MOPYHOPI
ADARS  TOTER  GAROU  ATTAR
RECIT  ETUDE  EWELL  WHORL
LETTS  TOPSY  SKYED  PARTS
```

75

```
ACCOSTS  PACAS  PIASTER
SHOUTAT  IRANI  IMMERGE
SANTAFE  TRENTONPERIOD
ORC  STEPHENAUSTIN  PIR
BLOCH  PLOT  PATES  SOSO
EIRE  ALUM  COTES  MALTS
REDROVER  AHLEN  VALISE
GEOID  BRAID  PAGE
SCRAPS  BEERS  COLUMBUS
COALS  CANAL  POLES  ONE
RAPS  LITTLEROCKS  ASIA
UTE  LORIS  SAMOS  ATTAR
BISMARCK  STIPA  PILOTS
AINE  CHOSE  MORAN
LAMINA  PHONE  LAMENTED
ABELE  VIEWS  BATE  TENO
TASS  TOEYE  RICH  CARTS
ELA  WALTERRALEIGH  REA
ROBERTLANSING  LOAFING
ANIMARE  NUDGE  DEPLETE
LESSPAY  EPEES  ASSURES
```

76

```
GROG  JOCKO  POCUS  CAJOLE
REMO  USHAK  IRANI  PRUNED
AGNI  THEYALEBULLDOGSONG
SLINKS  PER  DIKE  ATREE
SEATO  TIBIA  FIT  NOLA
OHHELL  DARN  PADISHAH
LITTLEMISSBLUEBIRD  HULA
ARAH  FPA  HAIG  ICY  GAMOW
MEMENTO  MACC  IDO  DIDOES
INAWAY  MONKEYS  TWOFERS
AERIE  JAR  BOLA  AUTO
SEAL  BONNYBLUEFLAG  NATO
DIRE  SEAU  OAF  LTCOL
RUBBISH  ATECROW  BOHEME
BALLET  UGH  GOAT  ROBERTA
ADEUX  TRA  POLK  AER  BROS
NAME  WHOBLEWOUTTHEFLAME
GRAYDAWN  ERNS  AMADOU
OONA  VIM  SAXON  XEBEC
PAINT  CHAS  MUD  MYSORE
ANDDARKBLUEISHEREE  IRON
STEERA  AURIC  OVERT  DAST
SHARDS  REESE  CADIZ  EXES
```

77

```
GOPAST  TOLA  MOST
MATADOR  ABACUS  CIPHER
ELIZADOOLITTLE  ORIOLE
SOO  HOVEL  HUNT  LAUREL
ASST  MERCY  PATIO  MTGE
SHEEN  SHUN  SENSE  WAT
LEAK  IMAS  ROSINA
ATLARGE  EARTH  NATIVE
RHO  ALEAF  ROIL  LEVEES
CEN  LONG  LOCKED  LARRY
ORGS  WEEHAWKENNJ  LAIC
LEILA  DROPSY  TEEN  DEE
ASSERT  SLAB  HOSEA  ISE
ELEGIT  TRUDI  TRICOTS
ATONER  OREG  RSVP
TIN  SILIC  GAHN  ELATE
INDO  NEGRI  FLORA  SCOT
ACCUSE  HENS  IRENE  EKA
RAISES  TAKEAGIANTSTEP
ASTERS  SKETCH  TAURINE
HYLA  DIET  ASIANS
```

78

```
A B R A S E ■ B E L A ■ ■ P O E T ■ A P T S
C U E M A N ■ H U R O N ■ B U R R O ■ W A R T
E S S O I N ■ E R I C A ■ A S T R O L O G E R
T H E I C E M A N C O M E T H ■ ■ E L E M E
W E D ■ A I D E S ■ T H E P A C E ■ B O A ■
O S A R ■ C O R O N A E ■ S O S O ■ D O R M
■ N E H R U ■ N E W S P A P E R B O Y S ■
T O O S M O O T H ■ I L I A ■ P A R O L ■
A W N ■ M T N ■ E N T ■ A L L Y ■ E S C A R P
J E S T E R ■ P O H ■ N E A ■ A S S E G A I
■ A T O ■ R A G E S ■ S O U P Y ■ O R E ■
B O N G ■ D O C T O R Z H I V A G O ■ A G E D
U N I ■ A D L A I ■ I O L E S ■ N O B ■
L E S A C R E ■ C P O ■ V E G ■ D U E T T O
G R I G R I ■ F A I N ■ E D A ■ B E T ■ O U R
■ L I V R E ■ L E A R ■ S T A N D E R B Y
T H E D E E R S L A Y E R ■ H I T O N ■
T R O T ■ R E N O ■ C A R A M E L ■ A T T S
R I M ■ A S K S F O R ■ N I C E A ■ H I C
I B E A M ■ T H E B E G G A R S O P E R A
N U R S E R Y M E N ■ A R E N T ■ F L O R A L
A N U T ■ A D A N O ■ S I R E E ■ A I D E D E
L E N O ■ P S T S ■ T E S T ■ T O S S E R
```

79

```
■ I D A S ■ M O P S A ■ ■ R E D B E A R
■ N O M E ■ A R R E T E ■ I D E A M E N
E D W I N ■ G R O W I N G U P A B S U R D
L U N G I N G ■ S E N N A S ■ M I S ■
S C H O L A ■ O I D ■ E V A N ■ T O U T S
A T I ■ E R A S T U S ■ E G A L ■ S N E E
S E L S ■ I F S ■ P H I L E M O N ■ D S C
■ E L E V A T E D ■ E T E ■ E X E G E T E
S A D E ■ E T A ■ S I D E D ■ D O R A D
■ L U N A R ■ N A T O ■ S R I ■ E T T E
F A L L O F T H E H O U S E O F U S H E R
U N T O ■ T H M ■ M O S T ■ P A R S E ■
N A H U A ■ E S T O P ■ L A P ■ A L B S
C R E S T O F ■ E S S ■ O V E R L O O K
H E W ■ T R A P N E T S ■ I R E ■ W A I F
A T A T ■ A L E E ■ O P P O S E R ■ R T E
L A Y O F ■ L A B S ■ E O N ■ V E N D R E
■ P U P ■ C R O T A L ■ R E N E W A L
H I G H E R T H A N A K I T E ■ A V A I S
U N O A R E D ■ T O U C H E ■ T E L L ■
B I G T O P S ■ S P E E D ■ A R K S ■
```

80

```
A M O R E T ■ C O M O ■ S A G A ■ P O R E S
L A M I N A ■ A V E R S ■ E V I L ■ A S A N A
T R I A L B A L A N C E ■ D O L L A R S I G N
O C T ■ A B I L L ■ A R T I C L E S ■ A M I D
N O S T R I L S ■ V A L E ■ E P I ■ E N E
■ A G E E ■ C A B I N E T S ■ I R O N E D
U N C L E S ■ T O N A L ■ P A R E N T S ■
R O U E S ■ S I M O L E O N ■ I D E S T ■
S E T S ■ S E L E N E ■ T O N N E R ■ A P I S
A L A ■ S E N T ■ T R I E S ■ C R E D O
■ M O L A S S E S ■ C E D E S ■ R A I N E D
E L E V A T E ■ C A L O R I C ■ B A N A N A S
R E L E T S ■ B O R E D ■ C E R E M O N Y ■
O D O R S ■ C O L O N ■ O L P E ■ W H F
S A N S ■ T A L E N T ■ S T E A L S ■ B I O L
■ T O A S T ■ G O L C O N D A ■ F O S S A
S T E L L A E ■ A U L I S ■ P A L E S T ■
C A R P A L ■ D E C A N T E D ■ A R L O ■
A M A ■ S E S ■ M I N G ■ C L A S S P I N
L A V O ■ S E R E N A D E ■ B E L I E ■ I R I
C R E D I T C A R D ■ O N E A S Y S T R E E T
A I R E D ■ C A G E ■ N O R I A ■ E T E R N E
R A S S E ■ O D E R ■ S E E R ■ D O S S E R
```

81

```
■ H A B L A ■ A T A V I S M ■ L A P O F
■ V A L U E S ■ R E T I N U E ■ I M I N O
B A R B R A S T R E I S A N D ■ M I N E R
U N D E R F I R E ■ P A S S A G E ■ S S E
R Y U N ■ S A S S ■ E E L Y ■ S A L S
G A P ■ P E T I T P O I N T ■ P A W N E E
■ D O Y E N ■ R U N S ■ L E D G E ■
S L A K E D ■ R U N N E R ■ P E A N ■
S C A R E D ■ W I N C E ■ I C E C R E A M
T U N E R ■ D A G G E R L O O K S ■ E V E
A R C S ■ B O B O ■ A T E E ■ A D I T
I V E ■ S P E A R H E A D E D ■ F I L A R
R E C O L O R S ■ A N T E D ■ T O R E R O
■ O T O E ■ H O T E L S ■ H E R E S Y
P A R T A ■ F E R O ■ E A S T S ■
I M P E N D ■ A R R O W S M I T H ■ R A H
A M O R ■ A C L E ■ S T E R ■ R I L E
N O R ■ S H E L V E R ■ A N Y O N E F O R
I N A N E ■ S W O R D O F D A M O C L E S
S I L E X ■ T E L L O F F ■ P I T I E S
T A S T Y ■ A T T E S T S ■ E T A T S
```

82

```
T O A D S ■ ■ B R O ■ I R A N I C ■ A S A D
O M N I U M ■ H O E D ■ S E N O R A ■ R O D E
P A Y D A Y W A Y L A Y N A Y S A Y ■ E M A N
O H M Y ■ O A T ■ S O C S ■ I S O G E N S
P A O D E ■ R E G A L E ■ H U B S ■ D A F O E
S H R O P ■ A D I R E F I R E W I R E ■
H A E ■ T E E V E E S ■ R O T A ■ A N D W O E
O H M ■ S O C I A L ■ B A R ■ V B S ■ W I N
P A I R ■ N O T ■ A M I ■ S E A T ■ M I L T
■ N E W ■ N A E ■ A G T ■ P W R ■ H A L S E
W H I T E C O L L A R D O L L A R H O L L E R
H E M I D E M I S E M I Q U A V E R S A V E R
A L O N G S I D E T O G U I D E T H E R I D E
T O D A Y ■ C O N ■ T R E ■ S S T ■ S I E
H I E S ■ P A L E ■ I S A ■ A S B ■ A W N S
A S S ■ E L I ■ S A G ■ D E V O T E ■ W O E
S E I S M O ■ D R E W ■ M A K E F U N ■ H R E
■ M A I N P L A N E L A N E ■ A G O O D
L I M N S ■ E E N S ■ E R A S E D ■ M O L E Y
A N O T H E R ■ A I M S ■ ■ E E E ■ A L A D
P U R A ■ A C O B B L E J O B L L W O B B L E
U S A F ■ T H R I L L ■ I D E S ■ A R I O S E
P E L E ■ S E T T E E ■ G E T ■ ■ S T O O D
```

83

```
J U T S ■ R A C E D ■ E B O N D ■ S M E W
A N A K ■ E T H A N ■ V I N C E ■ O U Z O
U R B I ■ T H E V A N I T Y O F ■ F E I N
N U L ■ T H O S E ■ I L E X ■ L L A N O S
T H E W O R S T ■ A C E S ■ P A I R S ■
■ T A R O ■ E A G E R ■ A R T I S T I C
C H A I R W A R M E R ■ F L O E ■ O E N O
H E L L S ■ S T E R ■ B L O B ■ A G R O N
A R K S ■ D U O S ■ C L O S E R T O ■
S E E ■ H O R N ■ R H E A S ■ A T O L L S
S O R B I L E ■ F O I S T ■ D I E D O U T
E N S U R E ■ R I A N T ■ B O N N ■ U G O
■ R E S P O N S E ■ D E W Y ■ S N A P
C A S E D ■ H U N T ■ S I D E ■ L I G N I
A L M A ■ L A G S ■ S T O O L P I G E O N
P L E U R I S Y ■ S C A R F ■ R O I L ■
■ A C U T E ■ C O U P ■ R U I N L I K E
G A R R E T ■ S O L D ■ V O L E S ■ Z E P
A M I A ■ L A M P O O N I S T S ■ M A N O
Z I N C ■ E R O S E ■ A L E R T ■ O R Y X
E D G Y ■ R A G E D ■ M E S A S ■ D D A Y
```

84

```
SAGES SAMBA RESAW CACTI
CURLY TRAIL OSELA ARLES
ADAMSNEEDLE JACKSONCENT
LIN TONSIL EAU AHSO VOL
POTIONS SEMIS ALIS MERE
IDLE LOTUS CLINICAL
ANNEE FIN REDOING ALAMO
MOAN VARAN NUGGET RENEW
INITIATIVE HRON OPPIDAN
RADICLE EOZOON ENSEMBLE
CHI INLAW SWEDE PAIR
CST SAJOU GEM INCUR YES
ATRI NONES REPLY DAB
SOUTACHE MAJLIS MORELLO
ALMADEN LIRA MOTIVATION
BEALE STERIC ANITA TNUT
ANNIE OATCAKE SLY RECTO
CAMENIGH ETAPE CERO
ARAN IGLO STALE TUSSLED
SOP HERS PES STUART NMU
HOOVERAPRON HARRISONRED
ESTER SINUS OCEAN REESE
STEED SNARE CELLO EDDAS
```

85

```
REPASTE LIEDER DACHA
ELECTED ANGRIER AGUES
CAPTIVEAUDIENCE TARAS
LITANY TRUSS EYRE TRI
ANA GESTES SAD ERSATZ
MELD SEAL ACCESS WISE
ESKER TRELLIS OATEN
MILS DIOR INTHERED
SPIGOTS PACING ITALY
VIE ASHEN FLORA OLIVE
IMAS TELEG ELAND YSER
LINER SAURY ARDOR ERS
MAUVE THREES EDUCERS
ANTENNAS ALOP ARTY
GRIEG ASPIRIN SACCO
ALAE HEAVES ORCA SLOP
FOLDER SAP FRIERS ELP
FUL BURT AGUAS MAGALO
ODETO BEHINDTHESCENES
RERUN IRONAGE CORTEGE
DRYAD NETTED AFEARED
```

86

```
AVOIDS RAINS OFFA FIRMS
CATNIP INTOW NAIL ASHOT
MARSEILLAISE SUNBONNETS
ELA STULMS EMEND UBOAT
FREE STETS BTES
DAV BIAS TOILS BILLYJOE
INEVERY BURSE SEEIT UPA
AGNATE EARTHENWARE SPIT
DEULS ANNES AONE WHINE
ELSE PRATE AEROS WHITEN
MAS NEPTUNESCUP THERES
FLORAE TAR BOILER
ALLIED MERCURYLAMP SCS
MAYORS TEREK HEADS EBON
ARTYS ARAG PENNY SCENE
NORD PLUTOCRATIC LECAMA
SNA FROES ROTOS MITERED
ESPALIER GAMER DASH DNS
TOSS ALTAR LENT
METOO PREEN LISTED MAT
SATURNALIA THEMOONSTONE
PRUNE REAM ICANT TCARTS
TINED MASS CANSO OSAGES
```

87

```
CRESS MESH BESTS
SHUTUP DACHA WALKING
PENCILPUSHER ARMINARM
URN TARS OLDTIMES PEA
DRIP TOTS FRATER BRAT
SYNOD PENS OPEN WROTE
GNAT RUMPLED CHILLS
SAWDUST BILLS FREELY
ALA BAIT LOS GRIEF
ROTC REUSED DOUBLINGS
AHEAD PRAY ROTI SNARE
HARROWING YACHTS GROW
RAINS DEN SELF RAE
SWILLS COAST DIAMOND
UPHOLD FOGHORN PLOW
POOLS BLUE MEOW LAMBS
BILE FRYPAN SWIG NILE
OLE PHIBETES ISNT NUN
WELLTODO DRESSPARADES
ROYALLY OVATE SURETE
TEHEE GARY HEADS
```

88

```
ANGLE RIATA HADES ADAGE
FORAY ONRED ADULT DIVAN
ALICEISLAND NELLANDVOID
RATE TAEL SADLY RELENTS
DART PURSE ASWE
NASTILY CAPRA AVIS UMBO
INAWAY PATTYWAGON CAIRN
CORAL TANTO HIC ARNIE
ERAS ONCE FLANAGAN NAG
NAH AMUSE PIE DARTLING
EKE BERYLLINGALONG CESS
NEAR EEL ALI OILS
MADS CLARAFICATIONS KIM
ERITREAN ELY ABUSE INE
DAP ARCATURE GNAT ERST
ABIES EOS HAIRS ACTII
LITUP EMMAGRATES SECEDE
SAYS DAIS LUNES SCOLDER
ORRA BONDS ETON
STAPLES MUSTY AVER POSH
HELENWHEELS MARIANHASTE
ALONE OSAGE ALACK ARSON
NATTY TOTED NESTS DROPS
```

89

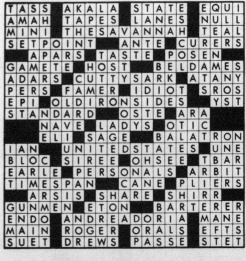

```
TASS AKALA STATE EQUI
AMAH TAPES LANES NULL
MINI THESAVANNAH TEAL
SETPOINT ANTE CURERS
APARS TASTE POSEN
GAMETE HOST BELDAMES
ADARS CUTTYSARK ATANY
PERS FAMER IDIOT SROS
EPI OLDIRONSIDES YST
STANDARD OSTE ARA
NAVE LADYS OTIC
ELI SAGE BALATRON
IAN UNITEDSTATES UNE
BLOC SIREE OHSEE TBAR
EARLE PERSONALS ARBIT
TIMESPAN CANE PLIERS
ARSIS SHARE SHIRR
GUNMEN ETON BARTERER
ENDO ANDREADORIA MANE
MAIN ROGER ORALS EFTS
SUET DREWS PASSE STET
```

90

```
APPT   ESSE  FLAMS  SIMBA
PULES  ONEIN AUTOS  KNEAD
PLASTICTABLECLOTH   ISTLE
OSU  INHALE NEURO   SETSIN
SEDANS DARED     RHODA
ERISTIC BISCUITMIX  NOTI
  THEDAY ACUITIES  STRUT
   RENE   ETNEAN  CAPERS
TAD RNWYS  AMS   BOLOGNA
DEFENSE EASELS   AUDIT
GROFE  DOLLAR    CRAVATS
SNORT PAPERNAPKIN  ATRIA
STOGIES  EGOIST   TOADY
  SALAT BASALT  BREEDER
LENTILS LEM   OSTEO  SED
AMIENS SOLIDS    RAMA
MINDS SPEEDERS  ANALOG
PLOT  SNOWMOBILE  SNIPING
  UNHAT    ASURE  TERROR
ROBROY  FIDOS  ROMAIN ASE
AWAKE FREEZEDRIEDCOFFEE
REBEL DERMO  DECEM  REFIT
ADAYS RESIN  EDAR   DENS
```

91

```
MUSHER  RANCOR  COASTS
ORIOLE  SOMEONE AMULET
DALLAS  ALETTES BIKINI
INKY OFTEN THIBET  DON
SIE GLUES  FEODOR  BERG
TANTRUMS TARRED  FUSSY
  RATE HELPS  YARD
DERIVE PALSIES  DOGMA
ENEMY SULLEN  EMOTIONS
CADS SHRIMP  PROPHETIC
AMS PLASTERSAINTS  OLE
MONOLOGUE ECLATS  GRIN
PROLAPSE SMOOTH  TREND
SWINE DEMILLE  PRUDES
VEDA MISDO  PLAN
CADET GUILES  BOOMTOWN
OMER TENNIS  SALTS  BOE
ROB MADDEN  UPSET  ALOW
ARABIC INGENUE  INSIDE
LATENT ECLAIRS  NEIGES
SLEEKS SEYTON   GERENT
```

92

```
COEDS ASPEN SWATSAT FTS
ONTAP SNIDE HASHISH AHA
ZENDA CONES ASTENSE CIR
DADDYIWANTADIAMONDRING
YEO PRI  NELL   SIENNA
SOLIDGOLDCADILLAC EDGES
AMA ARO  URN  LOP  RUSS
ANITA AWHALE ABELE OPTO
RICHEST AUSABLEFORKS
ENTERED  AFT   RELEASE
CHIC ADA ESTS EMS ESSEX
HIGHLY MINKSTOLE DEFINE
ALLIA APT APEX ABO OATS
STUNNED SAL   ITNEVER
CANDYISDANDY  REDMANS
FISH ASONE LEERAT SETUP
ASTI SUR FLU  CHE  ONE
RIALS PEARLOFGREATPRICE
ANGLER  PAON  AIT  TOO
PLEASESIRIWANTSOMEMORE
AIM ALAMODE AHAND AMISH
RNA MARINER MELES DENSE
TEN EXETERS ERASE EDGAR
```

93

```
MAIDS NAPA  ALOP  REBAR
INSET IRONCLADS  EARLE
SOLER MOONLANDINGSITE
SLADES SHOULD  EREBUS
YEN APSE MAG WEE  ESE
DEMIT IMP  READER
SPUN TERNES AMI  TAMPA
TEND SEATS ENCL  SPOOL
ADIME PRESENTEES TULE
RAVED SER VICEROY NYC
LENES  CREDO   PASTE
AIR RACCOON LOA  LEASH
LEST CORNSTALKS UNITE
TREES RUTS BERLE  SNEW
ASSET ASI NOGOOD ERRS
SULLEN ERE  PIEDA
BAM DAS ELA  FELT  IDS
OREADS  NEROLI  EARLET
REALESTATEAGENT PEWEE
ACTOR HEARTLINE  ENARM
HAYES ORLY ERST  STYES
```

94

```
SCAPA QUIT WHILOM  SHOE
HAVOC UNTO HECATE HENRY
ILIAC ADEL IRONON EXTRA
FLA OGLE ASCEND TIP HAP
TANTRUM MUCH  PITH  ETE
ODA DEGUST  ELOGE  GUS
FORHIMHATHTHINNENOROOME
ORION OVI SALADA  EDH
RET GOBIES LESE  ASSORTS
AGATTU DROLL AMAT WHEAT
ROSA  ROBB  IRISH  ELL
CHRISTMASEVEISCOMEANDLO
HOI ASIDE  ETRE  ECTO
OBOLI TERM ORATE THWART
POTENCY VISA MALAYA ZOO
NTH FICKLE BIT  VROUW
ONESMALLCHILDFROMHEAVEN
FAR AQUAE  SPIRIT  AYN
AVE TUNG  ELIZ  QUETSCH
TAW TEA VETOED GATS ARE
UHHUH TIESUP ADIT ELCID
BOONE ISRAEL YOGA EARED
SNOW CAYUSE STIR  NYASA
```

95

```
SLAP OBEYS  BAYS  FORA
LOLA FUGUE  GALOP  AMIS
ABOLTFROMTHEBLUE  DECK
VAGARIES TINES  CHINKS
TENN RINDS  TION
PAGING SINGE  BRAGGART
AMIND FINGERNAILS  SOI
NOVE SAGS  URNS  SCUP
TRI ONTHESQUARE  MORES
SENTRIES LUNGE  OATEN
GOADS BOITE  ARROW
STOLE CRETE  EMBALLED
BAHTS DOESONESBIT  ORE
RUES MEED  ATIT  SOIE
IDA SAWDAYLIGHT  BUSED
MIXTURES  AIDES  DURESS
AVID SNEER  ORIG
GOTHAM TACNA  STYLISTS
ALUI BURIESTHEHATCHET
MINT ATANY EARED  AONE
YOGI SEPT  SPARS  LEST
```

96

```
CRS ALES JINX AME
QUICKLIME ONEANDONE
PULVERIZED INSTALLING
RAVENS ARGON GINGER
AVERT ARGENTINE BAMRA
HERS RIDE EUROPA RAGS
ART JARS STREWING SYS
ZYME PAWED LOOM
GREENS BOLOS JADEITES
RELAX HELOT PATERNITY
ABEL PERIPHERIES AMUR
DEMOCRATS RAILS CREDO
SLITHERS LERES THESES
SIFT KEELS DIET
SAC CAITIFFS SUEZ DAS
IMAM BEATTO SPED SERT
TAROS RESOURCES CHOSE
AZALEA VRAIC TRADER
REMITTANCE GETHSEMANE
SENTENCER ENRAPTURE
LEO TOSS STEM ESS
```

97

```
FIREI TODAY WEWHO INIGO
ANAGS AMIDO AVION NOSAD
RINGA READY YELLS KAAMA
STANDINGROOMONLY BESHE
ISTOOD AYN AFTS GODHELP
GRIS ANA APO TRAP
THEPEOPLETHEMOBTHECROWD
SONO MOORES AMAH DOA
ABDUL TSIN ONEARM MYNAH
RETRIM SCOWL SLIES SONE
AETAS IRIDS LATA TEA
AHBROKENISTHEGOLDENBOWL
CAL NERO HORAS EMCEE
URET SISAL SANTA STANZA
PASHA NOSEAT DECS SLAYS
EAT NEON SHOTUP AIMS
JOSTLINGANDBEINGJOSTLED
ARTO NUS FUN ISEE
SNOWMAN PERM QUA ITCAME
EPEES MYCUPRUNNETHOVER
EVORA LEROI SATAN IMALL
TENON ADULT VSIGN TEHEE
CRAFT POSES PILES ERIES
```

98

```
PLATINUM SLOB TROUTS
PROVOLONE LAVA HISSAT
REVERENCE IRED INHERE
ISERE MAT DARNING ORE
MAST BASIC DESK ANER
AGE CON NARROWMINDED
LETSON GROANS TIES
HIER PRATE ROC NIE
AMANDA LACE LOVESONG
GRIDS TEACH FUSE PONG
ARNI BLACK TAPER IDEE
BIDE RISE VALET DELED
OVERTAKE WALL TRADED
REX HIE CELLI AERO
PEAN MELLON LINAGE
FASTTHINKING PAN DEV
MANS REST ESSAY FATE
ELD BURNETT HUM RAMON
SLICES ARAM OPERATIVE
TENANT MERE RELEGATED
ANGLES EDEN TRAVELER
```

99

```
CAPES SIRAT SCALE ATIME
OPART INUSE EAGER BONER
HARRYTRUMANCAPOTE LLAMA
ACTS HERON ALERT BALLES
NEY SANER OVERA GAZELLE
SOLI DOER AUGER
PATRICKHENRYJAMES REC
BOGOTA REGAN ELIS CLARA
ALIA CARA UNITS ROBOT
JESSEJAMESCAGNEY CERISE
ART BUSES ALLYN BLANDER
LONER HOI BLUME
ANOINTS ASONE CRANE SAM
SARNIA OTTOGRAHAMGREENE
ISLET START LANE ODER
DIODE LALA OPTIC DOSAGE
ESP EARLWARRENHARDING
BANTU GEAR NOON
CHARLIE BOGGY CLAIR BAH
HAROLD BURRO TRACT MANO
OVENS NORMANTHOMASHARDY
IRATE AIMED RICER ANGEL
RELET GLARE SNERD GEESE
```

100

```
SCOLD PARTED CHAM
STEREO ILOILO HALAS
CLARAANNFOWLER AVERTS
HERON CAFES MITRE IRA
EATS TOILS WESER SEAN
AVE THULE NANDA ONDIT
TERRIERS MANTA DHARNA
EAST ROTE YOUARE
ALLURE TOTARA ARRESTS
RAINA BASIL NITRE SIP
IDLE TULAFINKLEA BLEU
ELY CURER EELER FLEUR
LECTERN YOWLED SLURPS
HOLISM SOLD RHEE
STALIN ALTOS JOUSTING
PAULA BRAID BUNCH TON
ORCS CEIBA CRACK GETA
RAH PIANO CHINA ORRIS
TWOBIT ARCHIBALDLEACH
AISLE DERIDE LEGATE
NAYS EDITED IRATE
```

101

```
CROUP AMPHI WHEE HAWAII
HORSEPLAYER HANDMEDOWNS
INSIDETRACK ODDSANDENDS
DONAS ELKE SAMOA SISS
GLENNS DOW ANIMUS
EYE TUG THAN NAP SRA
NOTBYALONGSHOT AGT CHAR
EMCEE OHIO TOZ ECHOIC
RAU BEAK SADIE REELS
ASST PLAYTHEFIELD IAMB
ITCH TINES VAN INSPAIN
MAR TONGS MEX TOTUP KRA
SKATING WAN SODOM BEDS
ETRE UNDERTHEWIRE URSA
ASCUS AEONS OMEN NOR
TOHEAR SET EBER BREAD
RUED OFT ACROSSTHEBOARD
ITS SUR STHS ION UKE
STEAMY EEL CEDRES
OMOO NANAS ODOR ONALL
TRIPLECROWN DISCJOCKEYS
INTHESADDLE HOMESTRETCH
GOESAT ISSY ANOLD ESTOP
```

102

```
AMASS  EARACHES    HAREM
LIVEANDLETLIVE     TAMARA
PRECIOUSSTONES     ONEDAY
ARR  LOCO  SIGNSUP  NITA
COST  NERO  SETINMOTION
AREAS  DAVIT    ODOR
  RHS  NINEMAN  VISTAS
FLAGONS  DARERS  IBERIA
LAMEDUCK  SENT  SEINERS
ATAS  BOOS  DEISTS  SALS
RED    ULUS  SETA    SAI
EDAM  TRINES  RUGA  JUNE
SAVAGES  DRAB  DEPLORES
UTAHAN  WAFFLE  STALEST
PETALS  RESEALS    SOT
    ETAH  PEELS  SEATS
EARNSAMEDAL  CUPS  DRAW
ALAI  TEARGAS  GALL  RIA
RENEGE  REACHAGREEMENT
TRACES  SAVEONESBREATH
OTTER   TRESSURE  PARSE
```

103

```
ANITA  ANNAS  PROA  ARS
MOLAR  MEANT  REBS  BEV
SATIRE  BETSYROSSHOUSE
ATLAS  CODA  EWE  OUSEL
BEACONHILL  WALLSTREET
OUT   EASE  FOCSLE  DDE
TREASURE  TOOT  SCAB
    SIR  GIRD  OREN
MUTT  LILTS  CONCLUDE
GENRE  SALEM  RUD  LARA
ALSO  EMBARCADERO  ENID
GOAD  NEO  HIVES  RICES
ENFORCER  PERMS  USED
    EMIL  ENES  LIL
  EVAS  PARD  PRUNELLA
SCB  SMEARY  GLEN   OAR
THECAPITOL  ORANGEBOWL
ALLAH  TEL  RIND  TOKYO
GOLDENTRIANGLE  CHASES
ERE  AMEN  DEALT  LOSER
DOS  DUNE  DANES  ESTES
```

104

```
GASPE  ISEE  ENABLE  DAMAS
ADAMS  CARBONATION  PHONY
BACKTHEWRONGHORSE  LEMON
BRODIE  GONER  METRE  REDO
YES  MATIN  HOMIN  GRINNED
  BATON  COSEC  BILLET
MAKETHE  BURST  GAZES  OAS
EMILE  DEEPSEATUBE  EDUCE
DELISH  BARED  HIED  ESCE
ORLE  ADANO  ICONS  RAIDER
CIT  RIANT  INURE  CUDGEL
SCHOOLROOMS  SNAKEDANCES
AERIES  WILDS  FRIED  IRT
ENFOLD  ENLAI  POOLS  ISAR
DEAN  TREE  SPAWN  TANITE
ASTOR  HORSECOLLAR  SLOES
MET  AMESS  DOSES  ATTENDS
  ESTATE  NEUTS  CARET
ANDTEAR  BARRE  LABOR  ASS
ROCA  SABAS  ARSEN  LOATHE
ARABA  CONSIGNTOOBLIVION
ISLAM  ESCAPESONES  DOMES
LEFTY  SCOUTS  MESA  SWEDE
```

105

```
SHASTA  ICTUS  ICIEST
ELUVIAL  NOOSE  MUSTARD
SUGARPLUMTREE  BRESLAU
TIGS  ESTATE  CHORE  TIP
ACE   PITA  GAUDY  NONE
REDO  RICE  PATSY  SAFER
  ABACA  PERCH  PANTRY
COTTAGE  DEPTH  PORCH
OCHERS  GRAPH  DELAYERS
WAYNE  TEASE  DELES  EEK
ISM  GINGERBREAD  AVE
SEE  ALBIA  MAIDS  STREW
HYLOZOIC  DILLS  QUATRE
  AMORA  HANKY  PUNCHER
STEELY  FORTH  BRAKE
OSAGE  PUNTS  SOOT  TASS
LACA  MORES  DIRT   CWO
ARE  TELLY  ORDERS  ORAL
RIORITA  BASILRATHBONE
SNUGGER  ELEVE  CERISES
ASTERS  ESSES  TSETSE
```

106

```
5THS  AHILL  COMM  NAIAD
ORAE  PODIA  2ADAY  ESOPUS
5ANDIOCENT  3MENONAHORSE
OSSIP  KAYE  SPONGER  POEM
HAMITES  ROK  NARO  SENSE
  EERY  FINIS  AMOUR
QUINCY  DOSADOS  MEDICINE
UNITE  SIRE  DATA  NOTEMAN
EDNA  WISER  OPENAIR  NANO
DEAL  HAM  OPTIMA  ETNAS
ARM  REMISED  ASTO  CRESS
  13ER  STLO  DORR  EARP
ALFIE  SEEL  SNAPOUT  ORG
BILIN  SERVED  HUT  CIEL
AMIE  DISEASE  AGORA  ASEA
STOLLEN  STOM  PLUS  STOSS
SONDELIS  EMIGRES  STONES
  SALSA  ETAIN  THE9
ABOYS  TRIS  ALL  HEARTAS
TANS  BEANIES  ISIN  IAGOS
4LETTERWORDS  5CENTCIGAR
OTTERS  ANODE  TIRED  LINT
SOMAT  KENO  HOARS  SEDA
```

107

```
GUARD  ACT  STAIRS  CANOPY
OSTIA  FOR  CUTLET  ALBINO
NUTTYPINE  ANTIQUEDEALER
NAH  CORNELL  SAUCERS  YUK
ELENORE  BULB  NICLE  LAME
  BOAC  SAMOAN  TOY  HUMOR
ARMCHAIR  PRICES  DIRE
URIAH  YOKE  ODES  FEDERAL
KIND  RUSTIQUE  FIFE  ILE
ELK  APEX  ONUS  VASE  ICON
  EME  DICE  RESTAURANT
COMMODE  PLANTER  STRANGE
ADAMSAPPLE  MOST  EIN
MYNA  GOES  EIRE  MADS  TOE
ALT  CODA  STROLLER  BUDS
SELVAGE  SEHR  LOAN  CODES
  EASY  SENIOR  UNICOLOR
LAPSE  FHA  CREDIT  ALAR
EDIT  GUESS  SIRS  CROSSED
SHE  JANACEK  SESSION  EAR
SECRETDRAWERS  APPLIEDTO
ORENSE  EPERDU  YAP  ALAIN
NESSUS  REDOSE  SRI  LYNNE
```

108

```
WISTFULLY DRATITS TOM
AVERAGEUP RIGHTEOUSLY
NICECHAPS YPOTENTIALS
LETME PAINLESSLY GRAT
YDS SAY LAY LEN
NAMEDAY OPA ADAPTS
COMO DARN GLOP RUNHIT
ABET TRET UDDER NIDA
VITAM IIIA INFIDELIC
ARA GROUNDLESSLY
SPERO GOLDSMY LOWLY
SAIDIMMANUEL RIO
PRESENTLY DOOM OFWAR
ROME SEOUL VIBE TLRS
ODANTE RUBY ENON LYCO
DENTON ART WRIGGLY
EGO DAD ISA SAG
ITTY OCOMEOCOME DAKUA
MUHAMMADALI SUMMARILY
SAIDMARTIAL ELECTORAL
ONS CROSSLY DANDAILEY
```

109

```
STILE TASSO TIETO QUARE
KEMAL OTTER ENROL UNDUE
ITALIANHERO CHINESEWALL
NEMO RIENS FUOCO HERMES
AGENT GIMPS LANA
MATADORS PHASE FOREPAWS
ELUDES NOOSE BUSED RAP
DORIA SWISSCHEESES RAGA
INKED WISETO WHIR GABOR
ASIT OILER VEAL BONING
SOS ENGLISHHORNS ATEASE
HOMES OUT RUMEN
CITRON ITSGREEKTOME NAM
ABOARD NETS AROSE NIDI
NEWLY PLAY CURARE SIGHS
TRES SIAMESETWINS ETHEL
AIL SWATS HITAT SARTRE
BASELINE SILEX ENCLOSED
AUTO PINER TREES
IATRIC TREND LEARN EZIO
FRENCHLEAVE PERSIANLAMB
ANNEE ORDER ESSEN GENII
TENDS PROSY STERE SCENT
```

110

```
AMOS MESSAGE JASPER
COUTH SETUPSET ULTIMA
ULTRA PROMISER SPINBY
PELISSES DUSE ACHES
OCHOS AVERT SICKED
SPOKEN SHIRE MALAYA
HAKES CHARY TAMES DNA
IRON WRUNG OUTOF SPAR
EMU BEATDOWNBEAT WIRE
SATIRIZE ACER SANDS
CERE PALER MIEN
ICHOR BOCK BALANCES
POON OVERHANGOVER ONA
SOLO CENTS ORNIS SMUG
ELD LENDS LIEUS STERE
UBOATS DOSES CARIES
SPOONS WAVED CUTIN
ETHOS ARNE CARRACES
LOOKER GOTINGOT ATOLL
MOLINE ETONIANS PEMBA
ODDEST DENSELY DEEM
```

111

```
SMA MAIMS DIVAS JOWLED
CINQ ALDEN EMILE ENHALO
ACTU ILONA SPACE WEIMAR
NARA TENOR PINON ERMINE
SHAKERATTLEANDROLL WADS
EVER SWIG TEETH
CHERI STH EREBS TRIANON
HUMBLE HEIL EHEU OMAHA
AMBO TREMBLINGASPEN TAM
SPAN HUMAN NAIVEST PARE
MYRNA TEN MAPLES CURLED
ETAH MEWED AHME
CRETAN SEATER JAR ASTAB
HANS SKIDDOO BELOW ERMA
IDA QUIVEROFARROWS NOOK
CAMAU RAMI LORN WATTLE
ORIGINS ADAZE YES ETHER
ITICS NIAS HERE
BITT SHOULDOFSTOODINBED
ARHATS ATION TOPOG SORE
SEETHE KIMRI AWAKE EXAM
INTERN ICERS RECUR SISI
LEADUS NASAT SLAPS NET
```

112

```
DECOCT PLUME BATMEN
ENAMOR ELOPING ACHENE
ORRERY MASSAGE CREDIT
DOING SPITE ITAKE ISM
ABB ISAAC TANIST TULE
RESH TINE TRENCHERMEN
ASIDE CINE HELI
SOLAR LEONORA WIPER
LECTURE RAGS STREAMED
ORA DIALECT OTHO REDO
BARKINGUPTHEWRONGTREE
APIE GENT ENLARGE GAR
SINECURE DAVE SHOVELS
SALOP TARPOTS ODIST
MOTH ROPY CURES
TOTALRECALL ARMS ACME
ARAN ORACLE REPEL HEX
RIM BURGH CORES APART
SEALAB ENGAGED AVENGE
UNROLL SIERRAS HANGER
STABLE DETER ASTERN
```

113

```
COMES FEEDS SALAD GRAPE
AMATI RATIO CHOLO RAGES
BIZETSIGNAL HAYDNGOSEEK
STES ALLA ICONS NIPPERS
AILE SCOLD AIDE
AFFABLY SAIDA ERSE AZOF
MERLES LITTERBACH SHORE
ELATE TAXIS ASA EARNS
LONE MITE SCHEDULE BAT
INC SHARI ARA ISINLATE
ASK HANDELWITHCARE ITER
EWER TAI GOA RASH
ESNE BRAHMSBURSTING EME
RESTROKE EAT URGES GAR
NAT TROOPERS KAAN ERMA
AMERE LAN WILLS BRIES
NAIDS LITDEFALLA PRIERE
INNS NOAH RUTTY GRANGER
FERN DIMES BRIT
OFFERED TENOR OLIO AIME
VERDIDSHEGO RAVELROUSER
IMAGE IOTAS AREAL CRASS
DETER THESE TENTS CARAT
```

114

```
BIOG WAMP MEOW IMATMY
ARRA ISAR ALLE DISHED
MITT TINE YEDS ELPERS
ASH SHAGS WEPT SOIF
HELOT ASTI ESTA SILL
ELFISH NEATER ORTHREE
SOLE ENE CHAS LEU SOW
PRONGLESS ATI DONAT
YEW ROMEO LHAS NABOBS
ROAVE OSLO OAT AFAT
JOYSBEASTHEMONTHOFMAY
ALMS INA ATEL TESTA
SEEING YODH DRIFT YEA
ASOAK FRY SHRIEKING
ARD IVA TOFT AEF ISTO
DESERET HELIUM TINMEN
SOIL ISME OMAN ELGAR
NAIN EHEU KALES YON
TOMTOM TORR ALAN ADZE
ETAETA RULE REST LAOS
MAYDAY ORES ISTH EYAS
```

115

```
ALPACA ASPEN ANVIL RAMA
LIANAS MAINE SEATO ILES
LADYSSLIPPER PALACECARS
SRS PAYSAS MITE KAHILI
JAMESJ AMIRS ASSE
CIDER OENONE SILENCER
ONUS PUTUPONESDUKES RMA
PACT ANH INKY EASY LOCH
ASHE SHINTOS GAV POWER
LEER ANE PANE CORNEA
SCS KINGFISHERS FURNISH
STANDS NOONE MORGAN
AHEARTY QUEENSBERRY GSA
LAPRES BUSS ARE RGTS
CROON REE THETIME ELAN
APIS FOES FOAL NAN CONE
PIN COURTBOUILLONS ORCA
PATRIOTS ENTREE BUYER
ANTS BETSY TRIPUP
SPINEL OARS TIEBAR CPA
CASTLEWALK KNIGHTSSTARS
OTHE TAHOE HENRI TARPOT
TSAR STUNG ASSET ARISTA
```

116

```
LOEB DISCO FOAM BLEB
IRAE SUNTAN ANNI RAIL
DERM ADUANA TENS INDI
TOONERVILLE USANCES
SCHARF EENIE SLINGERS
ENSNARE EMILY STO
TOT TALC BLOC SINFUL
UTA ENLACE ANEMIC OVI
PERM CAROMS DEEP URUK
ACI ONETWO SPANGLE
TRANSSIBERIANRAILROAD
REDLACS SIERRA REI
ABLY OAST RIENZI GASP
IBI SCROOP IDGIVE BLA
NEBULA AGAR AMEN DEI
NAB RATES BREVIER
ENTITLES CLASP BRACTS
GOATEED CHATTANOOGA
ARIA CERO PEORIA ATOP
DING AMID SELECT REDE
SATE RAGE ENARE YSER
```

117

```
SEARCH CAPA AGA AMES
ANDAHUG CABAL LRS CROCE
MOUNTRUSHMORE FASTONTHE
ELBA RELIEVE MANWAY HOS
DYSON ENTO DEN ABIE
FASTESTGUN THEGREATRACE
APERCU PURSE RAT NIL
DELIAN ESNE RAMPART LEG
SLENDER CHEAM ISA AFAR
STOLID EXPEND HAILTO
SAJ WINESAP RISS TREES
TWOPINS RATRACE CHASERS
ANNAS AJAR ELECTRA TYE
TEATRO ATTEST EYESOF
URTH PFC RESET RETRIED
ESH SPIKIER RARE YELLOW
ABI SBS ISSUE PLEURA
RUNOFTHEMILL THEHUSTLER
URSA ESQ AYUB ARIDE
FAW ANNUAL REBUILD ARUI
FLIGHTAID APOLLOLIFTOFF
LIFES RCD RENAS SNOWSOF
ECTO EKA ADES GLOSSY
```

118

```
PASS MUCHOF POILUS
ENABLES ENROLL ARTIST
FORLOVEORMONEY ROSTER
FRT BERNE PEOPLE TSE
AMIS REED OATES LUI
CANNES TIS TIPS ADEPT
ENGIN MOTHHOLE CLUB
FORE HOES RARERIPE
BAFFLERS VAST LIMOGES
ANIL SCENEV RIIS HDS
RISE HELLENIZE CODA
BTH SANA NOMANS ORLY
EROSION TATS RATLINES
RAREBITS BOTH TEEN
CASE LICORICE NAMES
SOUSE FINS AGR BEGONE
AMT NORMS HETO ESSE
ROB MANTIS CAIRN EIN
TRANCE EASYCOMEEASYGO
REININ STONES SAPIENT
ESTERS SUNSET LEND
```

119

```
NAWAB TSARS SALPA ASFAR
ALIBI ROSIE CROON BOOLA
GIRLSCOUTSCOOKIES ARUIS
SMEE AURAE STINT STERNE
TRIPPER STIES CLEATED
SHA COED COLA HARSH
MOPPETS WOMENSCLUBS OSE
ASPIRE SHOER CLOTS AFOX
REEKS CHAPS PAUSE ANJOU
TARA TOILE DONEE GROUND
SUMMERSALTS TIRALEE
RAF IRIS HUE AONE YRS
ELASTIC STANDINGPAT
BACKIN FLIRT MONAS ACIS
ALEUT CRUDE GOMEZ PRONE
TATA CHIME SAGES HOTWAR
OSH CHEAPSKATES MANACLE
EMAIL IRUN BEST ALT
CAMETOA FANON CONSENT
AZURES DEIGN TIROL ACTI
NOSIR FIRSTGRADETEACHER
ELITE ARALU ONEAT FREAK
DECOR SKEET TARSI TERMS
```

120

```
RES LBS TREACLE SARGS
ENTAILS RANGOON SHEET
SHADROE ENDEMIC SUNNY
TARMAC OPT BROB GEOM
ANTIS APA STEERAGEWAY
ICER TRENCHER ITAL
NEDA ERN LEE ANELACES
LANA PELTING ENAMI
AGEOFDISCOVERY LADDER
CRAFT GAINERS SISLER
TART ANT DIP INGE
ETHICS CRASHED MEZEN
ACHENE THEINDIESTRADE
MILOT AGENDAS MANE
PAYCALLS AER SEI VEST
ECOL SIDEREAL EACH
GREATCIRCLE ART MASER
ROAN KNAR AMS FELINE
AMUSE ANIMALS DETENTE
SADES LEMORTE PLEDGER
SNEAK LESSEES STR SDS
```

121

```
LIFEIS CRADLE ARENOT
CAMPION LENIENT NERINES
LEPANTO OSCEOLA DARLENE
OTO EATSUP DRABBED SER
VASE SAUTES ARLES HEIDI
IRENE SPECTA GETSWINDOF
SESAME ARTICLES AIRLESS
MILA SELLER TYPEE
SCOTERS DEED ROSE AIDS
BEAR VITA TOGOUT DEGREE
APR REDUCE REMIT SUAVE
STOPIN MARGARINE STENOG
SILAS BRIEF TERRAE ITE
OMELET LISTED DEEM PAER
SERI USED SAID DESTINE
STRAD SISLER FOOL
SAVARIN CONTUSED NOISED
CREDENTIAL ITISAP KNAVE
AGREE ABBOT ENTIRE GLIB
LAD DYNAMIC EASELS ADA
ALAMEDA NOTHING DELUDES
RINGMEN ENHANCE INALINE
STRESA SENSES CAMENT
```

122

```
BKS SAAL BBC SPAR
ORE ACCESS SOLA TALE
SAILFLEETOFSPAIN ARIA
SANDEEL APRIL SNORKEL
LESS ERR ERICSON ANS
SOB SECRETS
AMBER SOOTH EIS NOSE
LOADER MAEWEST FEELER
FURSEAL REACT TRIEDTO
ANNE NEED TEHERAN SSS
TALESOFTHESEVENSEAS
LAC CONTOUR MEEK LIAS
ILLFAME PISIA SEDILIA
STEEDS BOTANIC RETOLD
POSE NER INNER TERSE
FRONTAL BRA
APE LETITGO RAM ORBS
SEXTANT UNRRA PENALTY
TRIO TOURISTCLASSFARE
RILE EBAN SEANCE MAT
ALES DER STET EPI
```

123

```
SALS COLON OBAN TAIPEH
TRAIT ALIVE FARE UNMADE
OMINO NINES FLAP STASIS
PACKUPYOURTROUBLES USES
ARLO STEER SUNLAMP
TRA IONS RATS STEPSOUT
HERESY ALP MUTE ODA RNR
ADEPT AXIOM NASA SATTE
ROASTED TWOWEEKSWITHPAY
ORCA HERE LETIN AHN
PRIMAL DORRIT RESH SONG
AES PIKE SIGHT REAP TEE
PALE PEAL SHARON LAMODE
LAB SARAH ESER DECA
INNOCENTSABROAD ESKIMOS
FIDEL HERR STEIN ARENT
ICH EPI REIN YRS AGENCY
LEOTARDS STAN MAME SEX
PATELLA APORT TADS
CAPN SEENONESEENTHEMALL
ALINES EVEN ANNUL AERIE
DANITE VIII LEONE LANDS
SIGNED ELLA TERSE ROOT
```

124

```
TRADE TIMOR RANCHED
PREMAN INURE FIREHOSE
RECANT NOSED OPERETTA
OVERGROW HOUSEPAINTER
SODA ERASE CAMEL EEL
ERE SNARED TOAD WORMY
DECREE FINN DIP
BLITHE DRIVE DILEMMA
SAINTE STORE COMENEAR
ATONED LIME WAVE HAIR
LANE HAMPSHIRE ANSA
OVER BONE TIDE LANDON
MISTRUST HONEY INDENT
EASIEST CANTO OTTERS
MSS FIDE PATTED
ASSET PISA MEDALS DEA
MAT PARCH ANOTE SEAL
BLABBERMOUTH RECREATE
LITERATE NOLAN HURLER
ENAMELED CREME ADVERT
RELATED HEROD PEARY
```

125

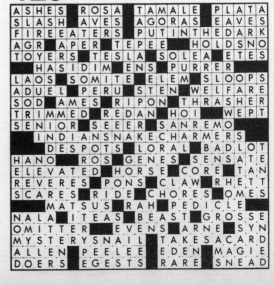

```
ASHES ROSA TAMALE PLATA
SLASH AVES AGORAS EAVES
FIREEATERS PUTINTHEDARK
AGR APER TEPEE HOLDSNO
TOYERS TESLA SOLEA ETES
HASIDIM ENS PURRER
LAOS SOMITE ELEM SLOOPS
ADUEL PERU STEN WELFARE
SOD AMES RIPON THRASHER
TRIMMED REDAN HOI WEPT
SENIOR SEEER SANREMO
INDIANSNAKECHARMERS
DESPOTS LORAL BADLOT
HANO ROS GENES SENSATE
ELEVATED HORSE CORE TAN
REVERES PONS CLAW RHETT
SCARES RIDE CHORES OMES
MATSUS RAH PEDICLE
NALA ITEAS BEAST GROSSE
OMITTER EVENS ARNE SYN
MYSTERYSNAIL TAKESACARD
ALLEN PEELEE EDEN MAGIE
DOERS EGESTS RARE SNEAD
```

126

```
PORCH BASE PARRS  TRE
ADIEU ALUM EBOAT ROES
RONDS KELP ABOMA EDEN
INCITIESFOULEDBYSMOKE
STELLAR  URNS    LETO
    LEM ARIA NEEDAREST
  BARBAROUSDISSONANCE
BALS  DRUM ECTON   DON
EMU GILAS ASHEN FAURE
EARTHDAY TRIES SILENT
   HALI GEARS MELT
REFUTE CRAKE COMMONER
ACIDS PRETE SAVES  ETA
ILO  CHEER APSE  PEON
 DARKBROWNISTHERIVER
STEARINES  OTES  OEN
   NEMO  STER ONSTAGE
CONGREGATIONOFVAPOURS
AREA ARIES DIRE ISLAS
NEAR NANAS EDER NAIVE
ALT  SMOKY DSTS ENCES
```

127

```
FLIPSIDE USSERY SCATTED
RIPSAWED NOTATE LOVEHER
ETIOLATE RUHREN EVILEYE
ETNAS ENTETE SPEE  LWOW
LESION EPHLAL APR  TIRR
DEF FUTUREPERFECT LACEY
AMI YSER NANISM  ITALK
MIRO TSANTSAS BIGWHEEL
PSYCHE NOES TEACHIN DOM
SEEAROUND DORRITS   WVA
IMWAS PSS BETAG  TALIEN
GUANASE EQUALTO ASFATAS
OFNOTE QUITE API  UNCLE
RFD ANOUILH SCHLEMIHL
SEB FLUTIST PUTA MENOTS
TABLEMAT FERNSEED AFRO
LUIGI USOPEN DDAY  TUI
HASNT SORORITYHOUSE HST
OSAN LMU 12THST  CHALET
ATMY EARP RAISEA SEEAS
GOTHURT ACROWD ITSASAFE
IOOOTOI COUPEE GOTITSET
EPOPTIC TWEEDS GRADETWO
```

128

```
STEAM ADMI SCAR SWISH
LODGE ERAS ALBO TITHE
ARDOR CURL MAIA STEEL
GEAR  SIE SUDSY  CARP
    ACACIA   DETACH
PAR ARAL SPISSKA  ORB
AMUSICAL EHEU   TAHOE
CAMPUSMARTIUS POORASA
ENBAS  ITER  CAPTURED
STANG APSES PARTHIANS
   RUBLES  TIPTOE
VESPASIAN PELES CAIRO
INNOCENT CLEO   ERROR
SCONCED QUINTUSENNIUS
BRUSH  UTES LESSONTO
YET UNTRIED PESO  GEN
   USURER  CIDERS
ALOP TONIC TAA   AMPS
HARPY JENA ANNA EXALT
ANNEE AGAR LOUD DORIA
BAERS NELL LESE ENTER
```

129

```
HASTO LEMUR ABBAS AMBLE
OLEAN INANE BLUNT CARON
PADRE MINIM CERVI TIERS
IMETALADYCOLDASIC STARK
SORELY STERE TALKTURKEY
    SORB OFAGE JAPE
SKS NEIN ARENEAR  AHA
TUQUE EIWOULDNOTWANTTOM
ABUT UNTORN AGRO  OOOOO
CLAIMS ARHAT RAIL TIMER
CARLOTS SOMA LAMA  SYN
 EETHERTWICESHEWASAM
HAM HERE IFHE  DOODADS
AMICE EGOS TRANS RUMSON
VALOR RUHR ERNANI AHME
ODELOFDECORUMIAIN SNEER
COS LATHERS DEFT  RID
   ABOU STERS SIRE
WILDERNESS ELIAS LALALA
ALOHA TNOLADYBUTIMWARUM
GAPES IDLER SATON HIERA
EVERT NOVEM ELENA ANNES
RAZES GRETA EDDYS TEARS
```

130

```
NOEL SLEPT STAR  ASTO
AURA HOARY EARL THEME
GRAYMATTER THESCARLET
   UINTA OOO ILIONE
PURPLEANDFINELINEN
ARU  DORS EON  KEEL
INSPACE RESAW DAVINCI
RATATAT MEUSE  MANGOS
  LITRES REST SONG
EDEN DREI AMAIN VIVE
SORT INANE MONET IMAM
PSST NASTY PESO OPTS
  HEAL IRIS STABLE
ASPELL MENTO ASSERTS
HOTTIPS ESTOP STATIUS
SOSO OAR HOAD    ANT
 WHITEELEPHANTSALES
DOWNON SMU  MAYAS
IVORYTOWER BLACKMAGIC
BEVEL SANE EAGRE NATO
REDE STDS TREES  AMOY
```

131

```
 PATTI PSI  PLOT  AGR
ARTHURWOOLF IONICFRIEZE
GATECRASHER CREPEHANGER
SHACK TIO AFAR PIA GALL
TARA HET CIA YELL CHIDE
   SAAR CADIZ LEE LANA
CASEIN OAR RUSK  DEEM
OXFORDANDBALLIOL MODISH
OLAF BNAI VAUD AMP ONTO
NEXT IGN HOW ELIAS GRAY
   HILL TACNA ANT DWELL
TWEEDLEDUMANDTWEEDLEDEE
IHAVE BAG TEREK  LION
RITE SAYSO WON FOG TACO
ENOL ORA FUJI COTE BLEW
DENVER KENNETHROSSTOOLE
  ELEM COIR OUT TOWELS
HITS ISH ESSEX  MEOW
PONCE STOA EHS BID OMAN
OPAL BTU VAYA LIL TWICE
REPANDERSON DRILLTOWERS
THEWILDDUCK SERGIOPOLIS
 TSP YEAH   MAE MOWED
```

132

```
A L L . I L E D . T H Y . . A M P .
O S E E . M A N O . H O E . C A R T S
E T N A . A B C S . E T A . R E S O R T
R E T R Y . O L E U M . R E A C T I O N
. R A N N . R O O T A . E O S . E B O N
C O N T E N D S F O R . R E T R O C E D E
L I D O . G I E . P V T S . F E L T .
I D O L . A S S I E R . O R B I T A L
. A P I G . A L E . V O U C H F O R
G I B E . R I D . S T E A M S . E T I O
L A B O U R A N D D O A L L T H Y W O R K
A T A R . A C T S O F . I S H . A O N E
S T R A P P E R . I M P . E V E R
I S N O T S O . N A O . T I E . K E P T
D O O N . C A N O . E R R . I N R E
C U T T H R O A T . S P E L L B I N D E R
O T H O . M R S . L E I L A . A G E D
T H E W O M A N . A D L I B . N G A I O
E T A M I N . F I B . E T O N . I R A N
R A I N S . A D O . E T R E . R E L S
. T I T . . T O R . N O S E . L D S .
```

133

```
D E S I G N . L E S A G E . C A P P . B A C H
A R E O L A . I M O G E N . A M A H . I C H O
I N Q U I S I T O R I A L . S O L I L O Q U Y
L E U . S T R E T T O . A T A S . M A T U R E
. E A T . K R E I S . C A B . R U D Y A R D
F E N N E L . A R E . B I N A T E . E P I .
L A T I N I S T . P E N D . O D D . E N A M
E G I L . Q U I N Q U A G E S I M A L . T E E
A L A . K U N . A U N T . M I L A N O . A N D
S E L E N O . S W O O S H . R E P I N . N E A
. P I R . E A R . O O P . L O G I C A L
S A L I C . A L B U Q U E R Q U E . T R E S S
T R I C K E D . M A T . O U R . S O I
U R N . E P A C T . T A B B E D . A N D M R S
R O C . R E M O R A . B R E E . A M S . O O O
D Y O . S E S Q U I Q U A D R A T E . A Z U L
Y O L K . S A U . R U N T . T I D E G A G E
. N U M . L E G S I T . G T T . I C E M E N
T H E M A K E . O A R . T A R E D . D E B
R I S Q U E . A S C I . A L I M O N Y . I T S
I N Q U I L I N E . N O L L E P R O S E Q U I
A G U A . S L O E . A N O I N T . V I S U A L
L E E T . O I N K . L A N C E S . A S S E N T
```

134

```
A M B I T S . E N T R E A T Y . B A T H S
C A R N I E . L O W E R T H E . A D H O C
T H E S O N A L S O R I S E S . O M E G A
H A R I . I L A . S I N E S . I C A N
. G U L L . N Y A C K . B R U N T
T I G H T E S T . C G S . A R T I E R
E M O T E . W H I R S . G R E A T . L A C
N A N . S T E E L E . C E L I A . T O G A
E G G S . E L O G E . O N E S . S A F E R
T O W N H A L L . D E N O T E . O T T E R
. I O U S . D O M I C A L . A M A H
M I T R E . I M P O S E . I N T E R E S T
A C H E S . B A E R . D E T E R . S W E E
M E T S . B E N N E . I N T U I T . I T E
A S H . S O R A S . U N D E R . A L L A N
E A T S I N . E N G . R O U L A D E S
T A W N Y . A D E L E . S N I P
A V I D . T R E A T . L I B . O L E S
M I N O R . T H E G R I P E S O F R O T H
E N D U E . R E C I T E R S . L A T O N A
R E S T S . A C T T H R E E . T R E P A N
```

135

```
C I V I C . D E L E D . E C C E . S T E T S
O T A R Y . O V A T E . O G H A M . T E R R A
M A D A M I M A D A M . T R I T E . O N I O N
B L E . A S I D E S . S T E P O N N O P E T S
. . O N E S . C H E S S . D I D I
A P R . S L I D . S O O T S . C A N O N L Y
B R I G A D E . M A N E T . L A T E N . I E S
L E S A G E . T A T . R O T A T O R . A V O W
E L E V E . P A T I O . A C E R . C R E M E
S A T E . P A L I N D R O M E S . M O O N E D
T W O . E A T E N . D E N E S . H O R M O N E
. V A N C E S . A F T E R . C A V E A T
S N O R T E R . B H E R A . S L I E S . O R T
T U T O R S . D R A W O C O W A R D . K N E W
A D E L E . S O U L . T R E S S . R E E S E
M I S E . P O L I T I C . D A S . T E E V E E
P S I . L I C E T . N A D E R . D E I F I E D
T R I A C I D . C A B E R . T E R N . L D S
. S T O E . C O D O N . D I E T
T O O H O T T O H O O T . T I P P I T . I A M
A N C O N . I D O L O . E R E I S A W E L B A
I T A M I . E A S E R . L E O N E . A M E E R
L O S E A . S L E D . M E N S A . S E X E S
```

136

```
A C T U P . I T H A D . E S T E . A I M S A T
B R A K E . D I A L A . E T A L . R O O K I E
B E P E R F E C T L Y F R A N K . O U T I N G
O P E S . I S I T . S O I L . S A M . E P E E
T E D . A L O N E . R E L . V A S . T E A
. A R T F O R A R T S S A K E . P A H
D E C I D E . L A S T . T A R . A D E L E
R U H R . R I F E L Y . B A R T . R O W E R
A L I E N . F I R E A T W I L L . E P H O R
C A P R I . I R A N . R O L L . G A T T O
U L O . P A S T S . P A R K . S U C H . L T D
L I N . I N T H E N I C K O F T I M E . E R E
A E T . N A H S . O C K S . L E D E R . T A A
. H A T T E . A L O E . H O P I . O P H I R
A L E P H . S T A N D P A T O N . D R I P S
R O S S E . P E O N . O B A N G S . A N S I
S A H I B . A T L . F I N I . T I N G E R
. O S U . B A L L I N G T H E J A C K
A B U . D E L . A N T . A D O R E . M A C
B O L T . M O O . D A R E . R I C O . P O L O
O R D E A L . S E L L A B I L L O F G O O D S
U N E A S Y . A G E E . B R A E S . A S S E T
T E R M E N . R O D S . S E N S E . B E E R S
```

137

```
. P O L A R I S . D E L T A . S H A M E .
M I L I T A N T . A D U W A . P A R E N T
E M I N E N C E . M A N O R . O R A N G E
R O V E . D I P L O M A T . B O M B A R D
G L E N . D O I N . I R A N . E C A D
E A R . B L E N D . T A M A R . C L E V E
. S A I N T . S A L E M . H O L D E R
. A R E N A T H E A T E R . S E R A
S L A C K S . E L A T E . H A N . S E R
T E N O R . A G I L E . S P A R E T I M E
A M I N O . W A T E R M A I N . R I G O R
L E N D L E A S E . S A B L E . T A N T A
E N E . L A R . P A R O L . D A R I E N
. . P I S E . M I L I T A R Y B A N D
T E N A N T . C A L L A . R E E L S
A M O N G . R A I L S . S T A R E . D S C
R U N A . E A R L . B O O S . L A T H
A L A M O D E . C O M E U P O N . A R E A
W A G I N G . P A R I A . O N E L I N E R
A T O N C E . E L A N D . S E V E R E L Y
. E N T E R . A L L E Y . T R E A D L E
```

138

```
AUBER  ODETS  ATILT  METRO
SNORE  FRAIL  SARAH  OARIN
ACOATOFARMS  HARNESSRACE
ILK  ARABLE  FER  DOIT  IER
REJECTS  YOYOS  DAUS  OLDS
ARKS  BRER  SECTIONB
INCAS  HAL  TWOACTS  PELAT
NAKS  DIEOF  ATRISK  ETAGE
CHEEREDFOR  ROAN  IONIZES
ATRACE  MOLDED  ORNAMENT
SIE  TEMPI  AGATE  ERDE
DST  DICER  SNA  ITSSO  SAD
ACHT  VISSI  GRAVY  SML
PARAPETS  BRAISE  SHEETS
PLENARY  BEAD  STEPINTOMY
LEEKS  SPURND  THORP  SPEE
ESSES  LEOTARD  ENS  SEDER
URANIANS  EVES  WEAR
IBIS  OCRA  ISILL  LACTASE
NOT  OAKS  COS  PISANO  WAM
TIESTHEKNOT  CAPEKENNEDY
ERROR  RIATA  ASTRE  ACRID
RESTE  SNEES  BOOTS  LOSES
```

139

```
ITO4AM  THE10TH  JUNE17TH
PATINA  HISDUE  ISEEYOU
IMINES  ANCONA  TODREAM
EAT  WHANG  WORSTS  ATE
CRIS  SKEIN  DOE  ARRET
EAST40TH  RIN  PROPOSES
AWAY  PONES  SITU
SPRIT  SANGOUT  LETSUP
TALENT  CROSSBAR  REUNE
HRUSKA  HART  SOAS  66CAR
ROM  STROVE  STIFLE  TIL
IYAR  SALA  76ERS  ENTIRE
PAGE80  MANATBAT  ECHOES
SNEADS  REGRETS  POUND
MARS  SHONE  EERY
ALLEYOOP  AMI  BREAKS100
FOURS  NO103  BATOR  SIAM
TAP  LASTTO  ASONE  TRI
EDITION  ERNANI  AMATOL
RUNSOUT  MUETTE  NICENE
125POUNDS  PESTER  STINGS
```

140

```
SUNDIAL  ASTACK  GIN  LAW
ONEACRE  PARLOI  ONESIDE
EIGHTEENTWELVEOVERTURE
STS  EASE  INTERN  ROE  IHS
ARS  ACTCOY  ENT  AWEOF
BAHN  OCTO  HOSTSA  MENUS
SHOTINA  MUM  AHEAD  SNR
ASUIT  POPSOFFTO  BASTES
RDS  PROCURE  TTUBES
HUGE  MACU  TEA  AHT  LIBRA
ALLPRO  ONTHEROPES  ADREM
STARED  MDI  GPU  CREOLE
ARSEN  GIFTHORSES  TUSKER
TASSE  ANR  ECO  AUGS  TETS
SWINGA  SAMURAI  NOR
CHASED  CASTAPALL  FRATS
LAN  RANTS  NAN  DELIGHT
NESTS  RUSTIC  CESA  EERY
DANSE  WAR  ITOVER  RBS
UNO  CLI  EBERLE  IOTA  AMB
SUCCESSSPOILROCKHUNTER
USEOVER  ONEAND  ILMETRO
PES  IRA  ESDRAS  EYEFULS
```

141

```
AMATIS  FACES  TABOOS
STAMINA  AROSE  AVENUES
WELTERWEIGHTS  GELATIN
EADS  OBERON  TOURS  ODA
ASE  OLES  EILAT  AFER
TENS  ONER  OMNIS  ABALL
LAMED  SNEAD  CLUMSY
CABALAS  ACTUS  GALLO
HELTER  PRAHS  METALLIC
ARIES  BERLE  EATEN  ENE
RISS  MARIACALLAS  CHAN
GAT  FATES  OMITS  CHIPS
ELEMENTS  FRATS  PURLIE
RANGY  SENSE  PERILED
ALBINO  ATLES  SRTAS
SEEDY  STAIR  SNEE  TUMP
HIES  PEENS  STAT  NOR
OST  AIRED  LOAFER  AUTO
RULABLE  PAULBUNYANSOX
EREGION  ANNUL  DODGERY
ESTATE  TEASE  STEEDS
```

142

```
MOC  OBTD  BAALS  GUBGUB
RIFLE  HAHA  AGRIN  ONEATA
AMBOY  ITER  SAMOA  BALLET
HOUSEOFTHESEVENGOBBLES
GEST  LOTH  EDS  MLLE
GOBBLEDEGOOK  DONEE  ISA
ANEYELID  ISTEPID  ENOL
FAA  FLT  GOBELINTAPESTRY
FIRST  THELEVEE  INSETS
ERSE  TOAMAN  DRAGNET  GOO
RAE  IMMAD  LOO  RERUN
GIGGLEGABBLEGOBBLEGIT
CUNEO  AHT  SAUNA  SEG
ATI  WATTEAU  SIGNET  AGOG
THEINN  FRIEDEGG  DROLL
MRSHEDDAGOBBLER  GME  BLO
AITS  MRMORSE  ROAMABIT
NEA  BOISE  GOLDENGOBLET
SORN  BAP  SOUP  OTOE
ANTHEGOBBLEUNSLLGITYOU
SPIREA  REBEL  ETUI  OHOHS
BEDAMN  CLANK  RUMS  NEUME
STEWED  ASSES  SPET  RRS
```

143

```
ATHOME  ANODE  PETULA
ETHANOL  DARER  ERASERS
THETYPEWRITER  BIRETTA
HELIX  CEILS  ORB  OUTER
INAN  STIFF  ORALS  PERK
CAS  STS  TIFF  MEAN  RYS
SITTER  LIFE  SNOOP
ACES  AERIAL  TORERO
BOSSTWEED  ECRU  ANDRED
REEK  STAD  DELTAS  OFME
INC  OLIC  RIOT  EAN
NORM  ANITAS  ESTS  ACIS
KNEELS  NIRA  SEATURTLE
SETTOS  GOBUST  RAVE
ASTER  NOVA  BESSES
BAR  STEP  NEMO  NAA  ALP
ANYA  SCUMS  ABBOT  ALLA
LIBRA  UBI  INLET  ASTIR
STIRRER  DICTATORSHIPS
ARRAYAL  AMAHS  NOSENSE
ADULTS  SPLAT  ENTREE
```

144

```
CABANA  ISLES  BRAT  ERST
ORATED  ACUATE  IOTA  NOPE
PICTUREWINDOW  DUTCHDOOR
YAK  RILL  PINSK  TATA  MON
  SCOFF  ROES  EGER  MOANS
BATH  TIMERS  PROS  SERT
AWAIT  NUNC  LENO  SPLITUP
RAINED  REHEAT  FANLIGHTS
ERRATIC  WELTER  SEAN  ETS
DES  HAHA  SIC  ACHAT  STET
  GERARD  CHARTED  BOORS
DAIRY  BANISTERS  SOBEIT
FERNS  DINETTE  SOBEIT
ABCS  TOTES  ROI  FOAL  RAJ
RAH  SADE  TRIUNE  PROFUSE
GRILLWORK  INTHAT  TROMPE
OSTEINS  IBEG  ASIS  SUPER
  ESPY  CLAN  ABELES  NUNS
FACTS  GAOL  CEIL  LEEDS
ALT  UCUT  MOUNT  ILEX  RDS
BLUEPRINT  BREAKFASTNOOK
LORN  OLIO  DIANAS  AREOLE
EYES  WEPT  TASTY  WARMED
```

145

```
SWELL  BAJA  CASK  SERIO
LEXIA  OLAF  OUTOFWHACK
GETONESELFINTOALATHER
DENTS  FOIST  PLOT  SRA
VERSUS  UXOR  PARCS
EDN  MARES  NIDE  HADAT
NOAH  YETIS  VARS  ENERO
DULAT  CHEAPEN  POSTERS
STEMWARE  LORGNON  APES
VAIN  RAMI  LURE  RAI
POINTTHEFINGEROFSCORN
ARD  LEAF  TEST  OTHO
SIES  ENLACES  UPROOTED
CONCERT  BADTURN  PLENE
ALCAN  YOLK  SNEER  EDDA
LEERS  MEED  FRAUS  BUN
  FLOWN  EIER  SERERS
GBO  AMOI  ASTEP  STELA
ALLOVERBUTTHESHOUTING
GOLDENRULE  EZIO  PIECE
ACADS  YSER  REST  SAFER
```

146

```
ABBOT  BIFF  PISAN  LEMOT
LEITH  EZIO  ENTRE  AMYLO
PILEA  LENA  ACARUS  TOSAY
IRO  TWO  MAC  ROTE  ETONS
NUX  FINIS  SEPOY  CHIEN
OTIDINGSOFCOMFORTANDJOY
  ORD  ALLONS  ISNT  OXO
SUSYQ  DATE  ABB  DITHER
ADOPT  UPON  AMBUSH  MANSE
PIN  SHORN  BROOM  ABEL
HEATWAVE  SATRAP  TABULAE
INTHEDAYSOFHERODTHEKING
SEAREED  TUFTED  LETHARGY
ETSI  ORION  CORSO  CUP
SUMAC  SPRING  COSA  LEAST
AGATHA  LES  ESOS  SADLY
IRR  RISE  UNLACE  EHE
LOVEINCARNATELOVEDIVINE
ENSUE  EARLY  BELEM  NOX
MULCT  NANS  EST  BSC  YEP
AROOM  ANTHEM  OSLO  OTATE
LAURA  TAUPE  WHEW  MALIC
ANSES  ALAIN  NEWS  EXACT
```

147

```
GPU  TIETO  STOLE  LSTS
SOAP  UNLIT  URGES  OTOE
URNS  SHIFTSGEARS  NORA
PETTICOAT  HAEM  ANGRY
  YACHT  PER  YAJE
BOWTIE  SELECTEDSHORTS
INAE  BETENOIRE  SHORN
KEIR  PAEAN  ARICA  NOIO
ITS  NECKTIETACKLE  MOB
NETWORKS  REDS  EVE
INSITU  AMIDE  WELLED
GAS  BRAE  THIRDAVE
SOP  LAWYERSBRIEFS  TEN
TRIM  LEROI  AIMEE  CENT
ALLEN  DONTSLEEP  ABSI
YELLOWSNEAKERS  DILLON
BANI  LED  HELLO
DONOT  TITI  SLACKSOFF
TAXI  HMSPINAFORE  OMOO
INEE  ABASE  TAKEN  FERN
MESS  LARES  EXIST  FRA
```

148

```
LALA  OAST  SHEK  TRAILER
ICEBERGLETTUCE  GRILLADE
SHOOTTHEBREEZE  RUTLEDGE
PENNA  ADEEM  ENTICES  YAK
ERIE  ASSTS  EMERGES  AWRY
DON  EST  ARARA  ALIS
NESTS  OSTIA  SNAG  DONNE
CHILLWILLS  CLARENDON
ARRAS  OPALS  KEEPME  SEWS
LEER  TRAIT  COLDHARBOR
INBETWEEN  FOAL  ALEE  MTG
SEESEE  TRALA  ADHERE
TEC  LEUD  OILS  COLDSORES
COLDTURKEY  CAVES  LENT
OWAR  LIVEON  CAFES  CISTS
KIDDIECAR  DEEPFREEZE
SNEES  ALAD  GREAT  BARBS
TWAS  TENET  LAR  UTA
TEIL  CUREFOR  BADIN  ATAR
ERN  DOSADOS  DIEOF  AUTRE
ESTEEMED  ROBERTLEEFROST
NEEDLERS  CALVINCOOLIDGE
STREETS  EPEE  AIRS  COOS
```

149

```
RACER  CANOED  OLAF
PAROLE  USURPED  BORA
DAYCAMP  PHILHARMONIC
AGOAL  LOO  TEATIME  ZIF
REFS  BAALS  HBS  LONE
ESS  JACKANAPES  CHANGE
UNITES  ERAT  AVAST
CANINES  TERROR  HUI
ESSEX  OOZES  ESOTERIC
ACHT  FORPETESSAKE  ANO
SOIE  ALLO  IALU  TBSP
EON  SWEETWILLIAM  OBIT
SPEWINGS  ANOLD  PRIDE
EDS  STYLUS  ROOSTER
TOTAL  ONEG  SORROW
SCORES  TOETHEMARK  AVA
ATMS  EAU  SLEDS  BROS
ROT  TERRIER  AES  EARTH
BOBUPANDDOWN  TESSERA
EMER  BELATED  ERMINE
RSVP  REMATS  REELS
```

150

```
AGG  AWS  GALAHAD  SESAMES
PARASOL  ABALONE  ALABAMA
STICKTOONESGUNS  LEBANON
ESTREATS  LEAR  CROCE  STD
ERN  TIER  ORANT  WHEY
ASTAS  TENS  GAMINS  MOODS
LAHM  BANK  CURBED  TOOT
ABE  BOND  PONIES  CALLFOR
TOTTERS  PURSER  SAUTERNE
ETHANE  PANDAS  PERT  NOSE
ROD  CARTON  LAME  MEL
FEES  ARMSANDTHEMAN  HATS
AVE  GAPE  BEATEN  AEC
RAMS  APAR  SULLEN  ATLAST
EDUCATES  TITLES  ANTONIO
RESALES  MINTED  PISA  NEA
KRIS  DANCER  HERA  EONS
SKEET  CONGER  POSY  ANNAT
PITS  DANTE  COPE  ETC
ALE  MEUSE  JOHN  TEAHOUSE
STELIAS  LOOKEDAGGERSAT
MIRACLE  ENTERED  GENESIS
SESTET  TASTERS  SRS  CLI
```

151

```
SAMITE  OCHER  EBB  BBS
IMIDES  ORALE  IRA  BALI
CATOTENTAILS  GARPIKES
HELENA  WRAITHS  IDEAS
SITE  NOTI  PERKY
REDO  NOSED  SAHL  ESS
AMORE  EXIT  HIS  DOM
SIXANDELEVENCENTSTORE
LANDED  REMORA  ELIZAS
CHET  PRIV  AUGERS
RAT  OASI  ELA  ELLE  NEY
INWORN  GALA  SNIT
AVOCET  HUSTLE  SHEBAT
TICKLESTHEEIGHTYNINES
ALE  DON  SANA  GLINT
NSF  LOIR  RONDO  KLEE
SITKA  ETNA  DORP
ANSER  MRNIXON  SCORIA
CAFEMENU  SEVENTHSENSE
KNOT  ELM  ENATE  ISOGON
SER  GYP  SOLID  DESERT
```

152

```
RAJA  SLEEP  LAPSE  CART
AMUR  OUTRE  AGIRL  OREO
TOPGALLANT  TOPSYTURVY
ERO  SOUL  AMINE  SAN
DENOTES  PLINY  BISTROS
DIO  TRODS  BRASSICA
ACTOR  AROID  RUNE  GEN
LAHR  MIDDLEMAN  SHAG
ITE  AMBOS  EDICT  AETNA
SCLEROID  MODS  CRAM
THECENTEROFATTRACTION
FLAT  AITS  HOLDONTO
ASTAR  SWISH  LISLE  DEN
NEWT  CENTERICE  HERE
ATI  SPAT  RECKS  GODOT
CONCERNS  POLIS  ALL
ENGAGES  TRAIT  BLEMISH
NNE  LEADA  AULA  DEE
BOTTOMMOST  BOTTOMLESS
AWOL  PASTE  LAITY  OATS
MERE  TREYS  ESTES  SLOE
```

153

```
AMBER  STEAD  RIVAL  OFFAL
RILLE  CARVE  ABODE  RIATA
GLASSHOUSES  CINDERELLAS
ULM  TART  RIDES  RELADLE
EYESORE  PARIS  STAG  MEER
ARM  SAGES  MIXTURE
COPSE  DIVERSIONS  LANCET
AMAH  CEDES  ODDS  TATTLER
MAP  MACES  FLEE  AARE  OLE
PTEROPOD  MAVERICKS  STEW
SERENER  MUSE  NOME  TAHRS
TEARAPART  KINESCOPE
CHILD  TURK  LIZA  CANASTA
HAGS  MILLIPEDE  MOMENTAL
IKE  GONE  NUTS  COVES  RUT
VERGING  VENT  CAPEL  RENO
ESSENE  PASSEDOVER  DUETS
RAYLESS  RIVES  LAI
KALE  METE  PERES  REMNANT
IRONMAN  WADER  DIVA  BOA
WOODENSHOES  CLAYPIGEONS
ISSUS  EARLS  TEPEE  EVICT
SEEMS  SLATE  STERN  DALEY
```

154

```
LAM  ASPO  HIP  CAKE
ANY  SWAN  ACE  OPINE
PTAH  PENE  REP  HORNER
REPEL  ERRED  LETSDRAW
ISHAM  TOUGH  PEA  HOTE
SHORTCHANGE  CARRIESON
MORT  AES  EATS  TEDA
SWAB  RAT  RRS  ALBERTO
EDER  STA  TAUNTERS
PILE  TRA  ERGONS  SAAR
ARROWSCUPIDSANDHEARTS
LIEN  POLISH  GEO  ANSE
LONGLINE  LAR  FORD
RESORTS  ANE  STP  CPLS
TBAR  OMNI  THE  ORAE
SCHOOLAGE  ANCIENTROME
IRED  CID  HERLS  COMBS
PARASITE  FRITO  UNIAT
MODELS  MAR  MOUE  ESSO
PEDAL  ORO  ENTS  TET
SYNE  DAM  ASHE  SEE
```

155

```
SANTA  ATLAST  ELBA  NODE
SPREES CHIMER  LILT  EBAN
PATACHOUENLAI  OMAR  FIDO
ARE HAG LEI  DIANA  ETES
CELT BAYOU STEN  CMDR
ESSEN MANPOWER  PETARD
MET TESSELATES  AIMEE
RAMPART  HELLESPONTIFF
USE RAREES  TITANIC  INEE
RID MELPOMENEMENE  CORR
ADAMS KAIFENG  SARA
LELAND SCAT ODDS  NECTAR
CYAN  REFRAIN  CARRY
LAMA BOHEMIAFARROW  APA
OBER OVERACT TEEMED  IAL
CORTINALOUISE  ERRANDS
HIGHS EMERSONIAN  TAT
SLEUTH  REUTTERS  GOLFS
ROAD FAST URALS  MALE
AREA TILLS SRI ELY  TOA
GELS PROA ALIBABAAURHUM
RASH IGOR REVILE  SLEETS
ALEE NENE GRASSY  HEEDS
```

156

```
IMAGI CHRONIST  ACRES
ARISEN RAISETHE  MAUVE
MARINA EINSTEIN  ARSON
ANA STRAND SMEETH  TKO
NICK IOTAS  ELMO  BRER
DALI OMEN DODDERSEED
ANEMONES FEN  SNEERS
OLIO DECEM  TARRIES
SANDS SEDATES  TEESUP
GOBO MATH MOTEL  TRA
RIBS OREIMPORTAN  BAER
ORR MRSAM IMET  INKS
WEEDER SCIENCE  TESTA
SEVERER ESNES  SHAH
INSTEP ITE TEAROOMS
MASTICATES TENN  PRAU
PATE ROSO PINSK  SANA
ALL BEATUP ALDENS  TAV
PAOLO SOCIABLE  OOLITE
AGNEW TRAMPLER  WIENER
LASTS SENATORS  LEDGE
```

157

```
QUAQUA TASKS ACCA  BLURB
UNTUNE HUTIA MOAB  RASED
ATLAST ETATS BURL  EMULS
ROAR MOLES UPGO  ABRA
TONTO MOME YELLOW  KAPPA
OTTER AVAST MAES  OBSESS
SHATTERITTOBITS  FIRTREE
VIN SOLE  COLE
ABRASING ACU STYX  APSE
TRAMPLE FLAGS ICI  KAHNS
RIVALS ELI HOOPLE  BLORE
AMATI BLOCKBUSTER  RETAN
ISLET APPEAR LOS  LETSGO
LULUS NAP TEPEE  GOATIER
PIRO ASYM AAR BOOKENDS
NINO ELKS  IRK
ZETAETA SMASHINGMACHINE
ELOISE COSI ARUBA  HAMUS
DOERS MONACO OMEN  ABIBS
CILI AYAH SANER  ITBE
LURID ROTI APORT  OBTAIN
ATONE STAB KORAH  TOATEE
BENES HESS ADELA  TATERS
```

158

```
CAPE CBD GASTON  GISH
HOAX MAUI UMPIRE  INTO
ABIE ARTS MOUNTAINEAR
WARMFRONT SUM ARN  PIN
PLYMOUTHROCK  DSTNS
HALLOS TRIO  TENET
AVOIR CABLECAR  EPIGON
NEC IAS RRS  VEERTO
GRANDBALLROOM  PENSEES
BLEAR MCIC ARD  ASE
CAPITALPUNISHMENT
NCO ADD LANE  ENOLS
OOLONGS WHIPSTHECRACK
CLOTHE BOY UTE  KAI
TARTAR LOOPHOLE  HIERS
ENSUE LONE  PATSYS
HEARD NIAGARAFALLS
OPS LAI GUY STEELPIER
SUNSETSTRIP 1001  ARCH
EROS TOHIDE DUNN  RACE
SETT ANOPEN ETS  TELA
```

159

```
SEDGE  PSHAW  SHOWS   PATHS
ECRIT  ATONE  TOLET   ETHIC
THEGOLDENTRIANGLE     THERE
SOSO  ADIGE  SNEAK  DEEPEN
   STAMINA  LADYS   BERNESE
BBC  MENS  LULU     ALEAN
ROILING  GIZAPYRAMID   TIM
UNREST  BELOW  SERBS  EASE
INCAS  SLAIN  FARCI  ARGOT
NELS  APART  MAYAS  ORIOLE
STEEPLES  HEAVEN  EXTENTS
   LIRE   ASO    ALII
REQUIEM  ASSORT  RIDERSTO
ICUMEN  ASHEN  OBESE  EQUI
FLAPS  SISAL  AXONE  SCULL
FADS  CEDAR  AVILA  NATALE
STR  CONEYISLAND  COLORER
ACHES   ASIS   BARS   ESS
CONRADE  METAL  HERMAID
EGGERS  SALIC  BEREA  DAIL
ALLAT  SPHEREOFINFLUENCE
REESE  PEACE  RADIO  TACËT
ASSER  TENTS  OSIER  ALERT
```

160

```
     CLAIM   STEAD    BEAST
SHASTAS  HILLER   CANCER
COMMECICOMMECA   ARCADE
ORB  ELOPE  FLIERS   DAS
ODAS  SLAP    ASIT   GINS
TASTE  STEM  ARISE   EASE
ETTES   IRONMEN    BLT
RASAS   SNEAD   ALASKA
MAMBA  TAP   HAN    IRK
MAGI  ILLS  RAISONDETRE
INRE  SUTE   PARC   REAR
TOURDEFORCE  MUSH  ASSN
TIM  REF   LAC   DEEPS
APRONS  TORAH    FERRO
UPS  BRANDED    GREER
FADS  CROOK  SARA  SALSE
AMIE  ETAL   DUMA  TOPS
VOL  SNARLS  ASPEN   AIT
ORACLE  DOUBLEENTENDRE
RATIOS  SPROUT  SEABEES
SLEET    EDAMS    STADS
```

161

```
TOR  ESP  SECEDER  PAD  AFT
ANA  ETO  PROVISO  OSE  LIE
FEDERAL  SADISTS  SLIDERS
TOIL  NIP  SELL  ESSE  ARTS
FOURCORNERSOFTHEEARTH
   DUE  AIRS  CORE   PIT
FACES  ATES  CARED  MECCA
AMOS  SHER  BOTTE  THEROOT
GER  SPAS  LURES  BEAD  ROI
ORNATUS  MORNS  GOAT  NRS
TIEROD  CEASE  EROSE  CUD
CREW  CORNERSTORE  LOCI
ASS  COALS  BETAS  MELONS
ENT  OUTS  PREEN  DEADPAN
AMO  LIPS  CLOPS  MILK  ITO
RANCORS  CHAOS  CAST  BAER
SNEER  BRINK  SORT  PASSE
   DAB  AUNT  SPIT  EAT
CORNISHCOASTOFENGLAND
SARI  TITI  TIER  NOR  AERO
TRICKED  ALINETO  VERNIER
AVE  ORE  NOODLES  ETE  GAT
BEL  SSS  SENSERS  LST  HRS
```

162

```
SWAM  IRISH  ABC  BESTOW
HOPI  MEDEA  PIO  ENTIRE
ERRS  PALET  PSI  ATAMAN
KICKOVERTHETRACES
   LOIRE  REAR  SHRIVEL
DESILT  FREELOADS  SANO
ETHNO  CREEDS  MIE  PEA
RHO  MELON   EARTHWORM
UAWS  WANDERLUST  EEROS
SNEERERS  DEARS   PRS
TERRORS  GENIE  SHEKELS
VBS  TAMAR  PHYSIQUE
ATSEA  RODANDREEL  TUMP
DAYDREAMS   OREAD   IBO
RUR  SMA  SWATAT  HONEY
EROS  TARPAULIN  DONORS
MISLAID  HURL   REBEC
ENVIRONMENTALISTS
MANANA  ANT  GORSE  TIES
CRAVAT  FEE  ELIOT  EARL
STEELE  TYR  DOONE  PLAY
```

163

```
ALORS  SUETS  SOCKO  PEBA
DIVER  INTHE  AFRIT  DANES
HEADINGTHEMOFFATTHEPASS
OGLE  ONION  REEKS  ECARTE
CES  TWEES  MITRE  SLOWEST
   CHITS  JOEYS  SKED
TROAS  SORN   TINE   CLE
THEYWENTTHATAWAYMARSHAL
ARGOS  IRONY  LOLLS  PALO
BIAS  SMEWS  OLDIE  GOESON
ALL  BABA   POEM   AARE
CLEAROUTOFTOWNBYSUNDOWN
   LENS  REAL  ESSE  PRO
BEGONE  TRIPE  NAMES  NEAT
ACRO  SHINE  BOXER  HANSA
THEFASTESTDRAWINTHEWEST
HOW  NEER   OLAS   AWARE
   DRAM  TUMMY  CALEB
MISTRAL  ARRAY  LURID  DUO
ASLEEP  ALIBI  REACT  MINT
MEANWHILEBACKATTHERANCH
ARMES  SARAN  ADIRE  ANGLE
NEST  TITLE  BATOR  FOYER
```

164

```
HATH   ROWENA   ROSO  ALAS
OCHO   ACORES   ALEF  TOBE
WHEELBARROW   MIAFARROW
BIGDEALS   NARROWBRIDGE
AEROSTAT   NEO  AYE   SAD
DREW       DDAY      EIDO
  ENAMOR   MASU   WONTON
SUNSHINE   PAN   RIANT
ENA  ONESTAR   WONDERFUL
APR  YES  EAR  ARK  LEONA
MURA  SPARROWHAWK   EXIT
EROSE  ARR  WOO  ENT  ETE
NEWSMEDIA  SKOALER   SOO
  EYRES  IKE  SLEEPOFF
CROSSE  TINY   ISDEAF
OENS    CANT        SHIP
RTE  LEO  VON  LEVITATE
DAVEGARROWAY   UNIVERSE
AROOSTOOK   POINTBARROW
GETA  ENCE  PURGEE  NOME
EDEN  NAKS  ESTERS  SWEE
```

165

```
PRETEST   BESIDE   EDITORS
LUCERNE   RELINED  TOTALUP
ANOMIES   ELIZABETHGOUDGE
ISLANDSINTHESTREAM   TAPE
NOO   SIDE  USEE  SNA   DAD
TUGOF  NOWS  NEMOS   BADS
STYLED   LACROSSE   CHUMS
   TEAL  LAINE  HASLET
TAS  SNOB  TAI  RICHARDNEY
OBAN  AVAS  SCOUTCAR  OISE
FORGE  ETH  ENLARGED  GSA
FUTURESHOCK   ALBERTSPEER
LTR  ASTEROID  EDE  CORNS
ETES  COSTUMED  LIES  DIET
ROSEMARIES  PER  TNTS  ASO
   LARYNX  REVES  SOUL
SALEP   ALEWIVES   TROPIC
STDS   GAMES   SETA  FORNO
TEA  GAB  AETA  SALA   EVA
OWNA  URISREICHANDFRASER
MACLAINEANDSHAW   ELOPERS
PRELUDE  GEEZERS  NOSENSE
STRIKER   ARRANT   SWATTER
```

166

```
  ROWAN   DOSE   BOBBIE
REBATE  SOTHIS  ALLINA
EDESSA  THRIFT  NEATASA
FIXHERBREAKFAST   CONES
  HATTER  SEPTA  KNELT
ESSE  OUTIN  LLAMAS
SPERM   CRI   ENSUE  BOM
THEWAY  HOSSES   RACINE
ASPIRES  NAIL  ABA  LOTS
  NOSE  INFIDEL  PEGAS
PRADO  TEN   ORE  RASPY
AARON  HOGGISH   ETON
STEW  ASS  ENCE  DISHOUT
SETSBY   STARRY  PIERRE
ESE  RESIT  AWE  TREAT
  ANITAS  PALAU   COLE
ECADS   LENTA   SPINAL
ALTOS  VACUUMHERFLOORS
TERRACE  ENLAIR  RESNAP
FAIRER   STAINS  ERECTS
SPADES    SERG    ETTES
```

167

```
SAFES   SATES   DUPED  SCRIP
TRACE   TREAT   INONE  PHASE
ARCHDIOCESE   ARMOFTHESEA
NATO  SLANT  SPIES  REAPER
   WHINY  SOAPS  MART
BESTRIDE  REUSE  DIVESTED
ELOHIM  NOTSO  AEDES   RAE
FIFES  TOOTHANDNAIL  SERF
OCTET  ORCAS  IERS  LEANT
RISS  GREAT  AMENT  MORSEL
ETH  BLABBERMOUTH  AUGURY
  OBEAH     OER    ANGER
OCULAR  THUMBTHROUGH  ERR
DELETE  HOSEA  AUNTY  DCII
ENDAS  SERI  ALICE  BEHAN
STET  SKINANDBONES  ABELS
SER  SPURS  ORLES  TRISTE
ARSENALS  TWEED  STRETTOS
  PARK  CHOIR  PURUS
SABOTS  VEINS  MANIC  WASP
LIONHEARTED  BOTTLENECKS
ANEYE  FAUVE  AURAL  LIMIT
GERMS  RISER  REINS  FRETS
```

168

```
TONTO   TIDIED   SENATE
AROAR   HAROLDE  RELATED
FIRMA   ONASSIS  AVEDONS
TOMENTOSE   TIPPECANOE
  TUR    ORIENT   ENL
HOSS  FACEISRED  TOSS
ABUT   THEPOPS   EYRE
REBALE  RENI  OBL  ATMO
PRUNED  TEARSHAIR  THAN
  RCA    OUTTHE    UNL
HUBERTHORATIOHUMPHREY
ANI   CORONA      AAM
LIAR  UNTANGLES  GULOSE
OSSE  USN  NITH  ALINES
  ANDS   REPAIRS  DDES
  DREE  SEAWOLVES  ESME
WEE  ATLAST      SET
EFFETESNOB   NATTERING
BRAVEST  PIEFACE  REFER
BEMISTS  UTTERED  MAFIA
SMELTS   SEAWAY   SLYLY
```

169

```
LILACS   GILT    PIUS   HEAP
ONOMATOMANIA    MUMBOJUMBO
GOBBLEDYGOOK    HYPOCORISM
ONES  RITA  NEMO  LAKE  LEM
SUS  COSH  PERE  COTS  BINE
    BAIT  GOSSAMERS  FIATS
REPAND  BROS  SALE  SIL
INERT  ZEAL  CULL  MALAGAS
BARBARISM  TORA  FIREBALL
ERS  BENTS  ALERTING  ILIA
SMILING  BEL  KINK  LAITY
   FOLD  BALLOTERS  CALM
BELGE  GALA  GAY  PULSATE
OMAO  SILLABUB  ATOLL  TAA
MIGRAINE  BLEU  RHOTACISM
ALERCES  PLUS  SOAP  TEASE
   HOG  TIAS  SOON  HISSES
CRIER  WHEATGERM  SOOT
RENA  BRED  ERAT  ECON  TEG
ACH  ALEF  DRIP  SDAK  SHOR
DOUBLETALK  TELEGRAPHESE
LAMBDACISM  TACHYPHRASIA
ETES  THRU  YSER  SEDENT
```

170

```
PEG   DECEM    BES    MID
AHNE  DEMERIT  ALTO  IDA
NICELYNICELY  BLOWBLOW
ANA  PATTI  ERG  ROLLIN
REMASK  LASERS  READDS
TAPS  ATILT  EAT  BAO
SEC  ABSALOMABSALOM
DUNDEE  AGAS  ETON
TOUT  WROTE  TOG  PEP
CHANEL  AHAB  USN  ALGA
MILESTOGOBEFOREISLEEP
DRAY  ENE  FIRN  CITARA
RED  PRE  TIOGA  PISH
HEEP  RARA  RATIOS
MERRILYMERRILY  RTE
SAR  NAT  IOOOO  NAVA
MORONS  GROSSA  YESYES
ANCIEN  YUL  DRIED  UNO
JOHNJOHN  TEMPERTEMPER
ORE  DODO  SERENES  CORE
RAS  PSI  PUNTS  INS
```

171

```
STATIC  ASCOT  ALAS  SEMIS
TAMALE  SPIER  ROLL  PROSE
ETAOINSHRDLU  ASSOCIATED
LET  OTIC  LISP  AVON  ERE
ARIA  REAP  ASTA  BALUSTER
   JOURNAL  MOIL  KALE
BECALM  LEO  MMES  SERUMS
ADORE  SPORTSPAGE  SINAI
NIM  SOTS  OPES  CUP  FIND
ALPS  RAINWEAR  SULLA  TIE
LEONIDS  OASTS  PROOFREAD
   SIRE  PIN  ARE  TEED
EDITORIAL  OMAHA  STEPPES
LOT  NEARS  PICAYUNE  TRAP
ATOE  DOT  ITSA  RARA  EVA
TERRA  COMICSTRIP  LASER
ERSATZ  HYPO  TAE  BAISSE
   SHOD  EONS  ASTOUND
REDEEMED  SAPS  TRUG  EAST
ACE  IBAR  ELAN  USES  NNE
CLASSIFIED  SOCIETYPAGES
KARAT  TELO  MOIST  EAGLET
STYES  ORAN  SPORO  DETERS
```

172

```
LAMS  OPCIT  PATHE  BIDS
ATOP  NEATH  OPIUM  ADAK
PAPAYATREE  POPGUNNERY
   CAPTS  MOLDS  LEGATE
CAPEMAY  PAPAS  SAVE
ISOMER  SITAR  BETIDED
RIPEN  PAPALSTATES  LAS
CAIN  SLUE  HEAD  PENT
ANN  OPANDPOPART  SEGUE
   SPINA  ONAN  SCRIBE
OLDTIRE  MOIRE  SHOOTER
MARINO  ECCE  ACORN
EDILE  FATHERBROWN  PAS
GIVE  BIDE  ECUS  FAMA
ADE  PATERNOSTER  BATON
   ALSORAN  ANTED  BATTLE
   APES  OTOES  CASHIER
RADIUS  AFIRE  SHIRE
IVANPAVLOV  POPULARIZE
MORT  REINE  LIETO  LOIN
AWNS  KNEES  ELDER  YOGA
```

173

```
GALLI   CHANC   LAOS    FROSH
ARIAN   MAJOR   ATLAS   IONIA
SNARK   INOVO   CHELA   SMELT
PORGYANDBASS    LOANSHARKS
ESSE  POL    BITE    DLO
    APRETTYKETTLEOFFISH
OWLAND    EHS   BIRLED    INNO
FIORE   BCDE   RECOAL   FSTAR
FLOUNDERABOUT   UNS   OHRID
ILK  TULU   YAH   STO   ORIOLE
SHEA   NUMB   KRAAL   ARME
HERRINGBONE   BLESSMYSOLE
    AREA   NANCY   TOPO   TROD
CAVIAR   TEY   LST   UELE   LUI
AMIND   SOL   FISHORCUTBAIT
NIOBE   EYECUP   EAST   HESSE
OSLO   CAESAR   RGT   PENTAD
THEWORLDSMINEOYSTER
    BUY    POEM   IER   LAGS
CATFISHROE   HOLYMACKEREL
ADULT   AITCH   RAMPS   NAOMI
REVUE   MOTHY   AGILE   ESSEN
POWER   TOES   SOREL   WHELK
```

174

```
RETAILS   WAVERED   LIARS
AXILLAE   AGITATO   INLET
GODSLITTLEACHER   SAMBA
BRIO   DIONNE   SRITA   SAT
ADE    ROUT    NEA    NATO
GIST   TOLTEC   PASS   ONER
SATYRINE   OBOL   KIND
    PUNS   TAMES   LETS
REPENT   CALMEST   ESTHER
ARADO   MALMO   EARL   SERA
FRI   FRANKANDSTEIN   MEM
TART   IDEA   CASAS   ADANO
STOWED   STEELER   TRINES
ADEN    HONED    REIN
INST   COST   DESCANTS
TACT   ASAN   STRESS   HEIL
UREY   LEI   HOSP   ARA
GIL   SCARP   CRONES   GRAS
GOOSE   WEIGHOFALLFLESH
ESSEN   ANTOINE   LARUSSE
DOTED   YEARNER   SWATTER
```

175

```
QUINQUE   MASSE   SEAFOAM
ERBIUMS   PALATAL   ENDURED
DENTATE   ANIMATE   ADORERS
SYSTS   DUNGAREE   POUR
1IFBYLANDAND2IFBYSEA
PCT   OVERSEA   SPLIT   AYR
AHOP   ETRE   DMUS   HOT   CLEM
RERAMS   SVT   STABAT   BOULE
SEPTI   EHS   IVYS   DONDER
ETERNAL   REEF   ETE   ASCOTS
RADIUMA   EYELASH   ECTO
SHOOTUP   SOLUBLE   CHORALE
TESS   RUSTIER   HANDBAG
KISSME   NIN   ESAU   OUTMIME
ERODED   EDGE   SSD   EAGER
YENAN   TWEEDS   TEC   BASALT
STAY   SHH   ROUT   BRAE   SILOTON
TON   SPEAR   GOTRIPE   LAN
ONTHE18THOFAPRILIN75
VERB   OVERSIDE   SOFTA
ANTIGUA   DENTING   BEETRED
WBEDELL   ARCADIE   ANAHEIM
LATERAL   SEXES   TASSELS
```

176

```
LIRPA   LOOF   XAOH
ESOOG   LLIF   ARES
EILLA   EOGI   MADA
SNR   LEHCAR   IROB
    ALABAC   SLARA
NEPOMA   IRPAC
RENO   SPAEH   TEA
ERUTCIP   EPAHSER
DTS   NAMUH   CELA
    NIGID   ECALAP
SENOZ   NEDIEL
TLAS   SRELIO   ESA
ETET   MOTA   REURT
TILA   ODNE   ETROA
STOR   NOEP   HACIM
```

177

```
CASPAR   PAJAMAS   CANADA
ASHORE   ALAMODE   APELET
STOLID   DIVORCE   ROMERO
CIVILSERVANT   PARDONME
ARETE   REES   MOAS
    EDAM   DESPOT   AWE
LIEN   MANNERSMAKYTHMAN
ADVERB   CRISPER   RIANT
WEASEL   OAS   ILES   INTER
DOSSIER   MALTA   TIDY
    DREADFULSORRY
SCAR   SMEAR   DEEPENS
WORST   TITI   JAB   PALLET
ABOVE   GERMANY   AHEAPO
PROPERBOSTONIANS   ANSA
SAM   EASTON   ATTS
    POLL   DIOR   AEDES
EXCUSEME   THANKYOUMAAM
BEARIN   CAROLER   PRONTO
UNMEET   CHIMERA   PISTOL
ROPERS   LAMENTS   OCTANT
```

178

```
CARIBE   AIDED   OSSIE
ALATED   IGNORES   VIENNA
TAKEAS   BOSTONTEAPARTY
CRIMP   DINA   STEAL   RUER
HIS   ANODYNE   ULT   SCIRE
CHARADE   EXTRA   ETHNOS
STIGMA   PIE   FLOP
BEYLE   GRANDOLDPARTY
BERATE   KOINE   RYE   ROUE
URI   ORDERED   DIOR   TARA
ROMP   ARAN   JESU   YSER
LIMA   PENS   BUSSTOP   TEN
ACER   UME   SONIA   RAVENS
PARTYPOLITICS   TIRED
    YEAN   MAL   TAROTS
STAPLE   UMBER   LILYPAD
ERROL   ARE   RELABEL   VIM
COMO   INERT   SIRE   ILOVE
TWOPARTYSYSTEM   KNOWIT
SERENE   SERMONS   RECEDE
LYRES   DEANS   ASIDES
```

179

```
STPS EBB  BISAYAS  TCE
AHEY NEA  ENAMELS  HOS
PENNAMES  GAMEWARDENS
OWN GIRT  GLOM   NICER
  ISBUT IMALABAMYBOUND
ASTRAY LAR  EMIL  ORCS
REAIR FLO  BARBEDWIRE
VITG  ORE EAT INSE ELL
ONEA PADDYWAGON  ARNIE
  DSC ARENTI  ELLECKS
ISITI  YEL HST  ATREE
ALTERTO EOLITH   WHO
GLORE CONVERSION  TSPS
TIO EATA END  RUS AERO
BLUNDERBUS  TDS  STRIP
REPP ENOL  GAD STEVES
PRISONEROFLOVE  POSES
MAGOR   TUES  GNAR TTS
LEAVENWORTH ROCKPILE
LOR  REGURGE EVE AMEN
YNS  RESTSON  EAR DEYS
```

180

```
SEDER SKI REAPS   WHO
AXONE ION EXEAT  RICH
LANDOFNOD PHONE MOTTO
ART ROCK TEIL REANTED
DCL DIE ARABIANNIGHTS
SHEKEL  NOTICE  ELSE
  TERSE DUST GUS  ROD
ETTE  RES  SPIN AVOWS
KOHLS GROAN IRRADIANT
ENESCO  STROLL UNDID
DEB  ABR OCTAL HAL TUB
 EERIE BACKON SEROSA
DEDUCTIVE HEWED SEDAN
ARBRE  CODA  TAO ARFS
GNU  PHI  ISLA LADLE
 GALA CARTEL ROMANY
HISTORYISBUNK  WIN MAE
EMBRACE SONS DATA LPS
SPIED ABORT NIGHTCAPS
SETS  HORNE ADE ERNIE
 LET  SATED GOD SIDES
```

181

```
GEARS  AMAS AGCY  EVENS
RELET TRACT VAREC XERES
ILLBEZINNIA IRISTOCRATS
PETUNIAOLDGRAYBONNET
SROS ORLY PETS   HEELS
  ANAD VASO SALAD  ATL
ASSESS  FARER ALENS CRO
STUMP SHASTASECOND SKIS
TAMIS METHYL TKOS CHAPE
EGAL CARAT  TUES  BLADES
REC TRILLIUMAIRE RAMADA
 CROAK  PAR  BASSI
TRUEUP PHLOXOFSHEEP SAT
HOMERS AEON  REELS  MYRA
WELDS TRAN STELMO FACET
ADAS VIOLETTHELAW RIATA
REU FILLE ROERS  HOLLER
TED RATED ORTS  BPOE
 REDAN  ALES ERLE  ELBA
 ANDSHELLDAHLIANOLIES
CALLASTOPTO ROSEISAROSE
AVIAN SWOOP OVERT  TONER
RABID  ESNE FESS  SYSTS
```

182

```
ALEP SLED  MATCH  SPADS
BEMA TILE  EMILE  TRACT
UTES AMRA  SALEM  AERIE
THEHAPPINESSOFPURSUIT
SERAGLIO VIS   SPTS
  RED SENECA  TETHER
ALIBI  PARADED ORIOLE
RASA STATS  LST  SMALT
CULM TALI ACTORS  EXES
ARABIAN RUBE RITE
 AMIMYKEEPERSBROTHER
  PEEL OTOE ENCORES
AFAR DRAINS ESME  LISA
SAMOA SIR  BATED  LATS
TRIUNE NACELLE  DYNES
AMENDS ENAMEL  SIA
 DRAG  SPA TORRANCE
THEHOUSETHATJACKBUILT
HARES TRAIL ONCE  TOOT
ILLAE ANNEE EGER  OBOE
SEEDS REARS YARS  SETS
```

183

```
SILTS  PAST  SPIRE  PST
GOCART ROMEO EARNER OUR
AMELIA APAIL TWOFER UFO
WEBOMBEDINNEWHAVEN IFFY
KOA  BANNEDINBOSTON
ANGI FORTE OLIO TENDING
TESTBAN ORR SCUD RAIDER
 SARDS ENO TOA SAIGA
DABBLE LATTENS RIO NORM
OWEA NOSHOW OVERMIAMI
CONCHAE EERY CEM  ASP
 LIKEGRANTTOOKRICHMOND
 TRE ISE RHES PAYLOAD
PHOENIXES KAYOED  ILLE
TRAP TEL THEREST ASSAIL
WISER REO IRA  ATNO5
ONTOUR SUMP SAF ASTOPTO
STORIES TOPS DIANA OLAF
 INSANFRANCISCO  ALA
YUMA PHILADELPHIALAWYER
ARE PIANOS LEONE UTHANT
PSI ARROWS LASER COACTS
SAN MEANS STET  KITTS
```

184

```
SAMP  PACT  NLAT  SNOW
IGOR HULLE EASES PEDI
RELOCATION IVORYTOWER
 RHETTBUTLERSPANTRY
DISARMS BIAS  HUGO
AMATI BETTI ABE ENTE
NAMES GARY MANOR BEL
EMUS LOBE OLGAS CARL
SSE COWARD NOIR LAKME
 LAINE ENSUE CAREER
PLANTER ILIAD SOSORRY
LODGER ARABY EVENS
ETALS CLAM SPADER DBA
ATMO RIATA ARAS SOUS
SIS ENTER RUIN BIZET
EENS SEE EWELL ADENO
 EAST SASS ALIENOR
SHELLEYWINTERSBARK
BADTOWORSE WILLYNILLY
ILLE SWABS EDIES CUTE
COED SPAT DEPR KISS
```

185

```
BRAIN THAI AGLEY SPARTA
MARNE ISSO SEENO LUSHED
THISWONTHURTMUCH ESTILO
 ETAS YSER LOVEHONOR
BAIT KEA EARNS OPEROSE
UMT ILLCALLYOU RIIS
LOCATE TKO IMPACT STOA
BRASSY HEWONTBITE LEHAR
ENCASE ORE LES AVERT
OAF SUNNYSKIES GWEN
LINPU TAN SOI BEARERS
ISL NEAREST LINCOLN XES
DRYICES ARA IOS DITCH
GRIN LOWERTAXES OWI
GLOAT BAD TOW ACROSS
POUTY ENDPAYOFFS ADROIT
SUPE QUASAR ULT TEENSY
SURE YOULLGOFAR MAP
SLASHER ASONE MAL DELE
HAPPINESS BEAN CASE
ORIENT THEHORSECANTLOSE
AVANTI OUTER PROD ETAIN
LANDON PREEN SONE MATES
```

186

```
HAVOC FASTAS HIST
CINEMA ASTARTE OLEO
BACKLOT KILLERDILLER
INKED CHE OLDADAM REE
DOOR CHARS WAN DERM
EER HOITYTOITY KUDOS
YVONNE RUNE AIR
PUDDING SUNSET GLOWER
ARIAS MINCE OENOCHOE
RACY HODGEPODGE ELD
ELKS DOMO BIAS REIN
TIO EVENSTEVEN ALTO
TARLATAN CHRIS OKEHS
ANYONE TERREO ASPERSE
SIR CION DIETED
HOTEL MUMBOJUMBO EAR
APAR IDA WORSE RABI
PIC ABARREL NAH TALON
NOLENSVOLENS ICEBERG
EMIR HELLENO GOCART
SANO LESSEN HOSTS
```

187

```
DORAD PILOT REBAR BEADY
ENERO OSOLE ERASE RATIO
ACIER PLAIN GUSTS ASTOR
RENAISSANCEARCHITECTURE
 AHINT TRET ALT
ADDS ENDOW ITSA BAS ABS
BROOMS HIC LAIT SLAW
EARLYAMERICANPEWTERWARE
AMIDS OXIME ERNE MADRE
MACAO NIBS ERIC STANDIT
TRAIL ESTE OATY INA
ANCIENTEGYPTIANCARVINGS
NEO SOSO ALDS EMEER
DOTTIER OLDE ANTI NOVEM
ACERS ABIE ABRIN INANE
MEDIEVALEUROPEANARRASES
ANON ICER POE AEGEAN
NER ACT SPOT TOAST ESSE
RHO ANIM SMOTE
TWENTYFIRSTCENTURYABODE
REDYE GNASH SALLE SAMAR
ORDER OFTEA STEEL EDITS
PEATY DOEST YORTY SETAE
```

188

```
UTURN MIXER SCALD ASSET
NIPPY ANILE PANAY MILNE
CRIME OFPASSINGINTEREST
LON TUREEN HEARD ENSETE
ELAS LIE HILLY SAD PAD
SERPENS PEINE OHM MIRE
ASMARA LIPSERVICE CAN
MESNE PILOTS ACTI ARGOT
LEAD CREEK LIBRA
IHS STUFFEDSHIRT DEEDS
MAT CARES RHEES PAW AIM
PIO REAR PEENS FARE UNA
ARC ELL COALS CAROL TEN
INKLE GOLDFISHBOWL YES
RESIN URALS COLD
STATE HATE MOUSEY PASTA
NED LYINGINBED BATHER
SADR BAS ALCAN HECTARE
ELB TAN BASLE POD AMMA
ATOSSA GASPE PHARES RIC
MENTALINSTITUTION OZONO
ENDOR CUTUP PARLE DECAD
WASPS ISERE SHEAR ANKLE
```

189

```
GALORE SCARAB BRAZIL
OVERACT ORMOLU EUGENE
SINATRA COMPEL ADAPTS
SAT CURLICUE WINE HAS
IRISH LIEUT MANY DYKE
PYLE WATTS DARK LOREN
APATHY MURK FEZ
OCARINAS CATS FACETS
CHICKEN PARCHMENT RAM
TITHES HATCHLING DEMI
EMEER WATCHBAND LAMPS
TESS RANCHHAND BAUBLE
SRI NORTHWARD MINGLER
ASHERY WORN FINCHERY
ICY PORE FORGET
QUIRK CARD MORTE ERGS
URGE HARK BIRCH CREEP
OSO BABA VENGEFUL VEE
TUREEN PRAGUE UTILIZE
ELOPED EASIER LEVELED
SATINY TWENTY SEVERS
```

190

```
ESTATE EMBER RIDE TAMPA
GIMLET MOIRE ONUS AREAN
GRASSHOPPERS BLOODYMARY
SEN SELLER ETRES UGANDA
LEOS ITHOT SNED
ADO TROY ISTRY CONTACTS
SORTIES ANOLE PLEA LAT
SOARED COFFEETEAOR SEBI
ANNAS OHROT USSS STALL
YEGG ARAT PRS CLARET
SSE OLDFASHIONED AIRWAY
BALLOF TOWNE ADITYA
ALLUDE SCREWDRIVERS TES
ROONEY LAD NINO MESH
ASSER HEAP STUDY HARTE
BESS MOONSHINERS SURFER
IRO BURN ASONE CHILLER
ASMILDAS PLEBS RIOT AMY
GADS HIVES TIER
ASSIZE RENEW EAGLES WED
BUTTERMILK HOTCHOCOLATE
AMOUR ALLE AWAIT ODDSON
SPARS PLOD TESTS DARINS
```

191

```
ISLET ETHOS SCS NOME
IMPUTE NHANG HAM ICER
TRITON CIRCS RSO NERA
SEVEN-THREE FIAT ELIS
STOATS ELEVEN+ONE
ATTU WINE OSAKA OTTO
CHARLOTTE ASPS ETH
CONGO NOSES EMERGES
EIGHT+SIX RRS EACH
SKI TOOHOT NES PERLE
PON ENGINE PILATE EAR
RACER GEE ANATID STE
ALAI REF FIVEXZERO
TANGLED CIVET OVERT
HAT ELLE EASTSIDER
TATS ANILS ENOW DESI
SIX÷TWELVE UNTROD
LEIF IRAE SIXTY÷EIGHT
OSLO SIR HONOR OFPOOR
TULU PEG INANE NOISES
SPAR SSE MELEE EELER
```

192

```
CATT SCANT RESTED PARIS
ULAR PALER ERMINE ABODE
ILLUMINATI FLAMETHROWER
CUCKOLDS ALLES OAKLEAF
APS ULL IDEE HETUP ILLS
FREEON ACE MARIS
INCANDESCENTLAMPS ALLAN
POOLS NIAS DEY CREASE
ARRA ADS CORES SARDINES
STU BUS HOMER PITY STAT
SESTOS POLIS KENT STE
SCINTILLATIONCOUNTERS
ANN TIER SPOON EARNED
SATS BEES STEWS MAR FEY
SPIELERS POSSE SOT LION
TOOLED LIL TRIO RESUE
SENSA THENORTHERNLIGHTS
DORIS NER ASSETS
ACTO LASSO CULL HAH ELS
CLOCHES VIREO FINESPUN
TAKEASHINETO FLINTSTONE
URIAL ELATES TELEO EDGE
PEONS SENAMS SEERS PEER
```

193

```
STARK EASTWARDS HASPS
HEMEN URIAHHEEP ONEUP
ANISE LAGNIAPPE UTICA
HENIE OCHER ARA SONAR
STOPLIGHTS AVERSENESS
SKINS KNESSET
PARODIZE CUIRS ROSTRA
ISAROSE CHATS AFLOWER
THRAWS CHELA UNDECENT
STERN FLORA AMNOT LEI
CAGE FLORILEGIUM AVGS
ABA SLOYD UREAL CLEAT
LUSCIOUS SMIRK FLOODS
ELEANOR NOPES TRAINEE
SASSER SORUS BEESNEST
QUITTER HEARS
GALLUPPOLL TENCENTERS
OMAHA ERA BRAZA OWLET
ROMAN CATHEADED TIOGA
AESO AGEOFGOLD EXPAL
SEDAN CERTAINLY STELE
```

194

```
STEAM HOSES  TMAN  AGER
CRAVE UNITED OATER LUTE
RATED NEGATE ALETA LEAN
ADORE GALLICISMS PRESTO
PENT MESA  LETO  STARS
EDE MARY ALARM SLUG WAW
OPALS AFAR ATTIRE  HUE
OCULIST ETTE SHAME DOSS
MATED RAREE STERE BASTE
ANOA RIGOR ALERT DANCER
NEF CAKE DESIRE BRITON
HEAVED IRING PROTEM
LODGES ENRAGE EELS ICA
PAUSED RANON NATAL KNOB
RUSES MISER DELED REGAL
OREL ROVER PARA ADEPTLY
VIA TOWELS ADAR NEATO
EEN ABET PENAL ADAM DAH
DATED CERA HEWN CITE
ASHLAR GRANDOPERA SANTA
PLOT TEREK ARARAT LINER
SOME AGATE SENATE ARENT
EWER ODER METER WORDY
```

195

```
NASHE SCUFF TREND
BONTON HORAL HOTTEA
TISNOWTHEVERYWITCHING
AMT REROBE RACES FOO
CIRC SABANA ILKS RIDE
INURE IBN BOGLE SEEIT
TIMEOFNIGHTWHENCHURCH
ESO TSE LTD YEN
RESPIRE LPS FREIGHT
ELA NATURAL AIL TORAH
CILI YARDSYAWNAN NILE
AHEMS IDS ELASTIC ELI
PUMPKIN ARI SCOFFER
AAF APR MOW HCL
DHELLITSELFBREATHESOU
ROVED ASTOR IAM EATUP
ARES ANIS ODELET SIRE
FAN AGASP INTROS RON
TCONTAGIONTOTHISWORLD
EUROPE OUIDA NEARED
TAPER KNEEL DETER
```

196

```
TARTS LOSES BLAST SUM
AMORE ABANK WINCH ONE
RELIC SIXCYLINDERENGI
ONEACAT EASE NEPER AN
NOTIP SANS STALAG
JONG OMER IDEA EDEN
EMEU PARALLELBARS TSA
SAULT RIDE RENTS DIPP
UNSAID LOTI NEE SACHE
SIERRAS NURE RANTS EL
BASAL PATH SAO ARI
MADISONSQUAREGARDEN
ATONE SLO IDLE STENO
SHOD PELTS EADS STAFF
CARAFES APC SELF STIL
ONAGER STEAR EIRE ENA
TEGEL ICECREAMCONE FR
SSE LANI SOTS ENGR LE
PASCAL MISS DONAU
ESTE ALTOS NEAT REVER
THREEPOINTLANDING ANI
REEVE SCEAT THROE SCO
EAMES EARNS SEEDS TET
```

197

```
ABATIS  FLEA  CLODS
LABORER SLEDS ASHEN
DRAWKCABGNIKOOL RUMBA
EDS STIRRERS CAME YAR
NOEL LIEAT SIMP MARL
STRIKEBACK FLASHBACKS
DOMINO ROIL ATH
BAT BIRD TOUP MOHAIRS
INAWORD FALLSHORT NET
BIKELS CALLSBACK EGGS
MELD WALKSBACK BABU
BASK PULLSBACK RESALE
ATA HARKSBACK DUSTCAP
HOBOISM BACK DERE KRI
AAR LACK MARATS
BACKTOBACK CAMELSBACK
ARKS TURK CORAL WERE
CBS BERG GOODSIDE REE
KEENE REGNANIKCABKOOL
OLAND SEATS TROUBLE
FATES SETS INNEED
```

198

```
BAREFOOT ASHIP CAMPUSES
OVERRIDE SHARI AMOUNTTO
DEGRADES TEPEE BERTLAHR
ARIES STRIP DEARE ANET
ODETS HOKE PALIR CDRS
BRN RHODES NAIR CEDES
ROAD ELAM DISPLEASE FAD
EGLI MARE ONCE ASPS AVE
SELFBORN ENGIRDS ESPIAL
TRYFOR SPLAT ATIC ARLO
EDER AETO SMOLT ITON
EVERYTHINGISFUNNYASLONG
DEME HOWDY ORSE ABEL
INAN ISAR MEADS LEAFED
LENTAN NOTSEEN THESSALY
EEC AGST HOBO AYAH SILL
SRI ASHAMEDOF SLUE ERIA
PILAU ARAD ASITIS TEN
CHAC MNEME YORE ESTAR
HATI APSES EDITS OSAGE
ANICONIC TOLDO OBTRUDES
FOOLLIKE HOSES COHERENT
FINESSES ENERO ONESIDED
```

199

```
EFF SCORN POKED ALAIN
CLUE HACHE ENOLA NAUSET
HILT ESTAR ATOMY DUBLIN
EXCERPT PORC DOT TRUANT
AIR AHAB LUEGO OTHER
PRAISEWESINGYOUNOELNOEL
MURANO TOP TATA GRI
PICARDY TROOPER ENLARGE
ETAGES MOA DOVER GAMEOF
KALE WYO JAW ACE EXIST
ELI CHER AVID HAMLIN
SOFTLYTOTHELITTLESTABLE
HATINH CLEO TRAY LAC
TRASH IRA SUN OVI AUNT
SHENSI CINCH TAR DODECA
ORGIAST VIRAGOS TUTORED
RUE JAPE OLA TURNIP
EMMANUELSHALLCOMETOTHEE
NOBLE ATREE TAOS ILL
DOREMI BON ENDS STENCIL
ANIMAL ISSEI UHHUH ECCE
DIVIDE ALONG LOIRE RUIN
TEASE NOMEN ADEEM OPT
```

200

```
HOOP COWED JOSH LABEL
ABLE ARARA UELE ABODE
WIDEANDFAR DRYANDHIGH
SERRATED NAY PILOSE
EASER BEGAT EMER
STAGER ALLENANDBURNS
WADE SEASEDGE PEACE
ARY STORK PEEPS DRIP
PTA THROE DUNDEE COE
UNDOERS DANDYANDFINE
DARTE ENC CHAOS
CARRYANDCASH CHORIST
LEO STEELE FLIRT URI
ATUB KORDA LOESS SUN
MAGOO MENSWEAR HACK
SHOVELANDPICK STONES
TETE TWINK COULD
KILROY HND HARRIERS
SODAANDRYE GOWNANDCAP
ERECT EINE ONAIR AHME
TOSEE NOEL DENSE YOST
```